On Story-Telling

PUBLISHED VOLUMES

Robert W. Funk,
The Poetics of Biblical Narrative

Burton L. Mack and Vernon K. Robbins
Patterns of Persuasion in the Gospels

Mieke Bal
On Story-Telling: Essays in Narratology

On Story-Telling

Essays in Narratology

Mieke Bal

Edited by David Jobling

SONOMA, CALIFORNIA

Polebridge Press, Sonoma, CA 95476

Copyright © 1991 Polebridge Press

Library of Congress Cataloging-in-Publication Data

Bal, Mieke, 1946–
    On storytelling : essays in narratology / Mieke Bal ; edited by
David Jobling.
       p.   cm. — (Foundations and facets. [New Testament]. Literary
facets)
    Includes bibliographical references and index.
    ISBN 0-944344-17-8 : $29.95
    1. Narration (Rhetoric) 2. Narration in the Bible. I. Jobling,
David. II. Title. III. Series
PN212.B28   1991
808.5'43—dc20   90–26587
                                           CIP

10   9   8   7   6   5   4   3   2   1

Contents

Acknowledgments

These essays were written over a period of ten years, during which I met many, many colleagues who had a decisive influence on my development. I must content myself with thanking them collectively, with only a few exceptions. At the beginning of my professional life, there were three decisive moments, when I would not have continued without the support and sympathy I was lucky enough to encounter. At the first moment, there were the late Jan Kamerbeek, Jr., and Aart van Zoest. At the second, Philippe Hamon. At the third, there was the "Synopsis II" conference in Tel-Aviv and Jerusalem in 1979, to which I owe my "international turn." Only those who were there can have any idea of what that event has meant to us all. I am deeply grateful to the conference organizers and participants, and wish to single out Jonathan Culler, Cynthia Chase, Brian McHale, Shlomith Rimmon-Kenan, and Susan Suleiman, who have become real friends.

With one exception, these essays have been published previously, but several appear here for the first time in English.

Chapter 1, "Narratology as Critical Theory," is an excerpt from *Femmes imaginaires*, 246–70. Translation by Elizabeth Castelli and David Jobling.

Chapter 2, "Tell-Tale Theories," appeared in *Poetics Today* 7 (1986): 555–64.

Chapter 3, "The Bible as Literature: A Critical Escape," was first published in *Diacritics* 16 (1986): 71–79.

A first, shorter version of Chapter 4, "Narration and Focalization," was published in *Poétique* 29 (1977): 107–27, and a longer version in *Narratologie*, 19–58. The English translation, by Jane E. Lewin, appeared in *Style* 17 (1983): 234–69, under the title "The Narrating and the Focalizing: A Theory of Agents in Narrative."

Chapter 5, "Description as Narration," appeared as "On Meanings and Descriptions" in *Studies in Twentieth Century Literature* 6 (1981–82): 100–48, in a special issue on *The Semiotics of Literary Signification*, edited by Nomi Tamir-Ghez. I thank Ann Jefferson for her help with this chapter. Translation by Robert Corum.

Chapter 6, "Narrative Subjectivity," is again an excerpt from *Femmes imaginaires*, 61–88. Translation by Gary Phillips.

Chapter 7, "Hypo-Stories: The Heuristics of Perplexity," was first published as "Un roman dans le roman: Encadrement ou enchâssement?" in *Neophilologus* 57 (1974): 2–21, and later included in *Narratologie*, 59–85. Translation by David Jobling.

Chapter 8, "*Chéri* and the Non-Existent Character," appeared as "Inconsciences de *Chéri*: Chéri existe-t-il?" in *Colette: Nouvelles approches critiques* (edited by Bernard Bray, Paris: Nizet, 1986), 15–25. Translation by David Jobling.

Chapter 9, "Zola and the Nature of Sin," was first published as "Quelle est la faute de l'Abbé Mouret? Pour une narratologie diachronique et polémique" in *Australian Journal of French Studies* 23 (1986): 149–68. Translation by David Jobling.

Chapter 10, "Perpetual Contest," has not been published before. It was presented as a paper at the "Conversations" conference, Princeton Theological Seminary, May, 1987. I thank Jane Carter for her help with this piece.

Chapter 11, "The Song of the Sirens: The Narrative of Disjunction," written in collaboration with Ernst van Alphen, appeared as "Wilde dieren, of de verscheurde eenheid: Over 'De Sirenen' van Maria Dermoût," in *Over verhalen gesproken* (edited by J. Hoogteijling and F.C. de Rover, Groningen: Wolters-Noordhoff, 1982), 97–124. The short story "De sirenen" by Maria Dermoût was published in her *Verzameld werk*. Both the essay and the story were translated by G. W. Lord and J. J. van Nes.

Introduction

1. GENERAL REMARKS

This volume contains a selection of my work on the theory and criticism of narrative, or narratology. What kind of theory, what kind of readings are presented here? I have been proposing a narratology not unrelated to my ongoing interest in three particular assumptions. First, narrative is not a genre in the sense of a limited corpus of existing, definable texts, but a mode of discourse, ubiquitous but variably present and relevant and with specific effects. One such effect is the truth-claim of virtually any narrative: its status as exemplum, as illustration, as a replacement for proof, when embedded within expository discourse; as report of reality, in journalistic discourse; as typical, as case, in realistic narrative. This effect cannot be ignored or denied with reference to sophisticated literary theories; it is the mission of such theories to explain it.

The second assumption is about the subject of narrative. My argument for a three-layered model—better, a multi-layered model—of narrative as against current structuralist two-layered models, is directed against two, opposed views: the monologic one of classical structuralism, based on a one speaker = one subject identification, and the dialogic, Bakhtinian view of narrative as an unordered multitude of voices: another dichotomy. The former view is rightly challenged by contemporary theory, often in the name of the latter. As against the former, my narratology tries to produce a non-coincidence between technical speaker, or voice, and ideological "speaker," or focalizer. Thus it leaves room for ideological subjects intruding into the speaking subject's discourse while the latter, by virtue of the narrative mode, can continue to perceive and present itself as unified. The model I propose recommends being systematically attentive to gaps, to the non-coincidence of speaker and focalizer, to the plurality of the subjects and

1

their discourses represented, but not exactly given a "voice," in the narrative.

Yet, as against the Bakhtinian view, the narrative mode is so deceptive precisely because this plurality is ordered. The hierarchy of embedding, discussed in various chapters but central in Chapter 7, exposes structures of domination between voices and focalizers. Opposing the idealization of chaos inherent in the narrative model of the carnival, my model is based on the argument that the freedom of plural discourse is no more liberating than the marginalizing containment of freedom in carnival.[1] In this respect, my argument against the ideology of freedom that underlies the dialogic model joins the above one against a deceptive because simplistic accusation of ahistoricism.

Because of the similarity between these two arguments, an important related point my model is also meant to convey has to do with time and linearity. Again, the theory and the narrative text have enough in common to make the confrontation fruitful. As has been amply demonstrated, linearity is problematic not only as a projection of historical development but also as a structure of "happening."[2] The enlightenment ideology of progress is projected in a sense of the linearity of the structure of narrative, and the notion of the non-coincidence of fabula and story, criticizable as it is in many ways, is valuable if only because it drives home the arbitrariness of that ideology.[3] But again, rejecting linearity, not only as a real thing but also as an imaginary projection with a cultural, hence real, status and influence, is throwing away the baby with the bathwater.

Linearity in narrative is as crucial a facet of meaning-production as it is illusory as a fact. Ignoring it will not do; taking it for granted will not do either. Only by problematizing notions like linearity can they be accounted for in a truly critical sense. A model which, on the one hand, acknowledges the modeling function of linearity and voice, while, on the other, assigning them their proper place as relative and fictional, will help to accomplish more than just paraphrasing the text. The mismatch between voice and focalizer which my model assumes is one way to do this.

This brings me to a final general remark. Much ink has been spilled over the concept of focalization. It has been brought into currency by Genette. It is his initial formulation of the concept whose status and meaning I have

---

1. See Moser's fine review of a collection of essays on carnival: "Des usages intellectuels."

2. On this problem, the literature is abundant. I refer only to Derrida's remarks in *Of Grammatology*, 85, 332, and to Foucault's more elaborated view in *The Order of Things*, 82–92.

3. The dichotomy between fabula and story, or story and plot, or whatever they are called, has been sufficiently challenged by many, among whom I wish to mention in particular Herrnstein Smith, "Narrative Versions," Chase, *Decomposing Figures*, and Culler, *The Pursuit*. Needless to say, a multi-layered model cannot attach the same meaning to such a non-coincidence, hence, cannot be dismissed with reference to the same argument.

revised more radically than I realized when I wrote my first essay on it. Focalization, to put it simply, is vision *in* language. The concept acknowledges and problematizes the part of visuality in verbal semiosis, which is usually confined to the arbitrary limits of the concept of description.[4] But that leaves the problem of what vision is.

Focalization is not necessarily related to the spatial; in fact, it has been designed to get away from the conflation between visuality and space. Focalization deals with three things: what others have called "the mind's eye," "the other's eye," and the "real eye." The first has been current for a long time under various headings and within various projects. To name only two divergent ones: Mitchell evokes it under the name of "insight," the vision one develops while reading, in ways similar to Gelley's discussion of Kantian schemata.[5] In a much more critical endeavor, Keller and Grontkowski[6] trace the ideological implications of, and the shifts of meaning undergone by, the very notion of mental seeing and its epistemological implications. The concept of focalization is not meant to replace either of these two sets of thoughts, but to provide a framework, a place, for the idea of mental constructs as the arena of heterogeneous subjectivities. Such a framework would accommodate the indispensable ideological counterpart, the other's eye, or the ideological mimesis that Bakhtinians emancipate a bit too radically by giving it the actual voice it lacks—a lack which makes it the more effective. Without such a framework, it becomes difficult to account for, and assess the respective importance of, widely divergent or even contradictory stances represented by the same narratorial voice, or in works by the same author.

This ideological aspect of focalization, and hence the critical potential of the concept which names it, is absent from, and in effect blurred by, Genette's unsystematic and rather unworkable definition—or lack thereof —of the term. The passionate refusal to discuss my objections, displayed in his emphatic repetition of the same problems in his reply to critics,[7] betrays a force that I have attributed to ideological stakes.[8]

A third aspect that focalization must account for without assimilating it unproblematically to the other two is the place of the "real eye," of visuality in a more physical sense. Visuality in narrative has a structuring and representing role to play, as my examples in Chapter 4 demonstrate. Yet the

---

4. I am currently publishing a book-length study on the problems of visuality and verbality and their interaction, entitled *Reading "Rembrandt": Beyond the Word-Image Opposition*. Gelley's recent *Narrative Crossings*, wherein he aims to deal with this same problem, shifts from description to space to fictional worlds, without succeeding in developing a plausible view that encompasses all three, arguably because Gelley ignores focalization.

5. Mitchell, "Spatial Form"; Gelley, *Narrative Crossings*, Chapter 2.

6. "The Mind's Eye."

7. *Nouveau discours.*

8. See below, Chapter 6, sect. 2.1.

irreducible difference between words and images cannot be easily discounted. The implications of this problem are the subject of my current research on word and image interaction, and in retrospect I can see how that interest emerges from unresolved problems left by this earlier work. In a volume which is to follow the present one, and in which I will reunite essays devoted to more broadly semiotic questions, this issue will already be further pursued.

2. RESPONSE TO CRITICISM

When the publisher of this volume approached me with the request to collect my disparate essays on narratology, published in less accessible languages or journals, into one English volume, my initial reaction was ambivalent. I decided to look and think, which entailed the somewhat painful realization that there was, at least materially, enough of a "past" to look back upon. A decade had run by since I started out in the academic world and wrote my first essay. Some of this ambivalence remained after I went through my disorganized archives. Therefore, and in keeping with a major trend in my work, I would like to open this volume, and end this introduction, by sharing that ambivalence with my readers. Those who do not care for methodological reflections can proceed to reading the essays and skip the rest of this introduction.

The essays collected in this volume represent roughly ten years of reflection on narrative, on the theory of narrative, or narratology, and on particular narratives, as well as the intellectual development of their author from emphasis on the pursuit of theoretical rigor informed by French structuralism to emphasis on social, especially feminist critique, informed by American post-structuralism. As for subject-matter, the conjunction, or mixture, of theoretical reflection and critical reading of both theoretical and literary texts has been recurrent in my work. I am myself more surprised by the continuity that has persisted than by the obvious shifts in focus that interaction with students and colleagues entails. It is noticeable in retrospect that the desire for rigor has turned out to have never been without some sense of the social relevance of that rigor, while the socially oriented concerns more emphatic in the later years of this decade tended to require, for their elaboration and argumentation, a certain kind of "formalist rigor"—only writable, now, "under erasure"—even if less explicitly and less painstakingly formulated. In other words, there is continuity as well as discontinuity in this work, just as in literary theorizing in general.

By way of introduction to the concerns underlying this collection, then, I will begin by addressing a question which no collection of one's past essays can afford to neglect: why bother, after all these years, to publish work written earlier and in different contexts? Given the historical embeddedness of any academic work, I feel there is something to gain in addressing this question explicitly. In the case of this particular body of work, the question cannot be begged by simply deploring the very notion of belatedness—on which more later. Specifically, why publish the essays now, after they have been both followed up by the work of others, integrated so to speak, and criticized? As usual, criticism has been mild and harsh, to-the-point and futile, serious and intellectual, but also highly personal. Some of it deserves comment here.

The serious criticism addressed three aspects. On the one hand, the intrinsic quality of the theoretical concepts, evaluated from pre-structuralist or structuralist standpoints, has been questioned; I will not address those comments here, partly because I do so already in some of the essays. On the other hand, the work has been accused of formalism, ahistoricism, and belatedness in general.[9]

In order to position the essays for a contemporary readership, these criticisms demand a response. Rather than eluding these serious points of criticism, I prefer therefore to run the risk of appearing defensive and to take up the challenge of, indeed, defending, not so much my own work as the tendencies for which it stands and the problematics with which it is engaged. And rather than bothering the readers of this volume with specific responses to all my critics, I will make some comments on these trends in general, choosing an example for each among the most serious and challenging critics. These remarks will give an idea of the reasons for the decision to publish the essays in this form.

2.1 Formalism

When I wrote my first essays, I was training myself in structuralist narratology. An understanding of structuralist writing could not be assumed in those days, and working with it was hardly done, especially in the context of Dutch academia. The common complaints against structuralism were twofold: on the one hand, its opaqueness and its failure as a hermeneutic tool, on the other, its never perfect formalism, objectivity, generality. Both sets of problems are justified, and have never been satisfactorily resolved. In spite of these problems, my terms of endearment with structuralism have a completely different and much more down-to-earth stake.

Going through the early structuralist texts has been decisive for my thinking, and still today I realize how much I owe to the exercise, and how much one misses without that phase. I was enchanted, not by the objectivity or generality never reached, but by the very pursuit of rigor. This pursuit

---

9. The sense of belatedness that the translation of my *Narratology* may convey has been acutely formulated by Schehr, "Review." While he seems quite critical of, not so much my book as the belated publication in English, he is at the same time so ambivalent as to suggest the kind of response I am going to give.

was a challenging and exciting experience, for reasons that I now don't hesitate to call ideological, or pedagogical. The success or failure of the enterprise in terms of its own goals is not at issue in my sense of its nourishing qualities.

The deep sense this pursuit has left me with is that intersubjectivity is valuable. I mean by the term no more than the accessibility, with an acceptable degree of common interpretation, of any of our tools for dealing with the world. Not that I ever believed a model would emerge that would account for every narrative ever produced. Personally I have never been able to find that an interesting project. But the side-effect of those efforts was an increasing awareness that the elaboration of a set of terms whose meaning we could agree upon would be helpful in discussions about interpretations. For me, the consequence of the structuralist constructions was an increase of teachability. This should not be misinterpreted.

What I emphatically never believed is that a model, however perfect, leads to intersubjectively verifiable interpretations.[10] Interpretation, although informed by cultural, institutional practices the members of a group share, is and must be a personal, subjective endeavor. The positivistic belief in models as purveyors of truth is an authoritarian ideology that, by concealing the subject, supports claims to proprietary rights over texts and meanings. Hence, such objectivism is not what I mean by a gain of teachability. In my practice as a teacher of literature on levels ranging from beginning high-school students to advanced Ph.D. students, the possibility of doing more than demonstrate personal cleverness has been a permanent concern. Teaching literature easily amounts to showing off, as it were, unintentionally intimidating students: the more they find interest in the interpretation offered, the more they feel personally incapable of doing something like it. Offering terms which allow them to couch their views in publicly accessible language was in my eyes an important gain to be drawn from these structuralist exercises.

But disillusion followed quickly. For the terms of structuralist jargon, if understandable at all, intimidated the students even more, and, interestingly, for the same reasons: because ultimately, they were *not* intersubjective, could not be understood. The solution to this problem has been one of my concerns, and has been one of two major motivations behind my emendations of Genette's model, presented in Chapters 2 and 4–6 of this volume.[11] Rigor, I learned from my teaching experience, is not a value *per se* for the student of literature, but helps to give access to the skill and to the

---

10. Schehr ("Review," 84) is mistaken when he quotes my theory as positing "a goodly amount of textual transparency."

11. The other reason is more ideological than pedagogical, although the two cannot be separated (see Johnson, *A World of Difference*). I discuss it below, in Chapters 4 and 6. My *Narratology* mainly grew out of this pedagogical struggle.

communicational needs that the practice of criticism entails. So in that phase, my goal was to make the terms more accessible: less ambiguous, more systematic, so that students could handle them. Yet again, disappointment followed.

A related problem with early structuralism was the degree of abstraction of the models. All the passion being invested in the logical tenability of the theories, examples were drawn from quite elementary narrative forms or tiny passages, and the sense of futility, the what's-the-pointness, never disappeared. The French structuralists were aware of the need to solve this problem if they ever wanted to conquer a large audience of practicing critics. Their attempts were revealing, and led to post-structuralism. To make the obtuse models operational, three of the French structuralist masters each wrote a book-length sample-analysis or "application": Greimas' *Maupassant*, Barthes' *S/Z*, both on a short story, and Genette's *Narrative Discourse*, on Proust's *Remembrance of Things Past*. All three exist in English.

These books provided evidence of the difficulty inherent in the very notion of "application" of a model, and thus quite usefully demonstrated that the desire for applicability is in itself a fallacy based on an ontology of discursive strata that has long since been undermined. "Application" suggests a hierarchy between discourses, which contemporary critics prefer therefore to replace with confrontation between two discourses of equal status. But aside from that problem, whose projection upon these three attempts sounds almost anachronistic, each of these three applications, successful in some respect or other, failed in a different way.

The first is valuable for the insight it provides into the workability of the model; for many of us, Greimas' theory has become accessible only with his *Maupassant*. But it failed to persuade us of the heuristic surplus value of the method, yielding only a quite uninteresting and predictable, and, besides, questionable, interpretation buried in lengthy and amazingly unreadable chapters. The claim to a scientific status for this less-than-novel interpretation was moreover undermined by the obvious interpretive decisions all along the analysis. The understanding of the theory brought a realization of its built-in interpretive steps.

The second has become a darling of literary academia. Barthes' fascinating and well-written analysis of Balzac's story engages, not least because it takes us along the paths walked by the text *and* by ourselves. In other words, Barthes' book is seductive mainly because, in addition to the brilliant interpretation of Balzac's story, *S/Z* is more anchored in semiotics and reader-response theory than in structuralist formalism, and demonstrates not a structuralist model but a set of hypothetical reading strategies.[12]

---

12. Suleiman, "Introduction," presents structuralism and semiotics as one category of

The third, which has in effect functioned as a model followed by many a critic, has generated criticism on both theoretical and literary grounds. Predictably, Genette's brave attempt to work with a long and complex text met with the accusation of reducing Proust's text to an example of the theory, while adapting the theory to Proust's idiosyncratic writing. Moreover, its structuralist rigor is more apparent in the set of rhetorical terms Genette develops than in a strict model of narrative; as far as narrative theory is concerned, the book is rather a systematization of pre-structuralist German and Anglo-Saxon concepts. Of the three exercises, this one represents the most obvious continuity with the past.

While Greimas' strict, formalist structuralism failed to help the critic and offended the humanist, and while Barthes' superb play with the story failed to yield the desired teachable model, to the extent that it spilled over from structuralism into semiotics, Genette's book took a middle position, both unsatisfactory and appealing for theorist and critic alike. Although none of these three books succeeded entirely in its mission, they did demonstrate some sort of working relationship between literary criticism and a strain of theoretical thought that has been associated, for better or for worse, with the term "formalism." It was in participation in this multiple and difficult, yet at times passionate, interaction that I began to work with literature. I never lost the need to work with a text when elaborating a theoretical discussion, and to examine a theoretical question while engaged with a text. I guess this taste for an integration of theoretical and literary practice comes from the assumption that the two are not fundamentally different, let alone hierarchically ordered.

I will not endeavor to write either the history or the apology of structuralism. What remains of the impasse produced by structuralism at its key-moment of demonstration is a general, widely applied criticism of "formalism." Conflating, in retrospect, the pre-structuralist New Critical autonomist movement and the structuralist pursuit of rigor, post-structuralist criticism faults it all because of its alleged claim that the text, and specifically its form, speaks for itself. Thus, Susan S. Lanser[13] criticizes my interpretation of Genesis 2–3 as "formalist," and she is not alone. I do not wish to elude or deny this charge; nor do I wish to admit to it. In the following remarks, I will simply try to shape up the idea of formalism a bit, so as to suggest a certain acceptability for it, under strict conditions.

I feel compelled to do this, because I am publishing these essays today; because they might, half-deservedly, be identified by others as formalist,

---

reader-response approaches. She can do so because Barthes' *S/Z* constitutes, precisely, the hinge between the two.

13. Lanser, "(Feminist) Criticism in the Garden." See Bal, "Sexuality, Sin and Sorrow," and now *Lethal Love*, Chapter 5.

and because formalism is, today, a bad thing. So bad, in effect, that one does not even need to define what it is in order to eliminate it from the stage, nor to prove that a text under scrutiny *is* formalist at all in order to dismiss it altogether. In a very general sense, formalism is rebuked as an approach to texts isolated from context, to form detached from content or the other way around, to structure indifferent to beauty, interest, or value; an approach to objects taken out of history, and, worst of all, to truth disengaged from ideology, to an objectivity which hides its subject. These are serious charges. I deny them all.

"Formalism," in all this, is a vague notion. In the first place, these judgments are based on dichotomies in which formalism is set off against some ill-defined other. Dichotomies have two inevitable consequences: they subsume all relevant phenomena under only two categories, thus restricting the possibilities and paralyzing the imagination—their centripetal quality. And they turn hierarchical, shedding off one pole as negative in favor of the other which needs to establish its value—their centrifugal quality. Hayden White[14] calls this latter aspect "ostensive self-definition by negation." Both features are at work in the above qualifications of formalism. In effect, the negative or deficient self-definitions of those opposites shape the image of formalism.

Contextualism, for one, is the vaguest of notions. It has not been explicitly theorized, but it refers to the attempt to understand a text in some sort of context. This opposition is going around quite generally. In her recent book on romance, Wendy Steiner,[15] for example, opposes formalism to contextualism and means by the latter term attention to the reader, rhetoric, history, genre, or intertextual relations. In fact, the notion of contextualism is only defined by its opposition to formalism—as well as *vice versa*. The logic of negation which implies that the negative is devoid of features makes such a mutual definition by opposition meaningless.

In addition, the opposition suggests that the two opposed concepts are comparable, while the one is in fact part of a larger framework for which the other is a synonym. If I want to address this charge in spite of its vagueness, it is because I find it important to stress that formalism is not the opposite of contextualism, but part of the semiotic enterprise the latter concept evokes. This is the case, not only because the text is a factor in the communication process—the "message"—but in a more immanent sense, because the text is by definition, *as* a semiotic object, reception-oriented, and any formalist approach does or should integrate that orientation in its method. The analysis of the text is presented, by all three sample exercises evoked above, as a complex manipulation of its readers.

14. White, "The Forms of Wildness."
15. Steiner, *Pictures of Romance.*

Similarly, the concept of formalism is taken by some to neglect content, while the theorists who came up with the term, the Russian formalists, emphatically claimed there was no such opposition, and no form which does not, simultaneously, produce content. Others make the quite hilariously contradictory assumption that formalism cares *only* about content,[16] a view which stems from the limitation of structuralism to a very narrow body of theory, that represented mainly by Greimas and Bremond in the wake of Propp. These and other presentations of "formalism" suggest that the term covers models and analyses which are primarily text-based, but not necessarily autonomist. A textual analysis can be, and in the best cases is, a reader-oriented analysis of its rhetorical, conative structure or discourse. Therefore, it does not preclude attention to context, effect, and ideology, but it grounds that attention in an interaction between the written discourse with its formal properties, and the audience it addresses, the social position that audience holds, and the social situation from which it emerges.

Lanser blames my paper on Genesis 2–3 for formalism by constructing an opposition between formalism and speech-act theory. This is another case of "ostensive self-definition by negation." Lanser simply *poses* my paper as formalist, motivated by the wish to dispose of it in combination with Trible's altogether different treatment of the same text.[17] She then reduces speech-act theory to inference, and demonstrates her method by means of an example of contemporary, colloquial dialogue. The combination of the sentences "I have a headache" and "I have aspirin," she argues, allows the first speaker to read the second sentence as an offer of aspirin, on the basis of the sequence. Granted. She then proceeds to interpret Genesis 2–3, an ancient, literary, monologous text, through inferences based on "normality," in the misogynist tradition.[18]

16. E.g., Gelley, *Narrative Crossings*, 80.
17. Trible, *God and the Rhetoric of Sexuality*, 72–143.
18. Lanser, "(Feminist) Criticism in the Garden." She has nothing new or different to add to the arsenal of sexist interpretations, nor is her account either text-based or theory-based. I would say it is a particularly pernicious form of "contextualism": it is based on the subtext of contemporary normativity justified by allusions to theories—Austin's, Grice's—which are not seriously engaged. And indeed, her major sources are Alter and Sternberg rather than Austin or Grice, and her interpretation is oriented by unargued universalized inferences, rather than by the words and strategies of the text. However, ambiguous as they are, or maybe because of their ambiguity, these should be engaged; not objectified as the sole producers of meaning, but taken up as subtexts in their own right, confrontationally engaged with the reader's attempts to give them contextual meanings. This resource Lanser wishes to refuse. For reasons that I will propose later, the term "formalism" comes up every time I discuss what the wording of the text actually is, rather than what the various sexist interpretations have made of it. To put it simply: good reading is judged bad. And I do not mean that the *meanings* of the words are actually there, only that the words themselves, and their order in the standard edition, can be taken for granted. I submit that Lanser projects her refusal to relativize and contextualize her own inferences, and their ground in contemporary "logic," on my alleged formalism.

"Formalism," then, is the term which shapes the bad consciousness of the critic engaged in ostensive self-definition. I will return to Lanser later on, à propos the charge of ahistoricism, because her own argument is open to the same charge. Here, I would like to oppose to the negative and vague notion of "formalism" the possibility of emphasizing that a reader-oriented analysis of a text, which adopts an interactionist position, can take the name "formalism"—or "new formalism," if you like—as a positive label. Its rhetorical purpose, then, is to call attention to the relative but crucial place of "good reading"—which is not exclusive, not imperialist, not objectivist, but a kind of adequate rendering of what can be rendered, in the sense that, whatever its ambiguities, the word "cat" is a noun and not a verb, and refers to an animal, not an inanimate object, a mammal, not a fish, a singular not a plural, and the like; it is the opposite of obviously bad reading. In contrast to the common assumptions, "good" reading must by necessity imply reader-oriented reading, awareness of the rhetorical strategies displayed, not by the text itself, but by the evidence provided by the text-plus-its-reception.

The theoretical essays in this volume are "formalist" in this sense. They propose theoretical ideas and concepts which try to formulate a framework for interpretations of narratives which bridges the gap between the text in its structural complexity and its effect upon its readers. Granted, the term formalism does not mean much in this broad definition, but at least it does not depend, for its meaning, on its opposition to equally vague other, "better," -isms. The question is not so much what exactly formalism is, or if the essays collected here are formalist—I for one don't care so much for this or any label—but what attitudes the alleged formalism entails. It is in those attitudes, more than in its content, that formalism as I understand it differs from, without being opposed to, approaches which I would qualify, for lack of a more specific term which would yet cover its different varieties, as more philosophical.

For the latter, the theoretical text is a subtext or rather a co-text against which the literary text is rubbed or bumped; a collision very close to collusion, an encounter leading to mixture. Such has been my own attitude in some of my later works. In *Death and Dissymmetry*,[19] for instance, Freud's essay "The Taboo of Virginity" was thus rubbed against and mixed with the story of the sacrifice of Jephthah's daughter in the Book of Judges, for a more critical understanding of each through the other. Freud's essay was there emphatically not used as a tool.

A "formalist" theory is more subservient and at the same time more ambitious. Like the philosophical approaches, such a theory aims at an encounter with the literary text. Also in accordance with the philosophical

19. Pp. 52–59.

approaches, it divides, breaks, and brackets literary theory in this encounter, because the theory never "works," because "application" is impossible. But, as distinct from the philosophical approaches, it is temporarily protected against itself, and used as a searchlight, a heuristic tool that helps to illuminate the literary text, which it appears to subject to itself, but to which in fact it is subjected.[20] For formalist theory, the literary text is more interesting, more worthwhile, than itself.

Related to this difference is a shift in truth-claim. Granted, structuralists like Greimas do, at times, appear to hold a positivistic claim to truth and objectivity. I am firmly on the side of structuralism's critics when it comes to this issue. "Truth" is a way of colonizing the text, of occupying it and posing as its owner. No method whatsoever can provide the true meaning of a text, because semiosis is not dealing in truth. "Truth," in interpretation, is, as in other semiotic practices, a matter of carrying conviction. And conviction is sought, by formalist discourse, through the presentation of contextual and co-textual evidence for its results, as well as through the intersubjective accessibility—minimal ambiguity, maximal clarity, and maximal systematicity—of its terms. The more arguments can be alleged for a critical statement, the more convincing the statement will be held to be. But the provisional help provided by convergence should not blind the critic to details that contradict the interpretation—for such a blindness leads back to unification, which is *not* part of the package offered by this "neo-formalism."

The status of theory as heuristic tool is bound to relativize the theory because it can only be accepted as long as it does, indeed, "work." But I contended earlier that it never does. I now wish to qualify that statement by an insight that has received growing attention in my work: formalist theory works to the extent that it doesn't. Which is not the same as saying that it doesn't work in any simple sense. Let me explain this odd statement.

In my earliest theoretical piece, here Chapter 4, the steps I took involved projecting a hypothesis about the text on the basis of a first confrontation between theory and reading—in the shape of a provisional set of "rules" the text was assumed to follow—and testing that hypothesis with passages other than those which helped formulate it. The heuristics then were double-edged: on the one hand, the confrontation exposed limit-cases, the places where the text seemed to obey the "rules" so strictly that the very obedience produced surplus meaning; on the other, transgressions, where the very disobedience produced special effects. In both cases, the narratological equipment was claimed to generate the interpretation which it also helped

20. The visual metaphors of light are intentional, but should not be taken as implying a truth-claim. Light can be deceptive, should always be suspected, and visibility is just one way of approaching reality, not a more reliable, privileged one *per se*.

verify—in the relativistic, rhetorical sense above. In some of my later work, e.g., the analysis of the Samson story, I use this negative heuristics in a more radical way. The same theory is brought to the text and doesn't "work" at all there. Precisely there where the theory fails, however, the text reveals its repressed problematics. In that case, access to the text was again provided by the theory, if, this time, in a purely negative way.[21] I think theory, in these cases, has a function and a provisional status which are different from, but not incompatible with, those of the theories used as subtexts in philosophical criticism. Yet such a use does not imply some sort of positivistic and colonizing truth-claim. I call this the heuristic function of theory.

A second, related aspect of truth is the explanatory function of theory. I do not mean to reopen the debate on causal versus nomological explanation, or on explaining versus understanding; I use the term in a much more colloquial sense. The explanatory function of theories can also mean "accounting for what happens," and answering the question "Why?" In the same Chapter 4, for example, the starting-point for the analysis was an enigmatic feature of the novel's reception. Why is it, I wondered, that readers of this novel, women and men alike, automatically blame the woman character totally for the failure of the couple's marriage? What bothered me was not just the partiality in favor of the husband, whom in my own, equally realistic reading I happened to dislike from the start, but, more importantly, the very compulsion to judge, which I shared. Sophisticated criticism does not, today, go about distributing moral judgments on fictional characters. Why do Colette's readers tend to fall back into this moralistic fallacy? This question turned out to detain me later even more strongly, when I began to work on the Bible, where the same problem obviously occurs.[22]

It may need emphasis that I did not bring theory to bear on the text in order to "prove" that these readers were wrong. I took their response for granted, and wanted to analyze the strategies of seduction, the narrative rhetoric, which appeal to the readers and which, in turn, the readers appeal to as arguments. In other words, by shifting focus, the analysis aimed at

21. *Lethal Love*, Chapter 2. More theoretical reflection on negative heuristics is included in the longer French version of that book, *Femmes imaginaires*, Chapter 2.2 (cf. pp. 126–31). My Samson interpretation has been criticized for ahistoricism, in particular because of the use of psychoanalysis for the interpretation of an ancient text. As far as I know, it has not been challenged in the same way as the piece on Genesis 2–3.
22. Especially in the chapter (4) on Genesis 38, "One Woman, Many Men, and the Dialectic of Chronology," *Lethal Love* takes its starting-point in the same problem. Again, the French version in *Femmes imaginaires*, Chapter 3.2, has more theoretical reflections, especially a critical analysis of Genette's temporal categories. The criticisms of my Eve piece show how much even sophisticated non-religious critics get excited, ultimately, about the question whether Eve is "good" or "bad." This moral problem is so predominant that critics don't even notice my attempt to change the terms of that question, and to look at *how* the question is enforced upon the readers, not *what* the answer is.

overcoming the thorny problem of the compulsion to paraphrasis which paralyzes much of literary criticism. The overwhelming force of that compulsion makes one feel critics are, at best, just doing the homework dictated by the author, which is quite the opposite of criticism's vocation, and, at worst, projecting their own response onto the alleged authorial intention. This interest in the explanatory function of theory, its potency to account for text-reader interaction, has persisted in my work ever since, and has become more prominent as I went further with my work on the Bible. There, the question became more heavily relevant, as the Bible, of all books, is the most dangerous one, the one that has been endowed with the power to kill.[23]

I am obviously not claiming here that it is the text that kills, or hurts, or makes people sick or happy, strong, and active. What I want to examine is why people who kill, or do other things that engage power over the lives of others, are able to carry persuasion for a certain reading of the text that allows them to do these things in the name of the text. In other words, if we turn the aporia in reader-response theory as sketched by Culler into a sort of dialectic without resolution, a heterogeneity as proposed by van Alphen,[24] it makes sense to use theory as an agent that fights back: as the confrontational other to which the text cannot but confess, and thus expose, its strategies of persuasion.

2.2 Ahistoricism

The second criticism addressed to formalism, and to my work specifically, is a notion equally pervasive and equally vague, namely ahistoricism. Here, too, I would on the one hand deny my ahistoricism and acknowledge the importance of historical specificity, and on the other hand still defend the ways in which I have allegedly bracketed history in my theoretical and critical work. And again, historicism is often practising ostensive self-definition by negation, and for good reasons: it is far from having solved its most fundamental problems.

Historicism, in spite of the nice phrase with which it is today presented as "new," is not in the least a new idea. If I may be historical in my turn: it

---

23. Without overdramatizing, it seems hardly exaggerated to claim that the Bible has that power still today. As one of the founding texts for South African Apartheid, for example, it allows the racist regime to get away with its murders, partly because the basis of Apartheid in a certain reading of the Bible appears plausible enough to enough people to still count. And the power of such arguments in a thoroughly Christian society can hardly be overrated. Juridical and political systems work with texts—in fact, the practice of law is nothing but an ongoing exercise in interpretation. Appealing to the Bible is a move similar in kind, though not in content, to appealing to laws. Fundamentalism, then, is the imposition of a way of reading as law. The truth-claim of fundamentalism is in blatant contradiction with everything semiotic theory has taught us; at least, the practice of law acknowledges this, or it would not need to go on. Hence, the debate we are today engaged in is not an innocent academic game.

24. Culler, *On Deconstruction*, Chapter 1; Alphen, *Bij wijze van lezen*.

should not be forgotten that the old historicism has been rebuked, in the last three decades, not because of the importance it attached to history and time, but because of its anti-theoretical eclecticism, its determinism, its ethnocentrism and its evolutionism. Nobody would, today, defend Taine's "race, milieu, moment" theory which suffers from all these faults. If, and if so, to what extent, recent returns to historicism are fundamentally without these flaws remains a question that I would not undertake to discuss here. As for evolutionism, the tenacity with which this ideology survives even harsh and persuasive recent criticism is telling; I have discussed its intricate relationship to biblical criticism in *Murder and Difference*. Insofar as I can tell from the implicit arguments brought against my alleged ahistoricism, it is mainly eclecticism that motivates that rebuke. But it covers more than just eclecticism, as I will argue below.

Let me first say that my own concern for the historical dimension of literature has been lively all along, and it has been one of the reasons why I turned from the contemporary French novel to biblical narrative. Yet, in spite of my concern for history, I do not claim to be a historian of literature. It has never been my goal to account for the historical *meanings* of the biblical narratives. I disclaim such a goal especially because this is usually understood as the author's intention and the original audience's understanding. Toward the end of her article, Lanser assumes that biblical criticism is historical in this sense. She writes: "To the extent that biblical reading attempts to reconstruct an 'intentional' text, a reader will be constituting what she or he imagines to be the probable context . . . in which the text was *produced*."[25] Significantly, she does not appeal to the speech-act theorists here, but to Sternberg's arguably circular argument which I have criticized as projectionist.[26] I cannot agree with this pre-New Critical intentionalism which Lanser passes off as speech-act theory.

One of the rhetorical failures of structuralism is that the revision of historicism it inherently demands has not been taken up but has, instead, led to an all-too-easy dichotomy of synchrony versus diachrony. Yet under the pressure of structuralist systematics, the relation between synchronic models of narrative and the historical reality of texts cannot but become an urgent problem, not of irretrievable intention, or of unstable meaning, interactional and therefore heterogeneous, but of what might be called the handling of texts throughout history. That is what I became interested in, and I guess this has been misunderstood by those who saw in my readings of biblical narrative attempts to eternalize modern readings.

There are other ways to "be historical," to ask historical questions and raise historical problems, than to pretend to retrieve the authorial intention. I have given up the question of the author ("intention") long ago, and

---

25. Lanser, "(Feminist) Criticism in the Garden," 77.
26. See below, Chapter 3.

decidedly turned to the reader instead, not without a sharp awareness of the instability of these two roles. This instability has been more acutely sketched by Culler and then by van Alphen.[27] Especially the latter's proposal to distinguish radically between different moments and locations of meaning-production provides a possibility of adopting the aporia Culler's analysis demonstrates, without giving up reader-oriented criticism. What I called above the rhetorical strategies of the text should not be seen as linked up with the author's intention. Instead, the textual strategies of persuasion, although obviously in one sense produced by an author, are as much produced by the social situation in which that author is able to write, and allowed to write, only what the society is able and willing to process; yet those strategies are not objectively inscribed in the text, but are only vital and effective when activated by the response that brings them, so to speak, to life. Authors are also readers, and readers, writing their own ("version of" the) text, are also authors.

Working on the Bible has made me more sharply aware of precisely that. Readers of the Bible are constantly engaged in writing it. In this sense, *there is no historical text.* The study of extant biblical criticism quickly revealed the problems of any historical statement about the context and social structures in which the texts were produced, let alone which historical factors generated them, and how. In other words, the precise relationship between text and social reality has never been adequately defined, and even modernist critics are hard pressed to give a satisfactory account of that relationship. Is it not a bit unrealistic, then, to suppose even the possibility of doing so in the case of these ancient texts? We are dealing with a society whose relationship to "texts"—if we can, without anachronism, call these documents "texts" at all—was less than stable, and which, with only very few and small exceptions, is only known to us through its representation in the very texts whose relationship to it is supposed to be analyzed.

The fallacies such an assumption entails come fully to the fore whenever an appeal to history—be it called history, context, or performance—is followed up with a statement about intention. Allow me to take up, then, my two examples, with apologies for using my critics as "cases." As I have already suggested, Lanser misconstrues my interpretation of Genesis 2–3 in an attempt to defend, allegedly a historical interpretation, but implicitly the projection of her own interpretation—a full acceptance of eternalized sexism—onto the author's intention. Mary Nyquist also challenges my Genesis piece for ahistoricism. Both begin their constructions of my argument with an unwarranted identification between my analysis and Phyllis Trible's.[28]

27. See above, note 24.
28. Lanser, "(Feminist) Criticism in the Garden," especially qualifies this conflation in the end-notes. In fact, her aims, methods, and interpretations do not overlap that much

I have indeed been quite polite in my criticism of Trible, for the strategic reason that I did not want to alienate her audience, and for the scholarly reason that I found her interpretation, although basically wrong as I do not fail to point out, a lot better than the mass of male criticism on the same text that I had gone through. I faulted Trible not with ahistoricism, because that was not my concern in that article,[29] but for her religious bias. In spite of my less than polemical tone, I do clearly distance myself from Trible's article, which is quite obviously different in approach anyway.

The conflation is remarkable because of the following basic differences between Trible's work and mine. Trible's method is entirely based in New Criticism and traditional literary biblical criticism, claims to be text-immanent, and works with patterns of words, ignoring rhetorical strategies altogether. It is much closer to, say, Fokkelman's work than to mine. If anything, it is formalist in the traditional sense, not in the sense of Russian formalism. My own methodological argument, in contrast, semiotic and narratological, was about how character is constructed, and how sometimes the reader's construction of a character fails to overlap with the text's, so as to leave an irreducible gap. Lanser completely ignores or misses this point when she keeps blaming me for proposing that "Eve," the character which emerges toward the end of Genesis 3, is different from the creature whose construction began earlier, in Genesis 2. That "difference within," as Barbara Johnson would call it, was my major point.

The consequence of this difference in method is a different status for the text. Trible claims that it speaks for itself, that it "fits" the analysis, and she gives it unity. I claim that the text is already a reading, that no unambiguous reading is possible, and that the text is not unified. These assumptions, in turn, are based on ideological differences. Trible's position is theological

---

with those of Nyquist, "Gynesis, Genesis, Exegesis." The conflation between Trible and myself, which I find quite painful given my own problems with Trible's work, is so frequent, and so easily repeated, that it deserves interpretation as a rhetorical strategy. Patricia Parker follows the lead, and writes: "Bal's essay, and its basis in Phyllis Trible's *God and the Rhetoric of Sexuality* . . . is subjected to a critique of its ahistoricism . . ." (*Literary Fat Ladies*, 264) in a chapter that is itself entirely ahistorical. It is discouraging that feminists, whose major quarrel is or must be with binarism, seem so hard pressed to get away from binarism themselves. The two dichotomies which inform these critics are clear: (1) If I do not accuse Genesis of sexism, I must be idealizing and eternalizing it as feminist; (2) if I do not spit on Trible, I must agree with her. I happen to dislike spitting on colleagues, but I am more than willing to point out my position even more explicitly than I have already done—see Chapter 3. I am happy to concede that I have underestimated the power of these dichotomies, and would have been better advised to be more polemical against Trible, as I have learned since.

29. In *Death and Dissymmetry*, 82–83, I do criticize Trible's ahistoricism in her uncritical acceptance of the translation of *zōnā* as "harlot" and *pîlegesh* as "concubine" (*Texts of Terror*). These two concepts indicating the status of women are hardly ever challenged; yet they are arguably anachronistic misconceptions of the Hebrew words and the concerns they represent. I find any biblical critic using these translations without discussing them, fundamentally ahistorical.

and religious, and her interpretation is part of a feminist "salvation history." Thus it serves an overtly ideological purpose—perfectly acceptable within a given strategy—to which the ambiguities are subordinated. My ideological position stems from a different feminist philosophy and is close to radical scepticism. I discuss religious readings as instances of the text's ambiguity, not as its meaning; I deny the text's unity or wholeness; and I refuse the *a priori* alternative of sexism versus feminism, both and together anachronistic. Most importantly perhaps, my interpretation is part of a theoretical argument from which it cannot be separated, as both these critics do. Hence, the conflation of these very different papers into a single Trible-Bal argument is strange, almost sexist—the feminists are lumped together as the "other"—and must be motivated by some strong, probably emotional force.

But I will not overdo *my* conflation of Nyquist and Lanser. Lanser speaks in the name of speech-act theory, although in a version I find hard to recognize as such, while Nyquist speaks as a renaissancist. Lanser projects her interpretation as universal, including the original audience *and* author, and, once engaged in that movement, her speech-act theory becomes identical with intentionalism;[30] Nyquist projects her "sentimental and logocentric" enemy, a positive, non-sexist reading of Genesis 2–3, onto me.[31] In both cases, the historicism of my opponents themselves is highly dubious. Lanser finds that my account leaves my view of language implicit. I can understand that, but only if she considers my point about the gradual construction of character irrelevant or, more likely, if she has missed it. Nyquist is, like myself, interested in historical readings of the story, in the text's history as a history of interpretations. She comes close to contradicting herself when her criticism of other interpretations suggests the possibility of a "clean" interpretation. But she constructs the feminist readings as a context for Milton's reading of Genesis, which is a strangely ahistorical move for a historian. Nyquist rightly argues against idealizing the story and thereby taking it out of context. By projecting that problem on my text, however, she misreads my interpretation as fully as Lanser does. Why do they make these mistakes?

As I see it, it is because both criticisms are based on two dichotomies.

---

30. This is, indeed, a danger inherent in speech-act theory, whenever it projects a simple communicational model. Yet the theory has been designed, precisely, to overcome the ideology of perfect communication, in that it worries about success or failure of speech-acts. The revisionist way Lanser uses speech-act theory as a pretext for a return to intention contrasts sharply with more radical uses, e.g., Shoshana Felman's seminal *Literary Speech-Acts*.

31. In many ways, and without irony, I share much of Nyquist's suspicion, and I wish to point out that I find her account of Genesis, including the criticism of extant interpretations, much more worthwhile than Lanser's. Although I feel she misconstrues my argument, the very quality of her own piece made me aware of the rhetorical flaws of mine.

Firstly, as I have already suggested, the text is seen as either sexist or feminist-egalitarian. Since the latter seems highly unlikely—especially within any evolutionist bias—the former is taken to be the only acceptable starting-point. The profound ahistoricism in both these attacks, however, lies precisely in that dichotomy. However difficult it is to imagine, deeply trained as we all are in binary thinking, it is not self-evident that binarism has always and everywhere been the dominant mode of thought.[32]

Secondly, the very idea of egalitarianism is a historical and non-mono-lithic one. Moreover, the extent to which gender problems were relevant issues in this story needs historical analysis. And in addition to all this, the construction of a monolithic ideology for this text, be it sexist or egalitarian, is grounded in a unifying view of language and texts, and their functions, that became "normal"—hence, is ideological—only with romanticism.

The conflict underlying these discussions is also a matter of the place of theory, which I earlier discussed as the difference between "formalist" and "philosophical" theories-in-practice. Lanser, especially, uses theory awk-wardly. Firstly, she reduces speech-act theory to inference from textual elements; thus she turns a radically non-autonomist theory into an autono-mist one. Thereby, she turns it into a theory which does *not* allow historical interpretation. Lanser locks herself up within a text, with her own sense of "normal logic" as her only tool. Secondly, this use of the theory makes it impossible to view her own reading as speech-act theory would: as another performance. Yet by taking readings to be performances, the theory implies the projection she, in fact, performs. The combination of these two aspects of Lanser's use of the theory leads to blatant anachronisms and denial of the text's otherness.[33]

32. This does not occur to Lanser, who takes it for granted that her inferences are universal. A hilariously circular argument results on page 75 of "(Feminist) Criticism in the Garden," where she claims that the consequences of the transgression, in Gen 3:14–19, *must* be a punishment, because there was a prohibition and because the prohibitor has the authority to punish. When she writes, not shunning ambiguity in her choice of the passive form, that "God is *expected* to deliver punishment long before he does so," she is projecting, like so many others, a modern sense of authority relations on a text where, I maintain, such a context, while perhaps not absent, is not necessarily relevant in any predominant way.

33. One example among many is her argument, "(Feminist) Criticism in the Garden," 73, that the earth creature *hā' ādām* is the man Adam and has power to name the woman, in spite of the obvious fact that he doesn't. This recuperation of a centuries-old misreading is justified by the argument of coherence, of unity: "the text has already generated the context in which 'call' may be inferred to mean 'call the name of,' despite the abbreviated surface form." What "the text" has generated is, of course, Lanser's expectations, based on everyday language. This is the "context" invoked. What is suppressed is the well-known feature of biblical narrative, that in repetitions the slightest difference points to the meaningfulness of near-synonymy: the telling misfit. Lanser does not seem to know this, although her sources Alter and Sternberg drive this obvious point home quite frequently. Instead of acknowledging as part of the context the difference between this ancient text and her contemporary colloquial discourse, and the tensions on which biblical narrative is gen-erally assumed to be constructed, the difference within, all the text's power to estrange the reader from herself is suppressed in favor of "my context, myself."

A symptomatic reading of Lanser's and Nyquist's attacks would fore-ground a sense of passion in their discourse, betrayed by the contradictory conflation of Trible and me, the insistent misreadings, the absolutist lan-guage (Nyquist: "profoundly ahistorical," "fully justifies the sentimental and logocentric conclusion"), and, most significantly, the "ostensive self-definition by negation" whereby the historicism of my opponents needs no further clarification. I think that the strong force[34] motivating these attacks has to do with three problems: my attitude toward theory, of which enough has been said; uneasiness and difficulty about the heterogeneity of the text—a historical problem; and misprision of my refusal to construct such a monolithic ideological interpretation.

And that refusal of mine is, I contend, if not historical, at least a refusal of ahistoricism. I do not know exactly how "literature" functioned in biblical times, and I do not know how people "read," although there are reasons for believing that literacy, linearity, and literarity were not the only ways of processing stories, nor was binarism necessarily the all-encompassing frame of mind. But I do suspect our ways of reading to be typical of our culture, and therefore I tried to undermine the unifying reading usually applied to the Genesis story. My point was that it is not all-of-a-piece, ideologically speaking; that there are sexist elements and non-sexist elements, and that their juxtaposition may be a problem for us. Especially, the *moral* interpre-tation, which underlies all attempts to make the ideology of the text into a unified whole, is, I think, anachronistic.

Aside from anger with what the later Jewish and Christian cultures have done to women in the name of this text, and suspicion toward any interpre-tation that seems to justify those horrors by discounting the sexist sting applied to the text—an anger and suspicion which women are well advised to adopt—I have a sense that my two feminist critics are also upset because I seem ambivalent. But I am not ambivalent in my treatment; without being historical but consistent with my, say, anti-ahistoricism, I am just refusing holism and binarism.

A second dichotomy which, I think, underlies both the argument against my alleged ahistoricism and the rhetorical move of conflating Trible's and my interpretations, is also directly related to the issue of historicism itself. I am alluding to the widespread, and in my view highly ideological, dichot-omy between historical and systematic thinking, which betrays a conserva-tive strand in American criticism. As I have argued elsewhere,[35] the term post-structuralism does not indicate simply a temporal succession, and the

---

34. In *Death and Dissymmetry*, where I devote a full chapter (5) to speech-act theory (!) I insist on the difference between force and meaning. This difference is at stake here, too: even if my opponents were right on points, the *force* of their discourse still deserves interpretation.

35. *Femmes imaginaires* is the most extensive presentation of my thoughts about this issue.

concomitant evolutionism that automatically values posteriority needs critical examination. Its implied move "beyond" structuralism presupposes and indeed demands a passage through structuralism. One cannot go beyond what one has not gone through; instead of a step ahead, skipping the previous step leads to a flight.

Thus contemporary criticism includes, along with post-structuralists, pre-structuralists posing as post-structuralists (with apologies for this dichotomy).[36] Those post-structuralists who have thoroughly gone through structuralism differ in their critical practice from those who haven't. Those who have made shrewd use in their deconstructions of the very terms they criticize, turn around, bump against the literary text; and in the end the deconstructed term, bracketed, radically different from what it was before, is still there for us to use, in a different sense of "use." Those who haven't triumphantly exposed the obvious and inevitable contradictions and ideological strands in terms they sometimes don't render adequately in the first place, end with empty hands. But worse, the tendency to reject rather than analyze and relativize the tools of systematic analysis leads to a position which is an anti-theoretical version of historicism, often without being truly historical.

I would suggest that this entails a return to excessive eclecticism and poor historical analysis. The reason why this regression is inevitable lies precisely in what I wrote above about intentionalism: the projection of subjective interpretation onto the author, and the refusal to check this by negative heuristics.

The opposition between historical and systematic analysis which underlies this regression is itself anachronistic. In addition to the modernism of these two approaches, the dualism that informs the opposition is paradoxically universalistic. This universalism is paradoxical because historicism is overtly anti-universalistic. But its projectional aspects tend to turn the so-called historical interpretation into the truth, the only right way to interpret the text, hence, to universalize in the very attempt to undo the universalism of others.

An illuminating example of the intricacy of all these issues can be found in a publication whose foundation in philosophy, the discipline which lives in and by historical and/as/with systematic analysis, makes it exemplary for our problem. In his recent book on the origin of perspective, a book whose very title polemically refuses the above dichotomy, Hubert Damisch[37]

---

36. A well known, and good, example of the former is, of course, Jonathan Culler; one among many examples of the latter is David Carroll, whom I choose to mention because I have justified this view of his *Questioning the Subject* in an article to appear in the second volume of these essays.

37. Damisch, *L'origine*. The word "origin" points at an historical issue, while the concept "perspective" inscribes the systematic concern without which such a study is unthinkable.

addresses the issue of historicism with persuasiveness as well as with typical but understandable irritation. He discusses the origin, hence, the history, of both the concept of perspective in writing and the use of perspective in painting, and thus demonstrates that the two cannot be separated. Damisch thereby relativizes and criticizes the concept, yet uses it, "under erasure." He has no other choice, as both the ideological fallacies in which the concept is embedded, and the reality of something we have to call, at least provisionally, "perspective," are undeniably present in history.

Throughout his long study, Damisch insistently asks two questions: "If there is history, *of what* is it the history?" and "What is the place of *time* in history?"[38] ; and he deduces from the difficulty of answering these questions the necessity of self-criticism:

> A history which would not pretend to have the last word on everything, and which could not be practised unless . . . the term which names the discipline were problematic, never self-evident, and unless the question of its different usages as well as its ultimate meaning remained constantly present . . . .[39]

The importance of this view lies in the demand that historicism specify its own concept of history and historicality, and that is precisely what I find lacking in most historicist attacks on formalism.

Neglecting these important questions leads not only to a defective because unself-conscious historical analysis, but also to missing the boat of what formalism can offer to help bring about such self-consciousness. The indeterminacy of negativity is again at work here: when they do not specify what formalism is supposed to be doing and in what respects it is ahistorical, the attacks are not focusing on questions of history at all. Hence, there is no way to formulate whether, and in what respect, the analysis is in contradiction with (exactly what kind of) historical knowledge—which is, of course, the primary justification for any rejection of systematic analysis. Jumping through history on the basis of a theme implies a generalizing movement which is easily led away from historical to universalistic concerns.

In addition to the ill-foundedness and want of specificity of the so-called historical alternative, it should be clear by now that I reject the argument

38. For the first question ("S'il y a histoire, *de quoi* est-ce l'histoire?), see Damisch, *L'origine*, 12, and throughout the book. The second draws support from Benveniste's remark: "Le temps n'est pas le facteur de l'évolution, il n'en est que le cadre" ("Time is not the creator of evolution, only its setting"): *Problèmes*, 5.

39. My translation. The original reads: "Une histoire qui ne prétendrait pas avoir sur toutes choses le dernier mot, et qui ne saurait être pratiquée comme telle que sous la condition expresse que le terme qui donne son nom à cette discipline fasse pour elle problème, qu'il n'aille jamais de soi, et que la question des différents usages auxquels il prête, aussi bien que sa signification dernière, reste constamment présente à l'horizon de la recherche, comme doit être celle qui en fait la réciproque: s'il y a histoire, *de quoi* est-elle l'histoire?" (Damisch, *L'origine*, 12).

also because, simply, I do not find formalism *per se*, or my own work for that matter, ahistorical, any more than I find it autonomist. The study of the rhetorical strategies of a text produces the gap between the text and its other, which is its other readings. That gap foregrounds diachronic difference. By exposing the differences, not only between the text and its readings but also within the text *as* reading, the "difference within" which Barbara Johnson so brilliantly demonstrates throughout her work, criticism is harder pressed to remain outside of historical self-consciousness than by doing thematic analysis under the guise of a historicity merely indicated by unelaborated allusions to "Renaissance poetics," "Elizabethan discourse," or "biblical context." In other words, precisely the terms that cover the ahistoricism of historicism are those whose specification and questioning Damisch rightly demands.

2.3 Belatedness

The polemical tone which transpires in these pages, in spite of my peaceful intentions, stems from my difficulty with the very notion of belatedness. On the one hand, I find Schehr's point well taken: one cannot, innocently, go on publishing work which is structuralist, formalist or whatever one wishes to call it, as if the last fifteen years of theory had passed unnoticed. Hence my willingness, or even happiness, to address the issues discussed. On the other hand, the sheer fact that studies have been published that challenge assumptions akin to those of my work does not *automatically* make the work futile. Such a view is itself based on a single-stream evolutionism. Just as post-structuralism, and deconstruction in particular, has roots that precede structuralism and is unthinkable without structuralism, so, symmetrically, structuralism today cannot but be affected by its "post-," which it in any case projected from the outset. In a deep sense, never more apparent than in Barthes' *S/Z*, post-structuralism is the *trace* of structuralism as much as the other way around.

An unproblematic notion of belatedness ignores this inherent belatedness of ideas, which a more complex sense of history cannot but acknowledge and, indeed, appreciate. Such an accusation presupposes that ideas depend on "fashion," which is to assign them a rather superficial and ephemeral status. Assuming that the "new" is new at all is a linearist fallacy; assuming that the "new" is automatically superior is an evolutionist fallacy. To put it once more polemically: declaring ideas *passé* without their being *assumé* is turning "post-" back into "pre-."

I wish to emphasize at this point, and against probable misreadings of this text, that I am not trying to justify an intrinsically reactionary position. In contrast, I am arguing to expose the reactionary scenario of a simplistic plea for academic progressivity, and claiming that there may be more progressivity in *not* rejecting the past *en bloc*. The problem with "fashion"—

that in the name of which the notion of belatedness is applied —is its incapacity to historicize itself. Something that, by its misfit with current discourse, conveys a sense of belatedness might, in contrast, very well derive its value from the way it produces awareness of its own historical possibilities.

3. THE SEQUENCE OF THE CHAPTERS

The essays have been ordered in a sequence which not every reader will wish to follow. They are divided into three sections, whose sequence, after long hesitation, is fairly traditional. The first section contains methodological reflections and background: reflections in which my own narratological concepts and views are embedded. The second section presents, then, the theory of narrative as I outlined it in my early work. The third section contains five essays of "applied" narratology which have never before appeared in English: confrontations between theoretical and literary (three French, one Dutch, and one Latin) texts. Each section is provided with a short introduction which maps the contents of the essays in more detail.

January 1990, Mieke Bal

PART I

On Method

This section offers some reflections on the methodological status of narratology. For some, this status may not need justification; for me it most surely does. The primary standard by which I wish to measure the contribution of narratology is that of *relevance*. Chapter 1 positions narratology between feminism, psychoanalysis, and German critical theory, represented by Habermas. Although I agree with Jacqueline Rose's[1] objection to Habermas' recuperation of the unconscious, an argument I did not know of when I wrote this essay, I would maintain the heuristic fertility of an assumed analogy between the individual and the collective unconscious; but I would, today, be more cautious in specifying their differences. This chapter is a fragment of those theoretical sections of *Femmes imaginaires* which were sacrificed in the reworking of the book for the American audience as *Lethal Love*.

Chapter 2 represents a more narrow methodological discussion. This piece was written as a review article of Peter Brooks' *Reading for the Plot*, a book which, for all its merit, I consider typical of the American "new narratology." As I will suggest below, the movement beyond "formalism" is necessary but not unproblematic, and I have chosen to include this review because it presents a case—one of the best, as it happens—of certain problems I saw emerge in that movement. The review brings three phases in the development of narratology, from pre-structuralist—Stanzel[2]—via structuralist—Genette[3]—to post-structuralist—Brooks—to bear upon each other.

Chapter 3 is also a review article, and is included because it represents

1. Rose, *Sexuality in the Field of Vision.*
2. Stanzel, *A Theory of Narrative.*
3. Genette, *Nouveau discours.*

yet another current of my work: "The Bible as literature" between "formalism" and feminism. It is more concrete than the first two, in that it presents a discussion of how the methodological considerations affect "field studies." In this article, the studies discussed demonstrate some of the points I argued in the introduction to this volume, for example, that lack of method—of "rigor," if you like—joins, or even entails, a lack of historical awareness and of feminist consciousness. Together, these chapters, written during the more recent years, give an impression of my position in the current debate on the roles and assumptions of criticism.

∎ 1 ∎

Narratology
as Critical Theory

1. INTRODUCTION

For a theory to be critical it must account for the permanent interaction between social and individual processes. The opposition between the two is problematized, indeed resolved, by critical theory. This presupposition implies some specific methodological requirements. To establish itself, criticism needs *tools*: without these, no criticism would be able to achieve an acceptable degree of intersubjectivity, that is, be plausible and transmissible. But these tools need to satisfy the demands suggested by the above presupposition; that is to say, they need to be connected to the disciplines that are concerned, in principle separately, with the social and the individual: social theory and psychoanalysis. Nevertheless, it is not sufficient simply to combine them. Only a systematic integration, without rupture, of the two disciplines can prevent the continuation of this split, which so much needs resolution. Up to now, these tools have been wanting.

Conversely, narratology is at an impasse. It has ceased to be perceived as fruitful, insofar as it has not succeeded in establishing itself as a *tool*, that is, in putting itself in the service of any critical practice. The result is violent opposition to "formalism," identified wrongly or rightly with structuralism. The ambiguity of the term "post-structuralism" attests to this impasse. Its success, in certain contexts, rests on a misunderstanding. On the one hand, it points to a movement beyond. But it points also to the kinship between the two successive currents. This is why the term "post-Saussurianism,"[1] indicating a structuralism following Saussure (in both senses), is perhaps more appropriate. The choice of the term "post-structuralism" has allowed this current to secure for itself a particularly brilliant success in the coun-

---

1. Belsey, *Critical Practice.*

tries where structuralism was adopted only with reticence. The temptation to take a giant leap over a phase which has still not been fully accepted plays a motivating role here.

What has been lost along the way is, in fact, the positive nucleus of structuralism, its real contribution to critical theory; a contribution whose efficacy lies less in producing models that can be developed in a multitude of (disappointing) ways, than in carrying forward the search for models, or the desire to furnish tools. It is less the structures, therefore, than the mindset governing structuralism which could bring about the advance of which Marx and Freud, each in his own way, were the precursors *avant la lettre.*

The problem, then, has been the following. On the one hand, the criticism of ideologies has shown a tendency to produce massive judgments, and to reject precisely the methodological "formalism" which could have remedied this fault. On the other hand, narratology, applied in and for itself, has lacked relevance. In order to pursue research beyond this impasse, my working hypothesis has posited a central place for the concept of the subject, which is a privileged concept in the three fields concerned— sociology, psychoanalysis, and narratology—without its status having been systematically elucidated. The three disciplines express opinions about the subject, but in a doubly paradoxical fashion. On the one hand, it remains attached to the human individual, even while this individual is itself called in question. On the other hand, in a situation where the prevalent linguistic theories proclaim the ambiguity of the principle of "the sign become signifier," the concept is never defined, even though it is with good reason considered a dubious one. I have tried to resolve this paradoxical situation without completely eliminating the paradox.

Before attempting a definition, it seems to me necessary to study the concept of the subject in its functioning. The ambiguities of the word "subject" in current usage have to be taken seriously. Only then can a working definition be attempted. Such a definition, then, will derive its authority from lexical and semantic study of the word: current usage will constitute a solid foundation for a non-humanist conception of the semiotic subject. Daily usage and a certain level of scientific rigor are less contradictory than one might think, if one considers the capacity to make manifest the underlying problematics to be an integral part of such rigor. This reflection on the subject will permit us to clarify the relationship between the social, the individual, and the narrative, through the perspective of semiotics, which is well fitted for the purpose. Based on this elucidation, a systematic study of subjectivity as the organizing principle behind narrative will become possible. This study will open the way to a criticism of the social function of reading. The distortions practised on texts by social groups, distortions which the dominant groups impose on others, and which contribute to the (re)production of ideological positions, can then be marked, described, and explicated. Where is such an approach to be situated? In the pages that follow, I will quickly trace out the course of the epistemology that led Jürgen Habermas to define his concept of *critical science*. Despite some reservations, it is in light of this concept that I would like, finally, to situate my work in this collection of essays. These reflections address questions raised by neo-positivist skeptics, rather than by post-modern thinkers.

2. PROBLEMS OF EPISTEMOLOGY
The Place of the Knowing Subject

2.1 Positivism and its faults

My treatment will address in particular the empiricist movement in literary studies currently in vogue in Germany. In a philosophy of the conditions of "sure" knowledge (worthy of confidence), students of litera-ture don't find themselves at home. On the one hand, under the influence of an inexplicable masochism, if not the persistence of Calvinism, they persist in wanting to line up under the aegis of a totally outmoded posi-tivism, or of its modern variant, critical rationalism[2] uncritically regarded as a superior law. On the other hand, one is aware of the well-founded objections addressed to different positivisms in the name of a critical philosophy developed, out of Kant and especially out of Hegel via Marx, by the members of the Frankfurt School, and coming to a provisional con-clusion in the work of Habermas,[3] from which my reflections borrow a great deal. Simplified, this opposition can be summarized thus:

(a) Whereas objectivist positivism "forgets" the relationship between the sciences and the process of self-formation of the human species, in other words represses the direct relationship between science and human inter-ests, critical philosophy requires the knowing subject to examine the conditions and the extent of the knowledge of which it is in principle capable.

(b) Whereas positivism takes a specific category of knowledge as a prototype, then as a norm, in order to generalize from it to the procedures which then become the very definition of knowledge, critical philosophy recognizes the difference between the possible forms of knowledge. The equations "knowledge=science," and then "science=natural sciences," it therefore rejects.

(c) Whereas positivism sets up faith in science as a dogma, thus pro-tecting itself from self-criticism and, by this scientistic attitude, replacing

2. E.g., Popper, *The Poverty of Historicism.*
3. Habermas, *Knowledge and Human Interests.*

epistemology with a philosophy of science where *laws* replace subjects, critical philosophy requires knowledge's self-reflection on its own conditions, so proclaiming a conscious and constant activity of the knowing subject.

(d) This opposition can be illustrated in respect of the place of logic and mathematics. In positivisms, these two disciplines become formal independent sciences—independent because they are formal. Their foundation is no longer at issue. They escape critical reflection, and can no longer be questioned concerning the validity of knowledges based on them. Critical philosophies, by contrast, affirm that validity has so many aspects that, always and on principle, every form of knowledge must be open to criticism. To a formal logic which is, in any case, far from being unified, they oppose the possibility of a dialectical logic, always mobile, always open to critique.

(e) The positivist current has given rise to the naive idea that knowledge (in its view synonymous with science) describes reality. It considers the world as existent, consisting of *facts* structured by *laws*. The a priori constitution of these facts is thus "forgotten." The critical philosophies oppose to this idea consciousness of the process which led to the constitution of the world: the *facts* are the results of our choosing to consider them as such. These choices being discussable in principle, the notion of objectivity is replaced by that of intersubjectivity.

2.2 Peirce and the discursive character of knowledge

The logician Charles S. Peirce took an important step in the development of a philosophy of knowledge. He specified that the task of methodology is to clarify not only the logical structure of scientific theories, but also the logical structure of the procedure by which we arrive at these theories. The frequent and fundamental confusion between process and result is denounced with aplomb by Feyerabend.[4] The difference is important because process implies the underlying *interests*, interests which analysis exclusively of the result allows to be obliterated. But the contribution of Peirce's work resides above all in the emphasis he places on the *discursive* aspect of the cognitive process. Peirce speaks of a chain of arguments whose beginning and end are not perceptible. There are no propositions that are fundamental, generally valid, not subject to proof by other propositions. Neither are there ultimate elements of sure and uninterpreted perception. It is therefore inconceivable to speak of *facts* without speaking at the same time of *interpretations*.

Every valid empirical base is mediated, according to Peirce, by inferences. These are represented by signs. In consequence, even perceptions are situated in the dimension of representation. What we take for "asso-

---

4. Feyerabend, *Against Method*.

ciations of images" are in reality associations of judgments. Any increase in a person's information implies, and is implied by, an increase in the information attached to a word. The word takes on the successive interpretants brought by each user.

It is from here that the curious Peircian semiotics is developed, a semiotics a little too trinitarian to be plausible. (But plausibility is perhaps not a decisive criterion.) According to this theory, signs denote what they denote on the basis of three principles:

Principle	Function	Type of sign	Domain of signification
analogy	to be the image of	icon	imaginary
contiguity	to refer to	index	existential
convention	to represent	symbol	arbitrary

These categories, even if they are grounded in an ontology that one can question, at any rate allow us not only to analyze literary texts, but also to follow the not always very clear arguments by means of which critics discuss interpretations of these texts.

2.3 Dilthey and the hermeneutic character of knowledge

In the work of Wilhelm Dilthey, a specific methodology for the cultural sciences is elaborated. Starting from a conception of understanding that corresponds in principle with the discursivity posited by Peirce, Dilthey establishes an epistemology with a more general value. According to him,[5] understanding is the projection of the self into something external, in such a way that an unfamiliar or past experience is re-presented in the experience of the self. This exteriorization of the spirit is the process which produces meaning. To achieve it, the subject must get a foothold in language. Whether it be in words, attitudes, or actions, the subject cannot objectify its experience until it has entered into the system of intersubjectivity. Then alone can subjects agree about something general in a specific fashion. They identify themselves to each other, they know and recognize each other. At the same time, they keep their distance from each other by positing themselves in their own inalienable identity. The symbolic community allows reciprocal (in both senses of the word) identity and the preservation of difference, of nonidentity. One recognizes in this dialectic aspect the ideas of Lacan. Self-understanding, indispensable to a social communication that can meet these demands, is constituted at the intersection of the mutual intersubjective understanding of others and the intersubjective understanding of oneself. This is why self-reflection has a socially indispensable critical function.

5. See Gadamer, *Truth and Method*, and Göttner, *Logik der Interpretation*, for summaries.

2.4 Intersubjectivity and self-reflection
The contribution of the cultural sciences

There is an abyss between a (lived) situation and its linguistic expression. The dialogical use of language[6] requires this abyss to be filled up. Hermeneutical understanding is in this sense indispensable. The hermeneutic corresponds to the distance which the human subject must both maintain and express between itself—that is, its identity and its structures in the history of (its) life—and its objectifications. Without this distance, the subject risks being reified by those to whom it addresses itself, since it would be identified with what it expresses. But without the hermeneutic, the distance would remain irreducible, intersubjectivity would be destroyed, social life impossible, the individual lost.

In the cultural sciences and in the natural sciences, the relationships between language, action, and experience are different. The nomological propositions that constitute the structure of the natural sciences grasp reality in terms of technical mastery. Under specific conditions, this mastery is everywhere and always possible. The hermeneutical propositions, by contrast, seize reality in terms of intersubjectivity, a condition of the mutual understanding orienting the action, from a given hermeneutical starting point. The expression "in terms of" indicates that an underlying interest orients the science in question. By "interest," Habermas understands an orientation rooted in the specific conditions of self-formation and of the reproduction of the human species. These interests are fundamental, directed not at the satisfaction of immediate empirical needs but at the solution of systemic problems. In the natural and hermeneutical sciences, the initial orientations are respectively work, which is a unilateral and monological mastery of nature, and interaction. Thus one can distinguish a technical and a practical interest. But reason and its use entail the desire to reason freely, whence a third interest, that of responsibility and autonomy: the emancipatory interest. It is directed at liberation from dogmatic dependencies by critical self-reflection. This interest is not simply superimposed on the others. The three presuppose one another. Only the emancipated subject is capable of communication as a nonreified subject. Only the subject capable of interaction can (re)solve systemic problems of a technical order. Technical mastery without reflection produces what we witness today, symbolized by a floating ship, loaded with nuclear waste, which has no place to go. The cultural sciences serve principally the second and third interests. They are nonetheless equally indispensable to the blossoming of the natural sciences.

Habermas distinguishes three categories of science: each elaborates sys-

---

6. As analyzed by Mikhail Bakhtin; see the introduction by Todorov, *Bakhtine.*

tematically one of the basic notions. I insist on the fact that this division is an overview, a matter of where one puts the stress: no discipline can be exclusively enclosed in one category. The categories differ on several points, of which the following schema gives a survey.[7]

	I	II	III
actions	monological	dialogical	reflective
social organization	work	language	power
directed by	technical rules	social rules	rules of criticism
based on	empirical knowledge of the world	mutual recognition	self-reflection
goal	mastery	agreement	autonomy
sciences	empirical-analytical	hermeneutical	critical
means	information	interpretation	analysis (self-)criticism
prescientific experiences	sensory	communicative	metacommunicative
cognitive interest	technical	practical	emancipatory
goal	acquisition of applicable/usable knowledge	preservation of the continuity of tradition as the condition of communication	liberation from relations of dependence and power

2.5 Characteristics of the critical sciences

The cultural sciences have as their object the functioning of communication itself. They do not study the faults and problems produced *along with* language or the communicative system, but the problems *in* the communicative system. The very capacity to communicate is disordered. If the system has broken down, this problem is of a systemic order. Likewise the solution must be of a systemic order. Consequently, a theory of communication is necessary. To arrive at a systemic solution, critical theories must clarify (*aufklären*) the problem in communication and also explain (*erklären*) it. The symptom of a problem must be first located and described, then interpreted, and finally explained as to its cause. How can one put such a theory to the test? As in all science, a first testing takes place in theoretical discussions. There, concurrent theories confront one another on the basis of arguments. The arguments can be borrowed from perception, from the empirical base, but just as well from other fields, such as the

---

7. This schema is based on van Alphen, "Visie"; see also his *Bang voor schennis?*

logic of technical and social implications, etc. I have drawn on such discussions in the theoretical parts of the present study. But there is also a practical test. The subjects upon whose situation the theory renders a verdict need to confirm the hypothesis in the course of what Habermas calls "therapeutic discussions." But there is a problem here. As long as the situation remains unchanged, the subjects have not come to terms with their own dependence, their subjection. Confirmation therefore seems impossible. Here again there is a parallel between the situations concerning inter- and intrasubjective problems. In the case of intrasubjective problems, we know that the disappearance of the symptom does not provide confirmation. It can be part of the subject's strategies of resistance. Nor is rational, or even emotional, confirmation of any greater value. These can be inspired by the desire to please the analyst, the wish to be done with analysis, etc. The only fairly sure confirmation is the successful continuation of the analysis. In the case of intersubjective problems, the situation is similar. Confirmations through the disappearance of the symptom, in other words through the release of the constraint in question, can obscure another constraint. This is indeed very frequently the case: emancipation, if limited to details without real importance, is merely apparent. Confirmation by mutual agreement can be based on discouragement, fatigue, misunderstanding. Only the successful continuation of the analysis confirms that it is on the right track. This problem is transferred to literary criticism in the study of reader-response.[8] In any case, a confrontation between the text and its rewritings turns out to be, if not a means of resolution, at least a possibility of verification.

A critical theory presupposes some norms on which arguments will be based. In the majority of scientific discourses, this normative side, always present, is implicit, but for that reason only the more powerful. For the critical sciences, which are overtly normative, Habermas proposes to found these norms on a model of ideal communication. By that he means the reconstruction of an untroubled communicative competence, free from relations of power: a form of intersubjectivity. It is obvious that this model does not represent an accessible ideal. It is simply the norm in relation to which differences can be measured. The presupposition of a rational subject is no longer self-evident, and raises, little as one may be concerned to demonstrate its validity, a series of problems. The necessity of calling such a subject into question constitutes precisely the reason for the present enterprise; as has become apparent, I do not hold to the hypothesis of the rational subject, even if, in order to interrogate it, it is convenient at first to take it seriously.

---

8. See the collections edited by Suleiman, *The Reader in the Text*, and Tompkins, *Reader Response Criticism*.

What lesson can one draw from these epistemological considerations? First of all, the conclusion is inescapable that the subject must be seriously studied, situated, made explicit. It must occupy a central place in theory. Then, it is important to recognize that every action is oriented by interests, and this opens up the possibility, and the opportunity, of locating, in the texts one studies, the symptoms of underlying interests. Are they the interests of emancipation or of domination, and to what subjects can one link them? Thirdly, the theory must be normative. By this I mean neither that the theory itself is constituted out of a set of normative propositions, nor that it normatively delimits its corpus; rather that, by describing its corpus by means of definitional concepts, it allows for a normative analysis of the corpus. The result is that the interpretations can, after all, enter into competition. Nevertheless, the norms must be derived explicitly from systematic reflection of an epistemological order, on the one hand, and, on the other, from a theory of narrative communication. Finally, the analysis must be, in its different stages, comparative. Comparisons can be set up between text and model, between texts, rewritings and interpretations, and between texts of the same genre or period or, conversely, of different genres and periods. But the third term of the comparison, the norm, must always be made explicit.

2.6 Psychoanalysis as a model

Habermas develops his ideas on the critical sciences through a discussion of psychoanalysis, which is, according to him, the only example of a science having systematically integrated self-reflection. My ambition is to see whether, in a modest way, a certain narratology cannot also merit the title "critical." Psychoanalysis does indeed fit perfectly into critical philosophy's line of thought.

(a) First of all, it shares with the other cultural sciences a hermeneutical dimension. To illustrate what he meant by this term, Dilthey took biography as a model for interpretation: the reconstruction, beginning from memories, of the structure of a life. In psychoanalysis, the material brought by the subject and its memories is emblematic for the activity inherent in all symbolic reconstruction (cf. Peirce).

(b) A second critical aspect of psychoanalysis is the systemic character of the distortions and omissions that analysis corrects. The symbolic structures are corrupted by conditions that are internal: internal to the subject, internal to the system (the unconscious). The disconnected fragments have a meaning that is recuperable through systemic research.

(c) Thirdly, analysis has to do with linguistic structures, notably semantic structures. It therefore rests on a model of communicative competence. At the same time, in its search for causality, it locates itself within diachrony. It deals with *corrupt texts*, in other words with texts where the author (the analysand) makes a mistake/deceives her/himself[9] about the model. This state of affairs requires not only "philological" work, but also a causal explanation *which starts from* this earlier work. Analysis seeks to discover what interests orient the author in her/his enunciation of the corrupt text. It endeavors to distinguish the "authentic" part from the alienated and inaccessible part. It is on the basis of this distinction alone that analysis seeks the causal explanation. Freud warns against jumping immediately into the depths: without the patient work of the philologist, there is a severe risk that the causal explanation will be arbitrary. Such caution needs all the more to be observed when the corpus is ancient.

2.7 Psychoanalysis and its critical procedures

How does psychoanalysis proceed critically? The first step is the search for symptoms. Certain elements are characterized by a deviation from the model, and so become incomprehensible. The model is here conceived of as a set of rules of language, of norms of action, of modes of expression culturally acquired. Can this scheme be extended to literary models: "deviations" from generic models, rhyme schemes, etc. (provided one does not take "ideal" and "deviation" in an aesthetically normative sense)? These differences are signs. Peirce used the term "symptom" to indicate signs involuntarily emitted, as opposed to "signal," and it is exactly this opposition that is at stake in psychoanalysis. The symptoms there are signs of a specific alienation of the subject-sender, to be spotted by their "ab-normal" character. In a different terminology, one could call them "a-grammatical." Their effect is to interrupt the communication of the subject with itself.

When one tries to situate these symptoms within relationships of power and dependence, and with respect to the concerns of the critical sciences, these relationships seem to function as restrictions upon public communication. But the dependent subject has an interest in preserving at least the appearance of intersubjectivity. In order to do this, the subject adapts itself to the restrictions imposed. There is thus established a private, "ex-communicated" portion of language which the subject cannot permit itself to acknowledge: repression. The subject learns in analysis to translate this private text into public language. Since, paradoxically, the subject does not understand its own private language—and for good reason, language being by definition public—the subject needs public language in order to understand itself. This is what I found to be at work, for example, in the dialogue between Samson and Delilah.[10] The act of understanding is itself an object of critical research.

9. *Se trompe*, which carries both of these senses.
10. *Lethal Love*, Chapter 2.

2.8 From psychoanalysis to a critical hermeneutics of literature

Before pursuing the methodological reflection, it seems useful to me to raise some questions concerning the possible relations between psycho-analysis and literature (not literary criticism), in a critical perspective, starting from some key notions of analysis.

(a) *Hallucinations* are defined as a dislocation between perception and reality. They have this trait in common with fiction. What is the usefulness of this dislocation? The function of language is to stabilize the processes of consciousness in such a way that what is internal acquire an external existence by being linked to symbols. This function can be related to the intimately personal character of some literary works which one reads in public without embarrassment, indeed quite the contrary. The usefulness of this process is obvious. By means of symbolic elements, one can "calculate" the possibilities of action, that is, project sets of alternative actions in order to test them. Without incurring real danger, the subject is thus in a position to put reality to the test. Reading contributes to this putting to the test, which then determines subsequent choices of behavior.

(b) The *dream* as it is described by Freud in *The Interpretation of Dreams* is an "a-grammatical" discourse, imaged, condensed, and de-formed. Putting aside the question of origin, which would set these two types of text in opposition, it is obvious that this description applies just as well to literature. The first aspect, the a-grammaticality, is the most prob-lematic aspect of the comparison. The dream also is, in this sense, a model of linguistic "ex-communication," related by Habermas to the archaic punishment of expulsion or ostracism.[11] A-grammatical symbols by defini-tion escape public communication. Their semantic contents are privatized. The situation is perhaps no different than with literary texts called "diffi-cult" because they use symbols whose meaning cannot be inferred from the public domain, but only, and with difficulty, from the text itself. As for the imaged, condensed, and deformed character of the dream, there are numer-ous studies on the relationships between Freudian rhetoric and rhetoric as such. The literary relevance of these problems needs no further demonstra-tion. The "publication" of privatized language is a critical activity. Daring to take this step is Boaz's heroism—just as anguish in the face of this "publication" is Samson's weakness.[12]

(c) *Identification* is a *topos par excellence*, as much in psychoanalysis as in literary studies. The infant, in its development, is constantly confronted by socially sanctioned expectations. By identifying with the figures who sup-port these expectations, the infant forms its superego. The superego is the

---

11. See also Girard, *The Scapegoat*.
12. See my analysis of the Book of Ruth in Chapter 3 of *Lethal Love*.

intrapsychic extension of social authorities. The infant forms it by appropriating for itself the socially proper roles. This apprenticeship is part of the process of socialization, a process which, moreover, does not end in infancy. The infant chooses its authorities as best it can, to the limited extent that it has a choice. Since social interaction goes on at the level of signs, the more substantial struggle is the struggle for power over signs, because possession of signs makes possible the representation of authority, and assures the possessor a place in the ideology under formation. Reading is just such a practice of struggle. The reader's identification with certain narrative roles rather than with others indicates the success of such a practice. Analysis of the positions of the subjects in texts constitutes for this reason a critical practice.

(d) *Grammar*, and more generally the systems put into play in analytic as well as literary texts, constitute, as we have seen, the norm by which one can enter the problematic of critical interpretation. One may suppose that grammatical connections weave themselves in between the privatized symbols and the distorted public text. This grammatical relationship is presented in analysis as a causal relationship between empirical events and rigid personality traits. Analysis dissolves this relationship when it brings about, through the disappearance of privatizing deformations, conscious control. Before this dissolution, the alienation of the subject in relation to this privatized part of itself gave it the uncanny[13] feeling which explains, at another level, the attraction *and* the repulsion, the familiarity and the strangeness, of numerous literary texts. Analyzing this process does not, as one might suppose, eliminate the pleasure of reading, but rather unveils and critiques its implicit function, and hence its ideological power.

(e) Another aspect of psychoanalysis has an analogue not so much in literature as in criticism. *General interpretations* occupy a privileged place in psychoanalysis as well as in literary criticism. In both fields, the abuses of "wild analysis" abound. They are embarrassing principally because they are strictly tautological. If one claims, for example, that every personality is formed through pre-Oedipal and Oedipal stages, then it is absolutely futile merely to indicate, in each person, the traces of the Oedipus complex. Likewise, while it is one thing to perceive that every text is constructed according to an actantial model,[14] it is mere paraphrase then to point out, in a given text, the occurrence of the actants in question. When they are understood and used well, on the other hand, general interpretations occupy a unique place between the researching subject and its object-

---

13. This translation loses some of the nuances of *"unheimlich"*; see Freud, "The Uncanny," and below, Chapter 11, sect. 6 (pp. 260-62).

14. Whether that of Propp, *Morphology of the Folktale*, Souriau, *Les 200.000 situations dramatiques*, or Greimas, *Sémantique structurale*.

field.[15] In contrast to theoretical propositions which remain external to their object, the validity of general interpretations depends on the success of their direct application to the object. The empirical rightness of these interpretations depends not on controlled observation and agreement between researchers, but on self-reflection and agreement between the researcher and the object (which in the case of psychoanalysis is oneself). Communal language being indispensable, general interpretation has the merit of reestablishing intersubjectivity. In philology, this principle recurs as the criterion of coherence between the interpretation and the corrupt text; in the interpretation of difficult texts, as the criterion that the best interpretation is the one which accounts for the maximum number of elements.

2.9 Methodological implications of the use of models

A short digression, inspired again by Habermas, on the use of models in the two disciplines, seems to be indicated here. By "model," a term useful because it is concise, I mean here a general interpretation; this is a specific type of model—I will take up later the notion of model in its more general sense. Like general theories, models make possible causal explanations and conditional predictions. But there the resemblance ends. General interpretations do not base these explanations and predictions on a neat methodological separation between the object-field and the theoretical propositions—quite the contrary. Habermas insists on the narrative aspect of models such as that of Oedipus. By "narrative" he means that one explicates an event narratively. That is to say, one shows how a subject is engaged in a *story*, in the narratological sense of the term. This story must therefore be presented, and to present a story is to claim that it is unique. But Habermas' model erases this uniqueness without departing from narrativity. As a story systematically generalized, it provides a schema for *many* stories, each unique but on the other hand predictable. In this sense the model looks like a *typology*. In other words, it is translatable into other individual situations. Whether analysand or reader, the subject can apply the typical case to its own case. Analyst and analysand, criticism and literary text, orient themselves not by an example but by a schema.

General interpretation is a model in the sense that it does not comprise individual names, but rather the roles that invest positions, which may be indicated by names (Oedipus), by classes of individuals (infant-parents), or by theoretical terms (subject-sender-object). General interpretation presents not contingent situations but recurrent configurations, represented by

---

15. The parallel between analytic and literary models emphasizes the interpretive side of the model—hence my preference for the term "general interpretations" over "theoretical models."

triangles, hexagons, arrows, etc. It does not employ an approach which reduces everything to the typical, but describes, by means of concept-types, the schema of an action with its variations. Since the terms of the model contribute to the structuring of the narration, their formalization is impossible and is not even desirable. Specific hermeneutical interpretation is not just a technical application that leaves theoretical deductions intact; it *completes* the background model. It determines a particular realization of the general interpretation.

2.10 The status of psychoanalysis

The criticisms addressed to psychoanalysis by philosophers of science, from positivism to critical rationalism and beyond, have been effectively refuted by many, among whom the Dutch analyst A. W. Mooij is particularly clear.

(a) A first unjustified and untenable position, as I have already said, is the exclusion or misrepresentation of other forms of knowledge than science, of other forms of science than the natural sciences, and of other scientific bases than logic. It is the untenable decision that the sciences form a methodological unity, based on the model of the natural sciences, which has made causal determinism the sole criterion for explanation and progress. The desire for unity which unavowedly motivates this decision deserves an examination to which psychoanalysis could no doubt contribute. It seems obvious to me that, as a desire, it cannot boast of being scientific.

(b) A second argument that Mooij advances is equally convincing. The presupposition, which enjoys the status of a thesis, that an activity is scientific only when it is directed toward the construction of causal laws, itself assumes a vision of the world regarded as "natural"; it is, therefore, an ideology, involving an extension of the scope of causal laws beyond physical nature. This assumption points in turn to a systematic reification of social and individual life, and thus constitutes a thesis about the world which can only be metaphysical; hence neither true nor false, but unverifiable. This thesis also necessarily entails the assumption that, at the level of the formation of concepts, causal determinism holds absolute sway. This approach, that of unambiguous definitions, involves nevertheless the exclusion of exceptions. This is why I have chosen to follow the opposite course. Adherents of the first view, meanwhile, hold cheap an alternative and well-known possibility for the formation of concepts, that of conceptual families. In this view, a concept includes a number of traits, of which it is sufficient that some be realized in order that the definition be applicable.

(c) One final presupposition deserves to be called into question in this debate, namely, that the relations between the terms of a theory are exclusively external. This hypothesis prescribes that term A cannot be part of the domain of term B, and that the relationship between A and B is accidental. The two terms must be describable independently of each other. One "forgets," in this approach, that internal relations exist between the terms. But rather than reject, in psychoanalysis, a refined and tested instrument for giving an account of the structure of textual subjectivity, and of the interaction between the social and the individual, we should interrogate further its potential to enrich a literary criticism which is truly critical. Without having been able to conduct such reflection within the framework of the present study, I have suggested that psychoanalysis, as a practice of narrativity, of interpretation, and of criticism, makes a valuable contribution.[16]

3. THE QUESTION OF IDEOLOGY

Finally, some words on the concept of ideology which, being common to psychoanalysis and critical theory, can serve as a key concept, provided that it be defined with at least some degree of clarity.

3.1 Ideology and art

In *Language and Materialism*, Rosalind Coward and John Ellis discuss the best-known theories concerning the relationship between ideology and art. The book opens with an Althusserian definition: ideology is the way in which the subject is produced in language, as capable of representing itself and therefore of acting socially. The permanence/fixity of these representations is thus a function of ideology, indeed its desired effect. What strikes one right away in this definition is its relationship to the notion of the subject. At the same time, the authors express at the very beginning of the book the need for a theory of the processes and positions which the subject occupies in relation to language and to ideology. I would add that this theory must also account for the semantic structure, or better, for the semanticization, of these processes and positions. Let us take up again the arguments of Habermas, who correctly refers, in relation to psychoanalysis, to the subject's putting reality to the test, and deduces from it some considerations concerning the meaning of a critique of ideology.

For the entire human race, the boundaries of what we call the real (that which resists symbolization, as Lacan says) are not absolutely fixed. A potential satisfaction can be transformed into an institutionally sanctioned satisfaction. Technical progress can make it more objectively possible to subsume necessary social repression under institutionalized social repression. What we call illusions are not therefore necessarily expressions of an alienated conscience. Their utopian contents can be freed from their fusion with the ideological elements in the culture, which at an earlier stage had

---

16. For a more extended discussion see Bal, "Psychopoetics—Theory."

been transformed into a legitimation of authority. Liberation from this fusion makes possible a critique of the structure of power, to the extent that this has become historically out-of-date.

A critical cultural science is capable of determining when theoretical propositions really concern invariable social regularities and when, on the contrary, they express relations of dependence ideologically frozen but in principle modifiable. Any such critique has a bearing which extends well beyond the domain of the propositions in question. We know from everyday experience that ideas often serve to justify actions. At the individual level, we call this rationalization. At the collective social level, it is ideology. The manifest content of the propositions is falsified by failure to critique the relation between the consciousness of the subject and the interests at work. Rationalization creates the illusion of autonomous judgment. But the critique of ideology, whether psychoanalytic or not, works on the hypothesis that awareness of these pseudo-invariable relations can release, in the person who is the object of the pseudo-laws, a process of self-reflection. Thus uncritical consciousness, which is the precondition for the existence of such laws, can be transformed. Critical awareness of the laws in force cannot by itself render them inoperative. But it can render them inapplicable. Transferring this to the literary domain, the correspondence is obvious. Readers remain, to a certain extent, the objects of literature, that is, objects upon whom certain pseudo-laws operate, laws which literature seeks to represent as natural. As long as they remain in this position, a critical interpretation of literature can contribute to weakening these laws by unveiling them.

The first wave of Frankfurt School philosophers already pronounced a great many judgments concerning the relationships between ideology and art. Even if these judgments seem less convincing today than when they were first articulated, the contradictions to which they witness are not themselves *passé*. In *The Dialectic of Enlightenment*, Adorno and Horkheimer affirm that art can justify current ways of life merely by representing them, since these representations prove that a way of life which can produce such art must be satisfactory! That is art's conservative side. At the same time, art maintains the possibility of a critical perspective, since it is by definition situated *off-center* in relation to life. This idea of non-identity, so dear to critical philosophers, coincides, in the quite different context of Peircian semiotics, with the concept of the sign as *other*, representing the absent and irretrievable object. And Aristotle defined his much-maligned notion of *mimesis* in a similar way. The truth-value of art, say Adorno and Horkheimer, lies in the disjuncture it preserves between concepts, images projected from nature and humanity, and the actuality of its objects. Adorno, who wrote extensively about art, especially about the art whose signifying character is the least obvious, music, demands that art prescribe changes of attitude by undermining appearances.

Even if, as we know today, art does not allow itself to be set this task, its truth-content can in fact still be derived from its capacity to reformulate the relations existing between subjectivity and objectivity, by preserving, in its own way, non-identity. The formulation that one can derive from Adorno's texts is clear: art brings about a vacillation between two opposite, false attitudes, by rejecting them alternately: subjectivism, the idea that the subject's conceptions produce the world; and objectivism, the idea that the world is a realm of pure objects, given independently of the subject. Art, including literature, is therefore at the same time ideological and critical. Without its ideological level, it would no longer be linguistic, and therefore would be unreadable. Without its critical level, it would be without interest.

3.2 The concept of ideology
and its relationship to literary concerns

Definitions of the concept of ideology proliferate in discouraging numbers. A collection by Vadée was recently summarized by Hamon,[17] in his study of explicit ideology in literature. I cite some of these:

Generalizing and atopical discourse, with no privileged location.

Non-professional discourse, opinion, the vague "it is said," rumors.

Discourse which is serious, assertive, monologous, dichotomous, discriminating (*tranchant*) between good and bad.

Unconscious discourse; misunderstanding.

Discourse of subjection, interpellation of the subject as a free subject (which is a contradiction in terms).

Tautological discourse, which describes and justifies a state of affairs of which it is itself an expression.

Imaginary relationship to a real world.

Implicit consensus.

System of beliefs which knows how to maintain its legitimacy in spite of the fact that it cannot be validated by rational analysis.

Ground of the norms which justify the vision of the world which justifies them.

These definitions, or rather descriptions, have several qualities in common. Beyond a tendency (itself ideological) to personification, which emphasizes the formidable character of ideology, they refer either to language and discursive practice, or to the unconscious, or to the subject who is "subjected."

(a) Insofar as ideology articulates itself only indirectly, across other discursive practices, it has much in common with *myth*. Myth, which some say is to literature what pre-history is to history, and which one can describe as at once unarticulated, implicit, and obvious, has been described by Barthes[18] as a form of representation which naturalizes certain meanings, which eternalizes the present state of the world, in the interest of the

17. Vadée, *L'idéologie*; Hamon, *Texte et idéologie*.
18. Barthes, *Mythologies*.

bourgeoisie. While Barthes could still, before 1968 and in a particular context, use the word "bourgeoisie" without appearing desperately out-of-date, many of us must now take account of other structures of power which intersect with classism, and are linked with it in a common cause: especially sexism and racism. But what Barthes says rings true: myth succeeds precisely when it passes unperceived, when it goes *without saying*, when it confirms a position set up as a protection against doubt, when it universalizes history by saying (without *saying* it), "That's the way it is." Myth says this when it narratizes the world, providing it with an origin. It is according to the equations "priority=proof" and "priority=primacy" that myth produces its effects. In this perspective, Christianity's rewriting of the Hebrew Bible is a veritable *tour de force*: preserving, but then turning upside down, the initial viewpoint, which was *pro*spective, it has no difficulty in monopolizing the history of the Jewish people, by reading their texts *retro*spectively as a *pro*jection whose realization is situated beyond Judaism, in Christianity. Thus myth is a tool of ideology: it "objectifies," by naturalizing it, one element of the "reality" created by human beings, one of the beliefs systematized in the ideology. It is from this characteristic of myth that my analyses of biblical narratives get their relevance.[19]

(b) It is no longer necessary to emphasize, in the current use of the concept of ideology, its relationship with *language*. As a signifying system, language is pre-established, relatively fixed, and obvious; it is normative, indispensable, and reifying. As a non-reflexive competence, it produces and reproduces thought, which itself proceeds by signifiers. Lacan says it very poetically: "I identify myself in language, but only to lose myself there as an object."[20]

(c) With respect to Lacan and language, the third aspect of the concept of ideology enters the picture, that of the *subject*: "The form under which language expresses itself suffices to define subjectivity." Or "The word always subjectively includes its response." Or again: "Human language would constitute therefore a communication in which the sender receives from the receiver its own message in an inverted form."[21] In other words, the subject is in large measure forced to adapt itself to the expectation of its interlocutor, to the interlocutor's "unsaid": to its ideology. Coward and Ellis, following Althusser, define ideology as a practice of representation, producing certain meanings, and requiring certain subjects to support these meanings. Ideology produces the basis for the activity of the subject, its conditions and positions as subject. It produces the coherence of this subject in the face of the contradictions of society. Inversely, the subject can be considered as the place where ideological signifieds are realized: as their

19. See *Lethal Love, Murder and Difference*, and *Death and Dissymmetry*.
20. Lacan, *Ecrits*, 299–300.
21. Lacan, *Ecrits*, 298.

support. It is this aspect of the subject which will recur in the following essays.

(d) This definition by Coward and Ellis also leads us into the fourth, eminently literary, aspect of the concept of ideology: *representation*. This certainly suggests a practice producing a specific articulation, "producing certain meanings and requiring certain subjects to support these meanings." This clause posits the instability of the individual, which can occupy several subjective positions, even contradictory ones, given to it in a plurality of representations. Althusser[22] sees in ideology the form of representation that a society gives to itself, and which has the character of a tendency toward closure (discourse which "discriminates," see above). It is this closure, whose non-obviousness criticism has to demonstrate, that we see at work in the reception of biblical texts.

(e) This leads us to the fifth relevant aspect, *presupposition*, a form of intertextuality which Ducrot defines and Culler proposes be systematically analyzed,[23] and which constitutes the underlying mechanism of ideological closure. Speech-act theory defines and delimits the "mental horizon" of the structure of closure which representation imposes. In the practice of representation, the subject "takes up a position" (*prend position*), in both senses of the term: to occupy a place, and to do things. But it does so in a non-reflexive fashion, believing that this position "goes without saying," that it is natural, eternal, objective, inevitable. In this sense, the positions are "pre-positions," established in advance, and "sub-positions," insinuated "from below," from "reality" itself, and serving as the *basis* from which one acts, as the stage on which one plays social roles. "That's the way it *is*," "that *goes* without saying," are slogans which summarize ideologies: implicit theories concerning competencies. "That's the way it *is*" refers to presupposed systems of classification; "it *goes* without saying," points to systems in their development, implying, in its diachronic aspect, prediction: "That will always be so." Understood in this way, synchronic classification and diachronic perspective reinforce each other. We can see this mechanism at work in readings of the Genesis story of creation.[24]

The implicit character of these "theories"—*as theories*, that is, having the appearance of unavoidability—renders them very effective. They are characterized further by the appearance of coherence, which is nothing other than the closure denounced by Althusser. This appearance of coherence is by no means threatened even by the most obvious contradictions. A well-known example is human equality: "All men are equal." The contradiction, which consists in the incontestable fact that men are "more equal" than women, is resolved in language, where "men" can mean either "men"

22. Althusser, *For Marx*.
23. Ducrot, *Dire et ne pas dire*; Culler, *The Pursuit of Signs*.
24. See below, Chapter 9.

or "men and women." The existence and use of certain words, structures, expressions is based on such presuppositions, and reproduces them.

In these essays, I mean by "ideology" representations of visions of the world which are general among the subjects of a society. The subjects are not ready to abandon these representations, because they account for central aspects of life; they are systemic, that is to say, interconnected with each other; and they influence the social and private conduct of subjects. Described in this way, ideologies contribute to the legitimization and the maintenance of social institutions and practices, to the unequal distribution of power, and therefore to the possibility of satisfying conscious and unconscious needs and desires, and, finally, to the masking of contradictions. Today, we can demonstrate the outmoded or mystifying character of the sources from which ideologies flow. They are at work in the interaction between literary texts and their interpretations.

3.3 Ideology and psychoanalysis

I confine myself to a few words on the relationship between ideology and psychoanalysis. The traditional split between the individual and the social, which even today one has a hard time overcoming, is an ideological construction created to subject us to the system, while at the same time making us believe in our own personal autonomy.[25] This split is on the way to disappearing, since the development of post-structuralist theories: psychoanalytic (Lacan), philosophical (Derrida), and semiotic (Kristeva). But studies like Jameson's show that the problems have not, for all that, disappeared. For example, the recognition in psychoanalysis of the importance of the social in the formation of the subject has not led to the reverse movement: reflection on the way in which the social is composed of a network of subjects. One of the results of this lack is a literary criticism which persists in trying to trace the residue of the process of social formation, but stays purely at the level of the individual. Jameson (1977), who explicitly tries to solve this problem, does not succeed in going beyond "research *on* the subject" and its development, its passage from the imaginary to the symbolic and the traces of this passage that one can reconstruct in the text.[26] The metaphor "collective subject" is not adequate, and neither are such substitute expressions as "the subject of the text."

Going back to an Althusserian definition of ideology, however, disentangles some possible approaches: structures of representation which permit the individual subject to conceive or imagine its relations with transpersonal realities, such as the social structure, or the collective logic of history. Such a definition has the merit of positing the necessary elements

25. Jameson, *The Political Unconscious*; cf. also his "Imaginary and Symbolic in Lacan."
26. Jameson, "Imaginary and Symbolic in Lacan," 373.

without substituting them one for another. These elements are the individual subject, structures of representation, and social reality. Psychoanalysis, in its theories of the superego, of putting reality to the test, of the transition from the imaginary to the symbolic, accounts for the process which forms and deforms the individual subject. The structures of representation which allow the subject to imagine its relations to the real comprise language, but also literary, generic, and other structures. The psychoanalytic cure, which is a cure by language and narration, and also a cure by drama, in the transference and countertransference, allows the subject to account for the positions it occupies in these structures of representation, for the way it talks about itself, "puts itself into the picture." From among the available "sociolects," the subject chooses an "idiolect," a language which befits what it is.

If, as we have already seen, reading is one such taking of a position and coming to awareness, through the identifications, "hallucinations," and "dreams" into which it incites the reader; and if, on the other hand, as has been so often shown,[27] writing is also partially identifiable with a cure, then it is possible that the author's transference, provoking the reader's counter-transference, can appeal precisely to those positions available to the individual within the collectivity. The analysis of a text or a work in itself remains the analysis of an individual subject. The analysis of a text *together with* its echoes, rewritings, and interpretations—which allows us to extricate, through all the structures of representation chosen and later recaptured, not only the work of the author, but also the responses, the interaction between text and audience; and this in a series of stages, since the rewritings have in their turn given rise to interpretations—can reveal the *drama*, that is the transference *and* counter-transference, played out between successive subjects.[28] Only so will we be able to disentangle, starting from the individual subject and going beyond it, the "collective" subject of ideology. But this will not be a collective subject in the current sense of the term; working its way through the structures of representation, analysis can be effective only if it succeeds in locating the subjectal semiotic network which I have called textual subjectivity. It is to the definition and description of this network that Chapter 6 will try to contribute. Ideology at work in narrative subjectivity: this defines the object of my work. It is necessary to disentangle the epistemic, functional, and genetic aspects of ideology. For it is not enough to demonstrate the epistemic errors in texts and their reception. Even when it is easy to denounce how, for example, the specific interests of a group are presented as general interests, or how subjective processes are presented as objective, it is still necessary to under-

---

27. Mehlman, "Entre psychanalyse et psychocritique"; Mauron, *Des métaphores obsé-dantes*; Verhoeff, *Les comédies* and *Les grandes tragédies*; and others.
28. See Gallop, "Lacan and Literature."

stand where these systemic errors come from, and what their effects are on the social practice of which hermeneutical dialogue is a constituent part, and what interests orient them. In the end, these essays share the presupposition that the production of meaning is by definition a *pro*position of meaning. By proposing a certain distribution of the legitimacy of values, ideology seeks to bring about the *im*position of meaning; but only the process of reception can determine to what extent the proposition has succeeded in imposing itself.

Above all, I consider interpretation as a use of the text, sometimes a good use, sometimes an abuse. In defending my position, I have given a modest, but already fertile, place to the concept of the subject. This concept, never safe from analytic dispersion, will be atomized definitively in Chapter 6. The atomized subject, *including* the unifying tendency that tries to resubsume its fragments, is the force that leads back to the discipline which, for the analysis of ideology, is the privileged one—narratology. Some of its traditional concepts will be put to new use—to clarify the "subjected subject" which I have discussed here. Paradoxically, it is from this subjected subject that narratology must begin its emancipation from irrelevance.

■ 2 ■

Tell-Tale Theories

"These relics have a history then?"
"So much so that they are history."
Arthur Conan Doyle, "The Musgrave Ritual"

1. AN EPISODE IN THE STORY OF A FIELD

The almost simultaneous appearance of Franz K. Stanzel's *A Theory of Narrative*, Gérard Genette's *Nouveau discours du récit*, and Peter Brooks' *Reading for the Plot* constitutes an interesting episode in the recent history of narrative theory, a tale in itself. The three studies occupy different positions in that history. Stanzel's work, of which the new volume is a consistent part, can be characterized as pre-structuralist, Genette remains faithful to his structuralist stance, while Brooks claims to go beyond structuralism. Each book's format is telling, too. Stanzel's is an attempt to construct one coherent instrumentalist theory, while Brooks presents a collection of essays which all have a bearing on his conception of narrative. In between, Genette's booklet, a review of reviews, has the format and the tone of a pamphlet. The trio as a whole, as well as the three books separately, write the recent history of a discipline which is in crisis because it has reached the point where it is difficult to evaluate whether the narrative paradigm has been over-exploited or not fully adopted. The following discussion focuses mainly on the most recent development, Brooks, and comes from someone trained successively in the three moments, and excited, but also dissatisfied, by the turn the field is taking. I will try to argue that the coexistence of over- and under-exploitation of the paradigm lies behind the present situation, and furthermore, that polemic and metaphor are both fruitful and paralyzing. I will make a case for the student's need, my desire, or literature's demand, for a clearer delineation of where the different narratologists really stand. The genre of the review-article entails an ambiguity which the present essay cannot escape: that of reviewing specific studies while at the same time paying attention to wider trends of which they are examples.

49

2. AN UNPLOTTED STORY

Linguistic and cultural boundaries have had their impact on the evolution of narratology. Stanzel's early work stands at the origin of narratology in that, unlike the Anglo-Saxon writer-critics who determined narrative analysis in the English-speaking countries, his was a purely academic attempt at theory-building. If only for that reason, the belated appearance in English of his 1979 book is worthwhile. There are other reasons, but since I do not have enough space to develop them here, I must refer the reader to the thorough account by Dorrit Cohn.[1]

The discussion between pre-structuralists and structuralists has basically been a methodological one. Structuralist studies have claimed to be more systematic, which in general they are, and to provide more reliable information, which in general they do not. One feature of the early studies has remained characteristic even of Genette's work: a pre-structuralist conflation of typologies and analytic tools. The problem is a reversal of order. Classifications of what will later be termed *narrative situations* have usually been a first, instead of a concluding step. Similarly, Stanzel's new book, however rich in critical insights and ideas, starts off with a telling typology, in the form of a Goethian wheel, which constitutes the basis of the theory. In a more refined and self-conscious way than in his earlier work, he then analyzes the different types into features. These are defined in terms of three factors, misleadingly called elements, each of which is said to be predominant in a type: person, perspective, and mood. These factors are, in fact, criteria for distinctions between the types; they are all relevant in each type, but their combination varies. The conflation of criteria relevant for each narrative situation with their results—the "elements"—forms a major methodological flaw of this type of theory (see Chapter 6, below). If one were to proceed in the opposite direction, and first determine which factors are at stake in a narrative situation, defining them clearly, and second show how they interrelate and in what different combinations they appear, one would eventually generate a typology of narrative situations. (This final step is not indispensable for analysis; all the tools required would result from steps one and two.)

Genette, as an exception among the French structuralists, knew and integrated Stanzel's work. Although his theory is much more systematic, he does adopt the above conflation and as a result, the part of his theory concerned with narrative situations (mood and voice) is not wholly structuralist, while the other parts (order, frequency, duration) are much more so. Brooks, on the other hand, has the advantage of coming much later and of having been educated both in the Anglo-Saxon and in the French school. His book has the critical richness of Stanzel's without the defensiveness.

1. Cohn, "The Encirclement of Narrative."

Brooks is polemical even in the presentation of his subject-matter. Whereas Stanzel and Genette are concerned with narrative discourse, Brooks starts at the other end of narrative, with plot, hence, with the Aristotelian beginnings of the discipline. A similar, although much more philosophical and systematic alternative has been chosen by other recent narratologists, and we may speak of a trend here.[2]

Claiming that his project goes "beyond narratology," Brooks can afford both to be as little concerned with criteria of systematicity as he pleases, and yet also to take stances in the narratology debate: the discussion has moved from theory-building and systematicity to relevance and mobility. There is, then, no continuity between pre-structuralism and post-structuralism. While a precursor like Stanzel seems to feel compelled to update his views, Brooks retrospectively dismisses the system debate by declaring the tools provided by narratology to be insufficiently relevant, however adequate they may be. Although I find his polemical position only partially convincing, his ideas are most interesting, his analyses at times brilliant, and his model, however speculative, challenging and fruitful. Methodologists may object to the model on the grounds that it is basically a metaphor, which it is, but my judgments, in combination, entail the necessity to rethink methodological standards. I will do so by trying to give an account of Brooks' view of plot, his master-idea—or should I say, his masterplot?—in this book, through a discussion of his use of metaphor. This way, I will be able to return later to the confrontation between methodological concerns and the qualities of the book. From that point, I will come back to Brooks' position in the history of the discipline.

3. PLOT AND THE LANGUAGE OF POST-STRUCTURALISM

In order to overcome the traditional, static models of narrative, Brooks adopts two basic metaphors common to psychoanalytic theory: the motor, as the metaphor of the energetic model of the mind and of plot, and exchange, as the metaphor of transference and of reading. They come together in the formulation of Brooks' project, which is to examine the "conjunction of the narrative of desire (plot) and the desire of narrative (the act of narrating, and of reading)" (p. 9).[3] Pavel[4] convincingly questions this conjunction as a general model of narrative, pointing to cases where the first-person narration is merely a conventional, stylistic device, as in Brooks' example *La peau de chagrin*. The conjunction is completely lost from view in third-person narrative, where there is a significant split between the two partners in the conjunction; unless one displaces the narrating function

2. See, for example, Pavel, *The Poetics of Plot.*
3. Page references not otherwise specified are to Brooks, *Reading for the Plot.*
4. Pavel, "Origin and Articulation," 357.

onto the character, as Brooks does in his analysis of *Le rouge et le noir*, but then the conjunction loses one connection, since the character, far from narrating, is *plotting* the narratability of its origin. The implausibility of the general validity of the conjunction is not a very consequential matter, however, since the larger and more interesting part of the book is concerned with the first of the two metaphors. Plot is the key-term here, with its complement, desire, as its motor. As the subtitle of the book indicates, plot is conceived of as both the design and the intention of narrative, but in the course of the discussion the term comes to refer to much more. Brooks defies the requirement of univocal definitions, and the course of his argument shows that he has good reasons for doing so. Although it is impossible to account for all the subtleties and the rich network of semes attached to the concept that is built up throughout the book, I will try to indicate a few of its features. Plot is, firstly, design, both as the interconnections between episodes and as the overall pattern of a narrative. It is the intention of the reader as well as of the text, its characters, and its author. It is the structuring operation deployed by narratives and the one that is activated in the reading of narrative (p. 113). This double process functions through masterplots, which one acquires through reading and which one also adopts, applies and corrects during this process. It is an active force and it shapes meaning.

Of the many features of the term provided by the *Oxford English Dictionary* Brooks retains: space or lot, diagram, outline, and plan or scheme. Hence, he combines the location where plot happens (its field), its structure, its organization, and its teleology. Plot, then, is neither fabula nor *sjužet*, but the work of *sjužet* on fabula. It is the interaction of Barthes' proairetic and hermeneutic codes, that of the sequence of happenings through time and that of enigma and answer. For a plot to function, the picaresque actor must engage the reader as detective in a common scheme.

So far, we may be grateful for Brooks' reluctance to adopt univocal definitions. The openness of the concept leads to a powerful and dynamic whole which combines features that we are used to conceiving of separately. Brooks' way of filling up the concept is paradigmatic for its content. Just as the plot of a narrative becomes its motor, its meaning-machine, so the critic's argument fulfils the same function within the theory. It has the same limits as well. The concept of plot is based on, expressed via, that of desire. Desire, in its turn, drives and consumes plots. Here we reach the limit where enriching openness approaches confusion, and where metaphors come to hamper rather than stimulate understanding. The slight circularity we see here comes back on other, related occasions. The metaphor of the motor is introduced in a discussion of Freud's model of the drives in *Beyond the Pleasure Principle*. Plot borrows its energetics from its analogy with the tension between Eros and Thanatos. Although resolution into nothingness is the ultimate goal of both life and narrative, the ending is avoided, delayed, by the detours that constitute narrative itself. The analogy has the appeal of explaining why we bother to read narrative at all, why we even like doing it: the tension evoked by it is one which we feel, but less strongly perhaps, in life itself. Here lies the strongest difference between this approach and the pre-structuralist and structuralist ones; while the latter two remain rigorously descriptive, Brooks' attempts to explain, however tentative such an explanation may be. Explanation becomes a plot in itself, which is driven by a desire to overcome the synchronic descriptive project. But when the machine of association moves on, and detour becomes a simile of deviation (à propos *Great Expectations*), for example, I feel, for reasons that I will explain shortly, that such machines occasionally go off the rails.

Most of Brooks' interpretations of a wide range of narratives from the nineteenth and early twentieth century, with their fine combination of critical insight and historical awareness of psychoanalytic and narratological concepts, support his approach. I enjoyed most his discussion of authority, and how Stendhal's resistance to it explains the necessity of the guillotine at the end of *Le rouge et le noir*; his treatment, at the other end of the book, of the problem of narrative authority as a key to interpretation of Faulkner's *Absalom, Absalom!*; and, in between, his fine narrative analysis of Freud's *Wolfman*. The range of texts discussed, wider than in the average structuralist study, shows a second additional element in Brooks. Not only does he try to offer explanations, but he also historicizes his corpus, relating the texts to one another and to the social context. He thus offers a fine counterexample to the reproach of ahistoricism so often leveled at both literary criticism and psychoanalysis. Significantly, the quality of the essays depends largely on the function that the model, hence metaphor, has in each of them. There is a significant difference between readings directed by and realized through the energetic model, on the one hand, and, on the other, pure thematic readings where the concept of desire is a simple thematic unit, as in Chapter 6 on Sue's *Les mystères de Paris*, the least integrated and in my opinion the weakest of the essays. I would venture to suggest that this discrepancy can be accounted for by the distinction between a concept as metaphoric model and as thematic label. Therefore, the place of metaphor in Brooks' discourse, as distinct from that of his precursors, can provide a key to the understanding of the history of the discipline.

4. TELLING METAPHORS

Metaphors are indispensable tools for compensating the poverty of language, for bridging the gap between abstract theory and concrete objects, and for filling a theoretical void with ideas borrowed from both daily life and other disciplines. Their capacity for condensation and for transfer of meaning makes them useful for the desired extension of knowledge. There is no way to avoid their use, nor is there any need to try. At the same time, the analogical structure that underlies metaphor is in itself as open to interpretation as the most poetic of metaphors. The difference between metaphorical relations is as crucial as the choice of a particular metaphor. Brooks uses more conspicuous metaphors than Stanzel or Genette, who are constrained by the rigors of methodology. The difference, however, is not, and cannot be, that between metaphorical and monovalent language, since the latter is an illusion. To give only one example: Stanzel adopts the Jamesian metaphor of the *reflector* which Genette replaces with that of *focalization*. If the latter seems more suitable, it is not because it is less metaphorical—which it is not—but because it lacks the idea of ontological adequacy implied in reflection as mirroring; because it implies directionality as a specific feature of narrative; and because it allows restriction of the field focalized. In other words, it is the difference between the respective features transferred by each metaphor, not a difference in degree of "metaphoricity," that is the criterion for evaluation. It is precisely for that reason that I regret what I see as Genette's regression in the work under review: in his attempt to reconcile his work with that of his predecessors, he has dropped what constituted its novelty—directionality—and stepped back into pre-structuralism.

Another aspect of metaphor in theoretical discourse becomes clear when one compares Stanzel's eclectic terminology with Genette's rhetorical terms borrowed from the Greek. I find the latter set of terms preferable, not because of their greater precision, but because of their coherence as a set, which replaces the one-to-one relation of vehicle to tenor with a systematic analogy between two networks, thus providing more possibilities for testing and control over the whole set. Brooks, in his turn, does use a few technical terms, but he is not concerned with the terminological problem, and his freer use of metaphor therefore provides new insights into the possibilities and limits of metaphor in theoretical discourse. Sometimes he adopts common equations, like texts as analogons of life (p. xii). This type of metaphor is adopted more self-consciously, and with theoretical bearing, when he assumes a similarity between the functioning of the psychic apparatus and that of the text, or between Aristotle's rules and Freud's theory of drives. At other moments, he equates his own theoretical terms with one another, for example plot with narrative situation (e.g., pp. 294–95). Here, the act of metaphor tends to replace argumentation, since (1) the conjunction between the two was the point at issue, while (2) conjunction is one, but by no means the obvious metaphorical relation; it is not the same as equation.

In general, the use of metaphors is more dynamic and self-conscious at the stronger moments in the book, and more unreflecting and common-place at its weaker moments. Thus Brooks quite innocently equates female sexuality to bestiality à propos a description of a woman's *face* as bestial (p. 160). The implementation of sexuality is the critic's own, and, given the transition from one metaphor to the next, is, in this case, a telling one. In the same essay, on Sue that is, the serial metaphor desire = eroticism = female body = prostitution, which is obviously meant to integrate this essay into the book as a whole through the insertion of the concept of desire, shows how metaphor can relate to ideology. Where it allows vagueness it prevents critique, and opens the door to paraphrase, which is the opposite of critique. In this case, the commonplace equation dispenses the critic from having to question the equations proposed by Sue.

Eroticizing language is another effect of the freer use of metaphor, char-acteristic of post-structuralist discourse. The equation between beginning and arousal, and then between arousal and sexual activity, leads the critic to equate the beginning of *La nouvelle Heloïse*, a text born, according to an external source, from a masturbatory reverie, with that of Genêt's *Notre-Dame des fleurs* which begins with the textual account of the act of mastur-bation. The word "similar," then, becomes misleading.

The most problematic metaphor to me is the one already referred to, that equates *detour* with *deviation* (p. 102), doubtless stimulated by phonetic and etymological reasons. It is part of the implementation of the idea, interest-ing in itself, that the Freudian theory of drives provides a dynamic model for narrative in that it accounts for both the forward movement and the repeated delaying of the end. Detour, then, refers to the mediating move-ment, in ever wider circles, to avoid reaching too quickly the death which is pursued. Deviation, in the common sense of difference from the norms, lacks the temporal aspect of delay which is so pertinent in the construction of the model. Detour is a topological metaphor for a temporal concept; deviation is a formerly topological, but nowadays only axiological, concept that fills the model with moral features or suggests mental illness. Within a dynamic narratology, however psychoanalytically flavored, or precisely be-cause of that flavor, it is utterly confusing to equate the two.

Although it is speculative to draw conclusions from the few examples discussed, I would venture the suggestion that metaphor in theory-building is more useful for its condensing capacities than for the slippery transfer of meaning it allows. Compared to the work of his precursors, Brooks is able to enrich the views of narrative in a way neither pre-structuralist nor structuralist narratology was able to do, because at both moments the discipline was too exclusively preoccupied with positivistic standards to allow metaphors to function in this way; but he has not been able to delimit the semantic range of his concepts. What we thus gain in insight, we may lose in grasp.

5. HOW TO BE HISTORY WITHOUT BEING A RELIC

Is such loss inevitable? I do not think so. In my view, it is due to Brooks' refusal to insert his work more fully into the tradition he too readily claims to surpass. Structuralism is for Brooks solely concerned with static, paradigmatic structures, while he is himself more interested in dynamic, syntactic structures. This caricature of his precursors deprives him, however, of a number of fruitful possibilities. This concern with intention, time sequence, and narrative exchange, now integrated solely through the conjunction of the theory of drives on the one hand, and the altogether different theory of transference on the other, could have been much more solidly anchored if it had been related both to psychoanalysis and to structuralist narratology. To name only a few ancestors: Greimas' actantial model, though mentioned by Brooks, is not acknowledged in its teleological structure, which could have supported the primal place of desire; Genette's narrative rhetoric could have been related to discursive intentionality, avoiding the sometimes confusing equations between the different levels of discourse; while Bremond's model of the narrative cycle displays the structure of the "design of happenings" which Brooks wishes to insert in the temporal sequence that is stretched out by desire.[5] The acceptance of metaphor would allow for the condensation required to integrate these structural models, and the psychoanalytic model would considerably enrich them, but they would conversely provide a more consistent terminology, a better applicability to discourse, and a more directly linguistic framework.

Why is this opportunity so often missed, since in this Brooks is but an example? In other words, is Brooks' refusal to place himself more clearly "beyond" structuralism in the sense of "exploiting the paradigm first and then moving on," due to a lack? Is he surpassing or skipping structuralist narratology, is he moving directly from "before" to "beyond," from pre-to post-? This is a hard claim to substantiate, for the book displays a thorough knowledge of structuralist publications (albeit not always *perceived* as structuralist). More importantly, the spirit of the book sometimes suggests that the answer to my questions is yes. When dealing with free indirect discourse, for example, and the (in itself) convincing argument against a mimetic interpretation of this device,[6] Brooks claims that it has rather the effect of disturbing clear-cut categories of discourse. The term he uses is "interference." Now, text-interference has been the subject of a lively debate initiated by Doležel[7] in the heyday of structuralist narratology. Had Brooks inserted his views within the latter's, he would not only have gained

5. Greimas, *Sémantique structurale*, Genette, *Narrative Discourse*, Bremond, *Logique du récit*.
6. Such an interpretation is the basis of Stanzel's discussion; for an overview of such approaches, see McHale, "Free Indirect Discourse."
7. Doležel, *Narrative Modes*.

a more interested audience from among the structuralist ranks, but he would also have been able to analyze the phenomenon more fully and to show that, in order for the linguistic systems to clash, they first have somehow to be represented mimetically.

Let me wind up this discussion by a return to the beginning: Conan Doyle's representation of Holmes' and Watson's dialogue.[8] Narrative, like the telling relics in Holmes' narcissistic baggage, *has* a history, and that history should be accounted for in narratological studies. Both pre-structuralist and structuralist studies have tended to forget this, and Brooks redresses the balance. It is also *about* history, an intermediate aspect that Holmes does not name but instead carries out, by telling it. Brooks'—and Pavel's and others' for that matter—insistence on plot is wholesome, but Greimas, Bremond, Doležel,[9] and others insist on it too. There is an important difference, however: where the hard-core structuralists did not really manage to overcome the paradox that their models of an inherently dynamic process like plot were static, Brooks and the other "new narratologists" make their models more iconic to their object. But also, narrative *is* history, and history is narrative, and the relation between the two is not only metaphorical. It would be interesting if historians who emphasize the temporal-sequential aspect of their discipline were to adopt Brooks' model of its intentionality. Brooks overcomes the too narrow text-centeredness of his predecessors (which did, however, have value in its time) by adopting the analogy between the individual life-story and the problematic individualism of the nineteenth and early twentieth centuries.

The analogy with Sherlock Holmes would have been more complete, had the critic stepped into a third level of meaning of the analogy. What holds for the relics in the case of the Musgrave Ritual holds not only for narrative but also for narrative theory, including both Brooks' own work and other post-narratological narratology. It *has* a history, that ranges from, say, Aristotle to today or, in a narrower scope, from Stanzel through Genette to Brooks. But then, it is inevitably also *about* history, in that it tells its own story. It can do so, however, only from the inside-focalizer's standpoint. Hence Stanzel's claim to have become a structuralist. Genette tries to show that he is not so different from the pre-structuralists, and Brooks claims more progress than he can substantiate. Internal focalizers mix up the temporal sequentiality by overdoing intentionality.

Narratology, however, also *is* history. It places itself in history by the very polemical discourse that claims to be about history, but which is more. In the Freudian era, it is almost compulsory to read discourse symptomatically. If we try doing that with the texts under review here, we notice a

8. Doyle, *The Complete Sherlock Holmes*, vol. 1, 387.
9. Doležel, *Narrative Modes*.

fragile dialectic that shows where insufficient integration leads to: to the mutual construction of caricatures which conceal missed opportunities. I would not in the least wish to deny that there is progress in the field, and Brooks' book magnificently shows it. But there could be more if less were claimed. "The Musgrave Ritual" teaches that, through Sherlock Holmes' exemplary narcissism. And who would deny that Holmes is a structuralist, telling his tale in a pre-structuralist era, but in a post-structuralist manner?

▪ 3 ▪

The Bible as Literature

A Critical Escape

1. THE BIBLE AND THE CRITIQUE OF IDEOLOGY

Recent flows of literarily oriented Bible scholarship and of literary studies focusing on the Bible, in other words, a stream from two directions, raise the question of the assumptions, the appropriateness, and the point of what is currently referred to as "literary approaches to the Bible." The titles of the three recent books discussed here—Robert Alter, *The Art of Biblical Poetry*, Meir Sternberg, *The Poetics of Biblical Narrative: Ideological Literature and the Drama of Reading*, and Phyllis Trible, *Texts of Terror: Literary-Feminist Readings of Biblical Narratives*—indicate each a different purpose. As I will argue, not all these titles cover the contents of the books, and all three entertain, programmatically, a specific relation to ideological criticism. It will be my contention that the confrontation between literary scholarship and the Bible should, but does not, challenge the traditional acceptance of social and theological ideologies that are assumed to underlie biblical literature.

Several motivations bring literary scholars to the Bible, and biblical scholars to literary theory. If the latter have become more aware of the need to account for biblical texts *as* literature, since, whatever its other readings, the Bible *is* undeniably literature, the former come to the Bible with more diverse and less conspicuous motivations. Some literary critics find the Bible a wholesome challenge to contemporary theory: an awareness of its anachronism, perceptible when we consider its relation with ancient texts, can serve to undermine universalism. Alter's undertaking clearly and successfully issues from that premise. Others, paradoxically, use literary theory to support biblical theology by stressing the poetic strategies of ideology without questioning them; indeed, often fully subscribing to them. Sternberg's book is the most extreme example of this tendency I have come

59

across. Trible's enterprise, along with other works of feminist interpretation of the Bible, is an attempt to analyze the "poetics of ideology" in a more critical way. It runs into problems that, again paradoxically, preclude a radical critique because of its anachronism. Thus, these three books form a circle that figures the problems of literary Bible-criticism: escaping anachronism, one escapes critique as well, since the enterprise is anti-normative; escaping critique, one subscribes to problematic ideologies, and criticizing these, one falls back into anachronism. Is there a way to escape this escapism?

1.1 Alter: poetics as critique

It would be unfair to attribute to Alter's enterprise, which he initiated with his companion volume, *The Art of Biblical Narrative*, a critical function that it does not pursue. Alter wishes to reconstruct the poetics of the Bible, of its narrative and now of its poetic art, in its difference from our modern poetical tastes and conventions. In his earlier book he analyzed, for example, the poetics of characterization, that cannot but differ radically from our realist and post-realist conventions. The Bible has no or few "inner views," almost no description, and much dialogue. Thus, the almost, but not wholly, verbatim repetition of narratorial preview and character statement serves characterization in ways that might escape the reader used to more analytic psychology and the convention of "inner view." Repetition in general, in fact, is a feature of biblical narrative that the anachronistic and arrogantly ethnocentric reader easily qualifies as "primitive," a response that historical-critical scholarship tends to repeat, obscuring it under the gesture called "separation of sources."[1] Alter's attempt to make sense of repetition by enhancing the difference in source, purpose, and effect of each member of the repetition is therefore in itself, it deserves to be stressed, a critical gesture.

Alter's poetic reconstruction is profoundly historical, in spite of its lack of appeal to historical sources. Even if it is extremely hard to claim with any certainty that the reconstructed poetics is the historical poetics, the very attempt to assign a poetics to the text as it stands, the refusal to force it into modern poetic principles, implies a respect for difference and an escape from universalism that is historical and, in its historicity, critical. In his new book, the author approaches biblical poetry with the same attitude. But here, there is a problem that he cannot solve because his enterprise rests on it. The choice of biblical poetry as the object of analysis presupposes the existence of such a category. James Kugel questions that assumption in a study that can be seen as one long protest against anachronistic poetics. Although Kugel in his turn does not always escape anachronism, for ex-

1. For a critique, see Bal, *Murder and Difference.*

ample when he questions the oral background of the Song of Deborah,[2] his attempt to undermine the prose-poetry distinction is solid, and too easily disposed of by Alter. Of course, it is legitimate to study biblical poetry even without assuming its autonomous existence, and its opposition to prose, and therefore Alter's refusal of Kugel's approach seems to me uncalled for. Nevertheless, as I will argue shortly, Alter's endeavor is successful enough as a historically critical gesture, and nothing makes this more obvious than his comparison between the prose and the poetry version of the same "event," the murder of Sisera. The same example will also show the other side of Alter's modest limitation to literary arguments, and the loss of critical potential it entails.

1.2 Sternberg: the poetics of biblical theology

In spite of the appealing title, Sternberg's study is limited rigorously to the least narrative aspects of biblical narrative: the ideological impact of the work of the later editors who established the canon. His basic assumption is an interesting one. The deity of the Hebrew Bible is, unlike what Sternberg refers to as "pagan" gods, not ontologically but epistemologically character-ized. Heretofore this has been amply recognized, but now Sternberg's thesis is that the poetics of the Bible is based on an analogy between this deity and the narrator: divine omniscience is expressed in omniscient narration. The biblical narrator's duplicating God's omniscience, thanks to divine inspira-tion, is, he claims, not a religious dogma which may be doubted, but a narrative convention which must be accepted as given. This way of putting it is, however, symptomatic of the critic's ideological commitment to the text and his use of poetics to support it, if not to impose it. Attributing to the narrator a divine power that "must be accepted" is, also, circumscribing the position of the reader who cannot but submit, passively, to what the text states. The phrase "the drama of reading" in the subtitle seems highly appropriate.

The position of the reader is both central and problematic. The more the narrator is assigned power over him (Sternberg's discourse is all-male), the more the reader is called to be active, in order for that power to work; hence, the more the reader is in danger of becoming autonomous. The aporia this leads to is obliterated by the conflation, in Sternberg's approach, of the intention ascribed to the narrator and his own readerly assumptions and reactions. Some of his analyses are keenly interesting, some less so, but they are consistently and overtly triggered by the "reader's" reactions, "the" reader being this particular reader, of course. Hence, the autonomy of the critic is only discursively attributed to the workings of the omniscient

---

2. Kugel, *The Idea of Biblical Poetry*, 77.

narrator; and, as a more critical writer[3] recently put it, just as God is created, invented by his subjects, so Sternberg's narrator is created by his reader. The intentional fallacy deployed serves to claim the inevitable right of the critic.

Sternberg is, however, not so naive. He is well aware of the existence of other readers besides himself, and he even discusses them. He does so by differentiating between sophisticated and lower readers, called "under-readers." In order not to let "underreaders" escape the ideological intentions, the narrator makes his text "foolproof." The arrogance of this elitist stance needs no further comment; it surfaces on almost every page, and implicitly or explicitly it systematically insults "pagans," Christians, women alike. What concerns me in the context of this article is the circularity of the critical standpoint that makes the argument of this particular reader, his own ideological input, as "foolproof," inevitable, as that ascribed to the narrator—and to his God. The basic advantage of recent reader-response criticism, the inherent subjectivity and hence the impossibility of a "right" reading, is erased, and we are left with a study in the New Critical mode, interspersed with needless anger at every critic who views the Bible differently. Since Sternberg too discusses the Sisera murder, a comparison between Alter's and his practice is possible.

1.3 Trible: anachronistic critique

Trible's book is hard to compare to the other two in that it comes from biblical rather than from literary scholarship, and in that it is explicitly feminist. Like many biblical scholars coming to literary theory, Trible lacks contemporary theoretical reflection. Hence, she is unable to overcome the contradiction inherent in her project: to propose an "intrinsic reading of the text in its final form." Although she does acknowledge that no reading can be intrinsic,[4] her critical practice is tainted by the contradiction. There seems to be a gap between her careful formal analyses and the interpretative conclusions she claims to draw from them. Where Alter wants to reconstruct the historical poetics of the text, and Sternberg the historical ideology of the editorial process, Trible responds from a modern point of view to the texts as she reads them, an ahistorical, and in its overtness fully legitimate, gesture. Where these texts have been so extremely influential, it is justified to look at them as they stand in our culture, and continue to shape human existences. My problems with the book start where she comes closest to Sternberg: although she is critical toward the characters who abuse women in the four impressive "texts of terror" she selected, Yahweh is somehow redeemed from the critique. Hence, the theology is saved from the ideology.

3. Scarry, *The Body in Pain*.
4. Trible, *Texts of Terror*, 3, 6 (note 11).

Trible's practice is at its strongest when she challenges received views, at its weakest when she rests her argument on them. Interestingly, she sometimes accepts current assumptions in order to criticize the text's ideology, where the common views are so bluntly anachronistic that criticizing them instead of the text would have led her to a much more radical and poetically more interesting critique. I will discuss one example below. One aspect of this problem deserves attention, since it affects all three studies. The in itself valuable, neat analysis of poetic form that prepares Trible's subsequent evaluation is tainted by a somewhat positivistic truth-claim that has never disappeared since the time of New Criticism. The relation between "description" and interpretation, which are assumed to be separable, is not problematized by any of the three critics, and the critic's own views are subsequently given more status than they deserve; but this turns against them, in that they come to hang in the air.[5] In Sternberg's book, this problem seems to have been tackled by the theory of "gaps," "ambiguities," and the like, devices that are claimed to be author-designed and reader-oriented. Alter, pleasantly modest and seductively clear, remains so much closer to analysis and so little sticks out his interpretative neck, that the problem seems to affect him the least. Trible, however, seems to believe genuinely in the positive reliability of her analysis and lets herself be hampered by it in her critical reach.

2. CRITICAL PRACTICE: THE EXAMPLE OF GENDER

Alter analyzes the scene of the murder of Sisera in the two accounts, the poetic version of Judg 5:24–30 and the epic version of 4:17–22. The comparison seems to be appropriate as the test for the critic's admission to the status of master in the guild: there is no other case of two accounts so close and so different, and the critic's skill (derived from the etymological meaning of the verb *krinein*, to differentiate) can be handsomely displayed. The case has been analyzed by linguists[6] and by literary, philological, historical scholars alike. The case interests me in particular because of its relation to gender. For the Song of Deborah is one of the rare pieces of the Bible generally attributed, if not to a female poet, at least to a female voice. In my book on the case,[7] I have analyzed the ways in which critics from different disciplines deal with the difference between the two accounts, and with the difference in gender of the subjects of the lyric, female and of the epic, male version. The general tendency to conflate the two accounts into one I showed to be related to gender, and I will not repeat the argument here. It is not fair, and it is not my purpose, to require from the critics a feminist

5. For a discussion, see below, Chapter 5.
6. Berlin, *Biblical Parallelism*, is the latest.
7. *Murder and Difference.*

awareness that they do not bring up themselves; I want to show how the lack of that awareness—and perhaps in one case, the strong commitment to sexism—prevents the critics from bringing their own endeavors to their most far-reaching conclusions. I choose gender here as the factor that limits the power of critique, but it would be easy to replace it with other ideological stances, like ethnocentrism, "present-centrism" or anachronism, classism, or what have you.

Sternberg only discusses Judges 4, the epic version, while Alter discusses both. He does so with the explicit purpose of showing the generic differences between poetry and prose. Since Sternberg is concerned with narrative, his exclusive focus on the prose-version is acceptable, although not without consequences. Starting from the assumption that prospection and suspense are reader-oriented devices designed to convey a "foolproof" truth, Sternberg has no business studying the lyric evocation of Sisera's agony, so impressively sung in the poetry. Yet, the complete lack of comparison makes it more difficult for the critic to differentiate between his purely personal input and the "design" of the narrator. Had he been eager to avoid the intentional fallacy, this was his chance, and he missed it. Alter, on the other hand, focuses strictly on genre, and he has no business discussing gender. Yet, his neatly formal analysis, by the sheer fact of the comparison, comes much closer to a critical perspective. Without touching upon the anthropological background and the division of poetic labor,[8] Alter prepares the ground for a feminist interpretation of the differences he ascribes to genre.

2.1 Alter: the limits of realism

The comparison between Judges 4 and 5 shows the generic difference to have a strong impact on meaning. Where the prose version circumscribes the murder itself with an extensive preparation, the poetry evokes the agony in detail, leaving the circumstances aside. Alter, with an acute sense of the effect of parallelism—the major poetic device—pictures the heroine of the story as "the powerful figure of Jael the hammerer, standing over the body of Sisera, whose death throes between her legs, kneeling, then prostrate, may be, perhaps, an ironic glance at the time-honored martial custom of rape."[9] This conclusion is not based on any discussion of rape other than what directly emerges from the text—the use of the vulgar word "womb" for captured maidens, evoked, as part of the booty, by Sisera's mistaken mother. Yet it is radical in its critical impact. Alter opposes this picture of Jael to that of the prose-version, where "Jael here is in turn seductress, ministering mother, and sexual assailant."[10] The narrative genre demands

8. See Lemaire, *Ik zing mijn lied.*
9. Alter, *Biblical Poetry,* 49.
10. Alter, *Biblical Poetry,* 49.

circumstantial detail, while poetry is able to evoke without describing the "logic" of the story.

I find Alter's analysis here, as generally in both of his books, reasonably subtle and convincingly related to form. Had he been aware of the ways ideological criticism can inform poetic, even formal criticism, he would have been able not only to take his interpretation much further but also to avoid being trapped by the realistic fallacy he so carefully tries to undo. Alter's account of the genre is never universalistic and often fairly insightful. Here, for example, are statements about the Song that allow the reader to follow—and adopt—ways of reading that are, if not "originally intended," at least fruitful:

> "Hammer" as a noun at the end of line 3 is then transformed into "hammer" as a verb at the very beginning of line 4, in accord with a general tendency of nominal constructs to generate verbal chains, of actors or agents to produce actions. Line 4 is a strong instance—not only between versets but even within each verset—of the use of a sequence of seeming synonyms that in fact are related to each other syntagmatically, each term closely following the preceding one in time, like movie frames.[11]

Reading the Song this way enables us to read it *as* song, and to leave behind the fallacies of realistic reading.

It is obvious that there is more to the difference between narrative-circumstantial and poetic-evocative modes. Not only, as it turns out, is the prose-account obsessed with circumstantial detail, but that detail also happens to be extremely apologetic, explaining how it could happen that a man, even if an enemy, gets trapped by a woman. The realistic "logic" of the narrative requires, firstly, an explanation of why Sisera entered Jael's tent at all, next, why he was so stupid as to trust her enough to go to sleep, and finally, why he did not resist her aggression. The Song, on the other hand, is not in the least concerned with the "logic" of circumstances. It evokes the agony, as Alter points out brilliantly, as a reversal of rape. Alter bases his conclusion on the analysis of parallelisms, and from there on it is but one step to acknowledge the complex gender-relatedness of the device that, figuring in a female genre, in a song sung by a female voice, deals with the agony of a man brought about by a woman. Unfortunately, and here lies the limit of Alter's enterprise as a critical one, his methodology does not accommodate that step. Nor does it prevent him from slipping back into realism. Wondering why the Song does not specify that Sisera fell asleep in Jael's tent, Alter does accept the generic convention, but assigns the responsibility of filling in to the reader, in a move toward Sternberg's method, when he says: "a separate report of Sisera's sleep is not allowed to intervene, though the audience would surely have presupposed that narrative datum,

---

11. Alter, *Biblical Poetry*, 45.

and without it Jael would scarcely have had the chance to pick up peg and hammer and strike the blow."[12] Thus he misses one of the most fascinating aspects of the lyric version: its particular "logic" that reverses the narrative order. Sisera is said in the next verse to fall—a fall that denotes not only his physical fall but also his ultimate loss of power. The fall is described in a tricolon, a device which serves to accent it. Reversing the "logic" of realist narrative, we may assume that the question of his bodily position is not raised in terms of circumstances, of possibility, but in terms of the inexorable sequence of the phases of his undoing: he stands in vs 26 in order to fall in vs 27.

I have suggested already that the realistic endeavor of the prose version is related to the issue of gender. As a matter of fact, the death of the leader of the enemy army by the hand of a woman has been already been predicted, earlier in Judges 4, as a punishment for Barak's cowardice. The female hand is humiliating, and the expression of the ideologeme that relates shame and honor to gender is put in the mouth of Deborah. But her words are embedded by the male, epic narrator. The detail of Sisera's apology further strengthens the ideologeme. Now the lyric version does not mention the issue at all. There is no relation established between honor and gender, nor any between cause and effect. This particular structure of the Song, so well described by Alter, is not generated only by the form of lyric poetry; the latter is in its turn generated by a different, in this case female, literary logic. Or rather, it is non-male: devoid of the male concern with honor and shame that comes up when a woman is involved in military matters. The involvement of the women in war, in theology, in murder, and in poetry—the Song is attributed to Deborah—is, in the Song, an entirely "natural," unargued integration. Alter misses here an opportunity to provide his poetic approach with a socially relevant backing for which he did initially prepare the ground. Slipping back into realism at this very moment is a significant gesture: on the one hand, it shows how powerful realism as a fallacy is, hence, how useful his historical relativistic stance is; on the other, it shows that the poetic approach is not in itself productive of a critique that bridges the gap between an esthetic and an ideological approach. It should be stressed that Alter rarely slips into this type of self-defeating mistake; the bulk of his critical practice is, within the limits he assigns to it, interesting, useful, and in its respect for otherness, ideologically respectable.

2.2 Sternberg: the limits of paraphrasis

As I have already suggested, Sternberg's commitment to the biblical ideology as he sees it is counterproductive for critique. Left with a circular methodology, he can only paraphrase, repeat what he thinks the ideology of

12. Alter, *Biblical Poetry*, 44.

the text is. This turns him from the literary scholar he claims to be, into a theologian. At this point I want to show how this paraphrastic approach affects the issue of gender in Sternberg's analysis of the Sisera murder in the prose account. In the light of this problematic, his silence over the lyric version, although arguably caused by the preoccupation with narrative, also displays a blindness to otherness. It turns out that, within the prose text, the critic is also focused on those aspects that are maximally different from the poetic version. The details that strike the critic most are those related to gender, but since gender is not what he is concerned with, there is no discussion of it, let alone critique.

The first surprise this reader experiences—and that is, therefore, presented as part of the narrator's intentional devices—is the unexpected appearance of Deborah. The character is presented as follows: "At the sequential position reserved for the deliverer, she springs at us from nowhere, complete with husband, national role, foreign antagonist, seat of judgment bearing her name: all expositional features calculated to bring her sex into marked dissonance with her offices past and to come."[13] The author elaborates extensively on the "incongruity" of this female deliverer, placed in a row with the left-handed Ehud as evidence of God having "picked his instruments in contempt of human [!] norms of seemliness and efficacy."[14] That the critic brings in a more strict division of labor based on gender than the biblical narrator, in other words, that he beats the Bible in sexism, is less disturbing than the fact that the methodology—Minskian frame-theory used as Iserian gap-theory—allows him to turn his own male surprise into the leading principle that structures the text. There is no room for a questioning of these primary assumptions. It is arguable that the phrase usually translated "the wife of Lappidoth" means "a woman of torches," a metaphorical expression for an inspiring woman, which, as a prophetess, Deborah is. Although Deborah's "husband" has been questioned in the history of interpretation, he is here firmly reestablished, as is the equally doubtful incongruity of a female prophet.[15] In order to drive his point home, Sternberg ignores the bulk of biblical scholarship as bluntly as he ignores the last ten years of literary theory.

When discussing the murder-scene itself, the critic does not fail to give full credit to the circumstantial detail of the account. Far from discussing the ideology that underlies the issue of shame and gender, he seems to subscribe to it unproblematically. The problem is not that the analysis is bad; it is, in fact, quite interesting and, for our purpose, revealing. It is its embedding within the theory that is used to protect the critical enterprise from verification and criticism that makes it so utterly gratuitous. For those

---

13. Sternberg, *The Poetics of Biblical Narrative*, 272.
14. Sternberg, *The Poetics of Biblical Narrative*, 273.
15. Boling, *Judges*, 95.

who subscribe to the narrowly male ideology the critic defends, the study as a whole, and this analysis in particular, will be a confirmation. And that is exactly what it should not be. As Jonathan Culler pointed out in the 1985 Modern Language Association session on "What isn't Comparative Litera- ture?," it is the critic's task, not to repeat but to criticize ideologies, religious and other.

As I have suggested, however, the critic does more than just repeat. He exaggerates, overdoes the text's sexism. Although the narrative, already integrated in a predominantly male, epic tradition, does display the dis- turbing but powerful ideologeme that relates honor-shame to gender, it also responds to a different tradition, whose lively existence is demonstrated by the Song itself. Hence, the appearance of the prophetess Deborah is less incongruous than Sternberg seems to wish. In fact, there are indications, in the epic text, of an attempt to recuperate the otherness of the Song. This is visible, among many other instances, in the theological aspects of both texts. The image of the deity, unproblematically pantheistic and natural- istic in the Song, is personified in the epic. Repeating a keyword from the Song within the entirely different theology of the epic is a form of inter- discursivity that is neither polemic nor mimetic but imperialistic. "Going out" in the form of a thunderstorm, a cloud, is tamed into "going out" as personified leader. These tensions between the two versions are lost when- ever only one of them is analyzed; and it is in the tensions that the gender- ideologies can be measured. The differentiating third term between text and critic is so utterly absent in this type of paraphrastic criticism, that it is even impossible to evaluate to what extent it is paraphrastic at all. The omniscient narrator is replaced with the omniscient critic, and the text, as well as its ideology, is veiled.

2.3 Trible: the limits of anachronism

In the beginning of her book Trible explicitly includes her own subjec- tivity, as well as her feminist interest, in the analysis she is about to elaborate. I will briefly present here how this position, which is relativist in a different way from Alter's and which stands at the other side of histor- icism, affects the method and results in one particular case, the analysis of Judges 19. The story is arguably the most horrible one in the entire Bible, and deserves more attention than it usually gets. It is Trible's merit to have brought it to renewed attention. It is the story of the rape, torture, and murder of an unnamed "concubine," whom I propose to name, for reasons that I have expounded elsewhere, Beth.[16] A feminist analysis of "texts of terror" of this type has to incur the obvious danger of paraphrasis. What else

16. *Death and Dissymmetry*, 89–90.

can we do but express indignation at this display of hatred toward women? And how useful academically is such an expression for the understanding of the process of reading?

Trible carefully analyzes the structure of the story, from sentence to sequence to plot to characterization. The woman is introduced as a "concubine from Bethlehem." In the second verse, a philological problem arises—or rather, in my view, is uselessly raised—that affects the ideology of the text. The translations vary between "she played the harlot against him," based on the meaning of the verb *znh* as prostitution, and "she became angry at him," based on a far-fetched Aramaic source and unique in the Bible.[17] The issue here is not to decide the philological debate, but to question the question itself. Those who argue for the first alternative fail to understand how the man could possibly go through so much trouble to bring the runaway woman back if she would only have insulted him by prostituting herself. The possibility that he made her angry allows for guilt-feelings to motivate the trip. Neither of the two interpretations account for the discrepancy between the initial attempt to make up after whatever quarrel, and the later abandonment or even positive rejection and the subsequent dismemberment of the woman's body. Trible raises both possibilities, and she does not fail to make clear that a choice between the two translations affects the guilt-question, hence our view of the two characters. Instead of taking a position, however, she leaves the question open. Why does she miss this opportunity to discuss responsibilities? I cannot escape the impression that it is because Trible is not much interested in it, since she has already built up her structure.

The opposition it is based on is that between the socially respectable Levite, who, as a priest, is, according to Trible, a symbol of respect, and the concubine, a wife of lowly status. Hence, she assumes from the outset that the story is sadly opposing male power and female powerlessness. Far be it from me to deny that this latter opposition is at play. I wonder, however, whether it is as simplistically dichotomistic as Trible and most other critics of the story seem to assume. The opposition is based on two anachronistic assumptions. Priests are not necessarily respectable in the Bible. Not only is Aaron the priest subordinated to Moses the leader. Closer to our story, Judges 17 and 18 depict a far from respectable and respected Levite, and the case does not stand alone. Priesthood had a thoroughly different status in the context of the story than the one we customarily accord it. But worse, the concept of the concubine as a lowly woman is derived from later Latin traditions. There is no way to match the Hebrew "concubine" and the Latin concubine: the biblical woman was, as most studies acknowledge, legally

17. Koehler and Baumgartner, *Lexicon*, 261.

married, while the concubine in Roman times was not. One need only distance oneself from the modern presuppositions to become aware of the issue that the whole story so obviously raises. The woman referred to as a "concubine," and whom I call Beth, is a patrilocal wife, a woman who, after her marriage, stays in her father's house (Beth means "house"). Like Samson's bride in chapter 15, she went back to her father. Competing with the latter, the "husband" came to take her back. From father to husband and back, and back again: this is the voyage this woman has to make, and there is no way she can survive it. In vs 2, she was not angry but simply unfaithful. The verb that later receives the exclusive meaning of harlotry, is earlier a more general word for unfaithfulness, and is in some dictionaries related to the father-marriage.[18] It is to the father, not to the husband, that she was "unfaithful." Questioning the "concubine" thus entails an understanding of the problem in vs 2 that allows us to connect the different episodes, to make sense of the beginning in terms of the end, to displace the question of guilt from the individual "matrimonial crisis,"[19] that cannot but be anachronistic, onto a social issue: the chaotic transition from one marriage-form to another.[20]

Anachronism is thus not only a historical shortcoming that can be redeemed by contemporary interests. It is also a limit of feminism as well as of poetic understanding. A strong case of the negative effect of anachronism is a brief comment on this same story in another book of Alter's.[21] As numerous critics have argued, Judges 19 is an almost verbatim repetition of Genesis 19, the better known story of Lot who, in order to save the divine messengers from the threat of homosexual rape, offers his two daughters to satisfy the "sexual" appetite of the inhabitants of the city. The intention is not carried out there, while it is here. The reasons why, in spite of the similarity—homosexual rape threat, heterosexual compensation offered— Alter calls the present case a "heterosexual companion-piece" of Genesis 19 can only be guessed. It is only too obvious that, in both cases, the threat of homosexual rape is not carried out, while in this one case, heterosexual rape is. The one case is not more or less homo- or heterosexual than the other. Whatever his intentions, the result of Alter's distortion is that the man, in Judges, is written out of responsibility. His active rejection of the patrilocal wife whom he had claimed to take to his own house, but whom he was unable to keep, is a submission to the patrilocal system that clearly shows where women, in this competition, stand: nowhere. It is this conclusion, relevant for Trible's project as well as for the poetic enterprise, that the story designs in its figuration of traveling from house to house.

18. Koehler and Baumgartner, *Lexicon*, 261.
19. Soggin, *Judges*, 284.
20. For an extensive analysis, see Bal, *Death and Dissymmetry*.
21. Alter, *Motives for Fiction*, 132.

3. ESCAPING ESCAPISM

Although there is an enormous progress, from the point of view of the critical project, in a move from anachronistic, ethnocentric paraphrasis to a respectful mapping of a different poetics, we have seen that the most successful of our three critics, Alter, fails exactly where he accepts the limits of uncritical description. He falls back into what he tries to undo because his methodology has not built in a critical middle term. Trible, on the other hand, does have a critical purpose but fails to use the otherness of the other culture as a heuristic tool. Hence, her reader-oriented poetics remains, at critical moments, uncritical. Sternberg does not want to be critical, and it would be unfair to blame him for what he does not claim. But his conflation of author-intention and reader-response makes his work worse than uncritical: it is actively ideological, and poetics is put to that use. Becoming himself the omniscient narrator, he allows not even a second, let alone a third term. It is no surprise, then, that his book is self-centered and self-contained. While it has an excessively elaborated index—the self-referential aspect, the entrance to the book—it has no bibliography, the exit from the book to other books. It is exasperatingly long, and could have been much better if half its length. It is no coincidence that both Alter and Trible write pleasantly, Trible somewhat too religiously for my taste, but both clearly and modestly. The style of the books is symptomatic, as are their titles, format, and size. While Alter's and Trible's titles cover the contents of their books, Sternberg's confuses "narrative" with "theology," and that is a confusion iconic of the contents. Alter promises a poetics of biblical poetry, and gives it. Trible promises feminist-literary readings, and gives them. Both books are limited, Alter's in its refusal to go beyond aesthetic concerns, Trible's in its anachronism. Where the one lacks reflection on the link with social concerns, the other lacks a feminist philosophy that would account for the relations between text and society. These two lacks, then, meet. It is at their meeting point that we must seek after a feminist hermeneutics of the Bible.

"Gender" is an utterly modern concern. Although there have always been sexes, it is questionable whether gender, and its consequence, sexism, have always been, everywhere, and the same as today. It is indeed certain that this is not the case. The two forms of patriarchy that compete in Judges 19, reflected in patrilocal and virilocal marriage, are equally "sexist" if we look at them from a modern feminist perspective. They are far from identical, and the position of women in each is different. The interest of that finding is that it shows the changeability of patriarchy itself. If it can change, it is not universal. Hence it can also be undone. But how can we use texts—fictional texts—to substantiate these claims, and how does the claim relate to poetics? I have tried to show, if briefly, that the poetic questions raised, especially by Alter, cannot be dissociated from issues of gender. The generic difference has to be related to the gender-difference both of the characters and of the authorial voice; otherwise, there is no check against anachronism. This is a most surprising result. It shows that the relation between fiction and reality is more fundamental than a simplistic "mimetic" theory of fiction assumes. It shows that gender is poetically relevant, and that fiction is socially relevant, as two indissociable aspects of the one problematic of the place of texts in society. If interdiscursivity, voice, focalization are poetic issues, they entail insight into social differences, from the status of women to the image of God, and thus they can substantiate Culler's view of what Comparative Literature isn't, but should be.

PART II

A Theory
of Narrative

This section offers elements of a narratology as I have been working to develop it; *a* theory, not *the* theory of narrative. The specific contribution of this particular narratology lies in the tension, crucial to my mind, between subject-orientedness and the pluralization of the subject. It is the only narratology to my knowledge which offers an alternative to the humanistic, holistic view of the subject-as-author, and which does not shun semiotic responsibility.

None of these chapters contains a full sketch of narratology; the English translation of my Dutch introductory book, published as *Narratology*,[1] makes such a survey unnecessary. Two chapters date from my early writing, one is later. Chapter 4 represents the initial step, my argument with Genette initially published in *Poétique* by Genette himself, exemplified by an analysis of Colette's *The Cat*. The essay has some historical interest in that it is representative of the kind of discussions held in French structuralism. This article initiated a discussion that went on for years after, some of which appeared in *Poétique*. Most of that discussion has lost interest today, but in order to give at least an impression, and also to clarify some details, I refer the reader to a response I made to criticism of my analysis of

---

1. This is an opportunity to point out that *Narratology* is *not* the translation of the French *Narratologie* but of the Dutch *De theorie van vertellen en verhalen*, written a year later. The Dutch book—now in English—presents a pedagogical survey of the field of narratology, designed for classroom use and conceived to be practical, usable, teachable, while the French, of which only the first chapter has been available in English up to now, was a discussion and try-out. The confusion is due to publishers' policy. I had initially entitled the French book *Exercices de narratologie*, which I still find a more adequate title, but I was not in a position to push that title through. On the other hand, the complex title of the Dutch book did not sound right in English, while the comprehensiveness of the theory did justify the general title. Regretably, the cost was an overlap with Gerald Prince's earlier *Narratology*, already well established on the market when mine came out, but which is fortunately different enough from my book not to suffer from conflation.

The Cat, which, if coming rather from the pre-structuralist side, does address the kind of issues under debate.[2] The main point of this discussion is the position of the subject, and can be summarized as follows. The "subject-centrism" of my proposal has been mistaken for a subject-holism; hence the attempt to recuperate the notion of implied author which I had disposed of. And the notion of focalization has been projected on a realist view of language; hence, its possible embedding was denied. Both issues are more extensively addressed in Chapter 6.

Chapter 5 provides an example of a detailed elaboration of one aspect of narrative which the general model comprehended without, however, spelling it out. The subject of description, which has been present all along in structuralism, has also been marginal from the outset, in spite of Philippe Hamon's powerful advocacy of its serious narrative status. Today, with the renewed questioning of plot-centered views of narrative and the growing interest in the visual, description is becoming a prevailing topic again. The theoretical points are developed through passages of Flaubert's *Madame Bovary*. The English translation and reworking of this early piece has been buried in a periodical that has no traditional readership interested in theory. The essay is characteristic for the play with concepts and models, distinctions and details, in view of a movement between extreme atomism and extreme integrationalism which I now like to see as an undermining of the dichotomy of the whole and the part, the primary and the detailed, in keeping with Naomi Schor's recent work. During the period when my primary focus was biblical narrative, my earlier thoughts on description slipped out of it; with my current interest in the visual, I am bound to take these issues up again.

Chapter 6 is, again, a fragment of *Femmes imaginaires*. It takes up the methodological debate, responding to criticism, and refining the initial model. In fact, I would be reluctant to publish the earlier model today without this essay as a companion-piece. In it, the problem of the subject is more consciously addressed, and as a result, the subject is both more consciously central and more problematic. Notably, I distinguish, here, between at least three meanings of the concept of subject itself: the thematic one, the genetic one, and the interactional one. This splitting of the agents of narrative action leads the model further away, both from the pre-structuralist holistic concepts and from the structuralist ones, with their claim to ideological neutrality. Between "formalist rigor" and post-structuralist critique, and between the split subject of the Lacanian strand of post-structuralism and the free play of language of the Derridean strand, this renewed presentation of the theory can find a mediating position. Examples are drawn from *Wuthering Heights*.

2. See Bronzwaer, "Mieke Bal's Concept of Focalization," and my response in "The Laughing Mice."

▪4▪

Narration and Focalization

1. NARRATOLOGICAL FIGURES

1.1 Introduction

In *Narrative Discourse: An Essay in Method*, Gérard Genette works out a typology of narrative figures[1] based on the three categories of tense, mood, and voice. The study of tense (Chapters 1–3), in which Genette makes very precise distinctions among order, duration, and frequency, forms a coherent system. Both systematic and relevant, it has received the wide attention it deserves, so there is no need to dwell here on its merits and occasional contradictions.

In Chapters 4 and 5 of *Narrative Discourse* Genette clarifies a theory in the most elusive and most "narratological" area of narratology: the narrating. The chief originality of his theory lies in separating two categories that are ordinarily combined—the categories of perspective and narrating agent.[2] Genette classifies them under mood and voice, respectively. Besides separating, he also joins. Under mood he includes not only perspective or point of view (that is, what constitutes the answer to the question "Who sees?"), but also distance, which has to do with the old distinction between showing and telling or the even older one between mimesis and diegesis. Under voice he includes not only the status of the narrator (that is, what constitutes the answer to the question "Who speaks?") but also the two

1. The French title *Figures* represents both the limits and the originality of Genette's study and should therefore be taken completely literally.
2. [Translator's note.] "Narrating agent" is the translation used in this essay for the French phrase *instance narrative*. In Genette, *Narrative Discourse*, however, the same French phrase was translated as "narrating instance"—but there it meant "something like the narrating situation, the narrative matrix . . . out of which a narrative statement is produced" (31, note 10), whereas here it refers to a channel or medium within the narrative—a channel or medium that is both active and impersonal: a subject.

problems of the time of the narrating and the different narrative levels (the narrative within the narrative).

The importance of the subject, the quality of the theory, and the great need finally to understand these areas of mood and voice are my reasons for undertaking the present analysis of Genette's theory. I will be careful to limit myself to the narratological aspects of the two chapters in question. There is no point in reconsidering the value of the often brilliant analyses and interpretations of Proust's *Remembrance of Things Past* which served some readers as illustrations and others as touchstones and to the author were guidelines making it possible to sustain steady and fruitful interaction between deductive theory and the indispensable induction.

Nor will I go into the details of some fairly blunt distinctions that are not part of the theory itself, such as the functions of the narrator[3] or some hard-to-verify variants like "alterations" and "polymodality." What matters here is to analyze and evaluate the basic principles of the theory and, wherever the theory reveals problems, to see the extent to which we can modify it on its own level: that of a typology of narrative figures, designed as tools for critical analysis.

1.2 Analysis

1.2.1 *Mood.* Wishing to pattern his theory on a linguistic model—that of the categories of verbs[4]—Genette demarcated the area of mood by taking as his basis the *Littré* dictionary's definition of mood as an aspect of verbs: the "name given to the different forms of the verb that are used to affirm *more or less* the thing in question, and to express . . . the different *points of view* from which the life or the action is looked at."[5] The first part of this definition becomes his point of departure for a theory of the difference between mimesis and diegesis. The second part gives rise to a theory of "focalization."

Noting along with Booth[6] that narration, by definition diegetic, cannot be mimetic, that it can only create a stronger or weaker illusion of mimesis, Genette, in discussing the difference between the two, distinguishes between the "narrative of events" and the "narrative of words." In the narrative of events, the contrast between mimesis and diegesis is relative:

3. Genette, *Narrative Discourse*, 255–59.
4. *Narrative Discourse* is divided according to the three aspects of verbs: tense, mood, and voice.
5. Genette, *Narrative Discourse*, 161. The words I italicize are those guiding Genette in the development of his theory.
6. Booth, *The Rhetoric of Fiction*. It is unfortunate that in analyzing the "narrative of words," Genette was unable to take into account the theories of Doležel, *Narrative Modes*, and Schmid, *Textaufbau*.

"Mimesis [is] defined by a maximum of information and a minimum of the informer, and diegesis by the opposite relationship."[7] This formulation does indeed account for the relative nature of the opposition; narrative can never be absolutely mimetic. In the narrative of words, in contrast, the situation is completely different, because there the narrated content consists of words and can thus be presented directly, without the mediation of an informer *within* this content. Yet there, too, degrees of mimesis are possible. Genette differentiates "reported speech," identifiable as direct discourse, from "narratized" or "recounted speech," in which the content of the discourse is reduced to the bare minimum and speech has become simply an event like any other. Between these two extremes—the mimesis and the diegesis of speech—is an intermediary state: "transposed speech" (for example, free indirect style). In transposed speech, the narrator adheres as closely as possible to the words of the character without yielding the floor; the narrator speaks, yet does not replace the character's words with its own narration of them.

"Who sees?" is a totally different kind of question. After a very convincing analysis of the theories of Stanzel,[8] Brooks and Warren,[9] Friedman,[10] and Booth,[11] in which he unerringly exposes in all these authors the same confusion between vision and speech, Genette proposes for the problems of point of view a three-term typology based on focalization.[12]

The narrative in which the narrator "says more than any of the characters knows" is the "non-focalized" narrative. If the narrator "says only what a given character knows," the narrative has "internal focalization," whether that focalization be fixed, variable, or multiple. By focalized narrative Genette means what Blin would call a narrative with "restricted field" and what Pouillon would call a narrative having "vision with."[13] The third type is the narrative with "external focalization," in which the narrator "says less than the character knows," with the latter thus being presented from the outside.

1.2.2 *Voice*. Chapter 5 of *Narrative Discourse* concentrates on the narrating agent: "Who speaks?" Under the heading of voice, Genette discusses

7. Genette, *Narrative Discourse*, 166.
8. Stanzel, *Typische Formen*.
9. Brooks and Warren, *Understanding Fiction*.
10. Friedman, "Point of View in Fiction."
11. Booth, *The Rhetoric of Fiction*.
12. Genette prefers this term because it is more abstract than the "too specifically visual" (*Narrative Discourse*, 189) terms "point of view," "vision," and "field." This seems to me an odd argument, as focalization is derived from the visual term "focus." He does not define the exact meaning of his chosen term or the meanings of the other terms he refers to. I will come back to this problem.
13. Pouillon, *Temps et roman*; Blin, *Stendhal*. The quotations in this paragraph are from Genette, *Narrative Discourse*, 189.

all the relations between the narrating agent and the narrated object: temporal relations, relations of subordination, and the "person" by whom the narrative is told. The chapter ends by defining the status of the narrator; the definition makes use of the last two aspects of the narrating agent, but not the first.

(a) The *temporal relation* between story and narrating is defined in the same terms as relations between main clauses and adverbial clauses of time: by antecedence, posteriority, or simultaneity. Moreover, a combination of the last two relations is conceivable and would occasion an interpolated narrating. Examining the temporal aspect of the narrating requires one already to take into account the "person" of the narrator, to the extent that (especially in a "first-person" narrative) the narrator is distinguishable from the character by the temporal aspect as well. With a "first-person" narrative the hero cannot be identified with the narrator, because the moment of writing down one's adventures is never the moment of experiencing them.

(b) A *relationship of subordination* exists between two narratives located at different narrative levels. We are dealing here with "metanarrative," the narrative within the narrative—not only narratives that are framed or embedded[14] (as in *Manon Lescaut* or *The Thousand and One Nights*), but also less obvious insertions within a narrative. In general, the narrator of such a secondary narrative is connected, by its function as a character, to the primary narrative; it thus belongs to the diegetic universe of that primary narrative. Hence Genette's statement that "any event a narrative recounts is at a diegetic level immediately higher than the level at which the narrating act producing this narrative is placed."[15] Here the passage to the second degree is presented as a passage to a *higher* level, whereas logically subordination would be denoted by the word *lower*.[16] This problem of terminology is all the more serious since a regular profusion of meta-terms with the prefix "meta-" has sprouted since the publication of *Figures III*. This abuse must positively end, for it produces an unfortunate looseness in terms that were created or introduced for their exactness. But, at the moment, what counts is distinguishing narrative levels and diegetic levels, their

14. Maatje, in *Doppelroman*, systematically analyzes the possible relationships between the framing narrative and the framed narrative. The idea of *Doppelroman*, however, does not overlap that of a "narrative with a frame." The latter has stricter laws about dependence, whereas the former requires, precisely, a certain minimum of independence. This difference is irrelevant here. Maatje's typology does not take account of different levels; it is based on the spatio-temporal relations between the two narratives. Genette uses only the term "embedding," which I will come back to. A propos "mise en abyme," see Dällenbach, *Le récit spéculaire*.

15. Genette, *Narrative Discourse*, 228.

16. It is obvious that Genette chooses "higher" so that he can use the prefix meta-, by analogy with "metalanguage." As he himself notes, the way the term functions here is the opposite of the way it functions in the model of logic and linguistics.

reciprocal relationships, and the place of the narrator within such relationships.

Between a metadiegetic (secondary) narrative and its primary narrative, three possible kinds of relationships can exist. The relationship may be causal (functioning as an explanation), as when the metanarrative explains what is happening in the primary narrative. Or the relationship may be thematic, involving no spatiotemporal continuity between the two narratives. This second relationship may be one of contrast and analogy, as in the *mise en abyme* so esteemed by the New Novelists. In this case the secondary narrative may influence the events of the primary narrative "by example," on condition, of course, that the secondary narrative be *told* to the characters in the primary narrative. The third relationship between metadiegetic narrative and primary narrative is strictly narrative: not the content of the "metanarrative" but the very act of narrating influences the events of the primary narrative. It goes without saying that the canonical example of this type is *The Thousand and One Nights*. From the first type to the third, the relationship is less and less direct: the importance of the content of the "metanarrative" for the content of the primary narrative decreases, while the importance of the narrating act itself increases. The crossing from one narrative level to another must be by way of the narrating. Transgressions of this rule are instances of "narrative metalepsis," a figure that consists of "taking hold of (telling) by changing level."[17]

(c) A propos the (grammatical) "person" of the narrator, Genette is quite right in saying that so long as that question concerns grammar, it is irrelevant. By definition, a "third-person" narrator does not exist: any time there is narrating, there is a narrating subject, one that to all intents and purposes is always in the "first person." The "person" of the narrator (this time in the "human" sense—the narrator as agent—since the question has been eliminated on the grammatical plane) can be distinguished only in terms of his/her presence or absence in the narrative at the level in question. The narrator who is present in the story s/he tells is "homodiegetic"; the narrator who is absent (invisible), or who tells at a higher level a narrative from which s/he is absent, is "heterodiegetic." Among homodiegetic narrators, we can distinguish in terms of the degree of presence: some homodiegetic narrators tell a story in which they are the main character (in which case they are "autodiegetic"), while other homodiegetic narrators are merely witnesses.

So with any narrative; we can define the status of the narrator both by the narrative level and by the relationship to the story s/he tells; s/he is always extra-, intra-, or metadiegetic, at the same time s/he is always hetero- or homodiegetic.

17. Genette, *Narrative Discourse*, 235, note.

1.3 Commentary

There, summed up very quickly, is Genette's theory. The distinction between "the one who sees" and "the one who speaks" is essential, and it very decidedly advances the theory of narratology as well as the practice of textual analysis. Never before has the confusion between the two agents been explicitly exposed, and never has the remedy for it been presented so lucidly.

It is appropriate, however, to examine the two categories of mood and voice more closely, bringing to bear the criteria of internal coherence and critical relevance.

1.3.1 *Mood.* Right away, we note a dissymmetry: while the chapter on voice focuses entirely on the subject and the object of the narrating—on the relations between "s/he who speaks" or tells and what is told—the chapter on mood is divided into two fairly heterogeneous parts. The part on "focalizations" in fact elaborates a theory about "s/he who sees," while the part on "distance" seeks to contribute to the age-old discussion of mimesis and diegesis, and in that part we are not dealing at all with the status of one of the agents of narrative. The *Littré* dictionary's definition of mood— Genette's pretext for the division into distance and focalization—includes the idea of "affirm[ing] more or less"[18] the content of a statement. That formulation implies a *degree* of affirmation. In contrasting mimesis and diegesis, Genette uses a quantitative criterion ("more or less") to distinguish *ways* (mimetic or diegetic) of affirming.[19] So his reasoning slides from degree, via quantity, to manner. What we have to examine is whether and to what extent distance actually belongs with the figures of mood. We also have to examine whether, in discussing focalization—which clearly does belong with the figures of mood—Genette's typology has a sound basis.

(a) *The superfluity: distance.* Genette classifies narratives into two groups: the narrative of events and the narrative of words. Both types will be more mimetic or less, more diegetic or less. Now, the criterion on which this typology is based is the quantity of information and, in inverse ratio, the quantity of the informer (or, to put it differently, the quantity of traces of the informer). For this criterion to be operational, we need to know exactly what is *information* and what is *informer*. By information, Genette means what is constituted by the narrated object—and from this perspective, the maximum amount of information is the object narrated with as many details as possible. Any "useless" detail, whether it be picturesque, circumstantial, symbolic, or indicative—in short, any descriptive element—constitutes the superfluity whose function is to "show" what Genette points to as

18. Genette, *Narrative Discourse*, 161.
19. It is not the actual quantity but the *proportion* that, in the final analysis, determines the *way* of recounting, according to Genette.

"reality." These details are "connotators of mimesis." The more diegetic the narrative, the fewer the details, for diegesis is limited to the series of *events* that form the story. Every description is mimetic, every event is diegetic—that is what this theory comes down to. We are simply, despite what Genette has said elsewhere, again in the presence of the old prejudice that denies to description any properly narrative function.[20] So long as the idea of event is not more clearly defined, it is impossible to perform the analyses necessary to classify narratives within the proposed typology.

While the narrative of events is defined only proportionally within the opposition mimesis/diegesis, the narrative of words, Genette says, "can, by contrast, seem condemned *a priori* to . . . absolute imitation."[21] Basically, that "absolute imitation" occurs in only one of the three types of the narrative of words. Indeed, reported speech, which is no different from direct discourse—the literal quotation of the words or thoughts of a character—constitutes a pure instance of mimesis. As to narratized speech, it represents "the most distant and generally . . . the most reduced,"[22] type. Of the three types, then, this discourse is the most diegetic, the most narrative. Now, the reason this discourse is called narratized is precisely that it is no longer discourse; it is taken in hand by the narrator and *integrated* into his narrative. Discourse has become an event like any other. It is inserted into the narrative discourse and, theoretically, is indistinguishable from the narrative of events. It is, therefore, radically different from reported speech: narratized speech is not speech. Reported speech is inserted into the narrative text by the use of a mark of transition, most often a declarative verb. With that transition the narrator yields the floor to someone else—to the character who speaks. That speech is thereby a virtual "metanarrative," a narrative within the narrative, for the same reason that the framed or embedded narrative is.[23]

Transposed speech, which according to Genette is a state midway between the two others, testifies to the narrator's effort to "give as much information as possible" about a speech, to recount it as mimetically as possible, but without yielding the floor, without changing narrative level.

20. In "Boundaries of Narrative," Genette's position is more moderate, but does not invalidate the principle of what he says here. For a comprehensive study of description, see below, Chapter 5.

21. Genette, *Narrative Discourse*, 169.

22. Genette, *Narrative Discourse*, 171.

23. "Reported speech" is not always a complete narrative. To be that, it must be produced as such by the indispensable agents of narrative. Fragmentary "reported speeches" could perhaps be units of the "dramatic" genre intruding into a narrative. If the nature of fragmentary "reported speeches" is still to be defined, their narrative level is nonetheless lower than that of the narratives into which they are inserted. If reported speech is not always narrative, it is at least always "meta-." The particular problems raised by the distinction between reported speech and narratized speech are shrewdly discussed by Schmid, *Textaufbau*.

We ought then to separate reported speech—"metanarrative" speech—from the two other types, and to consider it "metanarrative." The two other types would then constitute the two extreme states of the mimetic and the diegetic, paralleling the tpes of the narrative of events. Ultimately, then, the distinction between narrative of events and narrative of words—however interesting some of the critical results it generates—has only a provisional meaning: actually the two types of narrative are only one.

For the moment, let us accept Genette's theory with that modification. Let us also accept the possibility of defining with some certainty the idea of event. In that case the theory would be coherent, and for every narrative we would in fact be able to investigate the type—the relative type—of *distance* that predominates and the changes it undergoes in the course of the narrative.[24] But one difficulty remains, one that the author himself pointed out. The proportional opposition between mimesis and diegesis refers us to two other categories.

On the one hand, the "quantity of information" can be comprehended with respect to *duration*: that quantity determines the speed of the narrative, which is defined by the relationship between the duration of the story and the duration—length—of the narrative. The mimetic narrative will always be slow, while the diegetic narrative, in which narrative efficiency is greatest, will be fast. In Chapter 2 of his book, Genette clarified a theory of duration that is perfectly coherent and allows us to account for that aspect of narrative. Bringing the problem of duration into the chapter on mood blurs the clarity of that latter chapter as a whole—which is all the more unfortunate, since in the area of mood confusion reigns. It is true that traditionally the problem of mood has been incorporated into the study of point of view because point of view has been assimilated to "presentation," and this assimilation is precisely what Genette seeks to refute. For in this tradition, "presentation" covers practically all aspects of the text—indeed, the text itself, which is considered synonymous with the narrative: the narrative is the presentation of the story.[25]

On the other hand, the second part of the formulation, the "quantity of

24. Let me say parenthetically: in this part of the "Genettian meta-discourse" we are not dealing with *figures*. If in a pinch we could say that the theory allows a typology of narratives, it does not allow us to discern very easily any "distance" figure within particular narratives. The place where this section belongs is therefore not only outside of this chapter but even—if we take the title of the book literally—outside of the book.

25. In my introduction to *Narratologie*, of which this essay is the first chapter, I explain my disagreement with Genette on narrative hierarchy. His use of the word "narrative" (*récit*) is, I claim, imprecise, since it is equated with "narrative text," which sometimes means what results from the arrangement of the story and other times what results from the narrating; so basically Genette distinguishes only two levels, story and plot. I, on the other hand, postulate a third level, neither *histoire* nor *récit*, called "narrative text" (*texte narratif*). For a presentation of my developed theory of three levels, "text," "story," and "fabula," see now *Narratology*.

the informer," obviously refers us to the category of *voice*, since what we are dealing with are the traces in the narrative of the presence of the narrator.[26] We can, therefore, conclude that the section on distance, even when modified, has no place in the category of mood, whose systematic character it weakens. It is superfluous.

(b) *The deficiency: focalization.* Although Genette nowhere explicitly defines "focalization," he says he uses it as a slightly more abstract synonym of terms like "vision," "field," or "point of view."[27] Unfortunately, these three terms are not synonymous, and Genette's typology suffers accordingly. In his first distinction, the one between non-focalized narrative and narrative with internal focalization, focalization has a restrictive meaning. Referring here to Georges Blin's restrictions of field, Genette distinguished the narrative whose narrator is traditionally called omniscient (the narrator who knows, if not "everything," at least more than the character knows) from the narrative whose narrator knows only what a given character knows. This character, "from whom" the narrative is recounted, is the "focalized character." The third type of narrative, however, the narrative with external focalization, is distinguished from the second by a wholly different principle of classification. Now we are no longer dealing with a restriction, but with an inversion of functions. In the narrative with external focalization, characters also are focalized, but they are focalized from without. That means that the narrative's center of interest is a character (as it is with internal focalization), but its development is seen only from the outside.

It is true that, in moving from the first type to the third, the narrator's "knowledge" diminishes, and in this sense the series is homogeneous. But that difference does not have to do with point of view or focalization. The difference between the non-focalized narrative and the internally focalized narrative lies in the agent "who sees": is the agent the narrator who— omniscient—sees more than the character, or (in the second type) is the agent the narrator who sees "with" the character, sees as much as s/he does? Between the second and third types the distinction is not of the same order. In the second type, the "focalized" character *sees*, in the third type, s/he does not see, s/he *is seen*. The difference this time is not between the "seeing" agents, but between the objects of that seeing. This confusion will undermine the theory of focalizations. The following passage perfectly illustrates this difficulty:

26. Here one wonders whether Genette is not somewhat the victim of his own method. Analyzing the discourse of Proust's *Remembrance of Things Past*, the inductive occasion of his work, must have prompted him to speak, at whatever cost, about these problems of the discourse of the characters, in order to have an occasion for dealing with the "ideolectical speaking" of Proust's characters.

27. Genette, *Narrative Discourse*, 189. Cf. above, note 7.

External focalization with respect to one character could sometimes just as well be defined as internal focalization on another: external focalization on Phileas Fogg is just as well internal focalization on Passepartout dumbfounded by his new master, and the only reason for being satisfied with the first term is Phileas' status as hero, which restricts Passepartout to the role of witness.[28]

We see that the nonchalant use of a preposition is enough to overturn a theory. If Genette had thought to distinguish "focalization on" from "focalization through," he would never have ended up treating Phileas and his valet as almost interchangeable agents—treating the subject (Passepartout) or the object (Phileas) alike as "focalized." That mistake highlights the confusion among the various meanings Genette attributed to the term "focalization." If, in the final analysis, the decisive criterion were to remain the distinction between main character and secondary character, it could obviously be said that we have not made very much progress since E. M. Forster. Analysis would be doing no more than paraphrasing the ideological taxonomy of the literary text and hence would not be *critical*.

I would not go that far. Although Genette confuses certain ideas, his typology is not without value. That typology, it is true, cannot be defined by focalization—whose definition needs more precision—but solely and entirely by the narrator's knowledge, and this is betrayed by the very formulation Genette uses in defining his types: the narrator says more than, as much as, or less than the character *knows*. In that formulation, knowledge and speech go hand in glove with each other. Could it be that the distinction between mood and voice, between sight and speech, is less radical than it seems? Or, on the contrary, should we push it further? However valuable the distinction provided by this chapter on mood, one other distinction is needed: that between subject and object.

1.3.2 *Voice: The refractory absentee—the narrator.* Genette's typology of narratives according to the temporal relationship between story and narrating is convincing. In the great majority of cases the narrating *follows* the events narrated. Predictive narratives remain in the minority and are most often "metanarratives," rarely primary narratives. Simultaneous narrating, a sort of running commentary, is entirely exceptional, and belongs to the experimental novel. The epistolary novel, though, constitutes the prototype of the interpolated narrative, so that type is on the whole fairly widespread; by greatly simplifying, we can say in fact that the correspondents write each letter after the event which prompted it, but before the event which will lead them to write the next letter.

---

28. [Translator's note.] Genette, *Narrative Discourse*, 191–92. But the translation given here varies in one respect. In the original French, the crucial phrase, the one Bal's argument centers on, is *focalisation interne sur*—literally, "internal focalization on," as it is rendered here. In *Narrative Discourse* the phrase was rendered as "internal focalization through"—thus anticipating the point Bal makes here.

One small problem remains. Determining the narrating time in relation to the narrated time is possible only in cases in which the narrator appears. In other words, this problem of the temporal relationship cannot be separated from the problem of the status of the narrator. If the narrator, in one way or another, is present in the narrating—whether s/he be homodiegetic or heterodiegetic—we can determine the relationship between story and narrating. The narrator must tell its own story or someone else's "in the first person"; otherwise, the time of the narrating remains vague, indefinite, and above all uninteresting. The most widespread type of narrative, the one in which the narrator is absent or invisible (the narrative told "in the third person"), has no place in the typology. Who knows, for example, whether the narrator of Colette's *The Cat*, when s/he describes a quiet evening at home at the beginning of the novel, is already fully informed about the novel's unhappy ending? The question seems to me totally irrelevant, for this narrator, being absent, is removed from the novel's center of interest. Restricting the typology's applicability in this way does not in itself mean discrediting the typology, for with narratives whose narrators are visible, the typology has great analytical value. The idea of "narrative level" offers an important advantage. Its range of application is such that with it we can consider two different kinds of narrative from a single point of view: narratives within the narrative (of the *Thousand and One Nights* type), which have always been classified as a particular kind of narrative, as well as others whose changes of level are subtler, the "micro-narratives" (like the *mise en abyme*) that characterize the New Novel without thereby being absent from the classical novel. In analyzing some examples, Genette is entirely convincing. As with time, however, changes of level will be hard to identify in narratives whose narrators are absent or invisible. In one way or another the narrator has to mark the passage from one level to another, and this the absent or invisible narrator cannot do. To take *The Cat* again as an example: Alain's dream in the first chapter is clearly felt by the reader to be an interpolated narrative, a "metadiegetic" narrative. It does not enter into the series of events constituting the story of the novel, and it contains in itself an independent series of events. Where is the transition that lets us characterize the dream as "metadiegetic"? Denying it that designation is absurd, since the consensus of readers proves, albeit intuitively, that the dream is "metanarrative."[29]

---

29. The relations that can exist between a "metadiegetic" narrative and its primary narrative are defined only in terms of relations between the "metanarrative" and the narrating, which is logical since the narrating is what is being discussed. One could, however, also consider these relations in terms of the action and the actants. In my essay on hypo-narratives (below, Chapter 7), I distinguish between "framing" and "embedding" on the basis of the actantial function. This distinction can be added to the one Genette makes.

Classifying narrators as homo-or heterodiegetic is in reality the only possible way to classify them, if we rigorously restrict ourselves to voice. The group of heterodiegetic narrators contains two types that we traditionally differentiate: the "third-person" narrator—absent, invisible as narrator—and the narrator who is visible ("first person") but who tells a story from which s/he is absent. No difference of level exists between the narrator who narrates in the third person (the absent narrator) and the narrator who tells in the first person a story from which s/he is absent: but neither does any difference of level exist between the latter and the narrator who tells his own story—for in that story the narrator is present not as the narrator but only as a character. The narrator as narrator is always at the higher diegetic level; at the very most, s/he can as a person be identified with a character.

But the narrator is not a person, only an agent—an "it"—and therein lies the problem. We can appreciate Genette's systematic rigor, which kept him, in the chapter on voice, from going outside the realm of pure voice. But in the final analysis, perhaps this rigor is untenable. If it ends in a theory altogether too opposed to the reality of its object, one must no doubt look elsewhere for the solution to the problem—to systematics of another kind.

2. THE NARRATING AND THE FOCALIZING

2.1 Agents

In every narrative, the functions that give effect to the kernels of the action are fulfilled by what we traditionally call "characters"; we also call them "actants" or "actors."[30] The character is defined by everything that has to do with its function in the action, its identity, its personality, its history, its relationships with other characters. In other words, it is defined by everything involved in the answer to the question "Who is s/he?" But as we cannot yet even define the content of this personal pronoun, "he" or "she," we can use the more abstract formulation "Who is?"[31] Since the earliest attempts at narrative theory, critics have been preoccupied with finding the answer to that obviously pertinent question. From round characters/flat characters to Greimas' actants, critics have been speculating on the status of the character inside the story within which it develops and which it causes

---

30. Obviously, these terms are not synonyms. The differences among their respective meanings are not relevant here, but it may nonetheless be useful to redefine them. The term "actor" has the abstract meaning of "the agent that acts." "Actant" has a functional meaning, "the one who makes the action move forward." The term "character" refers to the actant in its own individuality, with the broad meaning conferred by tradition. For my part, I use the term character when I am dealing with narrative level, that is, when the meaning I want to refer to transcends the precise framework of the two other terms.

31. Its identity is in large part determined by what it *does*. Since we are dealing here only with the result of that determination, it seems to me justifiable to use the shortened formulation "Who is?"

to develop. If the question of the character's status is harder to answer than it would first seem to be, that is because the reader becomes acquainted with this "one who is" *through the medium* of several agents, which had best be carefully differentiated.

The reader can interpret—indeed, can pass judgment on[32]—a character. That is because, in one way or another, the character is readable, or shall we say "visible": the reader "sees" it. The reader sees it through the medium of an agent other than the character, an agent that sees and, seeing, causes to be seen. I will examine this agent, provisionally called the "focalizer" (a term I define below), in seeking to answer the question "Who sees?" For we must answer that question of mood (that metaquestion, if we may play this game with Genette's terminology) before we can say anything at all about the character seen, because the focalizer influences how the reader perceives the character seen. But our game does not stop there: we cannot determine "who sees" without taking into account the medium through which we perceive that sight: the narrating. So we must know "who speaks." "The one who speaks" is the narrating agent, set in motion by and representing the author (the answer to the question "Who writes?").

In interpreting narratives, too often—it seems needless to say—critics pass directly from the author to the character, with any resemblance whatever between the two being allowed to determine the view the critic takes of the character. The critic passes directly from the agent "who writes" to the agent "who is." It was a crucial moment in the history of the theory of narrative when it discovered the essential importance of the author's delegate, the autonomy of the agent whom the author deliberately entrusted with the narrative function within the narrative: the narrator. At another moment, just as crucial although more recent, another discovery was made—that of the presence of the one to whom this narrator in turn delegates a function midway between itself and the character—the focalizer. The significance of this distinction cannot be overestimated; credit for it belongs to Genette.[33]

The agents that function, *hierarchically*, in every narrative form the following series, which characterizes narrative as writing:

narrator	focalizer	actor,	each of whom has an activity:
narrating	focalizing	acting,	the objects of which are:
the narrated	the focalized	the object of the acting.	

32. Even if the verb "judge" will upset—and rightly so—the modern literary critic and theorist, let us not forget that the reader does judge. If we want to modify that reactive behavior on the part of the reader, we must start from that behavior as it is, or else be in danger of widening still further the gulf that exists—unfortunately and wrongly, but nevertheless substantially—between reading as a cultural and as a scholarly activity.

33. Genette separated the two agents, yet without seeing that they are positioned in a narrative hierarchy. While he is not the first to have *differentiated* the two agents (Henry James, among others, did that), he is the first to have separated them in theory.

Each agent effects the transition from one plane to another: the actor, using the acting as his or her material, produces the story; the focalizer, who selects the actions and chooses the angle from which to present them, with those actions produces the narrative; while the narrator puts the narrative into words: with the narrative it creates the narrative text. Theoretically, each agent addresses a receiver located on the same plane: the actor addresses another actor, the focalizer addresses a "spectator"— the indirect object of the focalizing—and the narrator addresses a hypothetical reader. In some texts these receivers are referred to explicitly, like the reader in Diderot's *Jacques le fataliste*, in others they remain implied. In either case, the only way to comprehend how narrative communication functions is to distinguish among these receivers.

The model these reflections lead to is indicated in Figure 1.

Figure 1

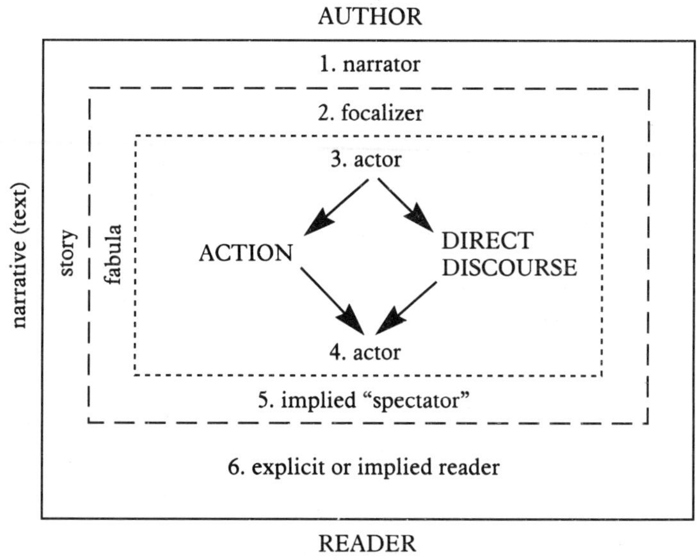

AUTHOR

READER

Now, every activity has its own object, just as it has its particular subject. If we confine ourselves, as I do here, to the agents that are peculiar to narrative and define it as a written genre, we must differentiate between the object of the speaking and the object of the focalizing, just as we must differentiate between the respective subjects of those two activities.

The agents that concern us here, therefore, are:

The subject of the narrating: the narrator.
The object of the narrating: the narrated.
The subject of the focalizing: the focalizer.
The object of the focalizing: the focalized.

By defining these four concepts, I hope to resolve the problems that Genette's theory neglects.

2.1.1 *The Narrator*. We have seen that only a single narrative "person" exists: the first person. The narrator in its narrating can be "visible," present in the narrative, or absent. Its presence is defined with respect to the very narrative being studied: to be present, the narrator must be *inside* the narrative. This is Genette's homodiegetic narrator, telling a story in whose fabula it itself appears. It can also be a heterodiegetic narrator, telling "in the first person" a story from whose fabula it is absent. The "third-person" narrator does not exist. If—in some of Maupassant's tales, for example—an I-narrator yields the floor to someone else who until then has been referred to as "he," this second-degree narrator immediately stops being a "third person" at the very moment "he" begins to recount: it takes first-person responsibility for the narrative it is about to tell the others, among whom the primary narrator, too, is present. This latter, who has been "first person," thereby becomes "second person," the extradiegetic recipient of the "metanarrative."[34] Both narrators can be homodiegetic in their respective narratives.

All this is understood, and my reason for dwelling on it once again is to emphasize the importance of the *change in level*, which is crucial for the status of the narrator. In his typology of the possibilities for the status of the narrator, Genette's implicit starting point is the hypothesis that the "third-person" narrator, the absent one, is automatically extradiegetic.[35] Since the extradiegetic narrator is defined by a difference of level, this implicit hypothesis of Genette's means that the absent narrator is located at the same narrative level with respect to the narrative it tells as is the extradiegetic "first-person" narrator of the type I have just described. Now, no indication attests the presence of this hypothetical level higher than the narrative itself. As Genette himself says, there is no narrator except as subject—thus, an "I," whether we see it or not. The most frequent type of narrator, the "invisible" narrator, achieves nothing by leaving no traces of its act of enunciating: regardless, it is well and truly the subject of the narrating. In this sense, it is as present as the other type—even though invisible.

---

34. Extradiegetic in relation to the narrative of which it is the narratee.

35. Actually, here the terminology slides a bit. The homodiegetic narrator is just as extradiegetic as the heterodiegetic narrator is, for every narrator "is at a diegetic level immediately higher than the level at which the story he is telling is situated." The "I" actor is not the narrator of its own story; the narrator in that instance is telling a story in which it is present as a character but is telling it by means of an agent who is hierarchically higher than that character. Genette implies that if the narrator is absent from the narrative, there is a still higher level, comparable to the one at which an extradiegetic narrator is located in relation to a "metanarrative." Basically, then, if we followed Genette's reasoning, the absent narrator would be doubly extradiegetic.

If the "invisible" narrator is nonetheless located inside its narrative, for the same reason that the homodiegetic narrator is, then, like the homodiegetic narrator (although in a different way), it must be present in its narrative. For like the latter it has an object: the narrated.

2.1.2 *The Narrated.* The narrated is composed of the words of the narrating. It is the statement. To define the status of the narrator, we sought an answer to the question "Who speaks?," and once we have the answer, we will ask, "What does s/he say?" Just as the object of an action *submits* to that action which the subject has performed, in the same way the object of the narrating is dependent on the subject, is *subordinate* to it. We can indeed say with Genette that every narrator maintains a hierarchical relationship with its object.

I continue to be unhappy with Genette's hierarchical inversion. I think that to indicate *dependence*, we have to replace *higher* by its opposite. To save the prefix "meta" for a more appropriate use, I want to propose, provisionally and for lack of anything better, that we speak of "hypo": "hyponarrative," "hypodiegetic."[36]

We have already seen that the narrator—present or absent, it makes little difference which—can yield the floor to a character. The character then speaks in direct discourse: this is reported speech—eminently mimetic, according to Genette. At that moment the *level changes*, the intradiegetic narrator becomes extradiegetic with respect to the new, hypodiegetic narrative formed by the direct discourse that the character-subject becomes narrator of. Clearly, not all direct discourse is necessarily narrative. It has to be brought about, if only virtually, by the agents that define the narrative. Otherwise it is still a hypo-discourse, but is in that case a "dramatic" intrusion in the narrative.

What the character talks about is located at a level even lower than the level at which the character-narrator is located, and the character-subject who talks ceases to be equal to the character s/he is talking about: in terms of narrative structure, the character-subject is higher than the character-object. We can sum it all up this way: the narrator tells that the character tells that a certain character does or is this or that, and if the character-object of the direct discourse is in turn supposed to speak, the series can be continued endlessly. We recognize Todorov's way of summarizing what happens in *The Thousand and One Nights*: "Scheherazade tells that Jaafer tells that the tailor tells that the barber tells that his brother (and he has six brothers) tells that. . . ."[37] When such a change in level occurs, the reader becomes aware, if not of the presence, at least of the activity (and thus of the

36. In "Métarécits," Scholes uses the term "metanarrative" with the logical meaning of "a narrative *on* a narrative." Using the term in this sense—even putting it in the title of the article—requires the introduction of another term to indicate its opposite.

37. Todorov, *Poetics of Prose*, 71, cited by Genette, *Narrative Discourse*, 214, note 4.

existence) of the narrator within the narrative. The declarative verb, or whatever other form the yielding of the floor by the narrator to the character can take, functions to *connote the transfer*, the handing over, like a sign indicating that the object of speech will in turn become its subject.

We can redefine the narrated object with respect to the narrator. The narrated is everything located at the level immediately below the level at which the act of enunciating is located.[38] From this formulation (which parallels Genette's definition of the status of the narrator) we can logically deduce that reported speech is fundamentally different from recounted speech: they are not located at the same narrative level. The narrated defined in this way is still an abstraction. It will be rendered concrete by its indispensable complement: the focalized, object of the focalizing.

2.1.3 *The Focalizing.* Now is the time to define the term "focalizing." We have seen that Genette's use of the term "focalization" is based on two concepts: point of view (I consider "vision" to be synonymous with this), and restriction of field. These two are neither completely different from each other nor completely identical. Furthermore, "point of view" is used with two opposite meanings.

Among the definitions in the *Robert* dictionary of "point of view," these two should be kept in mind: (1) "set of objects, scene on which one fastens one's gaze," and (2) "particular opinion." In the first definition, which is more literal than the second, we are dealing with the object of the gaze; in the second, with the subject who sees or considers. We recognize the difference between "internal focalization," which corresponds to the second definition, and "external focalization," which corresponds to the first. Ordinarily we say that "the story is told from the point of view of thus-and-such a character," where Genette speaks of internal focalization. In this case we are defining the *subject* of the "gaze"—the focalizer.

The term focalization is preferable to the traditional terms because it is more "technical" and thereby can be used in a way that is both more restricted and more extensive. The term excludes the psychological meanings of point of view, which is the reason Genette prefers it. At the same time, it can extend to any object of the "gaze," whether that object be a character, a place, or an event. Each of these elements is thus granted comparable status in the structures of narrative.

Genette's typology can be explained thus: "The story is told in *internal focalization*" means that the characters, places, and events are presented *from* thus-and-such a character. That character is the *subject* of the *presentation*. If the story is "told in *external focalization*," it is told from the narrator, and the latter has a point of view (in the radical, pictorial sense) on

---

38. The narrated is thus a statement, the object of the enunciation produced by an enunciator.

the characters, the places, the events. It is then not in the least privileged and sees only what a hypothetical spectator would see.

Restriction of field is a term that takes features from each of the two meanings of point of view. The object of the gaze is *limited* to what a spectator can see, but this spectator is not hypothetical: it is a character. This idea thus corresponds to internal focalization with respect to the subject of the gaze and to external focalization with respect to its object— which is why the term focalization as Genette uses it is not univocal enough to account for the whole range of narrative possibilities.

Actually, we can keep all the meanings of the term focalization, on condition that we carefully define and differentiate them. Immediately, extending the term beyond the purely visual lets us take focalization in the broad sense that, provisionally and for lack of anything better, I refer to as "center of interest." By that I mean, first, the result of the *selection*, from among all possible materials, of the content of the narrative. Next, the concept includes the "gaze," the *vision*, also in the abstract sense of "considering something from a certain angle"; and finally, the concept includes the *presentation*. The subject and object of these three activities, which can be summarized as *orientation*, are the narrating agents we are dealing with here.

2.1.4 *Focalizer and Focalized*. Thus there is a focalizer, which is not the narrator (as Genette has sufficiently said), but is also not the focalized. Phileas Fogg, hero though he may be, is, for the focalizing, subordinate to his valet. In a narrative with an "invisible" narrator, the focalizer too is often anonymous. But no more than the narrator is the focalizer expected to retain this power for itself throughout the narrative. As the narrator can yield the floor, the focalizer can yield the focalizing. That is when the narrative is "told from the point of view of a character," in internal focalization. Therefore, two possibilities exist: if a narrative begins in external focalization and changes to internal focalization, it is not necessarily the focalizer that changes; the change may equally well be in the focalized, with the character "seen from within" being not the subject but the object of the focalizing. The "knowledge" of narrator and character, a concept that is inoperative because purely figurative, can thus be left out of account. This use of the term focalization differs from Genette's in several respects:

(a) The use of the term is no longer limited to a typology of narratives that, with some rare exceptions, helps us characterize the great majority of narratives. It has also become an analytical tool, capable of accounting for the specific functioning of each individual narrative and discerning the figures within each.

(b) The term does not have the restrictive meaning it has in the distinction between non-focalized narrative and narrative with internal focalization, where focalization means that the narrator is the focalizer because it knows less than the omniscient narrator does.

(c) The functional difference—subject or object—that differentiates the narrative with internal focalization from the narrative with external focalization is made explicit.

(d) Parallel to the narrating, the focalizing too has levels. A change of level in the focalizing often goes hand-in-hand with a change in narrative level, but not always—far from it. Everything that has traditionally been looked on as author's intrusions, the traces of the implied author, can be analyzed as traces of the narrator and of the focalizer.[39]

(e) The focalized, when understood in this way, is not limited to characters. Things, places, events also form part of it. Thus, for a description for example, we can determine whether the object being described is focalized (that is, chosen, considered, and presented) by an anonymous focalizer or by a character. Needless to say, this distinction is important for the interpretation of particular descriptions, but also for the theoretical definition of the descriptive in general.

(f) The focalized can be perceptible or imperceptible. This distinction differentiates between what a hypothetical spectator can perceive—by sight, hearing, smell, touch, and taste—and what s/he cannot (the Genettian distinction between internal focalization and external focalization, but now kept strictly for the focalized). For lack of a better word, I will use "perceptible" to indicate the presentation of an external focalized; "imperceptible" is for a focalized that is solely internal, like psychological material. The important thing here is that the distinction has nothing directly to do with the focalizer, but characterizes only the nature of what is focalized.

In this theory the concepts of the focalizing and the narrating are symmetrical, and in this sense my theory, although based on Genette's fundamental distinction, utterly parts company with his. Yet if I seem to draw together what he disconnected, I am not invalidating his distinction but, on the contrary, radicalizing it. For to treat the agents of focalization and voice in isolation conceals the parallelism of their organization in narrative. And this parallelism is what must have caused the confusion that for so long dominated the theory and criticism of narrative. Ultimately, the way to keep that confusion from recurring is to elucidate and not merely denounce it. That is what I attempt to do in the few illustrations that follow.

39. The "implied author" also supposedly injects his "opinion" into the narrative. Needless to say, in my scheme of things, the author's opinion ("the ideological function of the narrator," according to Genette, *Narrative Discourse*, 256) comes under the focalizer and not the narrator. That is also true of the "ideological perspective" analyzed by Uspensky, *A Poetics of Composition*. The so-called identification of the narrator with the character is properly defined as an impersonal narrating (by an "invisible" narrator) with a character as focalizer.

2.2 Illustrations

The examples I analyze are taken from *The Cat* by Colette.[40] This novel is of the type that occurs most frequently, whether we define it as "told in the third person from the point of view of a character" or as "told by a hetero-extradiegetic narrator and with internal focalization." At the outset, let us say that the consensus readers have reached concerning the novel's technique does not extend to the novel's psychological, psychoanalytic, or moral stance. Of the three characters—Alain, Camille, and the cat—each has its fervent partisans, each its unremitting adversaries. That is why we can use this novel to illustrate two things: the coherence and relevance of the theory of agents I have just put forward, and the reasons that lay readers and experienced critics alike are necessarily misled by the technical aspects of the novel. For what Genette has not sufficiently seen is that the rhetorical responsibility for the ambiguity, moral and narratological, in the readers' response lies with the narrative.

2.2.1 *The Narrator-Focalizer.* Take the first sentence of the novel: "Towards ten o'clock, the family poker-players began to show signs of weariness" (p. 71). The situation is presented, but by whom? The information conveyed in the sentence is fairly plentiful. The reader is given information about the time (ten o'clock), the characters present (players), the relations among them (familial), their occupation (poker), and their reaction (weariness). No sign of the narrator, no sign of the focalizer. And

---

40. [Translator's note.] Otherwise unattributed page references are to the English version of this novel. Where the translation is too free for purposes of Bal's analysis, I have supplied my own translation in brackets.

Bal, *Narratologie*, 2, explains the problem posed by Colette's novel:

> *The Cat* . . . deals with the failure of a marriage, and the failure is tied to the presence of a cat. The question of the responsibility borne by the different protagonists seems an obvious one to ask, and does indeed figure consistently in the reception of the novel. Whose fault is it? In several ways the text invites the reader to side with the young man. The young woman, however, seems the more reasonable of the two. And, in the dispute dividing them, what *is* the cat's function? At the crucial moment, the cat defies her enemy and precipitates the catastrophe.
>
> The problem of fixing moral or psychological responsibility can be resolved only with a narratological investigation, which will explain how the problem is even relevant. The reason it is relevant—the reason the reader feels called on to judge—is that vision and voice are disconnected from each other. The events are presented in a certain way, in keeping with a certain vision, which may be that of the main character—but the main character is not the one who does the narrating. So the problem the novel poses is that of the relationship between the agent who *speaks* and the agent who *sees*. Moral responsibility therefore takes a back seat to narrative "responsibility."

Interpretation of this novel also has to do with the language in which one reads it. *Chatte* is the feminine form of the English word "cat," and while the title "character" is sometimes called by its name (Saha), it is most often referred to simply as "la chatte." That recurrent reminder of the cat's gender—of her sexuality—is unavailable in English but in French it strongly affects the reader's sense of the underlying dynamic among the three characters.

the word "signs"? It indicates that the behavior of the characters is such that a spectator can see and interpret it. This spectator, we know, is not the reader. The nature of narrative makes it impossible for the reader to perceive the content of the information directly. Nor is the spectator the narrator: the narrator is entitled to speech and not to anything else. The spectator must be the focalizer, anonymous and neutral, who sees "in place of" the reader. Since this focalizer is invisible, it has to be at the first level of focalization. The words "signs" functions as a *connotator of level*: it indicates not only that the "family poker-players" are starting to let their minds wander, to yawn, to fidget, but also that the narrative—told, certainly, by an extradiegetic narrator—is focalized, too, by an extradiegetic focalizer. The "signs" *given* are like winks from the diegesis at the extradiegetic agents: the focalizer and the narrator—and also the "spectators" (the recipients of the focalizing), the narratees, the readers. We see that at the beginning of this narrative, as at the beginning of many narratives, narrator and focalizer go hand in hand. As long as both those agents are on the same level in relation to their objects, conceivably they can be referred to by a term that recognizes their interdependence while respecting their autonomy. The term "narrator-focalizer," a formulation in which they are simultaneously together and apart, fulfills these conditions. Despite the unquestionable drawbacks inherent in such terminological exuberance—which will irritate, and rightly so, many a reader—my critical pursuit warns me against the too facile use of a single term. We will want to keep sight of every change in level.

2.2.2 *Limits and Transgressions*. It is self-evident that a change in the level of narrating, since it is denoted most often by a declarative verb and punctuation marks, is easier to see than a change in the level of focalizing. For that reason it may be worthwhile to dwell on some borderline cases with which we can more firmly ground the concepts put forth.

(a) Shortly after the beginning of the novel we find the following sentence:

> "Her eyes appealed to her fiancé, who lay back, overcome, in the depths of an armchair" (p. 71).

In this sentence it is no longer "signs" that are being recounted, but an appeal to fellowship issued by one character to another, and the situation of the other character at that moment. Despite the greater complexity of the object of the focalizing, the technique is the same: the appeal to fellowship is recounted in its external manifestation. Camille appeals to her fiancé with "her eyes," thus letting the "spectator" see what she sees. This spectator sees it at the same time that the character, Alain, the recipient of the appeal, sees it. As far as the agents are concerned, then, the functioning of the phrase in the first sentence: the sign—"signs" there, "eyes" here—

functions simultaneously at the diegetic and at the extradiegetic levels. In each case the sign is the point of contact between the two levels.

Similarly, Alain, "overcome, in the depths of an armchair," is "seen" both by his fiancée, who addresses herself to him, and by the extradiegetic agents (readers and the narrator-focalizer). In a case like this, in which the focalizer looks along "with" the character, the focalizing has a marked resemblance to a "transposed view," through analogy with "transposed speech," like free indirect discourse. In transposed speech the narrator takes on the speech of the character, adhering to it as closely as possible without effecting a change in level; in transposed focalizing, the focalizer assumes the character's view but without thereby yielding the focalizing. We have already seen that such speech is nothing other than narrating at its most mimetic. So we may say that here the focalizing is at the limit of the first level, and for the same reason: through the sign "eyes," the extradiegetic focalizer is able to retain its power.

(b) A more complex problem arises in the following passage:

> She watched him drink and felt a sudden pang of desire at the sight of his mouth pressing against the rim of the glass. But he felt so weary that he refused to share that pang and merely touched the white fingers with the red nails as they removed his empty tumbler (p. 72).

The verb "watched" in the first sentence denotes a change in the level of focalization. Alain, then his mouth, are the object of the focalizer Camille. Alain is focalized in the second degree, by the focalizer who is focalized. Camille, who "felt a pang," is still focalized in the first degree. Thus she is located at the first level as the focalized, and she functions at the second level as the focalizer. In the second sentence, the first level is reinstated. Alain is once again focalized directly by the focalizer-narrator of the first level. In the narrating, no change takes place.

The two sentences differ in another way, one that affects only the focalized. Twice in the passage a "feeling" is recounted. In the first—Camille's—her pang of desire is perceptible to the "spectator," all the more so as its expression is preceded by the verb "watch," a verb that is unlike "see" in allowing perception from without. Here, then, the focalized is perceptible. But the other feeling—Alain's—is of a different kind. True, as a rule fatigue can be read on a face and a refusal is perceptible in its consequences. But the *feeling* ("he felt . . .") of fatigue and the *decision* to refuse ("refused") could not be manifest at the very moment they were realized. Thus this passage is characterized by the following features:

> Both sentences are recounted at the first level.
> In the first sentence there is one focalizer at the first level (the one who sees Camille watch) and a second one at the second level (the one—Camille—who sees Alain).

In the second sentence there is only a focalizer at the first level (the focalizer-narrator).

In the first sentence each focalized is perceptible.

In the second sentence the focalized is imperceptible.

We see a correlation between the level of focalizing and the nature of the focalized. From that analysis, I will provisionally construct the following hypothesis:[41]

An imperceptible focalized can be focalized only by a focalizer at the first level, whereas a perceptible focalized can be focalized at any level.

(c) In the passage I have just analyzed, the change in level affects only the focalizing. Focalizer and narrator are thus dissociated from each other. In the following example the situation is even more complex:

"She's pretty," Alain reasoned, "because not one of her features is ugly, because she's an out-and-out brunette. Those lustrous eyes perfectly match that sleek, glossy, frequently washed hair that's the colour of a new piano." He was also perfectly aware that she could be as violent and capricious as a mountain stream (p. 73).

This passage begins in direct discourse. With the verb "reasoned," the narrator yields the floor to the character. It takes it back in the next sentence: "He was also perfectly aware. . . ." The verb "reasoned" functions to *connote a transfer*, to signal the change in narrative level.

The focalizing, in turn, determines the choice of this verb among all possible declarative verbs. The verb denotes a logic that should normally lead to the discovery of the truth. What we are dealing with is a young man's opinion of his fiancée, a week before their wedding. I contend that in that context—and, of course, in the context of the bourgeoisie in the 1920's—the denoted logic is connoted as misplaced, as a sign of a lack of love—or, at least, as ambivalent. The focalizer chose this way of presenting the content of the discourse, influencing with this choice the degree of "truth" the reader will attribute to the content: the reader will tend to react to the content with mistrust. S/he will, moreover, be interested in the point of view, in the focalizer rather than in the focalized. The first focalizer is very powerful here: by the use of an inappropriately logical verb, it reveals and exposes the inappropriately neutral character of Alain's discourse. While the narrator simply sets its power aside, the focalizer—before setting its own aside—momentarily tightens the bond between it and its object.

Within the hypo-story, Alain is the narrator and his opinion of Camille is the narrated. Alain is also the focalizer: he *chooses* the attributes of Camille

---

41. The hypothesis is still incomplete. This rule can be broken under two conditions, which I will specify in analyzing the dream.

that he wants to highlight, he *sees* Camille in his own way and *presents* her as he wishes. The change in the level of focalizing is thus parallel to the change in narrative level. The opinion about Camille is recounted in the second degree, and Camille herself is focalized in the second degree.

In the second part of the passage, after the direct discourse, the first narrative level is reinstated. The narrator again takes the floor, and Alain's thoughts again become the first level of the narrated. The same with the focalizing. The words "He was also perfectly aware that" are focalized in the first degree, just like the verb "reasoned" at the beginning of the passage, and the object of this focalizing—Camille and her attributes—is taken on by the first narrator-focalizer. This agent accepts responsibility for the focalized, the rather negative view of Camille, thus making this view more "true," since it is the object of a "neutral" focalizer. Selection of the neutral verb confirms that "truth."

But there is more. The word "also" reinforces the bond between the hypo-story and the primary story, inasmuch as the influence it connotes works against the influence of the verb "reasoned" at the beginning of the passage: the word "also" links Alain's opinion to that of the first focalizer, for it joins the opinion that has just been expressed in the second degree to the opinion now to be expressed in the first degree (the phrase "was perfectly aware" is synonymous with "knew," and likewise presupposes the unquestionable truth of the content of this knowledge). The word "also" confirms after the event the truth of the very opinion that the verb "reasoned" called into question. Thus, on the "moral" plane, the position of the focalizer contrasts radically with what it was at the beginning of the passage.

We can summarize the analysis this way:

The narrative level changes in the first sentence and changes back in the second sentence.
The level of focalizing changes in the first sentence and changes back in the second sentence.
Along with the first change in the level of focalizing, the first focalizer influences the focalized at the second level.
Along with the second change in the level of focalizing, the second focalizer influences the focalized at the first level.

We can easily imagine how such complex structures lead to the kind of confusion Genette denounces. Actually, that second influence—which is, to say the least, paradoxical, given the hierarchical relationship between the two focalizers—is responsible for some of the reactions readers have had, tending as they do to support Alain vehemently against Camille on the grounds that he resembles the author of the novel.[42] Probably these readers,

42. See, among others, Davies, *Colette.*

without being aware of it, are sensitive to the privileges that the presentation bestows on Alain.

2.2.3 *The Case of the Dream: Hypo-Narrative or Hypo-Focalized?* Finally, what about Alain's dream? This dream comes at the beginning of the novel, at the end of the first chapter, and takes up several pages (pp. 84–86). The passage begins in the following way:

> He loved his dreams and cultivated them. Not for anything in the world would he have revealed the successive stages which awaited him. At the first stopping-place, while he could still hear the motor-horns in the avenue, he met an eddy of faces, familiar yet distorted . . . (p. 84).

The dream is recounted in the first degree and, furthermore, that fact is explicitly noted—for several lines earlier, we read that "He did not talk about his adventures of the night." So the narrative of this dream cannot be a hypo-narrative. Nonetheless, it constitutes a relatively autonomous and fantastic story that, as a story, is apparently not at all distinguishable from the framed or embedded type of story. In such a case, the status of the dream can be accounted for only with the concept of focalization.

A dream, in terms of being the focalized, is by definition imperceptible. According to my hypothesis, therefore, it can be focalized only at the first degree. But how could it be focalized at the first degree here, since Alain himself is the only one able to "see" this dream and he is not the first focalizer? The problem this case raises is obviously a general one.

Let us suppose that the dream were recounted in the second degree. We would then have something like this: "Alain recounts, 'Last night, in a dream, I met an eddy of faces, familiar yet distorted.'" Such a narrative, which is clearly a hypo-narrative, is perfectly possible. It will be more likely to occur in a narrative with a homodiegetic and "present" narrator (for example, in a diary or an autobiography) than in a narrative like *The Cat*. The reason is that a homodiegetic narrator can more easily dispense with a narratee than a character-narrator can. If Alain had told his dream he would probably have told it to someone, which is exactly what he does not want to do. But at the moment, that does not much matter. The dream as a hypo-narrative, told in the second degree, will always in any case be an imperceptible focalized. The passage analyzed earlier, on the basis of which I constructed the hypothesis that an imperceptible focalized must be focalized in the first degree, will thus differ fundamentally from this one. In fact, it differs in two ways:

> In the sentence that had a focalization in the second degree, the second focalizer was not the same character as the second focalized: Camille was watching Alain. In a dream, the second focalizer, the one who "sees" and presents the dream, is also part of the focalized: he has the dream and he *presents* his own dream.

The change in level of focalizing was not accompanied by a change in narrative level. But in a dream hypo-narrative, the change in narrative level, which goes hand in hand with the change in level of focalizing, implies that the narrator in the second degree can become a narrator-focalizer who recounts an event at which s/he was present. In that case s/he is a homo- (and intra-) diegetic narrator-focalizer.

We must therefore revise the hypothesis as follows:

> An imperceptible focalized can be focalized only by (1) a focalizer in the first degree; (2) a focalizer-narrator in the second degree if it is homodiegetic; or (3) a focalizer in the second degree within a first-degree narrating if that focalizer is homodiegetic—thus if it forms part of the second focalized.
> A perceptible focalized can be focalized at any level.[43]

The hypothetical dream would go into the second category, and the dream as it appears in the novel must go into the third category: it is told at the first level, but focalized at the second level by a focalizer who is focalized. Actually, the focalizer is not constant. There is an alternation between the two levels. The following passage illustrates the difficulty:

> Each was furnished with one great eye and they circled round in an effortless gyration. But a submerged electric current shot them far away as soon as they touched an invisible barrier. In the humid gaze of a circular monster, in the eye of a plump moon or that of a wild archangel with rays of light for hair, Alain could recognize the same expression . . . (p. 84).

The content of the first two sentences of this passage is focalized at the second degree. The focalizer, Alain, is not named. The nature of the focalized makes it clear that the dreamer must be the focalizer. In the third sentence, Alain is named and thus focalized, and the first focalizer thereby reappears. The first focalizer sees Alain who sees the monsters who . . . see Alain, as the text of the dream will say a little later.[44] Such indications of the presence of the first focalizer appear throughout the passage, as if it were necessary to confirm regularly the fact that Alain is focalizing his own dream. It is like a clarification of the rule that holds that an imperceptible focalized is focalized by a homodiegetic focalizer.[45] If the dream is not a

43. It goes without saying that this rule is inferred for the moment from the particular narrative I am analyzing. Nothing proves that we are dealing with a general rule. A more extensive analysis of a large number of narratives is indispensable if we want to formulate the rule of the genre, or even of one type of narrative. However, it is quite likely that this rule will be valid for a considerable number of narratives. Given the realist mode of this novel, we may expect the rule to hold for realist narratives only.

44. I have analyzed this dream, whose sexual significance is apparent as soon as one superimposes the passage on other passages in the novel, in the second chapter of my book, *Complexité d'un roman populaire.*

45. This rule can be broken, as it is in some experimental novels. One can affirm the importance of rules just as much by deliberately setting out to break them as by strictly observing them. The experienced reader has no doubt seen another ambiguity in this dream, an ambiguity having to do with frequency: the narrative of the particular dream alternates with comments on the dreams Alain habitually has. Since this ambiguity does

hypo-narrative, it must at least be hypo-focalized. Thus it is partly like and partly unlike other dreams, hypo-narrative dreams. The formulation explains the reader's intuition while allowing a precise analysis of the technique brought into play in the narrative.

2.3 Interpretations

2.3.1 *Figures and Levels.* Every change in level constitutes a figure. In any given narrative, a certain type of figure will be found to predominate. For example, changes in level will be many or few. The changes in narrative level will be numerous or relatively sparse. The changes in the level of focalizing will benefit one or another character (one focalized character will often be imperceptible, another will always be perceptible). Or, on the contrary, the changes in the level of focalizing will be randomly distributed among the characters. The focalized characters may be exclusively perceptible.

From these patterns, we can set up a typology of narratives and then characterize a narrative in relation to other narratives. We can also give a detailed account of a narrative and describe its major cruxes, in order to lay bare its narrative originality. By carrying the analysis further, a critic who wants to interpret a particular narrative in depth will be able to study its narrative functioning and take note of any figure that is exceptional in terms of the type of narrative he originally classified his narrative as. After describing the characteristics of a narrative we can formulate its inner rules, the rules that it generally observes and that are peculiar to it. Again, some examples from *The Cat* can illustrate various possibilities of interpretation.

2.3.2 *Immanent Rules.* Every narrative can choose its stance with regard to the general rules of narrative. It can strictly observe them or, on the contrary, it can violate them, either as an exception or regularly. In theory the narrative will observe its own immanent rules, but there, too, infractions are possible, and the critic will wish to call attention to those infractions in particular. They might constitute the highlights of the text.

The narrative of *The Cat* observes the following eight rules:

(1) The changes in narrative level are limited to two levels.
(2) Camille is a narrator at the second level when the narrated consists of spoken words.
(3) Alain is a narrator at the second level when the narrated is perceptible or imperceptible and when it consists of spoken words (introduced by "he said") or thoughts (introduced by "he said to himself").
(4) The changes in the level of focalizing go beyond the second level.
(5) At the second level, Camille can be a focalizer when the focalized is perceptible.

not involve the agents of the narrative I will not linger over it here, although an analysis of that figure is indispensable to a complete interpretation of the dream.

(6) At the second level, Alain can be a focalizer when the focalized is perceptible or imperceptible.

(7) At the second level, Alain can be a focalizer when the focalized is, in turn, focalizer.

(8) At the second level, any other focalizer is a focalizer-narrator, and in such cases the focalized and the narrated must be perceptible.

This overall description, worked out inductively, can be verified. It lets us see at once that the privileged character is Alain. He can not only focalize another focalizer, but he can also narrate an imperceptible narrated and focalize an imperceptible focalized. Moreover, he is entrusted with the narrating and the focalizing much oftener than his antagonist is. To give an exhaustive description of the narrative in any case we will have to examine in particular: *the figures created when the rules are pushed to extremes, and the figures created when the rules are violated.*

It must be said immediately that this narrative is characterized by strict observance of its own rules. The only rule it breaks is the last one. I will present some examples of the rigor of this narrative, the faithfulness with which it abides by its own nature, to demonstrate that analyzing figures and formulating the rules inferable from the analysis do lead to interpretations. At stake here is the *relevance* of my theory to the criticism of narrative texts.

First Rule. This rule implies that the characters can recount, but that they cannot recount that someone else recounts.

> He got up from the green bench and assumed the important smile of the heir of Amparat Silks who is condescendingly marrying the daughter of Malmert Mangles, "a girl who's not *quite* our type," as Mme Amparat said (p. 95).

In this passage, the narrating passes from the first level to the second, and the narrator gives the floor to Mme. Amparat directly, without going through Alain. The focalizing, however, does go through him first, before he yields it in turn to his mother. This disconnection between narrating and focalizing, between speech and sight, can be looked on as the sign of a psychological disconnection. Alain sees Camille as his mother does, but does not yet dare to take that opinion as his own: he shares it without *saying* so. The narrative's strict observance of the first rule is a sign, a definite type of sign: a diagrammatic icon.[46]

Second Rule. This rule implies that neither the reader nor Alain has access to Camille's thoughts and feelings unless she ventures to express them. (Making her thoughts perceptible to the reader means making them perceptible also to the intradiegetic narratees, including Alain, whom she is almost always with.) In the occasionally stormy discussions between Camille and Alain, the reader can become acquainted only with what

---

46. For a presentation of this term for literary criticism, see Browne, "Typologie des signes littéraires," and van Zoest, "Le Signe iconique."

Camille *says*, whereas what the reader perceives of Alain is both words and *thoughts* (and the difference between words and thoughts).

> "Oh! the alterations! Don't tell me you're interested in those alterations! Admit"—she folded her arms like a tragic actress—"admit that you're going to see my rival!" "Saha's not your rival," said Alain simply. "How could she be your rival?" he went on to himself. "You can only have rivals in what's impure" (p. 105).

In this passage, Camille confesses her jealousy aloud. Alain reacts, but his *perceptible* reaction is not all there is. Mentally he reacts further. Quite obviously Camille's words have an effect on Alain's thoughts—they harm her case—but Camille is unaware of the influence her words have. Not only does she lack the (technical) means to know her partner's thoughts and therefore to understand him, but she also expresses her own thoughts, thus making them available to an interpretation she will never have access to. If she is disadvantaged on the narrative level, she is also—and as a consequence—disadvantaged as a character, in the novel's thematic and psychological structure. This disconnection, too, is a sign. The rule is equally strictly observed when Camille is alone, a wholly exceptional situation. The only time she is alone is the "assassination" scene. At that time no narratee is present at the diegetic level. After the assassination attempt—after Camille has hurled the cat nine floors down—the reader is vitally interested in her reaction. But the same solitude that made the assassination attempt possible means there is no character present for her to tell her reaction to— and the rule prevents her from "telling" her feelings inside herself.

> "It's as if I'd got thinner," she said out loud (p. 157).

It might surprise us that even at this crucial point in the novel, the rule that forbids direct access to Camille's thoughts remains unbroken. We see, however, that strict observance of the rule is not simply a technical means of guaranteeing the novel's formal coherence. Not only is this a way to reveal the moving intensity of Camille's feeling, but we can go even further and claim that, having taken her fate into her own hands and altered her life, she now feels disconnected from herself. Docile in her love until that moment, after the attempt on Saha she is profoundly other than what she was before. Her speaking aloud reflects the momentary estrangement she experiences: she is her own narratee. This interpretation is confirmed by the very content of the narrated, with the estrangement manifesting itself on the physical plane. The loss of flesh experienced is, to some extent, a change in the individual. We can add that she is not only alone—physically—at that moment, but that she well knows that her solitude, through her own action, is now beyond remedy. The absence of a narratee, then, is equally a sign. The figure of the change in level with the denial of an imperceptible narrated (the observance of the rule) is a complex sign that draws together a constellation of meaning on all levels—narrative, structural, thematic, and psychological.

Third Rule. As for Alain, he can transmit his most intimate and secret thoughts. Compared to Camille, he is privileged: readers know him better than they know Camille and better than she knows him. Psychologically, that advantage is relative and provisional. True, he can pick and choose among his feelings and transmit only what he wants to transmit. But since he does not express his thoughts at the diegetic level at which he "lives," he fails to put his thoughts into words and is thus denied the therapeutic function of speech. The example given *à propos* the second rule can illustrate this one too. In that passage, we see in particular that had Alain's reaction ("You can only have rivals in what's impure") been spoken aloud, it would have provoked a discussion that could have raised to consciousness an ambivalence in the area of sexuality that the observance of the narrative rule relegates to the unconscious.

In general, Alain recounts an imperceptible narrated more often than a perceptible one, which contributes to his ultimate isolation.

Fourth Rule. This rule produces a disconnection between the narrating and the focalizing. Besides the example cited *à propos* the first rule, we find some interesting instances that involve the domestic help. Here is one, from the final chapter of the novel. The day after the catastrophe in whose wake Alain leaves his wife, she comes to see him for the last time. She rings the doorbell, and with this simple gesture produces a miraculous effect.

> Behind the clipped hedge Alain could see the Basque woman retreating in disorder, her black silk apron flying in the wind, while a slither of slippers on the gravel announced the flight of old Emile (p. 185).

The first narrator-focalizer focalizes Alain, who focalizes the servants reacting to Camille's arrival. The verb "see," in its ambiguity, does indeed show what is happening: it refers to the physical action in its literal sense. Alain really sees the servants going by. But at the same time the verb has the figurative sense related to the *Robert* dictionary's definition of "point of view," with "to see" meaning "to consider." In other words, the substantives "disorder" and "flight" form part of an interpretation by Alain. In the literal sense his view is incomplete: "Behind the clipped hedge" where he is hiding, he does not see everything; so, too, in the broad sense, his view is incomplete: he interprets his incomplete (physical) view in accordance with his own reaction of panic. This hierarchical subordination of the focalized at the third level is a sign of Alain's great power over the servants. They are presented as being scarcely alive, they vegetate, and they exist only to the extent that they unreservedly adore the only son, king in his domain. The text of the novel is very clear on this point. The focalization has to pass through Alain because the servants do not exist except through him.

This rule produces the same ambiguity as the third rule. Alain's focalizing power is as great as his narrative impotence. He sees more and says less than he would have to, to maintain real communication and emerge from his solitude.

Fifth Rule. Camille as focalizer depends totally on what she can see. Focalizing for her is limited to direct perception, bound to the original meaning of the phrase "point of view." Thus, her sudden awareness of the impossibility of her relations with Alain comes via her perception of signs.[47] As an example of such a thematic sign that, by standing in for an imperceptible focalized which Camille is unable to focalize, transmits in a perceptible sign the signified of that imperceptible focalized, I quote three passages:

> "I can see your hair running," she called out. "It's crazy to be as fair as all that!" (p. 75)

> With his fair hair spread out and his eyes closed, he seemed to be sleeping on Saha's flank and to wake with a [sigh] only to see Camille standing there silent and apart, watching the close-knit group they made (p. 158).

> She was struggling to make herself understood and, at the same time, pointing to certain accidental [signs] about Alain which did indeed suggest [a somewhat delirious meaning]: the torn-off sleeve; the trembling, insulting mouth; the cheek from which all the blood had retreated; the wild crest of dishevelled fair hair (pp. 190–91).

The first passage comes at the beginning of the novel, the second after the assassination attempt and before the discovery of Camille's guilt, and the third at the end of the novel when Alain and Camille meet for the last time.

At the beginning, before their marriage, Camille, who is in love with her fiancé, already suspects that he "is not like other people." At that point she sees his fair hair as a sign of superiority. The word "crazy," still metaphorical, is used here in a positive sense, but essentially it already contains the literal sense it will have at the end. In the second passage, immediately after the assassination attempt, the dissension between Alain and Saha on one side and Camille on the other is more clearly manifest. The same sign—we can take the words "fair hair spread out" as synonymous with the words "hair running" and "fair"—associates superiority with the exclusion that is its reverse. At the end of the novel, the sign is explicitly perceived as such. The word "signs" appears in the text, as well as the word "meaning." The hair is deviant with respect to "normal" hair—for example, brown hair neatly arranged—in color and in outline. It is always in motion. Its motion

---

47. These signs are different in kind from the signs we saw functioning on the level of agents. These are thematic, and they function within the content of the narrated by means of a series of rearrangements involving the (unwitting) sender (the focalized) and the receiver (the focalizer). Strict observance of the rule is an absolutely narratological sign, unlike these thematic signs which can figure in non-narrative texts as well.

is less and less under control. At the beginning it runs, later it spreads out, and finally it gathers into a wild crest. The evolution of the outline of Alain's hair brings gradually to light the final meaning of the color of the hair and is a sign of the evolution of the person on whose head the hair flows, the person who is at first exceptionally superior and then becomes crazy.

But this development is not absolute. It depends on and is brought about by Camille's perception. Alain does not really change, for we have seen that at the beginning he is "crazy" on the strength of the color of his hair. His peculiar character becomes manifest only at the end. The sign, which consists of a thematic structure, can take effect only within the perception of Camille as focalizer. The observance of the rule is a sign of that sign: the focalizing brings about the sign.

Sixth Rule. The scope of this rule is limited by the general rule enunciated *à propos* Alain's dream. Alain can focalize an imperceptible focalized, but only if he himself forms part of the focalized—for example when he focalizes his own thoughts. The example used for the third rule (presented, however, in the discussion of the second rule), which illustrates the narrative power of this character, can illustrate this rule, too. I add an example in which Alain focalizes a perceptible focalized.

> But before he went out, he could see more clearly, at a distance, the dark circles round her eyes and the moisture which covered her temples and her smooth, unlined neck (p. 173).

The sentence comes at the point in the story when Alain is leaving his wife. He covertly observes her reaction. Rather than violate the second rule and let Camille as narrator tell her feelings, the narrative produces this second-degree focalization. The reaction that in itself is imperceptible is transmitted to Alain—and to the reader—by means of signs:[48] the dark circles round her eyes, the moisture on her face. Camille gives off signs without intending to: by remaining silent she wanted precisely to "build . . . up [Alain's] exit" (p. 172), as he himself puts it. She has chosen not to tell her reaction. Nevertheless, her reaction is "put into a sign" and this sign is focalized by Alain. A convincing illustration, it seems to me, of the principle that Alain, as a character and as an agent, is given the advantage.

Seventh Rule. This rule implies that Alain often sees things indirectly. His opinion of his wife in particular seems to a large extent determined, or at least confirmed, by those around him. The long conversation (pp. 135–36) among the servants, who are criticizing Camille, is focalized by Alain. The procedure, then, is the following: the first focalizer-narrator focalizes

---

48. These signs are different again: signs in the ordinary sense, such as occur in daily life too. Here they function at the level of the story, and not in the transmission of the fabula to the story. In addition, these signs are symptoms, not signals, as they are unintentional.

Alain, who focalizes (i.e., listens to) the servants, who focalize Camille. She is focalized at the third degree. In that way Alain receives the evidence of "prejudiced witnesses" (p. 137). This indirect focalization is obviously an iconic sign of the character's tendency to spy, to get information without speaking up. The passage, which is fairly long, is worth a detailed analysis, but this would carry us too far afield.

Eighth Rule. This rule brings about the exclusiveness of the novel's center of interest and is undoubtedly what has prompted some critics to look on Colette's narratives as novellas rather than novels.[49] In fact, the focalizing at the second degree is reserved strictly for the two main characters (whereas the focalizing at the third degree can belong to a secondary character, as we have seen *à propos* the seventh rule). I have found only one exception.

> At the foot of the nine-storeyed building, a gardener lifted his head and saw this white young man leap through the transparent wall like a burglar (p. 153).

The passage comes immediately before the scene of Camille's assassination attempt. Alain, a perceptible focalized, is focalized by a focalizer at the second degree who is a stranger to the story. So this focalizer is intra-heterodiegetic. This gardener is an unknown; this unknown person, whose view is limited to what is perceptible and is further limited by distance, sees Alain "the way a neutral spectator would see him." We recognize the formulation: it is how I defined the first narrator-focalizer. Why then does the focalizing pass to the second level?

The gardener sees signs of Alain's oddness: the "white young man" reminds one of a pantomimist, a fairylike creature, and the word "burglar" hints even at guilt, while "leap through the wall" partakes of the miraculous. This gradation, going from astonishment to mistrust and from play to unreality, is not unlike the thematic structure of the hair. But since Alain is alone here, he cannot be focalized by Camille. He could be by the first narrator-focalizer, but the latter, in delegating its power, lends its view more credibility, reinforcing it with a witness. Furthermore, the physical distance is a sign of the moral distance. Thus Alain's oddness, now "objectified," prepares the reader for Camille's desperate act. It is as though the reader, without having access to her feelings, were in this way being called on to understand her.

3. CONCLUSION

The rules underlying the system of narrative as a genre, some of which I have tried to formulate, produce rules immanent in each individual narrative. The differences of a given narrative from others of its genre must

---

49. Magny, *Histoire du roman français.*

necessarily lie in its compliance with the rules of the genre. Otherwise, it is not a narrative.

The rules *of* narrative produce the rules of *a* narrative, and these produce *the* particular narrative, its system of signs. In our analysis of *The Cat* we have seen some of these signs operating. In reality their number is limitless.

The signs that form part of the rules of the particular narrative produce in turn other signs, as we have seen à propos Alain's hair. In turn again, these other signs, hypo-signs produced by the signs of the narrative, form a network of significations, a structured constellation signifying the totality of the meaning of the narrative. The structural model I am proposing for narratives enables the critic to respond to the innumerable signs each one produces; as innumerable as the hairs on Alain's head.

▪ 5 ▪

Description as Narration

"Description" has challenged narratology from the start. It is difficult to define, to distinguish, to analyze, and to integrate. In this chapter, I will again take up the issue in relation to traditional views, and discuss it in relation to the project of a critical narratology. Description, far from supporting the realist fallacy, can be mobilized in favor of a subversive way of reading, wherein one kind of coherence combats another, more pernicious and fallacious.

1. DEFINITION AND DELIMITATION
A fortunate taxonomic impasse

Bob Assingham was distinguished altogether by a leanness of person, a leanness quite distinct from physical laxity, which might have been determined, on the part of superior powers, by views of transport and accommodation, and which in fact verged on the abnormal.[1]

The above excerpt presents no problems of classification. It is clearly a description. Problems arise, however, as soon as one attempts to define exactly what a description is. A good survey of what can and cannot be considered descriptive is Genette's article,[2] in which the author discusses common definitions of description, all of which are problematic either because the school of thought from which they evolved has been rejected, or because they are not specific enough; in addition, all the definitions are based on the distinction between descriptive and "pure" narrative text segments.

I shall consider a number of taxonomic proposals, which are schematically presented in Table 1.

1. James, *The Golden Bowl*, 72.
2. Genette, "Boundaries of Narrative."

Table 1

Basis	criterion	descriptive	narrative	source
Ontology	nature of object described	objects people	actions events	Genette[3]
	mode of existence	in space	in time	Genette[4]
Structural Functionalism	autonomy of the sequence	essential	optional	Genette[5]
	importance and function	secondary decoration or explanation *indice catalyse*	of primary importance *noyau*	Barthes[6]
Semiotics	coinciding or non-coinciding sub-codes	non-coinciding (wording successive contents simultaneous)	coincidence (both successive)	Genette[7]
Linguistics	verb complements	verbs with subject complements	verbs with no subject complements	Hendricks[8]
Narratology	sequence in fabula	non-diegetic or pro-diegetic elements	line of fabula not interrupted	van der Ven[9]
Logic	predictability	lexical predictability	logical predictability	Hamon[10]
	stability	predicates do not change	predicates change	Klaus[11]

1.1 Ontology

Before the emergence of structuralism, the distinction had been based on the ontological status of the object described. Actions and events belonged to narrative texts; things, places, and characters to descriptive texts. A similar distinction was based on the object's mode of existence: objects in descriptive texts existed in space; those in narrative texts existed in time.

The above descriptive passage by James can be classified with the help of these two criteria. The following fragment, however, satisfies only the first of the two criteria:

> Presently he told her the motion of the boat upon the stream was lulling him to rest. How green the banks were now, how bright the flowers growing on them,

3. Genette, "Boundaries of Narrative," 5.
4. Genette, "Boundaries of Narrative," 5–6.
5. Genette, "Boundaries of Narrative," 5–6.
6. Barthes, "Introduction," 91–97.
7. Genette, "Boundaries of Narrative," 7.
8. Hendricks, "Methodology," 169–74.
9. van der Ven, *Narrative Text*, 12–22.
10. Hamon "Qu'est-ce qu'une description?" 6.
11. Klaus, "Description and Event in Narrative."

and how tall the rushes! Now the boat was out at sea, but gliding smoothly on. And now there was a shore before him.[12]

Although this fragment primarily describes objects and people, it also involves a certain stretch of time. Intuitively speaking, this passage is a description. The first criterion, therefore, is more adequate than the second.

However, both criteria present certain theoretical problems. The most important objection is that the criteria are based on a classification of the objects of the texts and not on the texts themselves. Consequently, the criteria are not specific enough for (literary) texts since they do not lead to a definition of a specific type of discourse.

1.2 Structural functionalism

The structuralists of the 1960's worked from a functional point of view. Genette referred to description as the *ancilla narrationis*, a subordinate aid to narrative text segments. The paradox in this position, as Genette himself points out, is that although descriptions are secondary, they are nevertheless essential. It is, in fact, possible to imagine a descriptive text which contains no narrative elements. The autonomy of description is inversely proportional to its functional importance.

> One can imagine description existing independently of narration, although one never actually encounters description in such a state of freedom; narration, on the other hand, cannot exist without description, but this dependence does not prevent narration from always playing the primary role.[13]

In the terms used by Barthes in his pioneering article published in 1966, description in a narrative structure can only be *indice* (a thematic indication) or *catalyse* (filler), but never *noyau* (kernel).[14] Barthes' attitude toward description is not surprising since the model he uses is action-oriented. His criteria for determining the *noyaux*, the kernels of the fabula, are formulated in terms of actions. When one proceeds from this premise, the rejection as *noyau* of those text segments which contain something other than action can be criticized as being somewhat circular.

It is possible to relativize Genette's paradox further. Genette speaks of the autonomy of description, but he oversteps the boundaries of the area with which his article is concerned: the narrative text. Clearly, it is possible to imagine descriptive texts not only in poetry but also in tourist brochures and in the travel section of the Sunday newspaper. When, on the contrary, Genette attempts to demonstrate that the verb in the sentence "he seized a knife" is of a descriptive nature, his concept of "descriptive," suddenly shifts from a text (segment) to an aspect of every word.

12. Dickens, *Dombey and Son*, 297.
13. Genette, "Boundaries of Narrative," 6. (My translation differs.)
14. Barthes, "Introduction."

1.3 Semiotics

The last definition of the concept "descriptive" to be discussed in Genette's article corresponds to yet another development. It is a *semiotic* notion in which the distinction between the two sorts of text can be made on the basis of whether or not the expression roughly coincides with the content, these being the two primary sub-codes.[15] In narrative text segments, the expression roughly coincides with the content which also unfolds in time. This does not imply an isochrony, an identical rhythm, between expression and content, but rather a basic and general similarity. Descriptions do not display this similarity. The expression in a descriptive text segment involves a lapse of time, while the content unfolds in space.

This notion closely approaches the second criterion, and it too gives rise to similar problems when one attempts a delimitation. The contradiction found in the excerpt from *Dombey and Son* is not resolved. From a theoretical point of view it is easier to defend the semiotic approach, since the relationship between expression and content is accounted for. Working from this notion, it is possible to explain the embarrassment, shown by authors as well as by theorists, with regard to description. I shall return to this topic later.

1.4 Linguistics

Another approach to description comes from the *linguistically*-oriented structuralist school, the word "linguistic" being used in a non-metaphoric sense here. The early structuralists frequently employed linguistic terms without always precisely specifying their correspondences.[16] In the 1970's, various models were constructed in which attempts were made to isolate the narrative structure of the fabula as mechanically as possible. This objective—isolation of plot—indicates a relationship with the early structuralists. Proppians continued to predominate.

The influence of linguistics is apparent in the attempts at mechanization. These models can often be found in such journals as *Semiotica* and especially in *Poetics*. One representative example is an article by Hendricks who tries to isolate the plot structure by following a series of steps intended to *normalize* the text.[17] The last step of this series results in a number of similar propositions. One of the first steps is the elimination of *description assertions*. The indicators which are used for this purpose are linguistic. Hendricks characterizes description as sentences in which the verb has a

15. See, for this notion and its semiotic foundation, Eco, *A Theory of Semiotics*, 48–54.
16. This critique has been pointed out by Culler in his basic study of structuralism, *Structuralist Poetics*, 96–109.
17. Hendricks, "Methodology."

subject complement: generally speaking, the linking verbs. Difficulties arise when Hendricks' indicators are put into practice. For example, Hendricks himself considers the following passage from Faulkner's "A Rose for Emily" to be descriptive: "When the Negro opened the blinds of one window, they could see that the leather was cracked."[18] In this sentence, there is at least one verb which cannot be regarded as a linking verb ("to open"). "To see" also presents problems, but these can be settled with some effort. Intuitively, one would say that the sentence is partially descriptive, but it also contains a narrative segment. Unfortunately, Hendricks' method is unable to solve this sort of problem. It is quite easy to point to examples in Hendricks' own analysis which could intuitively be considered descriptive even though Hendricks does not regard them as such; the same is also true the other way around.

Apart from the problems connected with the practical application of this "mechanical" procedure, at least one theoretical problem must be solved. The correspondence between linguistic (linking verbs) and logical (propositions, two-place predicates) concepts demands to be more clearly elaborated upon.

1.5 Narratology

In a critical analysis and testing of Hendricks' model, van der Ven concludes that many elements which intuitively do not pertain to the plot cannot be eliminated with Hendricks' restricted criterion.[19] Although van der Ven shares the same objective as Hendricks—mechanical plot isolation —he chooses to resolve the problem of description by employing a *narratological* criterion. This necessitates his creating one large category from all of the pre-diegetic or non-diegetic elements, these being all those fragments that interrupt the continuing line of the fabula. This category includes all anachronisms with external time reference as well as all conversational fragments. Actually, van der Ven's approach is a return to Barthes, whose *indices* and *catalyses* include many other elements in addition to descriptions. I consider this return step significant. As long as the objective remains action-oriented, it is impossible to resolve the problem of description satisfactorily.

1.6 Logic

(a) Among the limited number of articles devoted to description itself, Hamon's remains the most important, and will be basic for the following discussion.[20] Hamon offers neither a precise criterion for delimitation nor a

---

18. Faulkner, "A Rose for Emily," 169.
19. van der Ven, *Narrative Text*.
20. Hamon, "Qu'est-ce qu'une description?" See also his recent book, *Introduction à l'analyse descriptive*.

definition of description, which is not essential to his main corpus (the works of Zola). He does, however, present an interesting characteristic of description. According to Hamon, description obeys the laws of *lexical predictability*, whereas narrative text segments are characterized by logical predictability. The term "logical" is to be understood here in terms of the (much disputed) logic of action à la Bremond. By lexical predictability, Hamon means that description consists of an enumeration of the components of the object described. In principle, this enumeration is exhaustive, and it is complete when the lexicon is exhausted. For example, the description of a character would be finished after all of the parts of the human body had been enumerated. Of course, one seldom encounters such an enumeration in reality. This characteristic of description is applicable in reverse, however. The description of a character, to use the same example, could never include components of other objects (such as a thatched roof or a garden gate), unless these components were used in a metaphoric comparison. One consequence of Hamon's approach is that description interrupts the fabula not only in practice but also in principle. The fabula obeys other laws.

(b) The most consistent, though not yet much elaborated, view of the nature and function of description is given by Klaus.[21] He defines description in terms of the logic of predicates, stating that description occurs whenever predicates are attached to a subject. Although this definition is more precise than Genette's paradox, it leads to the same scepticism with respect to the possibility of delimitation. Klaus, in fact, refuses to consider description in opposition to narrative; in his opinion, description is a function of the whole text rather than a segment of the text.

This same conclusion must be reached by anyone who thinks through the problem of description consistently, from whatever point of view. Even in the most action-oriented approaches, the fabula of a narrative text is defined as a series of events which are caused or experienced by actors.[22] It is both theoretically and practically impossible to consider events apart from the actors who cause them, from the places where they occur, or from the things or individuals who experience the consequences. Taxonomic efforts of the sort discussed here must, therefore, lead to an impasse.

Despite all of these difficulties, descriptions do exist. We recognize them intuitively. Moreover, precisely these text segments are cited by the literary critic as representative illustrations of an author's style or manner of writing. Descriptions, therefore, must be placed and studied within a narratological model; otherwise, the discipline might become so unintuitive that we will no longer be able to work with it adequately. At present, the

---

21. Klaus, "Description in Narrative."
22. See, for example, Bremond, "La logique."

only solution seems to be relative. Therefore, with Klaus, we will consider as descriptive a text segment in which the descriptive function is dominant. Such a relative criterion as this can only be employed to characterize fragments; it is useless for delimiting ambiguous fragments.

2. MOTIVATION
The unavoidable realism

Why do we make such a fuss about the question of what descriptions are? There is one explanation for our concern. Within the realistic tradition, description has always been regarded as problematic. Genette has shown that in the *Republic* Plato tried to rewrite fragments of Homer so that they would be "truly" narrative.[23] The first elements to be discarded were the descriptions. Even Homer himself attempted to avoid, or at least to disguise, descriptions by making them narrative. Achilles' shield is described as it is in the process of being made; Agamemnon's armor as he puts it on. In the nineteenth-century realistic novel descriptions, if not made narrative, were at least motivated. And despite its efforts to avoid imitation, the *Nouveau Roman* has continued to follow this tradition.

Working from the premise that descriptions interrupt the line of the fabula, Hamon has constructed a typology of the ways in which descriptions are inserted. Insertion necessitates *motivation*. The postulate of objectivity which Zola championed necessitates naturalization, the making acceptable of those interruptions known as descriptions. This so-called objectivity is in fact a form of subjectivity when the characters are given the function of *authenticating* the narrative contents.[24] If "truth," and even probability, is no longer a meaningful criterion, then motivation alone, according to whatever logic you please, can suggest probability, thus making the contents believable.[25]

Hamon proceeds from the assumption that most descriptions are motivated. This assumption could arise from the fact that descriptions are felt to be "unnatural" because they lack the semiotic coincidence between expression and content. One explanation for the irrefutable fact of this motivation (amply demonstrated by twenty centuries of Western literature) could perhaps be the need for iconism.[26] Narrative fragments are iconic. Roughly

---

23. Genette, *Figures III*, 186–89.
24. For the notion of authentication, see Doležel, "Truth and Authenticity."
25. For a discussion of the importance of motivation in an esthetics of *vraisemblance*, see Genette's article "Vraisemblance et motivation," in *Figures II*, 71–100. Culler analyzes several types of motivation in *Structuralist Poetics*, 131–60.
26. The notion of iconism is basic in a Peircian semiotics. Eco's extensive critique of iconism in *A Theory of Semiotics* (see above, note 15) is not altogether convincing, in spite of several points he makes. If carefully defined and applied, iconism is a useful concept that allows us to account for many interesting phenomena in language and literature.

speaking, they resemble their contents since both contain a lapse of time. Descriptions do not display such an analogy, however, since descriptions are *arbitrary*. The motivation for descriptions consists, then, in their being integrated into the time lapse so that they will be naturalized with respect to the narrative text.

Hamon distinguishes three types of motivation. Motivation is brought about by looking, speaking, or acting. The sequence in which he discusses these three types coincides with the frequency with which they appear. The most effective, the most frequent, and the least noticeable form is motivation via looking. A character sees an object. The description is the reproduction of what he sees. Looking at something demands time, and, in this fashion, the description is incorporated into the time lapse. But an act of looking must also have its motivation. There must be enough light so that the character is able to observe the object. There is a window, an open door, a corner, which also have to be described and therefore motivated. Further, the character must have both the time to look and a reason to look at an object. Hence the curious characters, the men of leisure, the unemployed, and the Sunday wanderers.

Given the fundamental arbitrariness of the elements of the fictional world, there is, equally fundamentally, no end to the need for motivation. The less obvious this motivation is, the more easily it can be terminated. In the following fragment, for example, the motivation is easily integrated into the description itself (italics mine):

> When they had washed they lay and *waited* again. There were fifteen beds in the tall, narrow room. The walls were painted grey. The windows were long but high up, *so that you could see only* the topmost branches of the trees in the grounds outside. Through *the glass* the sky had no colour.[27]

The sentence immediately preceding the description ("they lay and waited again") gives sufficient motivation for the act of looking. Hospital patients, particularly after their morning wash, have an ocean of time before them. Not only is the looking itself motivated, but also the contents of what the women see. And this is indicated by "so that you could see," by the boundaries of the area visible. The window motivates the fact that the women are not able to see anything at all of what is happening outside the hospital. Also, the restricted quality of the field of vision is emphasized: "Through the glass the sky had no colour." This lack of color has its own thematic meaning so that, even in this aspect, the description is fully integrated into the text.

Hamon refers to this type of motivation as a "thématique vide." A

---

27. Rhys, "Outside the Machine," 83.

diagram of the same is by definition incomplete; every motivating factor demands another motivation. We could sketch the following approximation: Character—notation of pause in action—verb of perception—notation of field of vision—object—motivation for looking—light.

When a character not only looks but also describes what it sees, a certain shift in motivation occurs, although in principle all of the above-mentioned motivation demands remain valid. The act of speaking necessitates a listener. The speaker must possess knowledge which the listener does not have but would like to have. The listener can, for example, be blind, or young, or amateurish. Hamon discusses yet a third form of motivation which resembles Homeric description. The character carries out an action with an object. The description is then made fully narrative. An example of this is the scene in Zola's *La bête humaine* in which Jacques polishes (strokes) every individual component of his beloved locomotive.

These three forms of motivation can be combined. Hamon does not take into consideration their different status with respect to action. However, they can readily be placed within the narratological model of layered meaning-formation.[28] Motivation occurs at the level of *text* when the character itself describes an object; at the level of *story* when the glance or vision of the character supplies the motivation; and at the level of *fabula* when the character carries out an action with an object. One clear illustration of *fabula*, which also demonstrates that a distinction between descriptive and narrative is no longer possible within this form, is the following "description" of a dead man:

> Then they went into José Arcadio Buendia's room, shook him with all their might, screamed in his ear, and held a little mirror in front of his nose, but they weren't able to wake him.[29]

Examples of the second type, motivation via focalization, are numerous. An illustration of the first type is the description of the Linton family as given by young Heathcliff in *Wuthering Heights*. He is forced to give this description because Nelly Dean has made him responsible for his escapades with Cathy and for the fact that he has returned alone.

Motivation is the relationship between elements made explicit. Precisely because these relationships are not self-evident in fictional texts, the motivation is never sufficient. And, for this reason, motivation is, in the final analysis, arbitrary.

---

28. For an account of the following three-fold model, and for its foundation both in narratology and in semiotics, see Bal, *Narratology*. Cf. also "Narrative Embedding."
29. Márquez, *One Hundred Years of Solitude*.

3. THE INTERNAL STRUCTURE
Contiguity

In spite of the theoretical impossibility of selecting descriptive text-fragments in an unambiguous way, it is possible to account for the internal structure of fragments intuitively characterized as descriptive. A model of the internal structure of description must be internally consistent, universally applicable, and yet only valid for the analysis of those text-fragments that are generally acknowledged as descriptive. It must also provide relevant information about the structure and meaning of the fragments. The best-known model that seems to meet these criteria is Hamon's.

According to Hamon, descriptions consist of a *theme* (e.g., "house") which is the object described, and a series of sub-themes (e.g., "door," "roof," "room") which are the components of the object. Taken together, the sub-themes constitute the *nomenclature*. They may or may not be accompanied by *predicates* (e.g., "pretty," "green," "large"). These predicates are *qualifying* when they indicate a characteristic of the object ("pretty"); they are *functional* when they indicate a function, action or possible use ("habitable for the six people"). Metaphors and comparisons are included among the predicates. In reality, it is seldom possible to distinguish between qualifying and functional predicates.

The model is constructed on the principle of *contiguity*. The relation between theme and sub-themes is *inclusive*. Predicates are represented only at the subordinated level of the sub-themes. But it is self-evident that the theme itself can be accompanied by one or more predicates. The model is hierarchic. A sub-theme can again be subdivided into smaller units, a fact

Table 2

THEME	(PREDICATE)
sub-theme 1	(predicate)
sub-theme 2	(predicate)
sub-theme 3	(predicate)
sub-theme 4	(predicate)

Table 3

THEME	(PREDICATE)
sub-theme 1	(predicate)
sub-theme 1a	(predicate)
sub-theme 1b	(predicate)
sub-theme 2	(predicate)
sub-theme 2a	(predicate)
sub-theme 2b	(predicate)
sub-theme 3	(predicate)
sub-theme 3a	(predicate)
sub-theme 3b	(predicate)

which Hamon does not take into account. If we momentarily set these complications aside, we are left with a simple and clearly organized structure (Table 2). This structure can then be adjusted to account for the above-mentioned complications (Table 3).

At first glance, this model would seem to present few problems. In practice, however, it must be slightly adjusted even for very simple descriptions. I shall give two examples. The first example is the description of the garden taken from Longus' Greek pastoral novel *Daphnis and Chloë*. The second fragment is the more frequently analyzed unconventional description of young Charles Bovary's cap. The garden:

> And that garden indeed was a most beautiful and goodly thing and such as might become a prince. For it lay extended in length a whole furlong. It was situated on a high ground, and had to its breadth four acres. To a spacious field one would easily have likened it. Trees it had of all kinds, the apple, the pear, the myrtle, the pomegranate, the fig, and the olive; and to these on the one side there grew a rare and taller sort of vines, that bended over and reclined their ripening bunches of grapes among the apples and pomegranates, as if they would vie and contend for beauty and worth of fruits with them. So many kinds there were of satives, or of such as are planted, grafted, or set. To these were not wanting the cypress, the laurel, the platan, and the pine. And towards them, instead of the vine, the ivy leaned, and with the errantry of her boughs and her scattered blackberries did imitate the vines and shadowed beauty of the ripening grapes. Within were kept, as in a garrison, trees of lower growth that bore fruit. Without stood the barren trees, enfolding all, much like a fort or some strong wall that had been built by the hand of art; and these were encompassed with a spruce, thin hedge. By alleys and glades there was everywhere a just distermination of things from things, an orderly discretion of tree from tree; but on the tops the boughs met to interweave their limbs and leaves with one another's, and a man would have thought that all this had not been, as indeed it was, the wild of nature, but rather the work of curious art. Nor were there wanting to these, borders and banks of various flowers, some the earth's own volunteers, some the structure of the artist's hand. The roses, hyacinths, and lilies were set and planted by the hand; the violet, the daffodil, and anagall the earth gave up of her own good will. In the summer there was shade, in the spring the beauty and fragrancy of flowers, in the autumn the pleasantness of the fruits; and at every season amusement and delight.[30]

The excerpt is constructed very conventionally according to the rules of *locus amoenus*. Even without embarking on a detailed analysis of this fragment, we are able to ascertain several problems. Should we, for example, consider the dimensions (length, breadth, height) as sub-themes or as predicates of the theme? More importantly, which hierarchy dominates this description? First there is a mention of trees, and then of flowers. But cutting across this division is the division between cultivated and wild plants. If we choose to regard this last division as the dominant one, then

---

30. *Daphnis and Chloë*, 189–91.

the former becomes a subdivision of the latter. As a result, the analysis does not account for the linear character of the description. Furthermore, there is yet a third division, that between center and periphery, which is difficult to place in relation to the other two divisions. The seasons, mentioned at the end of the excerpt, also create problems comparable to those presented by the dimensions.

Contrary to what we might expect, Hamon's model is more difficult to apply to this strictly conventional text than to the unorthodox description of the cap. One explanation for this may perhaps be found in the premise of lexical predictability. The convention of the *locus amoenus* is non-realistic, whereas the convention of the enumeration of the components of the described object is realistic. The garden is described according to textual, rhetorical conventions which are not at all related to the construction of the object described but rather to the euphoric expectations of the idyll. In a realistic sense, some of these elements can in fact be contradictory. In this case, a symmetry is first presented (between cultivated and wild trees, each accorded a rank); this is then further constructed concentrically (center and periphery), a concentricity which is difficult to harmonize with the symmetry first evoked. The difficulty is not apparent when one reads the description, but it does become so when one tries to draw the garden. It is a *textual garden* which is composed of words, words which are neatly arranged. Text and object are incommensurable in such a case. Therefore, Hamon's model must be adjusted to accommodate this description. The adjustment involves an expansion. The various divisions (wild-cultivated, center-periphery) can serve as predicates to all of the sub-themes in these divisions. The remaining division (trees, flowers) can be maintained, keeping with the order of the text. These two large sub-themes are then subdivided, first into cultivated-wild, and then into the sorts of plants mentioned. Dimensions and seasons can be regarded as predicates of the main theme.

The cap:

(La prière était finie que le *nouveau* tenait encore sa casquette sur ses deux genoux.) C'était une de ces coiffures d'ordre composite, où l'on retrouve les éléments du bonnet à poil, du chapska, du chapeau rond, de la casquette de loutre et du bonnet de coton, une de ces pauvres choses, enfin, dont la laideur muette a des profondeurs d'expression comme le visage d'un imbécile. Ovoïde et renflée de baleines, elle commençait par trois boudins circulaires; puis s'alternaient, séparés par une bande rouge, des losanges de velours et de poil de lapin; venait ensuite une façon de sac qui se terminait par un polygone cartonné, couvert d'une broderie en soutache compliquée, et d'où pendait, au bout d'un long cordon trop mince, un petit croisillon de fils d'or, en manière de gland. Elle était neuve; la visière brillait.[31]

31. [Editor's note] Flaubert, *Madame Bovary*, 22. The following analysis is untranslatable, so the original is quoted. The English version (p. 16) is as follows:
(For he was still holding his cap on his knees when prayers were over.) His was one of

The description can be divided into two. The first sentence is a general characterization and evaluation. The second sentence describes the cap in detail. An analysis of the themes and predicates is shown in the columns in Table 4. But two problems confront us. First, it is not possible to assimilate the difference between the two sentences into the *construction* of the schema. However, the difference between a general and a detailed description can be accommodated by *filling in* the schema. The second problem is more serious. It is impossible, using this model, to demonstrate the *connections* between the elements. Roughly speaking, the connections consist of a series of verb forms, some of which are accompanied by an adverb (see the bottom section of Table 4).

Hamon's analysis is restricted to the lexicon, and the connections which it fails to account for include a noticeable number of aspects which indicate a time lapse. It becomes clear that Hamon's model is connected with his opinions about the nature of descriptions. It should be mentioned that the use of pseudo-time indicators in description is considered (though not convincingly so) to be characteristic of Flaubert. His description of the wedding cake, to cite another example, is also built up of components which are connected by "first," "then," "lastly." Ricardou treats these aspects of Flaubert's descriptive style in great detail.[32] The procedure is so widespread, even in "natural narrative,"[33] that it seems to me unnecessary to criticize Hamon's model on that particular point. Ricardou considers it to be an indication of Flaubert's *modernité*, paraphrased as his *anti-mimetic* stand: the description is textual; the reference to an object is only secondary. This also appears to be the case with Longus. Ricardou criticizes Hamon's model, stating that such a hierarchic construction cannot be used when analyzing the paradoxical and complicated descriptions of Flaubert. It is understandable that a model such as this should meet with affective resistance. As I have pointed out, the applicability of the model is restricted to a lexical analysis. Within this restriction, however, the model functions reasonably well.

Ricardou presents an alternative which I consider unsatisfactory. Nevertheless I shall discuss it, since Ricardou is one of the few authors who has made important contributions to the study of description. Dissatisfied with Hamon's hierarchic construction, Ricardou designed a sort of tree diagram

those composite pieces of headgear in which you may trace features of bearskin, lancer-cap and bowler, night-cap and otterskin: one of those pathetic objects that are deeply expressive in their dumb ugliness, like an idiot's face. An oval splayed out with whalebone, it started off with three pompons; these were followed by lozenges of velvet and rabbit's fur alternately, separated by a red band, and after that came a kind of bag ending in a polygon of cardboard with intricate braiding on it; and from this there hung down like a tassel, at the end of a long, too slender cord, a little sheaf of gold threads. It was a new cap, with a shiny peak.

32. Ricardou, *Nouveaux problèmes*.
33. See Labov and Waletzky, "Narrative Analysis."

Table 4

THEME	PREDICATE
a. une de ces coiffures	d'ordre composite
b. une de ces choses	pauvre
c. elle	ovoïde
	renflée de baleines
	neuve

SUB-THEMES	PREDICATES
a. éléments du bonnet (1)	à poil
chapska (2)	
chapeau (3)	rond
casquette (4)	de loutre
bonnet (5)	de coton
b. laideur	muette
profondeurs d'expression	comme le visage d'un imbécile
c. boudins	circulaires
losanges	de velours
bande	rouge
losanges	poil de lapin
sac	une façon de
polygone	cartonné
	couvert d'une broderie
[broderie (soutache)]	en soutache compliqué
cordon	long
	trop mince
croisillon [en	fils]en fils
croisillon	d'or
visière	en manière de gland
	brillait

où l'on retrouve
enfin
a[34]
elle commençait
puis s'alternaient
séparés par
venait ensuite
qui se terminait
et d'où pendait
au bout de

34. Between "laideur muette" and "profondeurs d'expression."

with a central framework. All of the elements extend out from the theme, to which they remain joined. Ricardou distinguishes three relations. *Situation* concerns the relation of the parts to the whole; *composition* that of the whole to the parts; and qualification is distinguished by means of predicates. Because the relations are very poorly defined, and because they overlap one another, they are difficult to determine with any precision. But even if this were possible, there still remain more disadvantages than advantages to Ricardou's model.

Figure 1

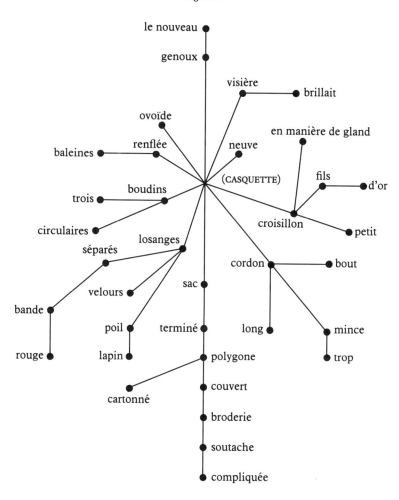

situation (object—next or higher object)
qualification (object—quality)
composition (object—parts of object)
comparison (object—exterior object)

Figure 1 shows Ricardou's own analysis of the description of the cap. The sequence of elements in the text is lost. The metaphors have been omitted, the general characterization has disappeared. And, strangely enough, the pseudo-temporal connections also disappear. Further, the model lacks the neat organization of Hamon's model. Although Ricardou is a creative and sensitive critic whose analyses can be very clarifying, his suggested model is not very useful. It does not provide new information about this description, nor about description in general.

Another, better-formulated objection to Hamon's model may be found in an article by van Buuren.[35] This article concerns the position of metaphor. In Hamon's model, metaphors were treated in the same manner as non-metaphoric qualitative predicates, which resulted in their being placed at the bottom of the hierarchy. Van Buuren demonstrates that, in addition to this sort of description, there are also metaphorically-constructed descriptions. When metaphor functions not as a predicate but as a principle of construction for the entire description, Hamon's model is not fully adequate and, as van Buuren concludes, a specific model is needed.

4. THE INTERNAL STRUCTURE
Specification

According to van Buuren, the construction of a description may follow one of two principles of organization: the metonymic or the metaphoric. Van Buuren uses the term metonymic in its broad sense as used by Jakobson: the components exist in a relation of contiguity with each other. In Peircian terms this relation is indexical. The metaphoric construction implies that "the coherence between the descriptive components is determined by a relation of identity between two terms." Van Buuren convincingly demonstrates that one of Hamon's own examples can be described more adequately when the (implicit) metaphoric construction principle is accounted for in an alternative model.

van Buuren's model is binary, consisting of two series. In Table 5, the elements of the described object itself, the *compared* (c^d), are on the left; on the right are the elements of the object with which the described object is compared, the *comparant* (c^t).

Because metaphoric relations are possible among the predicates, these latter are placed under the sub-themes.

One definite advantage of this design is that the interaction between c^d and c^t can be demonstrated. From both themes, a selection is made of elements which motivate and elaborate the comparison. This selection

---

35. Buuren, "Metaforische beschrijvingen."

Table 5

THEME c^d	THEME c^t
sub-theme 1	sub-theme 1a
predicate 1	predicate 1a
sub-theme 2	sub-theme 2a
predicate 2	predicate 2a
sub-theme 3	sub-theme 3a
predicate 3	predicate 3a

influences both the construction of the series and the choice of predicates. This is clearly demonstrated in van Buuren's illustrative analysis of a description by Proust[36] in which a second aspect of the interaction is also apparent. Elements remain implicit in both series and, consequently, the reader can fill in the series on the basis of the main metaphor. Because of this, for this sort of description Hamon's model cannot compete with van Buuren's. The various metaphoric elements could not be seen in coherent relation with each other. Where elements of the c^d remain implicit, elements of the c^t, according to Hamon's predicate with sub-theme model, would remain hanging in the air because of the lack of a corresponding sub-theme. I consider this model a welcome addition to the study of description. However, I do regard its status in relation to Hamon's to be problematic. van Buuren himself believes that his model can serve as an adjunct to Hamon's, remaining restricted to those cases in which Hamon's model proves inadequate. Such a situation has one serious disadvantage; since there could no longer be a systematic relationship between the two types of description, the theoretical status of descriptions could no longer be generally described.

Furthermore, such a division is not necessary. However tempting it may be to follow Jakobson's now classic bipartite division here, it should certainly not be considered a matter of course to do so. Many descriptions display a combination of both principles of construction. Genette analyzes the metonymic motivations of many of Proust's metaphors.[37] Moreover, metaphors can be introduced at the level of sub-theme and subsequently carried through, and the series c^d and c^t are both constructed according to the principle of contiguity. The simple reason for this is that the two categories are neither opposites nor alternatives, but rather complements.

It is possible to integrate both models, a step which would only involve adjusting Table 5. All of the elements, with the exception of theme c^d, are optional. Theme c^d can remain implicit. The components of the descrip-

36. Buuren, "Metaforische beschrijvingen," 50.
37. Genette, *Figures III*, 41–63.

tion are filled in along the vertical division. Whenever a sub-theme is not provided with a corresponding c^t, the right-hand compartment remains empty, and vice versa. Implicit, assumed elements can be inserted between parentheses, thereby contributing to the total formation of the image. The vertical division of the series remains contiguous in construction. If theme c^t is absent, the metaphor then appears at the level of the sub-theme. When the right half of the scheme is empty, we are left with Hamon's model. When both themes develop independently of each other, the line between the left and the right sides is unbroken.

This integrated model has several advantages. The specification desired by van Buuren is now possible. Moreover, all descriptions can be similarly analyzed, resulting in a greater generalization than was possible when using either model separately. Further, the relation between types can be investigated systematically. Because of these advantages, this model satisfies methodological requirements more fully.

With the help of this model, it is possible to develop further the interesting suggestions made by Lodge, in analyzing a number of descriptions of places.[38] He claims that the difference between "referential" and "literary" descriptions can, to a great extent, be attributed to the use of figures of speech. Although his argument is not as systematic as our present purpose requires, his analyses are creative and inspiring. A careful application of our analytic model enables us to differentiate roughly six types of descriptions. There are no absolute boundaries between these six types. The descriptions are classified according to whether they are more to the left or to the right of the model.

4.1 The referential, encyclopedic description

In principle, there are no figures of speech in this type of description, exemplified by the encyclopedia. The selection of components is based upon the contiguity of the content-elements. This means that the presence of some elements implies the absence of others. The missing detail can be filled in by the reader. General characteristics imply specific characteristics, unless the latter represent the former. The objective is to convey knowledge.

4.2 The referential-rhetoric description

The tourist guidebook rather than the encyclopedia is the model for this second type of description. The units are combined on the basis both of the contiguity of the components and of their thematic function. This function

---

38. "Types of Description." The following typology can be considered as a more systematic and extended version of the one sketched by Lodge.

is evaluative. The objective is both to convey knowledge and to persuade. Persuasion works through the wording (a pleasing rhythm, a style which reflects the value of what is described—for example, a sumptuous style to describe the Champs-Elysées) and through the contents; persuasion is also achieved through the choice of traditionally valued sub-themes, and by the addition of evaluative predicates. Even when a number of metaphors are included in such a description, the construction of the text continues to follow the principle of contiguity.

4.3 Metaphoric contiguity

Here again, contiguity is the dominating principle of construction: each individual component is metaphorized. Various *compareds* may, in fact, be omitted altogether and only the *comparants* found in the text, which is very metaphoric as a result. However, no contiguity relation obtains among the components of the c^t. Such a relation exists only among the implicit components of the c^d. One might think that this type of description would make an incoherent impression upon the reader. That such is not the case indicates that the reader is engaged in a filling-in activity. Lodge offers an illustrative example of this type of description which is taken from Forster's *A Passage to India*.

4.4 The systematized metaphor

This description is one large metaphor. The elements of the c^t and the c^d are systematically related to one another. Each series is built upon the principle of contiguity. The series balance each other. The question of which of the two series dominates the meaning cannot be answered without taking the context into consideration. Also included in this category are descriptions in which elements of both series imply each other, as in van Buuren's example.

4.5 The contiguous metaphor

The description is one large metaphor. The elements are contiguously related to each other. They form a coherent description which, taken as a whole, is the c^t of a c^d. If this relation can remain implicit, this type of description, when taken out of its context, cannot be distinguished from one of the other types. It is, then, only metaphoric if interpreted as such. An explicit c^t results in a Homeric comparison.

4.6 The series of metaphors

This description consists of a metaphor which is expanded without continuous reference to the c^d. The metaphor is repeatedly "adjusted," creating the impression that the c^d is elusive and indescribable. This classification clearly demonstrates the need for combining the models suggested by Hamon and by van Buuren. Although an extensive analysis of examples of all six types of descriptions is impossible here, I shall nevertheless attempt to clarify the typology by examining the following descriptions of Rouen. The first is an encyclopedia entry:

ROUEN (Latin Rotomagus), chief town of Seine Inférieure, 136 kilometers from Paris, on the Seine at the confluence of the Robec, population 107,739 (Rouennais, aises). Chief town of the 3rd military region. University of arts and sciences, commerce and industry, and professional school of medicine and pharmacy.

Port on the Seine, including, up to the Boïeldieu Bridge, a seaport, accessible at high tide to vessels drawing 7 meters, and a river port upriver from this bridge. Imports: American cotton, petroleum, coal, wine and fruit from Spain, wood. Exports: grains, sugar, beets, spirits. The city of Rouen is a large center for the spinning and weaving of cotton, flax and hemp, the manufacture of cotton fabric and calico, and a wool market. Cotton fabrics are often called "rouenneries"; lastly, there are many various industries: metalworks, soap making, dyeing, refineries, preserve making.[39]

This description of Rouen (R1) agrees with the conventions of the *encyclopedic* description. The topics which are mentioned are the same for all such descriptions of place: government, education, import, export, industry. Because of the generic conventions, it is possible to compare these descriptions with one another. Having read several different descriptions, one can compare cities with one another and conclude, for example, that Rouen is a more important city in many aspects (trade, industry) than Chambéry. There are no metaphors in the description. Elements which have been omitted can be filled in. For example, only the technical schools and schools for higher education are mentioned; their presence implies the existence of primary and secondary schools. The words "textile industry" are not specifically mentioned, since such a generalization would be too all-inclusive. Instead, the specific subdivisions of this industry are listed. The description conveys knowledge, but no attempt is made to force the knowledge upon the reader. The second description is from a prestigious guidebook:

a. Rouen, Seine-Maritime, population 124,577, former capital of Normandy, archdiocese and court of appeals, port on the Seine (5th largest in France), is a city of art and tourism as well as a commercial and industrial center. Because of its gothic churches, museums, picturesque streets lined with old houses, Rouen, the "gothic city," also called the "museum city," has maintained, despite serious damage from World War II, its eminent standing as a city of art. New neighborhoods have sprung up on both sides of the Seine; Saint-Sever, on the left bank, is dominated by the Tour des Archives, 88m. high, and by the new police head-

39. *Larousse*, 58. Translated by Robert Corum.

quarters . . . . b. One begins his visit of Rouen at the quais, where, from the Boïeldieu Bridge, one has a beautiful view of the entire city and port. It was from the Mathilde Bridge, which occupied the site of the present Boïeldieu Bridge, that the ashes of Joan of Arc were thrown into the Seine. Upriver, Lacroix Island is connected to the city and the suburb Saint Sever by the new Corneille Bridge. Downriver, the quai de la Bourse borders reconstructed neighborhoods which form a vast quadrilateral extending to the cathedral on one side, and from the rue Armand-Carrel to the rue Grand-Pont on the other. By going downriver from the quai de la Bourse, one finds to the right the rue Jeanne-d'Arc, a wide modern thoroughfare connecting the quais to the Rive-Droite train station. At the end of this street appears the new theater (1962), then, going back up the street, one sees, to the left, ruins of Saint-Vincent church, 15th and 16th centuries, of which there remain only the transept and the portal. A little further along, on the same side, is located the Saint-André tower, all that remains of the Saint-André-aux-Fébvres church. One ends up at the Place Foch victory monument, by Réal del Sarte, bordered on the right by the modern facade of the court building whose courtyard of honor opens to the rue aux Juifs. Next to it a parking garage has been built (576 places of which 380 are underground, 1961).[40]

This description (R2) is a combination of types 1 and 2. It is also intended to convey knowledge, namely more specific knowledge about the appearance of the city. The excerpt can be divided into two parts. The section which has been omitted presents a historical survey, and is therefore not descriptive but narrative. The first part of the description (R2a) very much resembles R1. Here too, a number of content-elements are mentioned. These elements are selected on the basis of the *contiguity* of the components, all of which form part of the city's image as a whole. Further, the elements are selected on the basis of their *thematic* character. The theme of the tourist guidebook is that of touristic attractiveness, largely determined by a locality's antiquities and its picturesqueness. The first sentence of the excerpt clearly illustrates how this type of description is constructed. The sentence is long and contains many elements. As a result, the reader receives the impression that the city is *interesting*; there is a great deal to be said about it. The first entry word, "former capital," recapitulates the importance of the city and its antiquities. Both aspects are repeated at the end of the sentence, here joined by "as well as." Each of the two subsequent sentences elaborates upon one aspect, and in the same sequence. The information is not very specific. The experienced tourist is made suspicious by the list of plurals (gothic churches, museums, picturesque streets, old houses), knowing that, in tourist guidebooks, quantity often disguises a lack of quality. A less attentive reader, on the other hand, is led to believe that the city has innumerable sights of interest. The reason why both aspects of the city, old and modern, are emphasized, is casually

40. *Guide Bleu.* Translated by Robert Corum.

mentioned in a sub-clause: the city suffered extensive damage during the Second World War.

The purpose of this first section of the description is to give readers just enough information to motivate them to visit the city despite its modern appearance.

In the second section (R2b), the rhetorical objective has already been achieved. The reader begins to walk, in reality or in his imagination. The description is built entirely around the principle of the (walking) *tour*. It is impossible to see all the objects described if one remains in a single fixed position. The narrative aspect is strongly emphasized by the form of the text. The strolling tourist is taken from one scene to the next by means of such phrases as "one begins—upriver—downriver—on one side—on the other—by going downriver—to the right—at the end—going back up—to the left—a little further along—one ends up—on the right—next to it." A respectable number of place adjuncts for such a short passage. Here again, the description conforms to the rules of the genre. All descriptions of places in tourist guidebooks are written in the form of a walking tour; the picturesque and the dynamic are emphasized in all of them. The analogy does not continue any further. In R2a, the elements which are mentioned are predictable. In R2b, the elements are selected according to the characteristics of the specific object (in this case Rouen) within the projected purpose and fixed theme of the guidebook.

> Then, at a single glance, the town appeared. Sweeping down in great tiers, plunged in the mist, it spread out far and wide beyond the bridges, confusedly. Behind it the open country rose in a monotonous movement, to touch the pale sky at the blurred horizon. Seen from above like this, the whole landscape looked still as a picture. In one corner ships crowded at anchor. The river curved round the green hills, the oblong islands looked like great dark fishes come to rest on its surface. Immense brown billows of smoke poured from the factory chimneys, to drift away in the wind. The roar of the foundries clashed with the clear chimes pealing from the churches that rose up above the mist. Bare trees on the boulevards showed as clumps of purple amid the houses; the rainwet roofs made a glistening patchwork all across the slopes of the town. Occasionally a gust of wind would carry the clouds towards St. Catherine's Hill, like aerial waves breaking soundlessly against a cliff. That mass of life down there gave her a dizzy feeling. Her heart swelled, as though those hundred and twenty thousand throbbing hearts had sent up to her all at once the fumes of the passions she imagined to be theirs.[41]

41. Flaubert, *Madame Bovary*, 273–74, translation slightly adapted. The French (p. 564) is as follows:

Puis, d'un seul coup d'oeil, la ville apparaissait. Descendant tout en amphithéâtre et noyée dans le brouillard, elle s'élargissait au delà des ponts, confusément. La pleine campagne remontait ensuite d'un mouvement monotone, jusqu'à toucher au loin la base indécise du ciel pâle. Ainsi vu d'en haut, le paysage tout entier avait l'air immobile

The third description (R3) is taken from a well-known novel. Let's call it a *literary* description. Like R2, this text presents a view of the city. It is possible to view the panorama from one fixed position. The large number of metaphors is immediately apparent: metaphors such as "in great tiers—plunged—as a picture—looked like great dark fishes" are the most obvious; in addition, there are metaphors that remain almost inconspicuous, metaphors such as the pronominal verb forms. The components of the c^d are selected on the basis of contiguity. They constitute the various parts of the panorama. The components of the c^t are not related to one another. For example, there is no contiguity between "tiers" and "great dark fishes." This description, therefore, may be included in the category of descriptions based on *metaphoric contiguity*. The components of the c^d conform to the rules of the panorama: only those elements which can be seen from a certain distance are described. The resulting image is both unspecific and static, compared to R2b.

An entirely different image presents itself when we examine the elements of the c^t. Here, the emphasis is on movement and confusion. The wide-angle view ("sweeping down in great tiers . . . the open country rose . . .") collides with negatively connotated elements ("monotonous . . . crowded . . . brown billows of smoke . . . breaking"). The passage is characterized by *contradiction*.[42] The city simultaneously represents an ideal, an illusion, and the disappointing reality of Emma's life. Both aspects shape the structure of the description. This same contradiction can be found in the preceding sentence as well. The amazement which is voiced in "at a single glance" is refuted by the imperfect iterative verb form in "appeared" (*apparaissait*).

On the basis of the context—the remainder of the chapter and the novel as a whole—this description can justifiably be classified as one large though implicit metaphor. Rouen with all of its contradictory aspects is then the c^t, and Emma's life, the fabula of the novel, is the c^d. Placed in context, the text can thus be classified under the fifth type of description. Because the c^d of this metaphor includes the entire fabula of the novel, the description may

comme une peinture; les navires à l'ancre se tassaient dans un coin; le fleuve arrondissait sa courbe au pied des collines vertes, et les îles, de forme oblongue, semblaient sur l'eau de grands poissons noirs arrêtés. Les cheminées des usines poussaient d'immenses panaches bruns qui s'envolaient par le bout. On entendait le ronflement des fonderies avec le carillon clair des églises qui se dressaient dans la brume. Les arbres des boulevards, sans feuilles, faisaient des broussailles violettes au milieu des maisons, et les toits, tout reluisants de pluie, miroitaient inégalement, selon la hauteur des quartiers. Parfois un coup de vent emportait les nuages vers la côte Sainte-Catherine, comme des flot aériens qui se brisaient en silence contre une falaise. Quelque chose de vertigineux se dégageait pour elle de ces existences amassées, et son coeur s'en gonflait abondamment, comme si les cent vingt mille âmes qui palpitaient là eussent envoyé toutes à la fois la vapeur des passions qu'elle leur supposait.

42. For a fuller discussion, see my *Narratologie*, 89–111.

also be regarded as a *mise en abyme*, a mirror-text. I shall return to this point in the next section.[43] I shall not discuss any further either the fourth or the sixth types of description, since van Buuren's analyses are sufficiently clear.

This description which, for the sake of convenience, I have termed *literary*, differs from the two other types in several respects. It is impossible to perceive the purpose of the description directly from the description itself. The text is thematically polyvalent. There are numerous figures of speech, and these are not restricted to metaphor and metonymy. It is impossible to classify the excerpt exclusively under one particular type of description. The rules of the panorama do not prescribe the selection of elements. The description is not *a priori* comparable with other descriptions of place in the novel; if descriptions of place should prove to be comparable, this may be attributed to the internal structure of the novel rather than to generic conventions of description. Finally, it is not possible to characterize the description adequately without taking the context into consideration. It is tempting to draw conclusions about literariness from these observations, but I find this impossible. It is easy enough to find journalistic examples which display the same characteristics. Nevertheless, I assume that these traits are characteristic of—or at least frequently appear in—narrative descriptions, because they account for the semantic dependence of description in relation to its context, as well as for the plurality of meaning.

5. PLACE AND FUNCTION
An integrated descriptive model

In order to characterize the internal structure of descriptions, it was necessary to expand Hamon's model and to make it more specific. In some cases, it also proved necessary, when using this typology, to refer to the context. The effect of the description is not restricted to the descriptive passage itself. Where the narrative structure is sufficiently flexible, the meaning of the entire narrative text may be laid open, predicted, summarized, transformed, or produced. As has often been shown by literary critics, descriptions provide the necessary flexibility. In this section, I shall discuss a number of aspects which influence the functioning of descriptions.

My working premise is functional. Every detail is related to the whole; nothing is superfluous; nothing is irrelevant; nothing is meaningless. Al-

---

43. A discussion of the "mise en abyme," a phenomenon which in some ways resembles the play in a play, can be found in Dällenbach, *Le récit spéculaire*, and in my review article on this book, "Mise en abyme."

though the rise of semiotics has rendered this premise almost banal,[44] it nevertheless refutes the premise of the Proppian structuralists. Proceeding from the primacy of action, this group could only accord description a marginal position, at best that of *indice*. Even Genette, who emphasized the need for description, regarded it as the boundary of the narrative—hence the title of his article. Hamon talks of the descriptive "expansion of the narrative," and thus agrees with Barthes. Ricardou, perhaps the most naive reader of the realistic novel, whose representational function he regards too literally, in order later to be able to react against it, moves from comments about the absolute uselessness and "gratuitousness" of descriptions to amazement at what he calls "l'inénarrable," an infelicitous and untranslatable term by which Ricardou means that the description succeeds in narrating that which cannot be narrated. This paradox must also be considered seriously. Does description narrate? And, if so, does it narrate that which cannot be narrated?

An investigation into the function of description can be organized in various ways. The possibility which will be presented here is nothing more than one practical suggestion, one which, at any rate, has proved useful to apply to R3. The analysis is carried out in three phases. First, the descriptive excerpt is itself described. Second, relations with the direct context are investigated. And finally, the excerpt is placed back within the text as a whole. In all three phases, both paradigmatic and syntagmatic relationships are investigated, as well as the connection between them. In principle, all possible data may be used: rhythm, sentence construction, lexicon, thematics, symbols, etc. The question which must be answered is the following: Is it possible, on the basis of this analysis, to offer an interpretation which differs from the current, general interpretations of the novel? If not, then it is impossible to continue to insist that description is more than an accentuated *indice* (thematic indication), possibly with some symbolic value. It should be mentioned that, in practice, analysis and interpretation are arrived at by a process of mutual interaction, and that it is difficult to distinguish them rigorously from one another. Further, the general interpretation of the narrative genre as an exciting, linear course of action must be taken into consideration. I shall return to this point later. The current interpretation of *Madame Bovary* may be summarized as "the collision between a stifling life in the provinces and romantic illusions, a collision which results in ruin." This interpretation is not contradicted by the analysis of R3. Rather, it is expanded in such a way that I am able to answer the above question in the affirmative.

44. See, for example, Lotman's well-known study, *The Structure of the Artistic Text*.

5.1 Stasis and movement

We have already seen that the stillness of the described object (criterion
"mode of existence" in Table 1) is not a general characteristic of descriptions. In fact, many descriptions are "in motion." This motion can reside in
the object itself or in the subject which observes and focalizes. Or it can
reside in both. Compare, for example, the following excerpts:

> Far in the distance, you could see an occasional church steeple between the
> green trees, other than this nothing of the surrounding world was visible, and
> then a wreath of rushes and flowering water plants which encircled the pearly
> surface of the water. On one side, exactly where the sun rose, it was impossible to
> distinguish the boundaries of the water. Now the cloud had disappeared again!
> The sun slowly rose higher and higher. And now a movement came from the
> water . . . . It actually looked as if a sleepy giant were stretching himself. It was as
> if a peculiar sound, a curious shuddering rose from out of the depths.[45]

> In the sky the planes look very small. On the runways they look very big.
> Therefore close up they should look even bigger—but in fact they don't. His
> own plane, for instance, just outside the window of the assembly lounge, doesn't
> look quite big enough for all the people who are going to get into it.[46]

> As the ship proceeded, sailing slowly on an azure lake of such transparency that
> sometimes the bottom was visible, the ring of mountains seemed to close in
> behind it. Presently at the end of the bay, close to the water's edge, at the foot of
> the mountains, the dazzlingly white town came in sight. A few small Italian
> vessels lay at anchor in the harbour. Four or five boats circled around the *Roi-
> Louis* to take off passengers.[47]

At first glance, we might say that in the first text the object moves, in the
second text object and subject, and in the third, where the observers are

---

45. Van Hichtum, *Afke's tiental.* I choose this example from a rather banal, moralistic
children's book from the 30's on purpose. Too often, complexity of narrative structure is
considered a characteristic feature of literature. I object to the taking for granted of that
position.

46. Lodge, *Changing Places*, 9. It seemed interesting to me to take an example from the
work of an author who proves in his theoretical work to be highly sensitive to the
differentiating power of descriptions. Furthermore, it is a contemporary novel without
being a theory-founded experimental one, like the works of the Nouveau Roman.

47. Maupassant, *A Life*, 57. This example is chosen because the novel resembles
Madame Bovary both in plot and in literary school, while at the same time it is recognized
to be more traditional in form. Thus the choice is implicitly polemic against Ricardou's
exaggerated insistence on the "modernité" of Flaubertian description, based on the
paradoxical movement that can supposedly be noticed. The same movement is to be found
in this Maupassant fragment, without the slightest effect of modernity. The French reads:
A mesure qu'on avançait, le cercle des monts semblait se refermer derrière le bâtiment
qui nageait avec lenteur dans un lac d'azur si transparent qu'on en voyait parfois le fond.
Et la ville apparut soudain, toute blanche, au fond du golfe, au bord des flots, au pied
des montagnes. Quelques petits bateaux italiens étaient à l'ancre dans le port. Quatre ou
cinq barques s'en vinrent rôder autour du Roi-Louis pour chercher ses passagers.

standing on a boat as it approaches a city, the subject moves (except in the last sentence, which resumes the narrative).

Roughly speaking, the above statement is correct, but there are some complications. In the first text, the sun rises; this is the object in motion. But it is more difficult to classify the movement of the water. This motion is described by three metaphors, two of which are synaesthetic. When a motion is so indirectly described by means of a personification (giant), hearing (sound), and feeling (shuddering), the impression arises that the experience, the *observation* (focalization), of an imperceptible change is being described, rather than a concrete, observable motion such as the movement of a cloud. Not only are the events of the sunrise related in this fragment, but, more importantly, the sensation brought about in the characters (inexperienced children) by this moment of the day is also related.

In the second fragment, only one aspect of airplanes—their dimensions —is described. The distance between the object described and the focalizing subject continually changes. Both are mobile. The person-bound focalizer, the character, remains the same. What changes is the moment of observation. This is possible because the character generalizes, and considers other airplanes in addition to the one in which he is about to depart. What is described is not one airplane, but the dimensions of airplanes in general.

In the third text, the focalizer (the two characters Jeanne and Julien who are on board a boat) moves as the boat approaches land. A passage such as " the . . . white town came in sight" is acceptable only if we consider the movement of the focalizer. Similarly, other, more subtle, phenomena can only be explained in this manner. If a considerable distance had not been covered between the two sentences, it would be impossible to observe the objects described in the second and third sentences respectively. This is emphasized by the adjective "small."

5.2 Focalization and interpretation

Focalization, the relation between the point of observation and the object described[48] is not important only for aspects of motion. The act of observation involves more than physical registration. As soon as we see something, we interpret it. In other words, every description is a depiction in words of our vision of an object. In the first of the above three fragments, movement-in-experience is described. In the second fragment, it is Swallow's view of the airplanes rather than the airplanes themselves which almost completely constitutes the object presented. In the third text, the

---

48. For this concept, see above, Chapter 4, and my *Narratology*, 100–15. Cf. also the controversy around the concept between Bronzwaer, "Mieke Bal's Concept of Focalization," and me, "The Laughing Mice," in which it is compared to related concepts like "point of view," "free indirect discourse," and "implied author."

city "appears" suddenly because Jeanne, now on her honeymoon, arrives with many pre-conceived images of the romantic Corsican city. The romantic aspect of her fantasy shapes the image of the city, set forth in a sentence which is significant both in its contents and in its wording.

Reality (fictive or "real") is misformed, transformed, mutilated, or idealized by our view of it. Or it is misunderstood, as is evident in the following description:

> In addition to the girl and the chickens and the geese, there were two men. And in the middle of the farmyard, standing as calmly as if they'd been standing there for hours, were two pigs. One of the pigs, the biggest one, leaned on the back of the other and wiggled its tail. It almost looked as if he were embracing the back of the other pig with his two forefeet.[49]

It is only when one of the men says, "If you watch how often Berend winks, you'll know exactly how many piglets are to be born" that an ironic twist is given to the metaphor "it almost looked as if he were embracing the back of the other pig with his two forefeet." There the c^t is actually the c^d, and what the six-year-old boy sees functions as an innocent metaphor for the real situation. When one analyzes a description, therefore, it is relevant to determine the point of view from which the object is presented, to determine who the focalizer is. In 't Hart's fragment, the focalizer is not the adult speaker, but rather the young child; in the excerpt taken from Maupassant, the focalizer is not the skeptical narrator, but the romantic bride.

In R3, Rouen is seen by Emma. She is not seeing the city for the first time. She is going there to meet her lover Léon. These contradictions in the description, in which euphoric and dysphoric aspects alternate with one another, may be attributed to Emma herself. She is trying to escape her stifling existence. Related to this desire are those aspects of the city which emphasize its openness, its space, its activity. But Emma does not succeed in fooling herself completely. "Reality" (within the fictive life of this character) also has its negative side. To this immanent realism correspond such aspects of the city as enclosure and suspension of motion. The combination of both sides leads to an accentuating of the contradiction in images such as "ships crowded at anchor" and "great dark fishes come to rest." Although these combinations are justifiable from a realistic point of view, they must be interpreted symbolically. Emma longs for movement, for travel (see, for example, her dream trip with Rodolphe). Ships and fish are travellers. It is highly significant that precisely these elements of the panorama are described and that the lack of motion is emphasized.

---

49. Hart, *De aansprekers*, 171. The example may also illustrate the possibilities of the concept of focalization for the analysis of metaphor.

5.3 Theme and motifs

Both of the aspects thus far discussed, stasis and motion, and focalization and interpretation, can be determined on the basis of formal characteristics. They become interesting when they can be related to the thematics of the description. By thematics I mean the semantic unity of which the theme is the (abstract) center. The theme is expressed by means of (concrete) motifs, put into words in the text itself. Thus, the theme can be determined from the motifs which it joins and motivates.

We have already noted a contradiction between illusion and reality in R3, between what Emma wants to see and what she is shown. This contradiction, with its components of illusion and reality, is the theme. One such motif is the metaphor of the inactive fish. Both aspects of the theme are included twice in the first sentence. "Sweeping down in great tiers," the spacious greatness (as well as theatrical—*amphithéâtre*—but this can only be interpreted in light of other scenes) stands opposed to and is negated by "plunged in the mist," and the same is true of "it spread out far and wide" and "confusedly." Sometimes, as in this sentence, both aspects are presented in succession, more or less independently of one another. And they are both sometimes contained in a combination of words such as in "monotonous movement," "pale sky," "ships . . . at anchor," "dark fishes," "bare trees," etc. The last sentence, similar to the first, again contains an emphatic succession of both aspects. The "aerial waves," preeminently a moving element, "breaking in silence."

An analysis of the theme can be combined with precise description of the *construction* of the thematics. The place of the metaphor is important for this purpose. As we have seen, in the sentence "the oblong islands looked like great dark fishes come to rest on its surface," the c^d denotes reality, and the c^t can be joined to the person-bound focalizer Emma. "Looked like" automatically raises the question about *who* considers the islands to resemble fish. When we assume that Emma focalizes, an assumption based on the preceding context, it then becomes clear that the contradiction in the image of Rouen is not a contradiction between the vision of the overall external focalizer, who represents realism, and the actor, the internal focalizer, who idealizes reality. *Both* aspects, the euphoric and the dysphoric, must be ascribed to Emma. Both are represented in the c^t "dark (dysphoria) fishes (euphoria) come to rest" which can be attributed to Emma via the verb "looked like."

The difference between the general interpretation of the novel and the meaning of this description gradually becomes evident. Critics often accuse Emma of romanticizing and idealizing life, of failing to see the more banal aspects of reality. It now appears that she does see the banal side, but that she does not wish to be conscious of it. She sees it and simultaneously represses it. The description, which can be attributed to her on the level of focalization and not on the level of narrative, makes this clear. As will later be shown, this small difference has several consequences. So far, we can characterize this description as an intermediate form between the second and the third types, and we can also classify it with the fifth type. At first sight, Rouen is described according to the pattern of the tourist guidebook, but the metaphors introduce elements of type three. The contradiction functions as an implicit metaphor, so that the whole makes a metaphor of Emma's attitude towards reality.

5.4 Style and rhythm

I understand style to be the choices which are made from the medium of language.[50] Rhythm, the linear aspect of style, may be regarded as a more or less regular movement. I introduce this somewhat vague concept here in order to demonstrate that, for the analysis of a descriptive passage, all of the data can, but need not, be used. An alternation between stasis and movement has already been noted in R3. The first half of the description is constructed according to a ternary rhythm in which this alternation is developed. The verbs contribute to this development. The resulting rhythm is equivocal. The alternation is, in fact, a mixture. Compare the verbs in the first three sentences:

1. "It *spread out far and wide beyond the bridges.*"
2. "Behind it *the open country rose* in a monotonous movement."
3. "The whole landscape *looked still* as a picture."

The verbs in the first two sentences express a standstill by means of an active form. In the third sentence, the stasis is absolute. The same is again evident in the following three sentences:

1. "In one corner ships *crowded* at anchor."
2. "The river *curved* round."
3. "The oblong islands looked like great dark fishes *come to rest.*"

The elements of the landscape seem, like Emma, to choose stagnation for themselves. This is suggested by the active verb form. This development is summarized in a comparison in the third sentence of each group. In the second half of the text, we (and Emma) approach the city, and the description consequently becomes livelier and more detailed. Motion now disappears, engulfed in smoke and mist. As has already been pointed out, the excerpt ends with the most mobile element, the clouds, in a state of absolute stillness.

The use of rhythmic information for interpretation is often regarded as

---

50. This definition is formulated by Todorov in Ducrot and Todorov, *Dictionnaire encyclopédique*, 383.

excessive, as an interpretation which merely confirms the one already held by the investigator. This is a real danger. For this reason, I have introduced these data only at this later stage. Rhythm is a difficult concept to grasp. Nevertheless, during the process of reading, rhythm is very penetrating. Everyone has at one time or another been aware of the extent to which rhythm, convincing or placating, can be used for rhetorical purposes. Political speeches, football commentaries, and advertisements all make extensive use of it as a manipulative device.

A special use of rhythmic possibilities consists in allowing the rhythm to coincide with the contents. Rhythm then becomes a sign of the contents, a sign which has meaning through a partial analogy: an icon. The effect of such an icon depends on a number of different factors. But in all cases, this phenomenon attracts attention. In R3, rhythm underlines the development from (illusory) motion to total standstill and stagnation. The iconic character of the description does not contribute to the meaning itself (this was sufficiently expressed in the thematics), but thrusts this meaning upon the reader.

This same phenomenon has another function in the following example from a well-known comic duo:

> They can neither read nor formulate properly in correct sentences the condition in which men are. Because they're too busy being men. Men? I think that they're becoming worse. And what have they accomplished in the last 20,000 years?[51]

The iconic nature of the first sentence is obvious. The sentence which states that men cannot formulate correctly is itself incorrectly formulated. The meaning cannot be said to be thrust upon the reader since it is stated explicitly enough. This sign has another function. The sentence concerns other people, and it is written "in the third person." The speaker identifies himself by formulating the sentence so poorly. He too is evidently a man. And, therefore, this same infelicitous rhythm proves the premise which forms the contents of the sentence. This is representative of Koot and Bie's humor. They identify themselves with the group they ridicule, and this makes their humor universally acceptable. It is evident from this example that the meaning and the function of iconic signs are not always purely redundant. The icon may contain information, not conveyed in the language-bound message, which is essential for a successful interpretation and explains the comic effect of the passage.

5.5 Interpretation

What can we do with the assembled data concerning the descriptive fragment R3? We can now read the description as a narrative text in the

---

51. Koot and Bie, *Calendar 1977*. This typically Dutch humorous calendar contains masterpieces of hardly translatable descriptions.

sense that things *happen* in the description. In addition to the shifting focalization, and the contradictory thematics, there is also a dynamic rhythm which is equivocal in detail (in the first half), and in general (the development to a state of total standstill). "Still" is expressed by means of development and motion. Following the equivocation of the first two sentences, the standstill in the third sentence is indicated by a metaphor, underlined by the presence of the modalizer ("looked like," "like"). The emphasis which is continually placed upon contradiction by various means indicates that this should not be overlooked.

The description is thus a set of *instructions for use.* The fragment must be read as a general metaphor. The c^t of this metaphor is the reality of Rouen; the c^d is Emma's idealistic vision. Both contribute to the image which she sees before her. The absolute standstill with which the text ends predicts the uselessness of Emma's attempts to bring diversity into her life. It predicts death. The instructions for use are concealed. The indications are hidden in metaphors, in indirect motifs, in rhythmic phenomena. The description also remains equivocal because the reader must not discover this predictive power too quickly or with too much certainty. For between (action-oriented) suspense and this form of *over-coding* there is a tense relationship.[52]

5.6 The direct context

The above interpretation is further motivated and justified in the chapter from which the passage is taken. The most important aspect which is manifest here is a phenomenon of frequency.[53] Emma goes to Rouen *every* Thursday. This habit has become an institution in her life. The emphatic and exclusive use of the *imperfect* underlines the fact that the entire scene is exemplary. Flaubert is clearly the predecessor of Proust here. How can someone who has been making this same weekly journey for such a long time be "surprised" by the panorama? This is explained in the sentence "afin de se faire des surprises, elle fermait les yeux" ("to give herself a surprise, she shut her eyes"): by cheating. The sentence which immediately precedes the description emphatically recapitulates the conflict.

The contradiction which we have noted in the description and which is further emphasized in the context, can be found in all three aspects of the narrative message. In the *text*, this contradiction is expressed in words and forms. In the *narrative*, we see that the focalizer cheats. And in the *fabula*, the event—the arrival in the dream city—is absorbed into a routine.

When considering the sequence of events in this chapter, we observe that the journey to Rouen "takes" longer (is presented more extensively) than the return journey. Even more striking is the fact that both the journey

52. For the concept of over-coding, see Eco, *A Theory of Semiotics*, 129–30.
53. See Genette's *Narrative Discourse.*

and the purpose of the journey, the visit with Léon, receive so little attention. The narrative rhythm can be termed realistic when we consider how unimportant a person Léon is for Emma. He represents a desire, as does the city in which he lives. Because Emma is unable to grasp her moments of happiness, these moments are very brief and they are over-shadowed by the routine which engulfs them.

When we examine the various elements of the entire journey, rather than the sequence of events, we become aware of a similarity between the arrival and the departure. This point can be treated very briefly. The final glimpse of the city, a glimpse which is symmetrical with the first, results in a shorter description, in which only aspects of confusion and incomprehension remain ("broad haze," "confused"). The relationship between the description and the direct context often provides information about the interpretation of the description. For example, the farmer's comments in *De aansprekers* were necessary in order to understand the confrontation between the child's view and the adult's; it was necessary to present these words *after* the description and not before it. In the fragment from *Changing Places*, the sequence from the general ("the planes") to the particular ("his own plane") was also motivated by the context. Immediately following his reflection about airplanes, the character boards his own plane.

If we examine description exclusively in relation to context, we shall never be able to attach more than an illustrative (redundant) and global meaning to it. For this reason, it is advisable to begin with the descriptive text itself. However, the interpretation of the description will have to be continually referred back to the context, a process which can be regarded as a form of testing one's interpretation. The context will support the interpretation. This support can take the form of confirmation, motivation, explication, or expansion.

5.7 Integration in the macrostructure

Placing the descriptive fragment back within the text as a whole has another function. The testing procedure is no longer necessary. Not the correctness, but rather the relevance of the analysis must be evident at this level. In other words, the meaning of the description is related to the general interpretation of the narrative text. As a result, the latter can *change*, *be further expanded*, or *be prematurely disclosed*. All three possibilities occur in the case of R3. These possible functions of the narrative description distinguish this type from the encyclopedic or referential-rhetorical descriptions, with their more restricted function. Because of lack of space, I shall present the methodological steps involved only briefly. Here again, the analysis follows two directions. The description has a place within the diegetic development. It is examined in the light of the situation existing at that moment in the fabula. Paradigmatically, the description can be compared with other descriptions from the same class. In the case of R3, a comparison of all descriptions of place can be made. The definition of the class is dependent upon the anticipated results. It would be rather useless to compare all of the descriptions first, and then to compare all the descriptions of place. Here again, a choice must be made. By working from a connection between the described characteristics of places and the state of mind of the focalizing heroine, we can further limit the series. For example, we could choose to examine only those places which Emma views with optimistic expectations. If we should do so, then the descriptions of Yonville, Vaubyessard castle, the dream city to which she will flee with Rodolphe, and Rouen, would constitute one class. In one respect, the first description of Yonville does not belong to this series. The focalizer is not Emma; instead, an anonymous though minimally diegetic pedestrian views the city at the moment that the Bovarys are on their way to Yonville.

An analysis of these descriptions reveals that there are a number of common aspects. There are more analogies, in addition to that based upon Emma as focalizer. All of the places are seen from a distance and from above. The scenes are panoramas. All of the descriptions are general and lacking detail. They have various elements in common, such as trees, water, and mist, which is particularly important thematically. Mist is related to the theme of inaccessible happiness, of confusion, and the change in this motif is striking. It can appear in both a euphoric and a dysphoric sense, without breaking away from the unifying theme. It develops from "mist—smoke—haze—veil" to "brightness." What changes in this series is the mood which is related to the motif. What remains the same is the theme of uncertainty, transitoriness, confusion, which is evident also in the motif of water which, in the sequence "country stream—river—wide ocean," remains connected with the impossibility of the desired journey. Thematic investigations can result in rigidity and reduction if we consider only the similarities between various motifs. A dynamic thematics enables us, by means of similarities, to see differences in their true perspective.

Here too, we have a paradox. According to the banal-realistic point of view, descriptions should be realistic precisely in their difference from one another, because the places described also differ in reality. Any similarities could be explained by their relation to the fictive character. Just the opposite is true. The differences can be related to Emma's wish to see the locations other than as they really are. The similarities indicate an immanent realism. In those instances where Emma continues to make the same mistake by attributing her dissatisfaction to the world around her rather than to her own expectations and passivity, "reality," her world, is unchangeable. This realism is a component of the fiction. It implies the predictability of misfortune, the inherently boring locations, the futility of cheating.

The diegetic structure of the novel contains a series of attempts in which

Emma tries to break through the mediocrity of her existence, attempts which fail. The fabula so formulated also demonstrates the effect of repetition. Repetition works cumulatively. Every failure is more disastrous, more definite than the one before. The character carries all of her previous failures with her.

According to Barthes, one characteristic of the diegetic structure is its predictability. In this case, the link that connects one episode with another, and that predicts the conclusion of each episode, is Emma's lack of insight. This lack of insight must somehow be conveyed to the reader. It is only after Emma's death that this predictability can be communicated by Charles, who misinterprets it: "C'est la faute de la fatalité" ("Fate is to blame"). It is only possible to speak of this fatality *afterwards*. Having chosen the realistic manner of writing, Flaubert cannot discuss fatality earlier in the novel. Furthermore, Flaubert does not wish to interfere so explicitly, and any information conveyed must therefore remain limited to that available to the character. Emma's lack of insight forces the same lack upon the reader.

Because of this situation, description, with all of its apparently innocent referential character, is employed. The meaning, the necessary and inevitable failure of every attempt based on contradiction, is placed in the description and transmitted in a concealed form. In this fashion, description completely alters the meaning of the novel as a whole. The suspense created by the question "How will it end?" disappears. We already know the conclusion. The novel becomes increasingly pessimistic, a phenomenon which occurs with the "fatalité" of the character which is not, as Charles believes, metaphysical, but rather is psychological. The essential conflict is made more profound by the intrinsic function of realism within the novel.

5.8 Maximal integration

For those who wish to do so, it is possible to continue the investigation. The various motifs in the description which have an integrating function can be analyzed elsewhere in the text. This is certainly worthwhile for the motif of *mist*. In addition, less obvious phenomena such as rhythmic characteristics may appear elsewhere in the novel and may then be related back to the description.

Not only is this model integrative for the object, the narrative description, but it is also methodologically integrative since it combines various approaches. The description is treated as a specific, isolatable discourse and yet remains within the context in which it functions. All aspects of the narratological framework have been discussed, including the combination of a simple narrator's text with complex focalization, and the diegetic side of description. Description in the novel is narrative. For this reason, an analysis which is limited to the description itself is not adequate. Yet a descriptive passage remains a description, and, for this reason, an analysis of the novel in which the descriptive fragments are regarded merely as illustrative material is also insufficient.

6. CONCLUDING REMARKS

Description is a type of *text*. It cannot be treated within a plot-oriented narratology. To do so would be circular reasoning. Nor is description an independent type of text, but rather an integrative component of the (usually narrative) text in which it appears. (There are, it is true, autonomous descriptions, but they are not included in this discussion; these descriptions do not cause the problems which have been raised here.) This essay has been concerned with the "marginal," subordinate descriptions in longer texts. None of the existent models proved adequate for the analysis of descriptive fragments. They had to be combined and adjusted. This combination led to the relativization of the opposition metaphor-metonymy. As a result, these two were regarded as the two extreme types of a sliding scale of six types. It is probable that further text analysis will result in an expansion of this taxonomy.

An analysis of the descriptive fragment only is insufficient, and often results in a superficial, overly direct, and unequivocal indication of symbolic meaning. This is avoided in the method suggested here. The relation between description and novel is *dynamic, indirect,* and *polyvalent.* In addition, the structural contribution of description to meaning is often more powerful than at first assumed. The function of a description is certainly not always limited to illustrating the meaning which is already present. Anyone who proceeds from the principle of redundancy will meet with difficulties in such cases as this passage, which appeared in a Dutch newspaper:

> The extremely zealous, kind, intelligent, and honest president Herbert Hoover, who, shortly before the crisis, had promised his people in his inauguration speech in March, 1929 a very prosperous future, remained fanatically devoted, month after month, year after year, to the idea that the crisis would resolve itself, that the American system was prepared for such shocks, and that it would automatically survive.[54]

The same president who is described as admirable by the first words of the sentence appears to be lazy, evil, stupid and corrupt in the rest of the sentence; the description can hardly be considered redundant or illustra-

54. *Trouw/Kwartet*, October 27, 1979. The example may seem provocative to the American reader, for which I apologize. It is, however, too clear a case of this frequent reversion of values in the description/narration cluster to leave out here.

tive. And this is just a simple newspaper sentence. It is possible, by means of descriptions, to criticize with praise and to praise with criticism. Or to transmit other, less obviously contradictory values.

I have omitted one important aspect of description. This is the status of the object to which the text refers, the referent. I have avoided two problems by my omission. The first is the distinction between the deictic and the anaphoric function. Descriptions refer to something which is located elsewhere, whether or not it "exists." This is their deictic function. Descriptions also refer to other elements of the text, and so contribute to textual cohesiveness. This is their anaphoric function. Both functions are indexical.

The second problem is the problem of fictionality. I have avoided this issue because it raises problems which are too numerous to discuss in one article. Furthermore, fictionality as a general problem is not specific to description. It is, nevertheless, desirable that descriptions be included in any such investigations, especially because the world which is evoked in a fictional text is constructed precisely in the descriptive passages. It is here that the illusion of reality is created.

The problem of fictionality concerns more than the description of that which does not exist. Whenever we must express in language something which does not exist in language, we face the problem which confronted Columbus. He had to make the unfamiliar familiar, to describe the exotic, the unreal, and to do so with such flair that the King of Spain would be willing to invest gold in the unknown. To evoke the unknown by means of the real, by comparisons as well as by differentiations, in such a way that the unknown becomes believable and the fictive becomes real: that is the task of the describer. But that is also a vicious circle, as is shown in Robbe-Grillet's "Le mannequin":

> A jug handle has, more or less, the shape of an ear, or rather of its rim; but it would be an ill-formed ear, overly round and lobeless, which would therefore have the shape of a "jug handle."[55]

55. Robbe-Grillet, *Instantanés*, 10. Translated by Robert Corum. The French reads: "L'anse a, si l'on veut, la forme d'une oreille, ou plutôt de l'ourlet extérieur d'une oreille; mais ce serait une oreille mal faite, trop arrondie et sans lobe, qui aurait ainsi la forme d'une 'anse de pot.'"

_ ■ 6 ■

Narrative Subjectivity

1. ANALYSIS AND RULES

1.1 The analytic attitude and the narrative text

"The art of analysis must be to suspend the certainties of the subject until the last illusions of certainty consume themselves," Lacan has said. We can readily hear in this statement an echo of Habermas, hoping for critical reflection to undermine the "obviousness" of ideology.[1] We will try to adopt this double position.

Greatly simplified, we can summarize the analytic method as follows. What is perceptible, namely the structures of representation put to use, is first analyzed into elements. Next these elements are placed in relationship to each other. The new elements thus formed, and the new relationships between them, are located at a different level. In the analytic dialogue nothing is either confirmed or contradicted. This corresponds, in literary analysis, to withholding hasty, immediate, or pre-analytic interpretations. Instead, a process of translation occurs: what is said/written is rendered in a modified form. These procedures include filling in, completing, establishing relationships, looking for parallels, contradictions, or mistakes.

In his description of psychoanalysis, Lacan comes amazingly close to a narratological formulation:

> Its means are those of speech in so far as they confer meaning on the functions of the individual; its domain is that of concrete discourse, considered as a field of transindividual reality of the subject; its operations are those of the story in so far as it constitutes the emergence of the truth within the real.[2]

1. See above, Chapter 1, especially (Sect. 3.2.).
2. Lacan, *Ecrits*, 257.

While acknowledging the differences which exist between psychoanalysis and literary criticism, it is possible to substitute for "speech" the narrative *text* as a linguistic mode possessing its own speakers and narratees; for "concrete discourse" the narrative level of the *story*, as modalizer, focalizer and bearer of ideologies ("the field of transindividual reality"); and for "story" the narratological *fabula*, which is the imaginary form given to "what happened" ("the emergence of the truth within the real," admittedly an enigmatic formulation but why not? . . .). The mirror stage, the turning point in the child's evolution and the beginning of the symbolic order, produces in the child an initial awareness of itself: in its image. The image is a symbol, in that it is *different* from the object it represents. As a representation, it can only *resemble* the modeled subject, never coincide with it: difference and *différance*, implying spatial and temporal displacements, constitute precisely the entry into the symbolic order. These, too, are characteristics of narration.

Spatial and temporal displacements therefore make it possible to carry out an analysis. By presupposing that the literary text is marked by the unconscious (which *is* the discourse of the Other), we can define the textual unconscious as that which is systematically eliminated from the narration and which can be interpolated into the gaps in the narration (which by definition remains incomplete). To interpret "psychoanalytically" would then mean to fill in the gaps that the text signals by its distortions, its incoherencies, and its violations of the rules of the implied systems; gaps on which we confer a meaning that explains their status as gaps. For the narrative text is not only an assertion. Like the text of analysis, it is also a product of, as well as an occasion for, transference. The transference is the competition between the dramatic and the narrative form. There the analytic subject seeks to play; to repeat the past, rather than to recount it. In this way, the subject of analysis privileges an open subjectivity rather than a deceptive objectification of the narration, a "direct" presentation rather than a past representation, and a dialogue rather than a narrative monologue. It is in light of this competition that we can view, for example, dialogues in reported speech in the narrative text (I will return to this later).

Hence the narrative text is an affirmation to the extent (and only to the extent) that is formulated in the indicative mood. But since negation also is affirmation, complexity is present from the outset. The narrative text is also an objectification; it is *about* something, someone, that does not participate in the locution. So there are already very unequal positions to be alloted. At the same time, it is an identification: the subject is formed here. It is a provocation, to the extent that it demands a reaction. This feature necessitates the study of the narratee, to be distinguished from real readers, but then to be compared with them. The narrative text is an apologia: it anticipates a reaction to which it already responds. The presuppositions which are inscribed within the text are manifestations of it. It is a frustration, for language is, by definition, insufficient, and representation imperfect. And since immediate expression is no more possible than access to the image of the self in the mirror, it is also alienation.[3]

1.2 Access to the public domain

Psychoanalysis shares with literature the fact that it is a practice of speech. Both are commonly thought to abstain from action. But speech *is* an action. It is an action which is characterized first and foremost by "publication": it goes public. What else is it? In both analysis and literary practice, the basic actions are *telling* and *listening*. To tell is to describe a proposition and an attitude. The attitude may be described explicitly in metanarrative utterances. It may also be implied. In this instance, it is possible to infer the attitude from the content. The attitude may vary considerably: affirming, asking, demanding, approving, ordering, and promising are but a few examples. The attitude may also be different according to either the content or the interlocutor. As a consequence, the effect, which is already in itself variable, may be either voluntary or involuntary (signal versus symptom, cf. Peirce and Freud). The choice of form of discourse adds further to these possible variations.

To listen is, among many other things, to examine the propositions and the selection that they represent—the attitude adopted, the form chosen; it is *also* to react. For the reader, whether "critical" or not, cannot avoid selecting any more than the analyst can. In every literary process, therefore, there is a double selection. The critic cannot be satisfied with examining a single selection; the very fact that one reads implies a second. Therefore, the interaction, the dialectical movement, is established right away. To examine the effects of a text is always also to examine oneself as interlocutor. This is precisely what critical scholarship must be—self-criticism.

The interlocutor also listens for the lack, for what is denied or omitted in the form itself; for a rigorously affirmative discourse can hide an affective lack. The interlocutor also listens for repetitions. They serve a purpose, whether to accentuate the recurrent content or, on the contrary, to hide some isolated detail through displacement. By reestablishing the censured content, as in the case of a dream, the critic completes the image, reverses the displacements, and analyzes the condensations. A prohibition imposed on the analyst applies *a fortiori* to the critic: one must not issue interpretations and judgments at the outset. Critic and analyst must hold back in order to become good listeners.

The excellent book by Mooij has a significant title: *Psychoanalysis and*

---

3. I am borrowing this characteristic of the narrative text from Mooij, *Taal en Verlangen*.

Rules.[4] The central place of rules in all symbolic practice is generally well recognized, but less well analyzed. The importance of rules in the public domain stems from the fact that they are constitutive, while at the same time differential or distinctive, guidelines. In contrast to natural or authoritarian laws, the rules that regulate interpretation are, in principle, open to debate. They demand voluntary acceptance based on the awareness that without them it is impossible to be understood. Rules differentiate and symbolize: they separate one activity from another by naming it. Likewise in literature, the conventions of genre enable a text to be placed under a category, to be understood precisely by the exclusion of other genres. The conventions name the chosen genre symbolically, which, in turn, permits deviation in relation to this genre. These rules also distinguish the subject who follows the rule from the object regulated, the symbolizing subject from the object symbolized, even if the latter coincides with the former. It is the absence of this type of rule which no doubt constitutes the unknowable that is the unconscious. It is unknowable precisely to the extent that its terms exist only in a differential relationship, in such a way that it constitutes a closed system. What is lacking in the primary process of the unconscious is the *subject*, defined as agency, capable of wanting, desiring, projecting, and acting. The rules of the public domain come to constitute this subject by offering it the possibility of conforming to them. And so, paradoxically, the rules free the subject from the apparent objectivity of things in the world, which, though it seems reassuring, renders the things inescapable. What appeared to be the eternal state of the world turns out to be constituted by rules which are contingent. This is why psychoanalysis is necessarily a critical theory.

1.3 The interpretation of relationships by rules

As we have seen, the relationships between actions and events are not only external and arbitrary, but internal as well. The latter constitute narration in literature. They are intentional and can, accordingly, be linked together to form a fabula. Between action and intention, the internal relationship refers to a subject which, in turn, refers to rules and to a language (which is also based upon rules). In order for there to be an action, the object which is the content of the intention must necessarily exist, and exist *for* the subject. However, the elementary process of the unconscious discloses only pseudo-actions: actions which do not refer to rules. Interpretation consists in linking these "actions" to an intention, and hence to a subject capable of making them real in retrospect; and to rules, to a public domain (the Other). In order to understand this, we must look more closely at the nature of internal relationships.

4. *Psychoanalyse en regels.*

Internal relationships are either of reference, of expression, or of obligation. The relations of reference lead to the two elements being mutually constituted, as in *Gestalt* psychology, where figure and ground are constituted in relation to each other.[5] In the relationships of expression both elements are mutually implied: the one does not exist apart from the other. Thus, the realization cannot exist without the desire, nor the action without the intention, nor the utterance without the enunciation. The relationships of obligation are expressed in speech-acts such as a promise, which, as we know, obligates.[6] Unlike external relationships, internal relationships differentiate themselves by their deontological status, which determines to what extent they are appropriate, suitable. The deontological status has no ethical value. The internal relationships—and this makes them very relevant for our purposes—are linked so as to form chains: a loss, which is a situation, implies a regret, which belongs to the order of emotions, bringing on tears, which are of the expressive order, forcing the subject to blow its nose, which is an action, etc.[7] They are also polyvalent, so that several possibilities can exist without their becoming arbitrary (like the external relationships). The interpretation of a text based on rules (of genre, of selected discursive form, of language) consists in supplying it with a context over against which it stands out in relief like the figure in a *Gestalt*. It is in this way that historical and individual variations may be understood in their relationship with the social.

2. CRITIQUE OF CLASSICAL NARRATOLOGY

2.1 Genette's theory

Expounded in *Narrative Discourse*, Genette's narratological theory, which has served for some time now as a manual for literary critics, has theoretical weaknesses which hinder its practical effectiveness. Having failed to reflect upon these foundational problems regarding the status of narrative, Genette has been incapable of reconsidering his own foundations.[8] I pause to examine this theory as an instance of theory which is non-critical in its very construction. It is constructed according to the model of traditional linguistics (the *Littré* grammar). However, Genette carefully keeps his distance from this model. He presents it as a heuristic metaphor and no more—convenient but not compelling. But he does not take up any

5. Reinhart, "Point of View in Language," explains this principle for narrative texts.
6. "Juridically," in the law of language only; see Ducrot, "Structuralisme"; cf. Felman, *Le scandal du corps parlant*.
7. Mooij, *Psychoanalyse en regels*, 90.
8. [Editor's note] In this section, there is a certain amount of repetition of Chapter 4, Part 1. This could not be avoided without disrupting the sequence of the present chapter. Between the original publications of the two chapters occurred what Bal takes to be Genette's failure (in "Discussion" and *Nouveau Discours*) to answer his critics.

alternative foundational models. It is this metaphorically-invoked model which inspires his basic categories: tense, mood, and voice. We note the striking absence of the subject in this initial division.

In order to discern the place accorded the subject by Genette, the chapters devoted to "Mood" and "Voice" better reward close attention than the chapters on "Tense."[9] The category of mood is structured on the model of the definition given by *Littré* of verbal aspect:

> Name given to the different forms of the verb that are used to *affirm more or less* the thing in question, and to express . . . the *different points of view*, with respect to which one considers the existence or the action.

Without revisiting in detail my criticism of the two chapters in question,[10] to which Genette really has not responded, the deficiencies of this definition nonetheless warrant our pausing for a moment. In effect, it juxtaposes two different verbs: *to affirm*, a declarative verb which indicates a discursive mode, and *to consider*, a verb of perception and interpretation, which in and of itself is as ambiguous as the expression "point of view." In other words, the distinguishing criterion in the first part of the sentence is quantitative ("more or less"), in the second, qualitative ("different"). The basic definition is doubly incoherent, and Genette's treatment suffers from this.[11]

The concept of focalization, which is central to and innovative in Genette's narratology, is never defined in his book. It is offered as a synonym for vision, field,[12] and point of view. These terms, however, are not synonymous. Vision has to do with the subject who sees; field, with the object; while point of view can signify both subject and object: compare the expressions "from my point of view" and "that is a good point of view." The original ambiguity of the concept inevitably returns in the typology of focalizations Genette then establishes. This typology has three terms: non-focalized narrative, narrative with internal focalization, and narrative with external focalization. The difference between the first two types lies in "who sees": in the first the subject sees "everything"; in the second the subject sees only what the character sees. The difference between second and third types has to do with the subjective position itself. In the second the "focalized character" sees, in the third it is seen, it is not the subject but the object of the vision. The following example, already quoted, is revealing:

> External focalization *with respect to* one character could sometimes just as well be defined as internal focalization *on* another: external focalization on Phileas

9. See *Lethal Love*, 91–95.
10. See Chapter 4, sect. 1.2.1–1.3.2.
11. The first part of Genette's treatment, "Distance," will not occupy our attention here. Cf. above, Chapter 4, sect. 1.3.1 (a).
12. In the sense used by Blin, *Stendahl*.

> Fogg is just as well internal focalization *on* Passepartout dumbfounded by his new master, and the *only reason* for being satisfied with the first term is Phileas' status as *hero*, which *restricts* Passepartout to the role of witness.[13]

Genette appears either to admit the impotence of his theory, its inability to interpret the narrative structure of the description of Phileas, or to suggest that the passage is narratively ambiguous. I don't think that either idea is correct. The problem is that the real problem is not indicated, namely, the interchange of functions. The casual use of prepositions (with respect to, on) masks the confusion between subject and object, which appears to me to be obvious. In spite of the criticism which I have offered of this confusion, Genette repeats it: "In internal focalization, the focus coincides with a character who then becomes the 'subject' of all the perceptions"; and further on, taking up the disputed example that I cite here, he simply repeats the confusion: "*As regards our information about Phileas*, both parts are *equivalent*" (Genette's italics).[14]

One does not respond to criticism by repeating words in italics; "our information about Phileas" is still quite at odds with "the 'subject' of all the perceptions." A bit further on Genette even speaks explicitly of Phileas as "*'object' of the narrative*."[15] I can only deduce from this a blindness to the question of the subject, and therefore to the very problematic which preoccupies literary criticism today. Genette appears to be indifferent to the fact that he is contributing to the gulf between "formal" criticism and socially relevant criticism, a gulf which I seek to bridge through the present study. It would be unfair to charge him with failure in an attempt he never intended to make. But what is more unsettling is that he does not even satisfy the criteria of his own methodology. By admitting that both analyses are equally possible, Genette admits to the impotence of his theory. It simply remains vague, and this weakness is very serious for the critic who wishes to find in narratology the tools for a sharper analysis. Moreover, by appealing to the notion of *hero*, Genette makes use of a criterion which is *foreign* to the problem in question. This theoretical error is of the first order,[16] especially from his own structuralist point of view. Finally, by appealing to the heroic status of the character, Genette does nothing more than paraphrase what is said in plain language in Verne's text, whose ideology he is satisfied merely to repeat. The concept which we have seen to be vague and theoretically insufficient is therefore *uncritical* as well. This problem crops up again in the relationships between the elements of the theory.

13. Genette, *Narrative Discourse*, 191–92 (my italics). For the following, cf. the discussion of the same passage in Chapter 4, sect. 1.3.1 (b), especially note 28.
14. The quotations are from *Nouveau Discours*, 49 and 50 respectively.
15. Genette, *Nouveau Discours*, 50.
16. See Ducrot, "Structuralism."

In the chapter on "Voice,"[17] the category of subject, without being explicitly analyzed, is implicated willy-nilly in two distinctions. The first operates between the extradiegetic and intradiegetic narrators, and concerns the different possible levels. The question becomes a relevant one as soon as an embedding of discourse is spotted. The second distinguishes between heterodiegetic and homodiegetic narrators, and concerns the non-coincidence or coincidence of the speaking subject with the acting subject. The concepts being dealt with here are based upon two distinct hierarchies: the one is inherent in narration, while the other is optional. The second, moreover, necessarily implies the first. Even if there is the tendency on occasion to confuse the two hierarchies, a tendency owing, no doubt, to the implicit character of the distinctions, Genette's reasoning here is coherent. What constitutes the problem, however, is that the structures of the two chapters are very different. By separating "Mood" and "Voice," Genette has provided us with the possibility of analyzing the problem, hitherto obliterated, of the confusion between "the one who speaks" and "the one who sees." But he carries this separation too far, and thus makes another mistake. By reserving a place for the subject in only one of the two categories, he retains the very polished image of a language which forms a *whole*, where the explicit (the voice) conceals the implicit (the vision transmitted) in a non-problematic way. Thus he takes the narrative text at its word; he believes what the words say. This explains why his entire theory, as well as being unsystematic and vague, can claim no properly critical effectiveness. By repeating Verne's ideology, which desires the master to be hero and the servant to be the impotent witness, Genette's theory does not go beyond the purely paraphrastic level. What it lacks is an analysis of the subject, and of the whole network of circulation of meaning and of responsibilities that it entails.

2.2 The role of typologies

It remains for us to say a word about the use that Genette makes—along with other classical narratologists[18]—of typology. Between the general model and the sentence-by-sentence analysis—the first being too superficial and the second ineffective—typologies, by enabling quick characterizations, appear to occupy a happy middle ground. But it is not so. Model, typology, and concepts of analysis form a series whose coherence is not obvious and must be questioned.

Before there is a model there must be a theory. The latter is indispensable for delimiting the object. In its simplest form, the theory consists of a definition of the object (for example, a narrative text), which will

17. See my discussion in Chapter 4, sect. 1.3.2.
18. One exception is the theory of discursive interference; see Doležel, *Narrative Modes.*

account for the nature of the object (for example, an object in a semiotic communication), the situation in which it circulates, if circulating plays a part in its nature, etc. This theory generates a model, that is, an abstraction which accounts for features of the object defined by the theory. In other words, the function of the model lies in illuminating their interrelationships. Without the model, the theory cannot connect to the object, and without the theory, the model cannot be properly constructed. Without a relationship to the nature of the object, the model would be arbitrary. In turn, the model generates operational concepts. These enable us to describe, to analyze, the object in its specific cases (each particular text). Based on the same concepts that have been systematically derived, these analyses render the different occurrences of the object comparable. Only thus is theory—in the broad sense, comprised of definitional theory, models, and operational concepts—as *generalizing* and *systematic* as it is *specifying* and *analytic*. It responds to (methodo-)logical demands which guarantee its intersubjectivity and therefore its persuasiveness, and it responds to critical demands. The systematic relations between theory, model, concepts, and analyses provide the scope required of criticism; on the other hand, critical reflection is protected from wild, arbitrary speculation by the movement back and forth, equally systematic, between the general and the particular. In this sense, method brings us back to the question with which we began (how to give an account of the interaction between the social and the individual), and to the principal characteristic of literature (which, while highly individual, takes up collective concerns, is expressed in intersubjective structures that follow general rules, etc.)

Neither Genette's nor other existing typologies—such as those of Stanzel, Friedman, Booth, Pouillon[19]—are constructed along these lines. They suffer from this lack, and prove inapplicable. The possibilities that they offer are either too limited (most often three, cf. Stanzel) or they overlap (Booth). The distinguishing criteria are vague (Genette), not comparable (Genette, Booth), or ambiguous (Friedman). By contrast, the authors who are dissatisfied with the available typologies and have made an effort to refine them,[20] end up by constructing charts that are so burdensome that their application can't even be imagined. One recent book[21] provides us with an example—virtually a caricature—presenting a typology whose criteria take nine pages to schematize! The author will have to pardon me for refusing to apply the whole thing (needless to say, the far-fetched criteria partially overlap), in order to analyze the smallest sentence: he doesn't even do so himself. And for good reason: the criterion of *simplicity*, as basic for intersubjectivity as for theoretical rigor, fortunately can't be

19. Stanzel, *Typische Formen*; Friedman, "Point of View in Fiction"; Booth, *Rhetoric of Fiction*; Pouillon, *Temps et roman*.
20. Petersen, "Kategorien des Erzählens."
21. Lintvelt, *Typologie narrative*.

gotten around. Not to mention the criterion which is fundamental for any theory, for critical theory *a fortiori*, namely that of *relevance*.

3. ELEMENTS OF A CRITICAL NARRATOLOGY

All these thoughts, a bit long but necessary, have as their object to prepare the ground for a theory which some might otherwise find contradictory: rigorous enough for the purpose of intersubjectivity, and at the same time normative enough for the purpose of criticism.

3.1 Basic model

The theory that I am proposing is based on that presented in Chapter 4; I will take up only the basic elements here. The definition which lies at its core, and governs the distinction sketched above, is as follows: A narrative text is a linguistic text, hierarchically organized, in which a subject recounts a story, that is, the vision, focalized by a subject, of a fabula. Several elements of this definition must be defined; I refer to my *Narratology* for these definitions.[22] The key terms are *text*, *story*, and *fabula*, which describe the three constitutive levels of the text; and *subject*, which entails an *object* as its necessary complement. With the help of the concept of *level*, derived from a hierarchical conception of linguistics, it is possible to construct the model of this theory.

And what of the classificatory typology? *After* the construction of the theory, model, and concepts, and only then, will it prove possible to construct a typology. This may be done along either deductive or inductive lines. Inductively, a typology may be derived from a large number of particular analyses, and will necessarily be limited by the historical status of the corpus. Deductively, the procedure consists of calculating the possible combinations, beginning from the model and concepts, by accounting, of course, for internal and non-reversible relationships between the two. This has a predictive power. The "empty" cases, possible combinations which do not in fact occur, prove useful rather than embarrassing, justifying themselves by serving as a control mechanism for the model. In other words, they provide a point of departure for causal explanation and criticism (why these, rather than those?). Inductive and deductive procedures may be combined.[23]

3.2 The notion of subject

(a) *The definition of "subject."* The model just described is characterized by the clear place it reserves for the subject, and it is this notion which we must now study in greater detail. For quite some time, the concept of the

22. *Narratology*, 5, 26–27.
23. The model is summarized in Chapter 4, sect. 2.1, Figure 1. Cf. the discussion there.

subject as an individual human being, forming a whole and consciously attributing meaning to objects, has no longer been credible. It has been replaced by a conception of the subject as a position, a place where different systems intersect. One of those systems is language. In a certain sense, the discourses which language produces are "common places."[24] Now the instability of the subject is represented in a particularly convincing fashion in the Common Place of the French language, known as the *Petit Robert*.[25] There "Subject" takes up an entire column. It consists of four groups of definitions. It is significant that the first definition in the series stresses the dependent condition of the subject, "who is in the condition of being dependent on a higher authority" (the Father? God?), and "submitted to a necessity, a law" (the Law-of-the-Father?). The second group deals with the semantic sense of the word: "matter, point, question, theme," and other synonyms. Then comes the logical or syntactic definition: "Term considered to be the source of an utterance . . . ." Only the fourth group deals with the individual human being, without, however, being exaggeratedly humanistic. It begins with "To be an individual, a person considered as the medium of action, of influence." This group seems to be inspired by Freud's dictum, "Man is not master in his own house," for it goes on to include passive and dependent subjects, such as persons who are subject to examination, or worse, patients in the medical sense, guinea-pigs and test objects, finishing up with the more or less idealist Kantian definition: "Thinking being, considered as the seat of knowing." I say "more or less" because, if the human subject is nothing more than the *seat* of knowledge, his seat is not a throne but a humble place—as in post-Saussurian theories.[26]

The different conceptions of the subject, as we have uncovered them in the dictionary, in no way justify a close link between the subject and the individual human being. In the context which occupies us here, it is more useful to try to define the subject as a semiotic subject. If the French language (and English is not very different) contains a word at once so crucial and so ambiguous, we need to analyze it. In conformity with the methodological guidelines sketched above, it is important both to construct a precise definition and to preserve the notion's complexity.

The first group of definitions (Subject 1) evokes the fact of dependency upon authorities or law. The fourth (Subject 4) is the seat of knowledge. The subject of the text (Subject 2) is the briefest summary one can hold on to after the action of the textual subjects has reached its end. The "theme" is close to being naturalized into myth, for it is the product of varied and intersecting activities of diverse narrative subjects. Since Subject 3, the source of the utterance or, we may say, of the narrative sequence, is often

24. See Valesio, *Novantiqua.*
25. The *Petit Robert* is a standard French dictionary.
26. Belsey, *Critical Practice.*

also the semantic center, it can easily become the determinant of Subject 2. Let us return to Subject 4. We have already noted in this group the idea of "seat" (*siège*). If we take this word literally, namely in its local sense, we notice that the same group contains "individual, a person considered as the medium of action, of influence." The juxtaposition of "action" and "influence" as predicates of "medium" is relevant here. It indicates that both sides of the semiotic process must be taken into consideration. There are subjects on both sides: action on the side of the sender, influence on the side of the receiver. In both cases, "medium" recalls "seat," a place where systems intersect.

Analyzed in this way, the word "subject," as used in common parlance, appears to be a defence and an illustration of post-Saussurianism. The pertinent features to be kept in mind may be summarized as follows:

1. submitted to laws
2. semantic center
3. point of departure
4. medium of an action or an influence

It is now possible to formulate a definition which, analytic as it is, will enable us to account for the way we project in language, in semiotic structures, our feelings about our own subjectivity. We find the elements of this analysis in the excellent entry in the dictionary of Greimas and Courtés.[27] The distinction between "pragmatic subjects" and "cognitive subjects" matches that between actor and focalizer. The latter pair is defined as a particular category of actants that the enunciator delegates and often installs in the pragmatic discourse, a definition which justifies, if need be, the distinction between factors which have no independent ontological existence. In the entry in question, nothing is said of the subject-object, about which *Robert* goes on at such great length. It is true that the subject's "object-ness" and dependency may be subsumed under the semantic level (thematic center); nonetheless, the absence of any mention of this aspect appears to me to reveal the "optimism" (or should I say "positivism"?) of scholarly discourse. At the same time, the semantic level is dominant, even to the point of exclusiveness, in Greimasian semiotics. Powerful as the Greimasian tools may be, they have no properly critical capacity. This flaw is attributable, in my view, to this exclusion of the subjectal positions and roles as *sources*—and, in the communicative process, as *effects*—of signification.

A definition which would integrate all the aspects adopted into ordinary language, without contradicting scholarly discourse, would consider the subject as *the medium of semiotic actions*, and could therefore be stated as follows: the source of its pragmatic dimension and the center of its semantic

27. Greimas and Courtés, *Semiotics and Language*, 319–21 ("Subject").

dimension, which combines, produces, transmits, and retains—and represses—certain meanings, in accordance with the rules of the systems in which it functions. There is semiotic action at different levels. As soon as a verb is used to describe what happens in semiosis, this verb can be attributed to a subject. Ordinarily, we summarize our description of semiosis as follows: a complex body of semiotic events which it is possible to analyze in terms of its elements. The goal of such an analysis is to account for what takes place in the semiotic process in the most subtle way possible. Its first step will be to analyze the different subjects under the generic name of "author." The analysis proposed above, which distinguishes between narrator, focalizer, and actor, as the basis of the model, is only a very rough beginning. Before we can go any further, however, we must situate this analysis in relation to the phenomenon of *embedding*, to which it is linked.

(b) *Narrative situations.* For the set of narrative subjects which are functioning at a particular moment in a text, I reserve the term *narrative situation* (NS). In every narrative situation a first narrator (N1) necessarily has at the same time the function of first focalizer (N1F1). From this basic situation two forms of embedding are possible:

NS N1F1[N2F2], complete embedding of reported discourse
NS N1F1[F2], embedding of the focalization only

These two basic types of embedding can be expanded, enabling us to account for complex embedding, which is in principle unlimited. Some examples taken from *Wuthering Heights*,[28] a novel replete with embedding, will illustrate the possibilities.

(i) *Simple embedding*:
"Before I came to live here, she commenced, waiting no further invitation to her story." Lockwood tells that Ellen Dean tells . . . : this is the basic narrative situation of this novel. Simple embedding, NS N1F1[N2F2], where N1F1 = Lockwood and N2F2 = Ellen Dean.

(ii) *Complex embedding with focalization*:
"This time, I remembered I was lying in the oak closet, and I heard distinctly the gusty wind, and the driving of the snow." Lockwood tells that Lockwood remembered the evening that Lockwood heard in his dream from which he had just awakened. . . . Complex embedding for the focalization only: NS N1F1[F2[F3]], where N1F1 = Lockwood writing in his journal, F2 = Lockwood the previous day, just after his awakening, and F3 = Lockwood in his dream.

(iii) *Complex embedding with mixed focalization*:
"He evidently wished no repetition of my intrusion." Lockwood tells

28. Brontë, *Wuthering Heights*. The four examples following are from pages 76, 66, 50, and 66, respectively.

that Lockwood sees ("evidently") that Heathcliff wishes ("wished"): NS N1F1[F2[F3]], where N1F1 = Lockwood writing in his journal, F2 = Lockwood interpreting the expression on Heathcliff's face, and F3 = Heathcliff wishing inside that Lockwood not repeat his visit.

(iv) *Simple embedding with mixed narration giving way to complex embedding with mixed focalization*:

"'Thou art the man!' cried Jabes, after a solemn pause, leaning over his cushion." Lockwood tells that Lockwood remembered the evening that Lockwood saw and heard in his dream that Jabes told that Jabes saw Lockwood. (The citation is part of a dream.) NS N1F1[F2[F3[N2F4]]], where N1F1 = Lockwood writing in his journal, F2 = Lockwood awakened from the dream, F3 = Lockwood in his dream, N2F4 = Jabes, a doubly fictional actor in the dream.

These examples show the simplicity and exhaustiveness of the notation system. Right away we see the gap between the embedding of the focalizer and the less complex one of the narrator. One can easily find counter-examples, where the embedding is primarily narrative. This situation being the classic one (cf. *The Thousand and One Nights*), I have deemed it more interesting to pause over the asymmetrical case which at the same time illustrates the relevance of the basic distinction. Without even linking these examples to the problems of the relationship between representation and effect, it is obvious that such structures are relevant to those questions. In order to press the analysis further, however, the various aspects of the notion of subject must be made operational.

3.3 Model of subjectivity

According to the analytic definition, the subject is implicated in diverse features of narrative semiosis. It is as much *source* (of the action) as *start* (of the process) and *center* (in its position). It can be represented in its abstract form as follows:

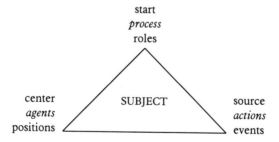

These features of the subject are to be juxtaposed to the features of narrative communication already introduced, which I now represent in the form of a triangle:

From these two analyses it is possible at last to define the different aspects of narrative subjectivity:

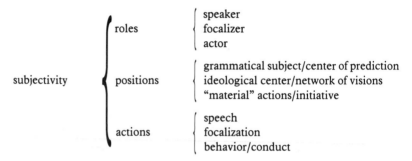

The thesis which much of my work is devoted to illustrating is the following. To manipulate these aspects is to manipulate the subjectivity of a text, and so possibly to blur the sources of signification, the themes and the effects. The ambiguities which can result from this influence the reader. Therein lies the critical relevance of such an analysis. I am happy to hold on to the term *subjectivity*, though *subjectal network* would have avoided any misunderstanding. However, I would not like, by choosing the latter, to abandon the former handy and eloquent term to the field of psychology, which would then maintain a monopoly over its circulation, so that from then on it could not be emancipated from a pre-discursive humanism. The "subjectal network" of a text is indeed its subjectivity; a subjectivity of the text to which other texts—metatexts—react by constructing another subjectivity around the "same" story.

On the basis of this analysis of subjectivity, we can formulate the questions to be posed to the text and its rewritings. Without going so far as to systematize them, I will give in the remainder of this chapter some examples of possible questions. They will be derived initially from the first term in each triad, that is, from the linguistic level. The results will serve as material for interpreting the relationships between this first term and the other two.

(a) *Roles.* This first group of questions deals with research into the subjects responsible for textual meaning. To begin with, they are simply *named*, enumerated.

(i) *Speakers.* The first speaker may remain implicit, or not. If it does, it can serve as a point of reference, of authority. It is this implicit character, for example, which enables us to say that God wrote the Bible. By being named, the speaker opens itself up, on the other hand, to analysis, to criticism. The speaker assumes responsibility for what it says.

With regard to the speaker, the question must be taken up of the discursive model to be adopted. This model will not be unrelated to the current model of power.[29] An initial distinction is to be made between dialogue and narration. Dialogue engages the speaker vis-à-vis its interlocutor. In principle the roles are interchangeable. Narration,[30] on the other hand, brackets the object. In the great majority of narrative texts, the primary level is dominated by narration, and the levels of embedded speech are frequently dialogical. However, we should examine this more closely.

Whence the question: Are dialogues truly dialogic or not? Instances of pseudo-dialogue are numerous. The formal model adopted is only partially actualized. In 2 Samuel 11, a pseudo-dialogue of this sort takes place between David and Uriah. Uriah takes the dialogical model literally, and thinks he can respond from his own point of view. But nothing of the kind: the offer was an order, and the king wanted only *to say what was going to happen*, as in a narration.[31] In order to analyze passages such as this, we must therefore question the relationships between speakers.

Whence a fourth question: What linguistic moods are used? The affirmative, imperative and interrogative moods possess a determinate linguistic structure, but this is not always used in a correct way, that is, in the way assumed by the pact between the users of the language. In the case of affirmation, it is possible that the speaker, far from reporting, ends up fooling, hiding, denying, or wrongly simplifying.[32] The analysis consists in confronting the speaker's claim with what actually happens. The imperative poses an analogous problem. Does the one giving the order have authority to do so? What reaction does the order produce? Under the form of a question, the speaker can issue what is really an order. Questions assume a distribution of knowledge: the one who asks the question does not have knowledge, whereas the interlocutor is supposed to know. If this is not the case, the question can be an order (Are you finished? = Hurry up!) A question to which an answer is impossible, superfluous, or undesirable functions as an exercise of power. When David asks Uriah how his army is doing, he is not expecting any information from him, but is looking to convince Uriah of his kind intentions (which they precisely are not) through the repeated use of the word *shālōm* (peace).

29. Kress and Hodge, *Language as Ideology.*
30. In the sense in which Benveniste, *Problèmes*, employs the term "histoire."
31. For the following, see Bal, *Lethal Love*, Chapter 1, which, in the original publication in *Femmes imaginaires*, immediately preceded the present chapter.
32. Kress and Hodge, *Language and Ideology*, 85–102.

(ii) *Focalizers.* In relation to speakers, focalizers can be either assimilated or displaced. As the speaker is the subject of the voice, so is the focalizer the subject of the vision. In many instances the primary focalizer can incorporate the view of another in an imperceptible way, while disclaiming responsibility for this view. This is what we have in the case of irony, for example. The question, "Who sees?," raised by Genette, therefore has great relevance. Similarly, the negative question can be relevant. Who is the character whose vision is never given? In 2 Samuel 11, for example, Bathsheba's perspective is not represented. It is systematically eliminated. This negative fact is a very clear sign.[33]

(iii) *Actors.* The primary question in this arena—"Who acts?"—is less basic than it appears. For, as we know, an action presupposes an intention. It can happen that an actor is but the one who carries out another's projects. It is clear that the questions to be posed concern power-relations. To what extent is the actor free to act? (For example, Uriah is not free to act.) Did he himself focalize his action? By unknowingly transmitting his own death sentence, Uriah is but the instrument for the actor David: since he does not have rights to the role of focalizer, he cannot assume an intention. In the same text, Joab presents an identical case. He is the focalizer of David's decision (he *does* read the letter), and he is therefore more responsible than Uriah. But he is not aware of the action to which the letter is linked by an internal relation, namely adultery. Quite characteristically, his role is that of one who is partly responsible. To the extent that he has the possibility of having an intention, he cannot exculpate himself with *Befehl ist Befehl* ("an order is an order"). But Joab's is only a partial and derived intention, limited to his obedience to the king and to the act of killing *on command*, whereas David's intention, in his capacity as embedding focalizer, encompasses the whole domain of this series of actions which constitutes Uriah's *murder.*

(b) *Positions.* The set of questions regarding positions is superimposed in a certain sense on that regarding roles. In very general terms, positions deal with the structure that the different roles form in relation to one another. If the latter are concerned with the sources of semiotic actions, the positions specify the centers of these actions. The fact that source and center do not always coincide—far from it—is the precise reason for drawing this distinction. Of course the analysis can be pursued at an extremely detailed level, as well as at a more global level: that of sentence, sequence, and discourse.

(i) *Linguistic positions: the grammatical subject versus the center of predication.* The instances where the grammatical subject is not the subject causing the action supply the paradigm for the displacement I want to consider, a paradigm capable of becoming a source of mystification. Here are some possibilities:

33. The *zero-priëm* of Lotman, *The Structure of the Artistic Text.*

In the passive transformation, the semantic subject of the sentence is no longer the cause but the effect. The link between the causal subject and the process is weakened. If the agent is not named, the process seems finished. At times the causal subject is irrecoverable. In this case, who can be held responsible for the action? Classification replaces causality. At the level of the narrative text, the network of actions may thus be entirely modified in relation to the underlying events. "The Greeks have defeated the Trojans" describes a narrative sequence which can also be enunciated as: "The Trojans are beaten" or "The gods have tipped the balance in favor of the Greeks." In the first version, the causal subject is also the semantic subject. The Greeks are highlighted. In the second version, they have disappeared. The Trojans are absorbed into the class of "victims," which characterizes them in a certain way. The third version attributes the responsibility to an external cause, which accentuates the arbitrariness, and nullifies the possible classification of the Greeks as heroes and the Trojans as victims. Compare the following: "This girl was raped" versus "A man raped this girl." Such manipulation of meaning is often to be sensed in the nominalization of verbs. The participants in the action are omitted. The process becomes the semantic subject. The process is presented as a state, the activity as an object, the specific becomes general, and the concrete abstract. Kress and Hodge[34] give the example of a sentence taken from Chomsky which uses the expression "the construction of a grammar," thereby "forgetting" to indicate that it is not a natural process but that he, Noam Chomsky, constructs a particular grammar for which he can be held responsible. In nominalizations, temporal and modal markers both disappear, which renders the utterance more vague. Moreover, the construction in question can be composite. The simplification of complex relations is the effect produced. Since newly-formed nouns can participate in new constructions, the reader will have neither the time nor the reason to analyze them. Thus things can be said without one's coming to terms with their being said. The phenomenon is also to be found at the level of an entire narrative text. The events which are accentuated as semantic subject are not always those which are part of the intentional action of the acting subjects. Bracketed in all kinds of ways—presented, for example, as an already classified and therefore inescapable state of affairs—the true motivations of the action are effaced in the linguistic surface structure of the text.

A comparable phenomenon can be seen when negation is incorporated in the verb. The grammatical subject does not indicate the causal subject, but rather the secondary, reactive subject, which is thus held accountable for an action not its own. Verbs such as "to ignore," "to refuse," and "to

34. Kress and Hodge, *Language and Ideology*, 29.

refrain from" present a grammatical subject which, while being the semantic subject, is not the acting subject. Negative action is considered positive,
so that the relations of power and responsibility are reversed. We have
already seen how, by refusing to return to his home, Uriah thinks he is
declining an offer, when in fact he is disobeying a deceitful order. Placed in
the context of the linguistic position, Uriah is held accountable, as grammatical subject of the sequence "Uriah refuses to go home," for an action
which he does not perform. In other words, this form effaces the difference
between not-wanting-to-do and wanting-not-to-do; the subject, the significance, and the object of the wanting therefore remain vague.

(ii) *Cognitive positions: ideological center, network of visions.* The choices
made at the textual level already outline alternative networks, of which one
is grammatical and the other semantic, and which together provide a
picture of the ideologies at work. The distribution of responsibilities and
powers will be compared to the position that each focalizer occupies in
relation to the set of roles. In Book Four of the *Odyssey*, for example, the
narrative of Helen contains her version of the glory of Ulysses. Semanti-
cally, it is indeed striking to note that while speaking of Ulysses she speaks
about herself, her cunning and her loyalty. Her favorable view of herself
will be questioned immediately by Menelaus, who, while introducing his
discourse with a "You are right," in confirmation of the frank perspective
upon Ulysses, displays in his focalization a story which partially contradicts
Helen's. For even though he corroborates her cunning, he not only shows
that Ulysses surpasses her in this area, but also that her loyalty is questionable. So the analysis of the whole perspectival network must be able to
account for this succession of stories. In his final position, Menelaus may
well have the last word, thus being in a position to undermine retrospectively Helen's perspective.[35]

(iii) *Pragmatic positions: center of action, center of initiative.* Although for
many reasons it is not possible to adopt Greimas' actantial model in the
context of the analysis whose approach I have been detailing, the position
in question here is not unreminiscent of the actantial subject.[36] The question here is as follows: Who guides the action? Who takes the initiative?
This question cannot be considered in isolation. The grammatical analysis
having already established the network of positions and pseudo-positions,
the actantial analysis proper, which has to do with the place of each actor in
relation to the narrative program(s), will progress on this basis. It will

35. For an exhaustive analysis of this passage, followed by a putting into perspective of
Helen's general position, see Bergren, "Helen's 'Good Drug,'" and "Language and the
Female."
36. *Sémantique structurale.* The primary reason for my reticence is the structural
character of both Greimas' model and my own, which prohibits me from detaching one
element of the set from the one, and reintegrating it into the other.

therefore prescind from the mystifications which result from implicit negatives, from passive transformations, from nominalization, or from other ways of bracketing the causal subject of the action.

(c) *Actions.* The third set of questions has to do with the activities carried out in the three domains. What activities are carried out, in what proportion, and with what result?

(i) *Speech.* Do the respective speakers speak much? The question here is the distribution of speech. The number and length of utterances are not necessarily relevant in and of themselves, but the comparison between these and other data can disclose lines of force, and in each instance the question of the success of the speech proves to be implicated. Do the speakers speak well, that is, in an adequate way, in relation to the functions of the linguistic modes they use? And does their speech have the desired success? In the case of a question, success is measured by its capacity to obtain the required answer. The order obeyed, the assertion understood, etc.: these nuances are what we have to analyze here. The second question concerns the changes of speaker. These may be brought about in several ways. The analysis will focus on attribution,[37] the formulae used to hand over the speaking to a speaker at the next level. The meaning of these formulae influences the truth-status that is conferred upon the words spoken thereafter. Equally relevant are the possible interruptions. We know also of dialogues which really consist of two separate monologues going on at the same time without relationship to each other, as in Edward Albee's play, *Who's Afraid of Virginia Woolf?* From this point of view, the alternation of speaking between Helen and Menelaus in Book Four of the *Odyssey* could be investigated anew.

(ii) *Focalization.* The nature of focalization is analyzable initially under two categories. We can distinguish physical perception, which—though never, as we have seen, free from interpretation and judgment—can nevertheless be defined by a certain intersubjectivity. This category is concerned with the field of view accessible to the perception of other beings than the focalizers in question. Verbs such as "to see," "to hear," "to feel," etc., and their equivalents, which are traditionally classified as verbs of perception, introduce such focalizations. On the other hand, mental actions, which are expressed by verbs like "to look," "to listen," "to love," etc., point to focalizations whose objects are not accessible *a priori* to an external witness. The distribution of focalization is obviously to be compared with the distribution of speech. As for the changes of focalizer, the attribution of focalization is often more difficult to spot, because it is more implicit than that of speech. Exact analysis of a text enables us nonetheless to make the em-

---

37. Prince, "Le discours attributif."

Table 1

	Role: Delimitation of subjects Basic question: Who?	Position: Hierarchy of subject/object Basic question: From whom/around whom?	Action: Organization, distribution, result Basic question: What, why, how?
language	identity of speaker: implicit vs. explicit (authority vs. responsibility) linguistic model used: dialogue vs. narration role-exchanging vs. elimination of object dialogue vs. pseudo-dialogue linguistic modes used: affirmative vs. mystifying imperative vs. lack of authority legitimate orders vs. illegitimate interrogative vs. imperative question vs. request who never speaks?	casual vs. grammatical subject: who is the semantic subject of both? agent-process-effect casualty vs. classification nominalization of verbs unique vs. general; concrete vs. abstract negation in verb grammatical subject vs. reactive subject causal subject vs. secondary subject who is responsible?	distribution of speech: number of utterances for each speaker length of utterances effect of utterances: is speech adequate to the function of the linguistic model used? are utterances successful? transition formulas

vision	identity of focalizer: is focalizer identical with speaker? reflective vs. nonreflective focalization mode of focalization: verb of perception vs. mental acts direct vs. indirect focalization who never focalizes?	two alternative versions of one event first vs. last focalizer attribution of focalization: explicit vs. implicit evaluation privileged focalizer vs. lack of visibility distribution of focalization spatial position of focalizer	distribution of focalization: number of focalizations for each subject distribution related to place in text distribution related to place of event in fabula kind of focalization: checkable vs. inaccessible to others object internal vs. external to subject relation to focalization-speech: who focalizes more than s/he speaks?
action	identity of actor: actor-character vs. actor-object relation to action-focalization: does actor focalize his/her action? relation to actor-sender: free vs. delegated actor who never acts?	direction of action: who takes initiatives? who accomplishes central action? relation to actor-narrative program are there transformations in the fabula similar to linguistic transformations (e.g., mystification of causal subject)?	distribution of actors on actional chain: number of actions for each actor importance of their actions place of actions in fabula effect of action: successful with respect to intention successful with respect to program relation to action-focalization-speech: are actions effective? are they carried out as a result of eval- uation by focalization or by speech?

beddings stand out, as well the systematic elimination of certain focalizations. This form of censorship also deserves to be accounted for.

(iii) *Behavior/conduct.* The same questions crop up again. How do the actors behave? The distribution of actions is involved here, as well as the effectiveness of each action in relation to the program. It may be relevant to ask to what extent the actions, effective or ineffective, are carried out in the wake of speech (whose?), or of judgments on focalizations (by whom?)

In order to facilitate overall comprehension, Table 1 offers a comprehensive view of this model, accompanied by questions which are derived from it.[38]

4. ANALYSIS—AND AFTERWARDS?

An analysis along the lines indicated above is only an initial step in the critical examination of a text. It provides a picture of the textual subjectivity. Deviations from the linguistic and narrative models, as well as violations of particular genres (heroic epic, psychological novel, etc.), will be pointed out along the way. It is on the basis of these deviations that the analysis will be able to rejoin the critical dimension. The procedure will be the following. The rewritings of the text at our disposal will be numerous in the case of texts whose ideological functioning is the most indisputable: canonical, mythical, and popular texts. Up to now in my analyses of biblical writings, it turns out that the "deviations" which constitute the nerve-centers of the text have always been the object of subsequent manipulations. Such will be the working hypothesis adopted here, since these manipulations undoubtedly attest to the problematic character of the points at issue.[39]

The urgent need of the receivers of the text to modify its subjectivity on these precise points indicates the turmoil felt by these collective subjects *à propos* a certain problematic subjectivity. It is therefore over these points that the individual subject and the social subject meet. The example of 2 Samuel 11 has already been analyzed on this point. The textual impotence of the female actor clearly creates a problem in the reception. By attributing to her a degree of responsibility for the events which the text in no way justifies, some receivers[40] appear to contradict the subjectivity of the text. By no means! Through the metaphor in vs 21, receivers succeed in making the woman-victim into an executioner. On the one hand, the text sanctions this distortion. On the other, it carefully avoids making it explicit: this

38. This table also appears in *Death and Dissymmetry*, 248–49, where I explain the differences.

39. [Editor's note] This paragraph needs to be read in its context in *Femmes imaginaires*, where this chapter preceded the analyses of biblical texts now found in *Lethal Love*, Chapters 2—5.

40. E.g., Sternberg, *The Poetics of Biblical Narrative*, 186–222.

disconcerting point creates a problem precisely *to the extent that* it remains unconscious. Those receivers who, in a certain ideological (patriarchal) context, identify themselves with the roles of the powerful, were able, by means of this "putting of reality to the test," to accept the distortion by eliminating it in favor of their own ideology, and then to base the ideology on the subjectivity of this authoritative text, henceforth "cured" of its problem! It remains to be seen just how far a causal explanation of this disturbing phenomenon, which consists in naturalizing an equivocal ancient text (giving it the benefit of the doubt) in a fashion more sexist than the text itself, can get us, in an age when we can readily claim to be emancipated. When, on the basis of an analysis well grounded from the start in the subjectivity of the text, we succeed in proposing an alternative interpretation which, for its part, leads subjects in a different direction, then and only then can we hope to show the way taken by the social subject, in accordance with its own interests. For it is true to say that a different evolution would have been possible, on the basis of other interests. I have offered some analyses along these lines.[41]

Where and how does this model of subjectivity join up with psychoanalysis? The points shared in common by psychoanalysis and narratological criticism are numerous, extending over the objective, the theory, the method, the results, and the status of the model in the two disciplines. In each case, the objective is a critique of relationships between the individual and the social, amounting, eventually, to nothing less than a critique of culture. The interaction of different subjectivities is what is at stake. The theories of the two approaches resemble each other in a striking way, nearly term for term, as the comparison with narratology in the Lacan quotation showed.[42] In both instances the evolution of a subject is retraced, starting from the vestiges in the text of the primary non-narrative process, which make manifest a privatization of language. The method is structural, implying a form of predictability based upon norms which are discovered as the system becomes established. The method is analytic, that is, the atomization of the textual material into elements precedes the establishing of relationships between these elements. In narratological analysis, answering the questions suggested here will implement this establishing of relations, which is a "translation" and implies a process of careful listening (a process equally indispensable in psychoanalysis). Discovering the *aspects* or narrative attitudes (affirmative, imperative, etc.) also forms part of the method.

---

41. [Editor's note] The original reads, "The preceding chapter offered the beginnings of a demonstration. In the present chapter another, more detailed, analysis will demonstrate that a way is opened up for hermeneutical critique if it grounds itself in a narratological theory anchored in an analytic conception of the subject." The "preceding" and the "present" chapters are now Chapters 1 and 2 of *Lethal Love*.

42. See above, note 2.

In both disciplines, the hoped-for result is comprehension, in both senses of the word. Hermeneutical understanding is only the first step. It acquires meaning to the extent that it prepares the ground for the causal explanation, by means of a systematic establishing of relationships among the problematic elements. The status of the proposed model is comparable to that of analytic models. The provisional atomization of subjectivity, derived from the current use of the word "subject" in language, provides an entrance into critique. It provides for the setting up of roles, positions, and actions which constitute, in the guise of variable networks of subjects, structures of displacement and condensation which constitute in turn the underlying system of a particular text. It is on the basis of the schema thus established that text and criticism, analysand and analyst, text and re-writings, are oriented. It is in this interaction, finally, that the relation between individual and social, to which the present outline offers a first approach, takes shape.

PART III

Narratology at Work

The five essays in this section present the indispensable, yet dubious "illustrations" of the theory. Illustrations are indispensable because no theory can be automatically "applied"; no analytic model yields relevant interpretations in and of itself; the model must be shown "at work." But such working pieces always entertain an ambivalent relationship to their theoretical framework; they tend to be more autonomous, more free-standing that the notion of "application" suggests. The dubious relationship between theory and application is so crucial to any theoretically informed criticism, that I wilfully endorse the dubiousness of this relationship.

Chapter 7 is the first article I wrote, before I entered an academic position, and quite nicely foreshadows my critical strategies of the years to follow. In it, the negative heuristics is fully at work. The essay was generated by my perplexity at reading, for the first time, a novel by Marguerite Duras, whose work was much less known at the time: *Le vice-consul*.[1] The relations between this novel and my own sense of self as a critic are intricate. Duras's writing consistently works through formal experiment and social or ideological concerns, without ever separating the two. The confrontation with this congenial intricacy was at the same time challenging, to the extent that structuralist models had tended to work only with traditional texts. Here was an experimental text so powerful that my model's attempt to domesticate it was bound to fail. It was already in this work that I realized how the *failure* of a method could be its strength. My later analysis of the Samson story, a traditional tale if ever there was one, worked in a similar vein.[2]

1. Although it has become widely known since then, good critical texts are few. The best book on Duras to date seems to me to be Willis, *Marguerite Duras*.
2. See *Lethal Love*, Chapter 2.

Chapter 8, on Colette's *Chéri*, on the other hand, was written much later. In it I argue that this arguably classical, fully realist novel does not in the least represent an unproblematic subject. The attempt to relate narratology to psychoanalysis reveals the open character of a subject-oriented narratology. The theory, here, "awakens" a text which current criticism had reduced a little too easily to a tragi-comedy of sorts. This novel was one of my favorites through high school and college, so much so that in my earlier work I stayed away from it, afraid as I was to "spoil" it. Only when I was able to relativize the pursuit of "rigor" and to establish relations between narratology and other approaches, was I able to work on this personal favorite.

Chapter 9, also on an allegedly realist novel with subject problematics, *La faute de l'abbé Mouret* by Zola, introduces a historical dimension through intertextuality. The concept of character, which was the leading question in my Genesis 2–3 analysis,[3] on which I continue to build here, is again conceived of as a projection of unity *as* ideology. The place of Christian thinking in the change of literary form is projected from the standpoint of Zola's post-Christian revision of the myth of paradise. The novel thus becomes less than realistic: a dream based on projection and retrospection, rather than reality. This essay gives an analysis, or rather, a snapshot of ideological development through literary representation, and thus constitutes another argument in favor of the integration of "formalism" and critique that I have been pursuing.

Chapter 10 was written as an occasion-piece: an invitation to speak at a conference at Princeton, a gathering of theologians with interdisciplinary interests, called "Conversations." The text, an autobiographical fragment on the last days of the Carthaginian martyr Perpetua, was chosen by Margaret Miles, the organizer of the panel, and three papers were presented on the same text. For me, working with this text was a thrilling experience. The demands of the conference fitted my interest in crossing between fields and between approaches. In the essay I play with narratology and visuality, with generic ambiguity, with the self-deconstruction of narratology and of the narrative by whose potential I had become fascinated. Responding to a recurrent question from the audience, I have added at the end of the paper a polemical statement on the use of psychoanalysis for historical texts. If nothing else, its rhetoric was quite effective in the oral setting in stopping short the commonplace and mistaken objection; I can recommend its use.

Finally, Chapter 11 is the result of my most personal experience as a scholar. I am pleased to be able to present the paper together with the story, "De sirenen" (The Sirens) by Maria Dermoût. The article was written at a turning-point, with difficulty and with delight. I was supposed to address the question "Does your method travel?", and by chance I found this story

3. *Lethal Love*, Chapter 5.

about travelling. I was asked to write a piece of criticism for a collection of essays on Dutch narrative, a field I had never worked on and did not know well at all. My prejudice against Dutch narrative was that it tends toward simplicity, and I found this amazingly complex text. It made me aware that the apparent simplicity of the best of Dutch narrative is part of a deceptive complexity.[4] In addition, I was to write the paper in a strongly anti-theoretical academic setting, and found a text that seemed absolutely unreadable without theoretical help. And then, typically, the editors had not included any other woman critic, nor were any of the other essays on work by women authors. Caught between tokenism and the total suppression of women, I stumbled into this colonial story that in many ways thematized these very issues, and I fell in love with it.

Most significantly, at the moment that I was struggling with the problem of the subject, when the unity of the subject was acutely undermined, the story I found displayed that very problem, with its double subject, its double ideology, and its double ending. My perplexity at the non-coherence, at the radical impossibility of subsuming the story under one interpretation, led to the most radical consequence of my confrontational habit. Lest I should have been tempted to cheat and force a solution to the drama of reading, the confrontation between the text and the theory obliged me to double myself, and invite a co-author. This co-author had to be congenial enough to see the dilemma, and different enough to make the non-coherence, the misfits, and the conflicts, the *difference within*, productive. In short: I needed a feminist man. I found one in Ernst van Alphen, and writing the paper with him was among the most pleasurable and challenging experiences in my academic life. I purposefully end this volume with this double-edged paper.

4. Maaike Meijer calls "complification" this opposite of simplification, in her wonderful analysis of deceptively simple Dutch poetry by women. Van Alphen (*Bij wijze van lezen*) demonstrates how apparently simple, compulsive story-telling is the major post-modernist strategy of the novelist Brakman. A collection of "complified" Dutch literature would be a nice publishing project.

▪7▪

Hypo-Stories

The Heuristics of Perplexity

0. INTRODUCTION

The reader of *The Vice-Consul*, by Marguerite Duras, is struck by the alternation, in this novel, of two narratives which tell stories apparently far removed from each other. The narrative with which the novel begins describes the march of a young Cambodian girl driven from home because she became pregnant, a march which lasts ten years, and during which she goes mad. After ten years she has arrived at Calcutta, where she has joined the begging lepers. The other narrative describes how a group of whites in Calcutta pass their time for three days, a group who form a circle around Anne-Marie Stretter, the wife of the French ambassador, and among whom the French Vice-Consul in Lahore has lately arrived. The two narratives alternate in the first half of the novel, each taking up, twice, twenty pages of text. In the second half, the narrative about the whites predominates, and is only rarely interrupted by a few lines about the mad woman; she, though, begins to figure within the narrative about the whites.

To what extent are these two narratives related to each other? This is the pressing question for anyone who wants to give a coherent account of the novel. Are the two narratives in a relationship of coordination or of subordination; in other words, are they at the same level, or is one integrated into the other, and if so, how? Literature knows plenty of works in which there is an alternation of two or several narratives. I would like to tackle the problem by comparing the structure of *The Vice-Consul* with that of the best-known example of the type, *The Thousand and One Nights*,[1] a structure which is generally referred to as embedding (*enchâssement*). The

1. I have chosen this example of popular literature deliberately: the simplicity of its structure allows me to expound my point of view.

main narrative, which contains the others and which I shall call N1, tells how a king, having been deceived by his wife, thereafter kills each of his new wives following the wedding night. To avoid being killed, Scheherazade tells the king captivating stories. The stories she tells are the embedded narratives, and will be indicated by N2 . . . NX, a formula which expresses their limitless number. The relationships between N1 and N2 . . . NX constitute a double subordination, on the level of actors and on the level of action. Scheherazade, an actor in N1, recounts N2 . . . NX: she is the narrator. Told by an actor in N1, N2 . . . NX are therefore subordinated to N1. Further, N2 . . . NX have a function within the action of N1: as long as Scheherazade tells the stories, the king does not kill her. The working out of the action of N1, and its dénouement, are determined by the existence of N2 . . . NX. Because of this functionality, one can think of N2 . . . NX as an actant in N1, as playing the role of *sender* in Greimas' actantial schema:[2] they enable the subject Scheherazade to attain her *object*, survival.

Though the term *embedding* is commonly used for all works where there *is a story within a story*, I propose, for the clarity of the analysis, to use it exclusively for works in which there is a double subordination comparable to that of *The Thousand and One Nights*. If the subordination occurs on only one of the two levels, I propose to use the term *framing (encadrement)*, introduced by Balzac in reference to his *The Lily in the Valley*.[3] In that novel, the one who recounts the framed narrative N2 is the subject of the framing narrative N1: so there is a subordination of actors.[4] But in this case the function of N2 in relation to the action of N1 is to provide an explanation, only after the fact, of the conduct of the subject in N1.[5] Since this conduct has already been decided, the fact that N2 is told does not influence the course of N1; it does not open up any alternative,[6] as in *The Thousand and One Nights* (death or life for Scheherazade). Here, therefore, it is a matter of simple subordination.

Let us go back to *The Vice-Consul*. Does it show simple or double subordination? The answer seems obvious. But it is only partly so: subordination on the level of actors is indicated from the first sentence of the novel: "She marches, writes Peter Morgan." The one who writes the girl's story, the narrator of N2, is an actor in N1, just as in *The Thousand and One Nights* and *The Lily in the Valley*. Nevertheless, the link is weak, in that Peter Morgan, and his novel, appear—at least if one considers the story of

2. Greimas, *Sémantique structurale*, 172–91.
3. See also Rossum-Guyon, *Critique du roman*, 134.
4. Whether or not the subject of the two narratives is the same actor is of no importance here.
5. For a typology of the relationships between the narratives, see Genette, *Narrative Discourse*.
6. A criterion used by Barthes to distinguish a *noyau* (kernel) from an *indice* (thematic indication); "Introduction," and see above, Chapter 5, sect. 1.2.

Anne-Marie Stretter's affairs to be the center of N1, which is, to say the least, doubtful—to have no more than a secondary function in N1, in contrast with Scheherazade and Balzac's hero, who have indispensable roles.[7] So far as the level of action is concerned, the problem is more complicated, firstly because the term "action" is hard to apply to this novel. The only spectacular action in N1, the vice-consul's killing of some lepers, is situated in the past. This action has no link with any other; it leads only to certain reactions, some vague opinions, and nothing gets decided about punishing the vice-consul, or about his future. So far as the other characters are concerned, they do nothing. At the very most one might discern in the description of the three days a love intrigue—even this feeble and uncertain —around Anne-Marie Stretter. On the level of events virtually nothing happens. How, in such a case, can we analyze the action of the novel? Such an analysis would generate several different actantial schemas, attached to each of the characters, but this would entail a fragmentation in conflict with the novel's thematic density. In schemas of this kind there would be, for example, no relationship between the vice-consul and the mad girl, and very little between Peter Morgan and the vice-consul, even though these relationships turn out to be essential. Instead of this kind of analysis of the stories, then, *The Vice-Consul* calls for an analysis at the narrative level which can provide a point of departure for an examination of narrative functioning in the novel. In order to be able to formulate the connections between the two narratives, it will be necessary to examine the thematics, the characters' reactions, and the analogies between motifs. Only thus will we be able to account for the novel's complexity. This analysis will then enable us to draw some conclusions about the formal functioning of this double narrative.

1. RELATIONSHIPS BETWEEN CHARACTERS

At first sight, everything conspires to cut the links between the characters in N1 and N2. The situations of Peter Morgan and the mad girl could hardly be more radically opposite. Peter Morgan is a man, while the one of whom he writes is a victim of her femaleness: she has lost everything as a result of her pregnancy. Peter Morgan is rich, the girl is poor; he is European, and integrated into his milieu, she is Asiatic, and has been irremediably expelled from hers. The situation is paradoxical: Peter Morgan is an expatriate, but at home in Calcutta, while the mad girl, on the continent where she was born, is doubly alienated—exiled from her country and from

---

7. The indispensable functions—subject, object, sender, receiver—are to be distinguished from the secondary functions in a number of respects. A very handy criterion is numerical freedom: the number of helpers and of opponents is in effect unlimited. Cf. above, note 2.

her social class. This paradoxical situation has its counterpart on the level of communication.[8] The mad girl, though Asiatic, speaks not a word of Hindustani (sic), and so cannot become integrated among the inhabitants of Calcutta. Peter Morgan, European, speaks English, the universal language. The girl's difficulty in communication is doubly aggravated: during her march she has completely forgotten how to speak; having no one to speak to, she has become dumb, then mad. Peter Morgan, by contrast, is intelligent and expresses himself very well. For several reasons, which dovetail and intersect, there is no communication possible between these two. But this very absence of relationships on the level of "reality"[9] creates new links between N1 and N2 on the literary level. In the absence of any possibility of getting information, Peter Morgan has to *invent* the girl's march. He is free to do this however he likes, which reinforces the links between him and his subject. He does not repeat a story that others are telling (cf. *The Thousand and One Nights*), or tell one which "really" happened (cf. *The Lily in the Valley*); rather, he invents, he is a creator, and this must increase his importance for N2. By this act of creation, the girl, who is a "person" in N1, becomes a character (*personnage*) in N2.[10]

However, since, as I have said, the importance of Peter Morgan in N1 is secondary, this direct actantial link between the two narratives is weak. But there are other, indirect, relationships, of which a certain number can be grouped into relationships between characters (reactions), and analogies of theme.[11] I intend to analyze each of these two groups of relationships. In this analysis I shall observe as far as possible the following order: first I shall speak of the mad woman, then of the whites, and finally of the character in between, the vice-consul. I shall keep to this order likewise for the analysis of each of the themes.

1.1 The mad woman: attraction

As we know, the mad woman is not only a character in N2 and the object of Peter Morgan's personal preoccupation; she also figures in N1 and fulfills there a very important role: she provokes reactions and reacts in her turn. Her own reactions are appropriate to her situation: she is dirty and mad, and she is looking for food. These features determine her conduct vis-

8. The theme of communication will be analyzed below. But it is necessary to introduce it already here, since it is essential to the subordination, at the level of the actors, of N2 to N1.

9. The terms *real* and *reality* are used here, it must be understood, in terms of the perspective of the heroes of the main narrative upon the narratives which it incorporates; they refer, therefore, to diegetic "reality."

10. The word "person" is used here in the same perspective as is "reality" in the preceding note.

11. It goes without saying that these few themes do not exhaust the subject. In particular, the temporal and spatial structures of the novel create very solid links between the two narratives, but these will not concern us here.

à-vis the characters of N1; she *follows* Anne-Marie Stretter, because the latter distributes food, but she amuses herself by *frightening* the whites with her dirtiness and madness. Her reaction therefore includes both attraction and aggression. She cannot carry to the limit either of these opposed tendencies, since she must remain at a certain *distance* from the whites. She cannot follow them except at a distance, which prevents her from scaring them too deeply.[12] We shall see that the different attitudes which characterize the conduct of the mad woman vis-à-vis the whites—attraction, aggression, and distance—recur in the reactions of the whites vis-à-vis the mad woman and the world she represents.[13] But the proportions change: in the behavior of the mad woman attraction predominates.

1.2 The whites: distance

The majority of the whites, those who have been in India for some time, have become gradually accustomed to the sight of the suffering around them. When they first arrived, it used to give them pain, just as they used to suffer from the change of surroundings and from the heat, but they have become just as inured to the inconveniences of the climate as to the suffering of the Indians, and they no longer feel more than slight discomfort —enough to provide a topic of conversation, but nothing to lose sleep over. When they speak of "the sorrow of India," they are talking of all these inconveniences at once, putting on the same level misery and heat, leprosy and blinding sunlight, beggars and dust. The following description of Calcutta, as a city where everything is already fixed and impermeable to change, shows the extent to which the elements of India's sorrow, of the sadness of the tropics, are mixed together.

> It is five weeks since Jean-Marc de H. arrived in a city on the banks of the Ganges which here will be the capital city of India and called Calcutta, the number of whose inhabitants remains the same, five million, as does the number, unknown, of those dying of hunger, and which has just entered today into the twilight of the summer monsoon (35/23).[14]

So far as the relationship between the text and the narrative is concerned, the reader is struck by the impersonal character of this description: the

---

12. Once, she tries to break this rule which she seems otherwise to accept: she approaches Charles Rossett, an Englishman recently arrived in India. He flees, and by doing so reestablishes the threatened distance.

13. The world the mad woman represents, to which the whites would rather close their eyes, is recreated by Peter Morgan. The representative—and therapeutic—function of his novel, in which, by contrast, the whites are keenly interested, constitutes a relationship of subordination on the level of action: it is *because* Peter Morgan writes about the mad woman that the whites react to her presence (see below, Conclusion).

14. [Translator's note]: Page references are to the French and English respectively. The latter are for reference only—the translations are my own, and deliberately literal.

indefinite article suggests that Calcutta is just any old city among other similar ones; the words "remains the same" indicate the permanent character of this misery, which is accepted as inevitable: "inhabitants" and "those dying of hunger" are put on the same level. The administrative style of the sentence reinforces this effect. The general description becomes particular through the indicator "today,"[15] which is used in relation to the climate: the misery is equal everywhere in India, but the climate is harder to bear in Calcutta than elsewhere.[16] Climate also seems to dominate in "the sorrow of India."[17]

As we have seen, the whites make the misery into a topic of conversation. They speak of it constantly. The tone of these conversations is impersonal: "All the same, the suicides of Europeans during the famine, even though it never affects them, it's odd" (161/128). The word "odd" in this sentence is a litotes, a figure of speech which signifies only too well the speaker's real feelings: it is a sign of the deliberate distancing, a weapon of defense to push away the suffering of the Indians. This taking of distance is very important in the novel, and it assumes several forms. Its most material and at the same time most symbolic form is the motif of the *railings*. This motif, which occurs more than twenty times, becomes more important as the novel progresses. This progression corresponds to the fact that the distance between the two worlds is more definitive at the end of the novel. The contexts in which the motif appears are significant: within N2 it occurs only at the moment when the girl enters into contact with the whites, when she succeeds in getting rid of her child. Absent up to this point, the word "railings" appears five times in the pages which describe the giving up of the child (56–68/41–51). In N1, the word is very frequent. "The railings erected against begging" (202/160) must protect the whites, must keep intact the irreducible distance between the two races. These railings are part of a system of self-protection which the whites have set up against the whole range of tropical inconveniences: they lower the awnings, shut the doors, leave as rarely as possible the gardens of the embassy, stay up all night and go to bed when the city wakes. In all the descriptions of Calcutta one finds, more or less explicitly, this distance. In the following description,

15. This indicator makes the text into a "represented discourse," in Doležel's terms (*Narrative Modes*), comparable to Genette's *discours transposé* and Schmid's *Textinterferenz* (*Textaufbau*).

16. See also p. 43/30.

17. The three days described in N1 occur at the beginning of the summer monsoon, the most unpleasant season. The girl's giving birth in N2 likewise takes place during the monsoon. On page 152 (120) the possibility is even raised of a suicide attempt by Anne-Marie Stretter and her lover during—or because of—the monsoon. The importance of this season lies in its fatal influence over human reactions: it has the effect of making everything harder to bear. The start of the monsoon brings about a *crisis*, in Racine's sense. The monsoon is therefore a doubly significant *metonymic metaphor*.

for example, a large number of words (printed in italics) relate to the theme[18] of distance and separation:

> *Far off, blue* palm trees. On the banks of the Ganges, the lepers and a *scrimmage* of dogs form the first *enclosure, broad,* the first around the city. The ones dying of hunger are *further away,* in a dense *swarm* to the north, they form the last *enclosure.* The light is dim, it is like no other. In infinite pain, unit by unit, the city *wakes* (164–65/131).[19]

The term "enclosure" concretely expresses separation; distance is likewise signified by all the words which denote expanse (far off, broad, blue)[20] and confusion (scrimmage, swarm), in that these words take away from the sufferers their individuality and even their humanity. In this sense, the personification of the city, juxtaposed to the collective presentation of the natives, reinforces the effect.

1.3 Anne-Marie Stretter: equilibrium menaced

In the reaction of most of the whites we see recurring the two tendencies which we established in the mad woman, sympathy and aggression. But they are attenuated; sympathy, in the form of pity, is limited to flat conversations, while aggression, transformed into fear,[21] is attenuated by the distance which dominates the relationships between the two groups.

Adapting to India is more difficult for Anne-Marie Stretter. Even though she too has been in the tropics for a long time—for more than 17 years—she does not react like the others. This has to do with difficulties she experienced at the beginning of her stay; it is said that she almost had to return to France. Where does this sensitivity come from? Everything leads us to believe that she exemplifies the general notion of female sensitivity; to all appearances, Madame Stretter fulfills to perfection her social function as a woman of high society. People find her kind, find her charity admirable—she distributes leftover food and fresh water to the beggars. On account of this charity, she is followed about by the mad woman, even when she leaves Calcutta. On the other hand, when someone talks about the mad woman,

18. In line with accepted usage, I understand by *theme* a more or less abstract unit of meaning, such as love, death, motherhood. I consider the theme as the referent of the story. Separating myself to some extent from structuralist usage, I designate as *motif* a smaller and more concrete unit, such as the railings, the gardens, the bicycle. By its metaphoric value, a motif contributes to the signifying of a theme. A motif is part of the narrative and is put into words in the text; a theme is not, necessarily. In principle, all the segments of a narrative are motifs; but I take into consideration only those motifs which have significance mainly or even exclusively through their relationship to the theme.

19. I underline only those words in which the sense of distance is obvious; it is clear that, in its context, this whole description has this sense.

20. The palms are "blue" since they are seen from a distance; so it is less color than distance that the word denotes.

21. The railings, on account of their frequent appearance, are a material incarnation of the aggressive fear which inspired their erection.

Anne-Marie Stretter suddenly falls asleep (181/145), and so avoids thinking about her. This topic of conversation is apparently disagreeable to her, even though the other elements of "the sorrow of India," the heat, the light, the boredom, are her constant topics of conversation. If one thinks of this sleep as a form of escape, one sees how Anne-Marie Stretter differs from the other whites. For her, the misery is not simply mixed together with the other disagreeable aspects of the tropics. Sympathy is expressed in her charity, and aggression, transformed, in her need to escape. These two tendencies remain, then, however feebly, and a stable equilibrium between them can to some extent be achieved, given that distance is maintained.

1.4 The new arrivals: painful apprenticeship

The whites who have arrived in Calcutta more recently have much trouble adapting. Charles Rossett, an Englishman and Anne-Marie Stretter's latest lover, suffers much, mostly from the climate, to the point of being tempted to request a transfer. He hopes to find a remedy in love. Love comes, in the person of Anne-Marie Stretter, but is incapable, as he himself says, of saving him. When this love does not run smooth,[22] Charles Rossett wants to leave the grounds of the hotel where Anne-Marie Stretter and her friends are spending the weekend.

> He tries to leave the boulevard, takes side-paths, falls against the railings erected to keep out beggars, turns back, resumes his search and finally finds a gate in the railings, goes out, realizes that he has been afraid, absurdly afraid of being unable to leave that part of the island which has been reserved for his greater security (202/160–61).

This attempt to leave the zone of security betrays Charles Rossett's desire to get out of the too-narrow world of the whites in India. The very rhythm of this exceptionally long sentence indicates his panic, notably by the rapid succession of verbs of action. A little later the situation is reversed. After succeeding in getting out, Charles Rossett meets the mad woman, who approaches him. He offers her money, then is afraid again and runs away. This scene signifies by metaphoric iconicity the difficult process of adaptation to life in the tropics. When the mad woman approaches, that is, when she threatens to diminish the distance, Charles Rossett takes to his heels; she chases him, and he becomes afraid of not being able to reenter the fenced-in grounds. His final reentry is a symbolic, definitive reentry into the world of the whites: his fear in the face of the mad woman's aggression has got the better of the suffocation he was experiencing in the narrow circle. He has finally come to accept the distance, the protection of the railings: he

22. This love had to fail because it was dead from birth, because it brought nothing new, because it was too predictable.

has placed himself on the side of the whites.[23] After he has reached the protecting railings, the first sensation he experiences is striking:

> Sweat, the body sweat comes from, streams, this heat of the monsoon drives you mad, ideas no longer hold together, they burn themselves up, they get in each other's way, fear reigns, and it alone (206/164).

We recognize here how the inconveniences of India are mixed together; for Charles Rossett madness and his fear of it are in close connection with the climate, at least as much as with the misery. The danger he has just escaped, the danger of going mad, stems from the heat.

In this classification of the whites according to the degree of intensity of their reactions, Peter Morgan also has a place. Let us see how he is presented: "Peter Morgan is a young man who wants to take upon himself the sorrow of Calcutta, to throw himself into it, so that he may get it over, and so that his ignorance may end when he has taken on the sorrow" (29/18). He refuses the distance that the others maintain. He wants to experience the reality of the sorrow, he doesn't want to exclude it from his own existence. The idealism in his attitude is no doubt related to his age; he is twenty-four, while all the other characters are between thirty and forty.[24]

He goes for walks in the city, follows the mad woman. He wants to find out how, through the misery, the heat, the light, she lost her reason, and to write a novel on the subject. But how to discover the truth, when the madness itself gets in the way of finding anything out about it? His only resource is his creative mind, but by inventing his novel he separates himself from the reality of the mad woman, and therefore can never realize his ambition "to throw himself into it." His attempt poses the problem of the authenticity of all literature. This literary problem signifies at the same time the moral problem of the life of the whites in the tropics: no real improvement in the condition of the indigenous population is possible so long as the rapprochement between the two groups remains partial. Peter Morgan's search for the truth about the mad woman is in vain, in just the same way as are Anne-Marie Stretter's distribution of food and Charles Rossett's excursion outside the railings. A manifestation of this powerlessness of Peter Morgan is his effort to get information from the others. He compares his data about the mad woman with the information given by Anne-Marie Stretter about the sale of a child at which she was present seventeen years before. The dates don't coincide. In agreeing to use such information, he gives up on finding out the reality. He accepts the fiction, since no other time exists than the fictive time which permits such devices.

---

23. The symmetry between his starting and finishing points is a sign of the uselessness of the attempt.

24. Is it a subtle irony on the part of the author to confirm the usual clichés in this area? The sensitivity loses whatever authenticity it may have had left through its being shown precisely by a woman (cf. above) and by a young man.

Hence he accepts, in his own fashion, distance, which saves his literary enterprise but destroys the real identification he has begun to have with the one who inhabits the alien world. Since the success of his novel seems to be the condition for his adaptation to life in India, one can conclude that in his case, too, distance—admittedly on another level—has got the better of attraction.

1.5 The vice-consul: equilibrium destroyed

Into the midst of all these characters who wrestle, or have given up wrestling, with the difficulties of the tropics, has come, a few weeks before, the vice-consul of France in Lahore. Who is this enigmatic character, who occupies central place in the novel, and gives it its title? We learn only that "he was transferred following incidents which were considered intolerable by the diplomatic authorities in Calcutta" (35/23–24). These incidents are not specified; they are indicated by diplomatic formulae like the one just quoted. Much later in the novel it is said that he killed some lepers and screamed in the night, but we cannot be certain of anything. He himself says nothing about it. All the characters in N1, without exception, are trying to find out why the vice-consul did what he did. Two possibilities emerge: it was a reaction either against his childhood or against life in Lahore, that is, "the sorrow of India." The vice-consul's only relative, an old aunt living in France, writes in a letter intended to provide information for the authorities: "Why go back to his childhood to explain his conduct at Lahore? Shouldn't you look also at Lahore itself?" (42/29). This question, which threatens the fragile equilibrium, the peace of mind of all the characters in N1, crops up all the time, and never ceases to trouble them. The tenacity with which they all want to look into the vice-consul's childhood indicates a refusal to accept the possibility of an adverse reaction to the difficulties of adapting to India. This refusal is the result of a deep disquiet: if they were forced to admit that the violent conduct of the vice-consul was the result of a reaction against life in the tropics, they would have to face the possibility that this life, to which they have all adapted, is unlivable. In the vice-consul's behavior attraction and aggression have become inextricably mixed, and the protective distance has been destroyed: the vice-consul has breached the whites' unspoken pact. This is why his behavior is so basically *scandalous*.

The central function of the vice-consul in N1 lies in the fact that his unusual reaction itself provokes reactions.[25] The attitude of the other whites to the vice-consul casts an indirect light on their true attitude to the relations between the two races. By killing the lepers, instead of letting

---

25. The reactions of the whites to the vice-consul's reaction constitute in my opinion the real center of the story of N1. The love intrigue around Anne-Marie Stretter is peripheral to the story. This displacement of the traditional center of interest in a novel is one of the reasons for the painful impression a reading of this novel leaves.

them die quietly like the others, he has forced everyone to think through the problem again. He cannot be completely excluded from their closed world, as the Indians can. They all avoid him, but "It's funny how this man forces you to think about him" (153/121). They resent this troubling fascination which emanates from him: "How harmful he has been to us" (100/77). Since the position of the vice-consul can be considered as that of an "intermediary"[26] between the Indians and the whites, the whites' reactions to him deserve a brief analysis.

It is significant in this regard that Peter Morgan, who voices so eloquently his sympathy for the poor, cannot stand the sight of the vice-consul. It is he who, after the reception at the embassy, makes the vice-consul leave, shows him to the door, and has the railings shut after him. Charles Rossett makes an effort to accept the vice-consul, talks to him, but ends up by going along with the others.[27] We have seen how, after his encounter with the mad woman, he returns definitively to the whites' camp. This scene can also be viewed as a metaphoric icon[28] of the relationship between Charles Rossett and the vice-consul. He has a brief pang of conscience (191–92/153–54), but it is quickly snuffed out by the others. Anne-Marie Stretter performs a charitable act towards the vice-consul, analogous to those she performs towards the mad woman and the other beggars. She invites him to the reception because, as her husband puts it, "we strive, my wife and I, *as far as protocol allows*, not to exclude anyone" (44/30, my italics). During the reception she seeks him out,[29] but in the end she chooses not to be bothered. She has him removed in a double sense, from the reception and from the city: she promises the others that the vice-consul will be given an appointment very far from Calcutta.

The vice-consul serves, then, as an intermediary in the N1 story. But he has the same function beyond it. He prevents the characters in N1 from maintaining the distance between the two worlds, but also between the two

26. From the moral point of view, to the extent that the whites' attitude towards him explains and makes explicit their attitude towards the Indians. He is a *pariah*, just as much as the mad woman, but a pariah whose isolation is problematic, since the vice-consul is *like* them. Despite themselves, their sense of responsibility towards him weighs heavily on them. From the structural point of view, since the different themes which link N2 to N1 intersect in the vice-consul. See below, part 2.

27. One might believe that, in his case, jealousy also plays a role: Charles Rossett and the vice-consul love the same woman, Anne-Marie Stretter. Given the analogy between Charles Rossett's attitudes towards the vice-consul and towards the mad woman, and the peripheral position of love in the N1 story, I am of the opinion that this jealousy is only of secondary importance.

28. See Zoest, "L'iconicité métaphorique." On page 169/135 we see a scene similar to that of the abortive rapprochement with the mad woman. Charles Rossett has been forced to go up to the vice-consul's quarters after the reception. He feels ill at ease: "Charles Rossett realizes that he is feeling a slight fear. When the vice-consul gets up and approaches him, he draws back."

29. There is also, in this approach, some love. Nonetheless, I think I am right to separate these two motives, since the part played by charity in this fleeting rapprochement is the dominant: it gets the upper hand in the end.

narratives. Where Peter Morgan had found an apparently satisfactory solution in fiction, the vice-consul destroys precisely *this* equilibrium: the mad woman begins to figure in N1. The subordination of N2 to N1 reassuringly reflected colonial subordination; the association of the vice-consul with the Indians, and his likeness to the mad woman, betray the impossibility of this separation, and betray simultaneously the impossibility of Peter Morgan's literary enterprise. So it is precisely the latter who gives less support to the vice-consul even than the others do. The case made by the whites, who try to present the vice-consul as an inhuman monster so as to eject him from their circle, unconvincing as it is, does succeed in exposing in him the same falsity which he finds in *their* relations with the natives. He has a "wheezing," "impersonal," voice, "as if it were grafted onto someone else"; his face is "dead," "white," "not belonging to him"; he "staggers" as he walks. This presentation, focalized by the whites, identifies him with the mad woman who is no longer even human.[30]

2. THEMATIC ANALOGIES

The various relationships among the whites on the one hand, and between the mad woman and her world on the other, and the crisis which the presence of the vice-consul brings about in these relationships, form only a part of the structure which links N2 to N1. It is filled out by a large number of thematic analogies which, taken together, establish the interdependence of the two narratives. It is neither possible nor necessary, within the framework of this analysis, to take account of all of these analogies. I have chosen some of the most important themes: motherhood, love, communication, and death. These themes—which I treat separately for the sake of clarity— are linked to each other to form a great constellation, embracing both characters and motifs, which is precisely the structure of *The Vice-Consul*.

2.1 Defective motherhood

Given the paucity of women in the novel, mothers are relatively numerous: in N1, Anne-Marie Stretter, the vice-consul's mother, his future, imaginary wife (211/168), and the mother who sold her child 17 years before in the presence of Anne-Marie Stretter; in N2, the mother of the mad woman, the mad woman herself, and the white woman who adopts the mad woman's child. In N1 as in N2 the relationships between the mothers and their children are defective, shot through with sadness and abandonment. The mad woman was thrown out by her mother because she was to be a mother in her turn, with the disastrous results that we have seen. After this separation, the mother does not disappear but the relationship remains painful: the girl struggles with her desire to return to her mother, she has

---

30. See below, on the theme of death.

nightmares in which she sees her mother again and is again abandoned by her. In her turn she abandons her child, is forced to do so, and experiences this abandonment as a relief. At the same time, the absence of the child is a lack, for the girl no longer has anyone to talk to. The rupture in the relationship between mother and child destroys all communication, however elementary.[31] The woman who adopts the girl's child is forced to do it by the girl's insistent look,[32] but also because her own child refuses to let the baby go. We recall that while the white woman was making the necessary arrangements, her own daughter stayed outside with the girl. This in itself amounts to a threat of abandonment—for the white woman to refuse the baby might imply an abandonment of her own child.

Anne-Marie Stretter, who is an "irreproachable" woman (100/76), seems to earn this epithet in particular in her capacity as mother: she pays great attention to the education of her daughters, she goes out with them, they resemble her and she is careful to accentuate this resemblance by the way she dresses them. She gives every appearance of being a perfect mother, which puts her in opposition to the other mothers in the novel. Nonetheless, she is not first of all a mother; her motherhood takes up only a very limited part of her life. She has another life, with her lovers, into which her daughters do not penetrate; and in any case the daughters play a completely impersonal, almost ornamental, role, serving only to fill out the image of perfection which Anne-Marie Stretter creates for herself. Her perfection in this area is just as superficial as her social charity. Moreover she plays a maternal role, likewise not very deep, in relation to other characters: she wants by her love to save Charles Rossett from the dangers of the climate, but this casual love is doomed to failure; she is the only one to be even a little bit kind to the vice-consul, who loves her, perhaps, because she is maternal (perhaps she could replace his own mother who abandoned him), but she ends up abandoning him in her turn; she comes to the aid of Peter Morgan by providing him with the subject for one episode of his novel, precisely the episode about the sale of a child.

The vice-consul's mother abandoned her child because she could not imagine, any more than the mad woman could, the possibility of being encumbered by a child. First she sent him to boarding school, and then she left him for good when she went off with her lover. For the vice-consul, too, the abandonment has affected the possibility of communication.[33] He expresses himself poorly; furthermore he has never been able to love a woman. When he speaks to the manager of the European club about his

31. "To the child, she used to talk. To whom now? To her old mother in Tonle Sap, the origin, the cause of all her troubles, her errant fate, her pure love" (67/50). This love-hate, like hunger, will go away only when madness arrives.

32. I shall return to the look, that dangerous means of communication.

33. See, in this connection, the theme of communication, particularly the motif of music.

future wife, he imagines her in childbirth during the first year of marriage, and his reverie seems like the confused vengeance of an abandoned child upon the mother of his own child: "In her face there is terror; when she looks at me she will be afraid" (211/168). His wife will be afraid of him, just as he was afraid of his mother.

The analogy between all these relationships of mothers to children signifies fatalism; since the most fundamental relationships between people are already so flawed, they have little chance to make a success of life. It is significant in this regard that, except for the vice-consul himself, all the children in the novel are girls, that is, future mothers who, in their turn, will have inadequate relationships with *their* children. The whites have no past, their families are never mentioned. The failure of motherhood has as its fatal consequence a rootlessness which life in India serves only to increase.[34]

2.2 Dead love

The theme of love is infected with the same pessimism. In N2, love is missing from the life of the mad woman. As a girl she "fell pregnant, from a tree, very high, without hurting herself, fell pregnant" (20/10). The pregnancy befell her by chance, like an illness, which didn't hurt at that moment, but which has destroyed her bit by bit. Without having known love, she has become its victim.

The situation of the whites allows them to give themselves over to love, their inactivity even incites them to it. For all that, their love life differs only in appearance from that of the girl: it is just as impoverished.

Anne-Marie Stretter left her first husband. Her present marriage is no happier. With her lovers she experiences casual love, which helps overcome the almost insufferable boredom of life in India, but which gives no satisfaction since communication is missing (a link between the themes of love and communication). It is this defective, empty, worn-out love which so disappoints Charles Rossett:

> . . . suddenly, while they are kissing—he wasn't expecting it—he feels a discordant pain, the burning sensation of a new relationship glimpsed but already foreclosed. Or as if he had loved her before, in other women, in another time, with a love that was . . . what (189–90/151)?

The love which didn't exist in the life of the mad woman is already dead in the life of the others. Between these two absences of love is situated the

---

34. We see that the maternal relationships in N1 are analogous to those in N2, however different are the realities evoked: the differences relate only to different external situations. Here again, N2 is a mirror of N1. On this point the novel diverges from most of Marguerite Duras' novels, in which the relationships between mothers and children are very intense.

nascent love of the vice-consul. Up to his arrival in Calcutta, he has never been able to love a woman: "I have never been able to stop trying to love" (77/58). The absence of love relationships in his life scandalizes the other whites: this is yet another element of their code that he eludes. However, he begins to feel love for Anne-Marie Stretter: "I feel a sort of attraction to her" (172/137), and this love fills him with hope. The vice-consul is attracted by the motherliness of Anne-Marie Stretter and by her sadness. She alone demonstrates—is able to demonstrate, since society allows a woman to do so—the deep sadness which the others repress. This love contains all sorts of new possibilities, which, no doubt, is what attracts Anne-Marie Stretter: is this, at last, the grand passion which she has never known before? This hope, this fugitive temptation are not made explicit; it all remains below the surface, but increases the already great tension during the reception. When, at the end of the evening, Anne-Marie Stretter weeps before Charles Rossett, she says: "It's nothing, it's just the glare of the daylight" (164/131). The grief caused by this lost opportunity for real contact, for passionate love, is already inextricable from the sorrow of India; it has attached itself to the boredom, and to the light of the monsoon daybreak. Charles Rossett glimpses, without altogether grasping it, the real cause of her tears, and this is why he can't stop himself from talking about it to the vice-consul. The latter, though, is just as incapable of assessing the real extent of Anne-Marie Stretter's feelings. He is no more able to understand her than to express himself: in this area he is still a child.[35] His budding love has no chance to flower, because it is rejected: Anne-Marie Stretter, like the others, prefers peace and quiet.

2.3 Impossible communication

The positing of this universal incapacity in the realm of love leads us to another theme with which it is in close relationship: that of communication, the precondition for love, and its negative counterpart, isolation. Several motifs play a clearly defined role within this theme: the word, the look, the smile, singing, music, and cries. All the characters in the novel experience the need to communicate with others; they all prove incapable of it. They differ from each other only in the way in which they accept this incapacity. As we shall see, the analogies between N1 and N2 are here again significant.

(a) Verbal communication. We have already established the irremediable impossibility of communication between Peter Morgan and the mad woman. After becoming mad, the girl used to talk only with her baby, who was not in a position to respond. Since reaching the Plain of Birds, the

---

35. Abandoned as a child, he is condemned to remain a child. He is incapable of becoming an adult.

original goal of her march, she has spoken no more than a single word, Battambang, a word which, for her, signifies her whole childhood, but which no one understands. Communication fails here because it is unilateral. The communication among the whites is equally defective, though they talk a great deal. The dialogues admirably express the meaninglessness of what is being said. They speak of other people's past, about which nothing is certain: of the vice-consul's past, which they hope might explain his conduct at Lahore, but of which they know nothing more than what the vice-consul himself has chosen to tell (and even that they don't believe); of Anne-Marie Stretter's past, of which they know only insignificant scraps; of that of the mad woman, completely invented. They speak only in speculations, and what they say tells us more about the speakers than about the topics. They speak of the present only indirectly; they commei what goes on around them. Not only are the topics of conversation often without foundation, but the dialogues show that the characters are not communicating with each other; they speak for themselves, without listening to each other. Often the sentences themselves are incomplete, a feature which signifies, by diagrammatic iconicity, the stagnation in communication: "He speaks very softly, look how he . . ." (126/98).

Between the mad woman who cannot speak and the whites who talk a lot but have nothing to say to each other is situated, once more, the vice-consul.[36] He expresses himself with difficulty, and others avoid talking to him. He refuses to explain himself concerning the incidents at Lahore, and the reasons he gives for this refusal are characteristic of the situation in general: first, he is convinced that, given his isolation, his explanation would make no sense: "Neither any outside authority nor our own administration would have any real interest, I believe, in what I might say"; second, he knows himself to be incapable of breaching his isolation: "I shall simply restrict myself here to stating that I find it impossible to give a comprehensible account of what happened in Lahore" (39/26–27). The fact is that he finds himself completely alone in Calcutta. No one talks to him. The only person who makes it his business to converse with him does so to find out the causes of his conduct in Lahore. This is the manager of the European club, who meets him each evening at the request of the diplomatic authorities. This man is, however, not a real interlocutor. He is a "drunkard," he regularly falls asleep while the vice-consul is talking, and, in his doze, does not answer him directly. As soon as an important question is put by one of the two, the other starts to talk about something else, or

---

36. This intermediate position, which I have already discussed, is concretized also in the way he is named. Between the mad woman who has no name—she is referred to as "the girl" or "the mad woman"—and the whites who are always referred to by their full names, the vice-consul is called Jean-Marc de H. Of his surname only the initial is given, which is reminiscent of police files: let us not forget that he has committed a crime.

doesn't react at all. The manager takes the role of examining magistrate: he interrogates, and passes on the results of these interrogations to the authorities for their consideration. He himself has no opinion at all about the vice-consul, or at any rate does not express one. Even though the two men speak a great deal during these evenings, there is no communication. The manager becomes really interested only when the discussion is of schooldays. For the vice-consul, this was the happiest time in his life: "Having fun at Montfort consisted of tearing Montfort apart" (84/63). Each of them tells about his memorable pranks at school, and the pleasure he experienced in destroying things. The authorities will be relieved to hear these stories, for here is a character trait, demonstrated already in childhood, which might explain Lahore. But the odd thing is that the stories the two men tell get mixed up; they make mistakes, each telling of things that actually happened to the other. The manager passes on this confusion to the other whites, for during the reception someone says, "That reform school in Arras . . . makes you think" (99/76), even though the vice-consul, who is being spoken of here, was at school in Montfort, while it was the manager who was at Arras! What we see here is a genuine interference between the actors' texts. Such confusion obviously takes away any explanatory value from the stories told by the vice-consul, and suggests once again that it is not enough to examine childhood only. As well as being a proof of the communication block, the confusion does away with the difference between the vice-consul and the other whites, a difference which *they* want to see as irreducible.

The vice-consul glimpses a possibility of communication with Anne-Marie Stretter. As we have seen, she is the first woman he has been able to love. I have already suggested that her motherliness may partly have inspired this love. Another of her characteristics may also have helped confirm it, namely her sadness, which is a sign of life[37] in this world "of fake chandeliers, futility, sham, and glitter" (93/71).[38] The vice-consul himself aspires to communicate with her on this basis.[39] In the description of the embassy reception, which takes up sixty pages, or nearly a third of the novel, the vice-consul's final attempt to establish contact with Anne-Marie Stretter has an important function. He dances with her, they converse for a few moments, observed by the guests, whose comments the text interpolates into the words of the two dancers. The moment when the vice-consul invites Anne-Marie Stretter to dance is a moment of general tension:

37. In the strong sense of the word. I have already noted (1.2) that the whites of Calcutta lacked vitality (and cf. below, 2.4, on the theme of death). This is a sign which functions on the story level, emitted and perceived by the actors.

38. These words occur in a description of the room where the reception is given. I think it is in order to cite them here, on account of their obvious metaphoric function.

39. He himself says it explicitly, in a conversation with the manager: "I would get access to her through her sadness, says the vice-consul, if I were given the chance" (80/61).

"Now all of white India looks at them" (121/94). Will the vice-consul succeed in breaking through his isolation? Will Anne-Marie Stretter find out the truth about Lahore? One senses that the outcome of this initiative will have grave consequences for the life of the whites in Calcutta, for their peace of mind. It is obvious why: if the vice-consul confides in Anne-Marie Stretter, they will know what happened at Lahore. His conduct will have lost its troubling character, the matter will have been duly filed away. If the vice-consul should succeed in winning the love of Anne-Marie Stretter, it will be necessary to accept this stranger not only as their equal, but even into the elite, into the circle of privileged friends of this woman who occupies so central a place in their milieu. The whites will have to call everything into question again. It is clear that this prospect scares them as much as the opposite possibility fills them with hope. At the beginning of the dance the vice-consul has difficulty speaking, as the spectators perceive by the pitch of his voice (124/97). He does not succeed in broaching the subject that preoccupies him (his love); he starts to talk about leprosy, a topic both banal and dismal, which serves to defer what he really wants to say:

> "Why do you talk to me about leprosy?"
> "Because I have the feeling that if I tried to say to you what I would like to say to you, everything would crumble to dust . . ." (125/98).

He goes on to speak of himself in the third person, and succeeds by this device in expressing at least a part of what he wants to say: "Lahore, it was still a sort of hope" (126/99). His conduct at Lahore had a positive side, in that it at least differed from the indifference shown in the "correct" behavior of the other whites. No doubt he intends this statement to mean that he is more human, more alive and therefore more capable of love than they. When finally Anne-Marie Stretter approaches him and says: "I understand the inevitable side of Lahore" (128/100), a great silence ensues,[40] and she refuses to carry the communication further. After the dance, Anne-Marie Stretter answers Charles Rossett, when he asks her who the vice-consul is: "Oh, a dead man . . ." (128/101). The vice-consul is condemned to remain alone, as alone as the mad woman; like her, he no longer has the right to penetrate into the world to which he belongs. He does not immediately accept this once-for-all exclusion; at the end of the party he starts to shout. He shouts, he pleads, he wants to stay. He expresses his feelings and forces the others to listen to him, something which is forbidden in this world: "People are scared. The vice-consul's moment has arrived. He shouts" (146/115). He is sent packing, shown the door. He has to leave the embassy

---

40. An ambiguous silence, full of mystery, hope, and misunderstanding. This silence will prove empty: in the end the tension, the illusion dissipate.

grounds, and the gates are shut behind him; like the lepers, like the mad woman, he is behind the railings. The only possibility of communication that is left to him is to start shouting again, as at Lahore, as at Neuilly, after his mother left. One can see the meaning of this shouting motif, so frequent in the novel (it occurs more than thirty times): it is the sign of failed communication, the last desperate attempt to escape from isolation. The shouts set up a communication below the level of words, which by its negativity betrays the blocking of verbal communication.

(b) Non-verbal communication. Besides shouting, a mode of expression situated at the limit which separates the two sorts of communication, there are other means which substitute for the inadequate word. The mad woman looks at the whites, and her look has a communicative power. By her insistent look she forced her child on the white woman. When she looks at the whites in Calcutta, they feel uncomfortable. Among the whites themselves, the importance of the look contrasts with the meaninglessness of words. In the meeting, at the reception, between Charles Rossett and Anne-Marie Stretter, a look is decisive, as one sees from the following ironically solemn sentence: "A single look, and the doors of white Calcutta softly open to him" (107/83). The look sometimes has a positive significance, more often negative,[41] and occasionally both at once. The vice-consul gazes at Anne-Marie Stretter's bicycle because it represents its owner, serves as a substitute for her. This look is suspicious to Charles Rossett, who sees its intensity without understanding its meaning; but he himself looks at Anne-Marie Stretter in an extremely aggressive way, after the first deceptive kiss: "He continues to look at her to the point of dismantling her, to the point of seeing her seated silently with empty eye-sockets in her corpse in the middle of Venice" (191/152).

The smile has a function similar to that of the look. The mad woman smiles, not from enjoyment, but to get what she wants. She smiles at the white woman, she laughs as she holds out her child to her (55/40). She smiles at Charles Rossett, who is frightened of her smile. The vice-consul smiles when he is in the depth of sadness; he scares the other whites by his inappropriate smiles. Elsewhere, the smile is intended to establish contact, but the effort fails; smiles effect communication only when they are out of place.

Singing and music generally have a communicative value, but it is not always the same. The mad woman, when in Calcutta, constantly sings a song from Battambang.[42] This repetition, which is itself a sign, a *metaphoric icon*, of the impossibility of communication, becomes another kind of

41. "Positive" and "negative," obviously, from the standpoint of the story, with the sense of "success" and "failure" in the pursuit of the object "communication" or "trust."

42. One wonders how she can sing this song when she can't speak. Perhaps she hums it—the text is not clear on this point.

means of communication: it wakes up the whites, preoccupies them, and finally obsesses them. It disturbs their tranquillity. This song, which the mad woman had learned at school, is all that is left to her of her relatively happy childhood. Further, it forms the point of departure for Peter Morgan's novel: it provides an indication—the only one—of her place of origin. So it constitutes a relationship of dependence of N2 on N1.

The vice-consul also sings a song, or rather he whistles it, since he has forgotten the words. This song, *Indiana's Song*, is first mentioned in a daydream he has:

> Thus, in his mind, it is a drawing-room, everything is in order, the grand piano is closed, on the music stand there is a score likewise closed, whose unreadable title is *Indiana's Song* (33/22).

This sentence evokes his house in Neuilly, empty since his departure. If one takes the effect for the cause, the situation becomes more dramatic, and real in a different way: it is because the house was empty, abandoned by the mother—it was she who used to play the piano—that the vice-consul himself left it. Probably it is also on account of the mother's departure that he has forgotten the words of the song, a forgetting which recalls the mad woman's complete forgetting of language.[43] The song the vice-consul sings symbolizes his lost past, but also his ruined future. It represents India for him, since it was all he knew of India before going there; but his stay, his confrontation with the reality of misery, has taught him that this image is false, and, lacking a past to stabilize him, he has not been able to "keep his head above water." This becomes even more obvious if one puts by the side of the passage just cited another, taken from a conversation with the manager of the European club: "Tell them: 'He is frozen with horror. A young man in the deserted house breaks the lights and asks himself why, why'" (88/67).

Crashes and shouts are the expression of disorder, of despair, and take the place of the mother's music which signifies the order created by affection. It is significant in this connection that the attraction which Anne-Marie Stretter exercises upon the white men is linked to music: like the vice-consul's mother, she plays the piano. She often plays a piece by Schubert which evokes, for her English friends, the time when they became acquainted, and, for Charles Rossett, Anne-Marie Stretter's imaginary childhood in Venice. For everyone, music is therefore linked to the past, real or imagined.

We have seen that, if there is communication in this story, it is to be found in large part beyond words, in connection with things, with vague

---

43. We know that the vice-consul has difficulty expressing himself, a defect with which this failure of memory can doubtless be connected.

impressions. The vice-consul, whose possibilities for communication are, because of his isolation, even more limited than the others', realizes this. This is why he hangs around Anne-Marie Stretter's bicycle: for want of anything better, he takes advantage of this opportunity for indirect contact, contact which can be established only through a lifeless object.

To the extent that verbal communication occurs in this novel, there is a very strong concentration on the phatic function.[44] Just as the vice-consul has "never been able to stop trying to love," the characters in the novel never reach the point of giving up trying to communicate. But even when they do talk, no one listens; they leave their sentences unfinished as if unable to complete them; they never say what they really want to say. Never does a true "message" reach the one to whom it is directed. So it is by no means surprising that non-verbal means must often replace the ineffective word. In a dead society, one communicates through dead objects.

2.4 "Death in the midst of life"

This reversal brings us to my final theme, that of death. The world depicted in this novel is a dead world. The mad woman and the other Calcutta beggars are often presented as inanimate objects: "enclosure," "pile," "mixture of lepers and dogs," "agglomerations of lepers"; they are almost always asleep. When the girl is turned out by her mother, the latter condemns her to death, and justifies this sentence in the following words: "my duty is to the survivors" (10/2). The girl is already fated to die when she begins her march. This death progresses, gradually reaches into every part of her being: she loses her hair, she is consumed by her unborn child, she becomes dumb, she goes mad and in the end becomes sterile. Nevertheless she does not die all at once, she has to go on living a life that isn't one. This vegetable state is defined with remarkable exactness by the vice-consul: "'Death in the midst of life,' says the vice-consul finally, 'but it never catches up with you? Is that it?'" (174/139).[45] The mad woman is already "too dead" to be affected by the leprosy by which she is surrounded. Her immunity to this disease strikes the whites powerfully, for they dwell on it in their conversations. One may connect their astonishment with the fear they have of leprosy: it is because they are afraid of it that they talk about it so much. This fear leads them to take security measures which guarantee the separation of the two races. At the same time, the ironic analogy between their own immunity and that of the mad woman—ironic because

44. See Jakobson, "Linguistics and Poetry."
45. He is reacting here to Charles Rossett's remarks about the mad woman. He has never met her, nor does he pay attention to her as the others do. There is no doubt that he is capable of comprehending the mad woman's condition—a capacity which is astounding in one who usually expresses himself so poorly—because her life resembles his own. He is himself "a dead man" (128/101). He speaks here as much of himself as of the mad woman.

the causes of the immunity are opposite in the two cases—extends to the entire life of the two groups, so different at first sight. The whites, too, vegetate in their artificial world; like the mad woman and the lepers, they are the living dead, in their idleness, in their cloistered life, in the falseness of their relationships, in short in the stagnation of their life in India. In this perspective, the whites' efforts to shelter themselves from leprosy reflects their efforts, on the moral plane, to not let themselves be touched by the suffering of the natives. They opt for a superficial but secure life, sheltered from suffering and leprosy. They choose immunity. This choice may significantly illuminate Anne-Marie Stretter's attitude towards the vice-consul. He attracts and intrigues her, because he doesn't hide his feelings, because he isn't like the others, but this attraction is dangerous. It threatens the equilibrium in just the same way that leprosy threatens cleanliness. This is why Anne-Marie Stretter will refuse this love.

The immunity of the mad woman and of the whites is a result of their dead life, which is reflected in their inability to love and communicate, an inability which has as its cause and effect the failure of relations between mother and child. This closes the thematic network, and the closure itself contributes to the process whereby the stifling atmosphere which penetrates the novel is signified.

3. CONCLUSION

Let us return to our starting-point. To what extent is N2 subordinated to N1? The thematic analysis has adequately shown the answer: every important theme of N1 is to be found, pushed to an extreme, in N2, which is therefore a *mise en abyme* of N1. It is important to note in this regard that the development of N2, the movement towards madness, towards total isolation, is already finished at the point where N1 begins. The outcome is known, not only to the reader, but also to the characters in N1. The thematic analogy suggests on every page that the outcome of N1 is going to be similar to that of N2: isolation, definitive abandonment of all hope, of all continuity. This stagnation is not signified only by the thematic analogy; the very fact that this analogy, visible to the reader, is invisible to the whites, makes the failure unavoidable. Not only the vice-consul, but also Anne-Marie Stretter, Charles Rossett, and Peter Morgan, give up, each in their own way, their initial hope for communication. Across the board, expectation vanishes, and they give themselves up to "death in the midst of life." The whites' encounters with the mad woman and with the vice-consul are the stages in this degradation. One understands why there is almost no action in this novel: the mirror story of the mad woman *predicts* the impossibility of action; the fact that Peter Morgan writes a book about this story, and talks about it, *establishes* this impossibility, since it is the mad woman as a topic of conversation that allows him to penetrate the world of the whites.

Thus we *can* call N2 an *embedded* narrative; its subordination to N1 is double, as in the case of *The Thousand and One Nights*. Nonetheless, the relationship which N2 establishes with N1 is a dynamic one, as we have seen, and its technical subordination goes along with a great power of prediction and determination. Because of its hypo-narrative function, N2 surpasses the limits assigned to it. Hence its subordination, clearly indicated by the novel's first sentence and confirmed, at the historical level, by the colonial situation, is constantly put in question. The railings protect the whites, but also imprison them. The fictive status of N2 in relation to N1 is pushed into the background when the mad woman, *with* her story— she *is* her story, and does not exist except through it—straddles the boundaries, the railings of the narrative. One no longer knows which of the two narratives is the hypo-narrative. They reflect each other equally. Peter Morgan's incapacity to write equals the mad woman's incapacity to speak.

The narrative structure, at first so clear and reassuring, signifies its own impossibility, to the same extent and in the same way that the colonial structure signifies its self-destruction. Destruction, like leprosy, is contagious: the two narratives infect each other. We no longer know whether the image of the society begets the narrative structure, or vice versa. N1 and N2 are both hypo-narratives. What is lacking, in this novel, is the *Narrative*, the mother-narrative which would ensure the fictive status of the world which the novel brings to signification.

∎ 8 ∎

Chéri and the
Non-Existent Character

The theme of the colloquium for which this paper was written was "New Critical Approaches to Colette." There is a need for such new approaches. Colette's status in criticism is ambiguous: an author eminently popular but, perhaps for this reason, ignored by recent criticism; an author almost too accessible, and hence of no interest to specialists in literary theory thirsty for the enigmatic and the avant-garde; a period author, but not of any canonical "great period," belonging neither to the nineteenth century nor to the post-modern era, and hence rarely taken up in research or the university curriculum; an author cited as an example in scholarly manuals of style and composition, and therefore holding no surprises for educated readers; a woman author writing about women, but studied at least as much by men—as witness the colloquium—and who created unique and disturbing male characters: her work has not been as fully integrated as one would wish into modern literary study. Analyses have remained for the most part thematic and stylistic; they deal with the entire *oeuvre* rather than with a single text, trying to draw out the characteristics of the *oeuvre*, or of the author, rather than penetrate into each particular novel. The novels suffer from this approach, being treated as symptoms rather than as autonomous signs; they are seen as stages in an evolution rather than as specific creations; they are related to the life of the author rather than to the moment in history when they began to have an impact.[1] Sometimes the studies are inspired rather by love,[2] or disappointed love,[3] than by scholarly interest, and in the bibliographies one finds writings by Colette's husband[4] side by side with those of professors. Structuralism, already passé for many,

1. E.g., Phelps, *Colette*; D'Hollander, *Colette*.
2. E.g., Raaphorst-Rousseau, *Colette*; Houssa, *Le souci de l'expression*.
3. E.g., Ketchum, *Colette*; Duquette, *Colette*.
4. Goudeket, *La douceur*, "L'oeil du témoin."

internalized by others (including me), has scarcely touched Colette's work. Psychoanalytic criticism has not been systematically integrated. Deconstruction would find the novels not complex enough; social criticism would find them insufficiently anchored in history; reception-criticism, despite the novels' great popularity and the full documentation available on their reception, has ignored them completely. Michèle Sarde has called Colette a feminist—a rather cavalier characterization—but feminist criticism has paid no attention at all. Only modern philology, the editing of texts, and the study of manuscripts—paradoxically coexisting with the new post-structuralist approaches—have systematically tackled the work of Colette.

There is no point in trying to explain this state of affairs. Better to change it. The colloquium was an attempt to do so. To integrate all these approaches will be beyond our scope, but that is not the point. If we could reintegrate the *oeuvre* into current literary study, show that there is something to be gained and that it is worth the trouble—that it is not too "a-social" for social criticism, for example—that would already be an interesting achievement.

For my part, I would like to propose a first step in psychoanalytic criticism of *Chéri*. My choice of this novel is motivated not only by its incontestably superior quality, but above all by the fact that its theme paradoxically obliterates its unconscious content; I will return to this in a moment. My approach will be equally paradoxical. Colette's autobiographical texts are so replete with psychoanalytic *themes*—fixation on childhood, nostalgia for a lost paradise, love of the mother—that one forgets their status as symptoms: too attached to what is *said*, the critics take these texts at face value and not sufficiently *according to the letter* (à la lettre), and in doing so miss the flagrant contradictions, between the *said* and the *unsaid*, between the autobiographical and the fictional, whose key symptom is the dominating presence of the mother in the autobiography, and her absence, flaws, or absurdity in the fiction. Starting from this symptom, I intend to invert the usual perspective and to begin with the hypothesis that the mother constitutes a burden on the child. In other words, that it is the position of the child who opposes or rivals the mother—a position occupied sometimes by a woman, sometimes by a man—which is the thematic center of the novels, *Chéri* being no exception. From this perspective, the mother's "wisdom" in the autobiographical writings becomes a bit irritating; generalizations about "the facts of life" are juxtaposed to the ridiculous repetitions, in the fiction, of the ridiculous old women. The negations, absences, indirect focalizations, are symptoms of a deep negativity, of which Chéri's suicide is only one instance, along with the desexualization of Léa, the whiteness of Edmée, the description of Chéri decolored by the light behind him, the omission of any account of the first months of the separation, Léa's complaint that Chéri talks as if in Chinese, the play of mirrors and the games of hide-and-seek, Chéri's desire not to hear the voice of his mother, her silence being presented as the height of happiness, the absence of the father and of the law, the absence of work or social occupation, the inability to speak, to communicate, to which is added for Chéri the inability to live either with or without Léa. In this sense, his suicide is no more than the natural conclusion to his life; never having existed, he needs only to disembarrass the world of his disturbing pseudo-existence. This is a first answer to the question implied in my title, Does Chéri exist? Very little.

And Léa? Might she be a representation of Colette (who, in her prime, played the role of Léa in the stage version)? The warm mother, in contrast to the old women in the Peloux house? But, as such a "good mother," Léa bears more resemblance to Sido, Colette's mother, as represented in the autobiographical writings. So who represents Colette? Is it not rather Chéri, who suffers from dependence, from fixation? The suggestion is disturbing, but it is analogous to the one I ventured in my little book on *The Cat*,[5] in which the neurotic Alain, fixated on childhood, on his mother, shows himself for that reason unable to live adult life as represented by marriage. The negativity of my title is related, therefore, to ambiguity in the character-identifications. It is time to move to the text itself, to try to show how the psychoanalytic hypothesis of unconscious meanings leads to a new interpretation, but one which subsumes the traditional interpretation. There, exactly, lies the point of which I would like to persuade you: such an approach is not opposed to the achievements of criticism; it integrates them, places them on another level so as to explain them. Thus it allows us to go beyond paraphrasing the conscious thematic. Let us read again the first page of the novel.

Immediately there is a conflict between two positions, that of the mother and that of the child, between two beings equally defined by the negative. The well known opening to the novel witnesses to this. Let us take it *according to the letter*, in order to extricate its unsaid:

> "Léa! Give it me, your pearl necklace! Do you hear me, Léa? Give me your necklace!"
> No answer came from the big bed of wrought iron and chiseled brass, which shone in the shadow like a suit of armor.
> "Why won't you give it me, your necklace? It suits me as well as you, if not better!" (13/3)[6]

Chéri, the speaker of the first word, begins his existence with the name of the other, and with a statement in the imperative mood. His object is an object of value,[7] the pearl necklace, which condenses two things in its

5. *Complexité d'un roman populaire.* See also above, Chapter 4, sect. 2.B.
6. [Translator's note] Page references are to the French and English respectively. The latter are for reference only—the translations are my own, and deliberately literal.
7. See the entries "Object" (216–17) and "Value" (364–66), in Greimas and Courtés, *Semiotics and Language.*

Freudian symbolic value: money—which, for people like Léa, rich but outside the law, stands for existence itself, the number of pearls, forty-nine, being a synecdochic metaphor for the age of their owner—and the *bisexuality* underlying the author's identification with Chéri, whose masculinity is so little developed. The imperative mood, as the philosophers of language[8] and the ideologues[9] tell us, does not succeed as a perlocutionary speech-act except when the speaker has the authority to use it. How can Chéri possibly have it, if he does not exist except through the other, as the opening to the novel, and so many other passages, show? His very repetition of the command turns it into an infantile, and therefore ambiguous, insistence—the insistence of the powerless. "Do you hear me?" implies doubt as to whether the existence of the speaker has been recognized.

The second paragraph shows that Chéri—his assumption of authority as well as his words—is indeed disregarded. But it does not help define his interlocutrix. Over against the necklace there stands the bed—the setting for the drama, the center of the world with which one must become acquainted, in opposition to the necklace as external value. What is presented to us is less a character than conflict itself. Before entering the scene through her words, Léa is represented by her weapons. She is well armed, and precisely by this bed, though it stands throughout the novel as the haven of security. The paradox will be definitively resolved by Chéri's words at the end, after he has understood: "Oh! How well you have poisoned me!" (153/134) He thus sums up his situation, of death, of non-existence, in line with his earlier, fatal diagnosis: "With you, Nounoune, I'm likely to stay twelve years old for a half-century!" (148/129) The security Léa offers is, in this sense, her weapon, and she strikes home.

The third paragraph, again spoken by Chéri, pursues the issue of sexual ambiguity—"It suits me as well as you, if not better!"—while introducing a new, related motif, that of rivalry. Chéri is in competition with Léa, a competition which starts as a banal beauty contest, but in which the real stake is the conflict between generations. The young child tries to monopolize the mother's goodness, then her beauty, then her position, in order to supplant her: this is why the novel had to begin with a command, which is resumed here, but which will be realized, negatively, in the prohibition at the end, when Chéri's "I forbid you" (151/132) strikes home, and condemns Léa to give up for good the position of mother. To supplant the too-powerful mother, to render her superfluous, to grab her position: this, in my opinion, is what is unconsciously at stake in the work, what it strives by all means to achieve. But the struggle is too hard, utterly unequal, and unhappy in its result: between suicide and solitude, the relations between

8. See Ducrot, *Dire et ne pas dire*
9. Kress and Hodge, *Language as Ideology*.

the sexes, which seem necessarily to be a competition between generations, turn out to be the way towards androgyny or non-existence. The setting for the unequal struggle is presented in these terms:

> In front of the pink curtains shot through with sunlight he danced, all black, like a graceful devil against the background of a furnace. But when he turned back towards the bed, he became all white again, from his silk pyjamas to his suede slippers (13/3).

The situation is set out in terms of colors. The curtains which enclose Chéri in this haven of security destined to become a prison are pink, like the pearls, like Léa, like soft flesh, like the inside of the body, translucent but not transparent. Chéri, by contrast, is colorless. Though graceful, he is also diabolical, and in relation to him the pinkness becomes a furnace. Turning himself from black to white, he passes, in the implied photographic terminology, from a positive to a negative image, one which is the exact opposite of reality. On the next page this suggestion recurs, and the word image is used, in connection with a key motif of indirection—the mirror.

> He stood in front of a long mirror attached to the wall between the two windows, and contemplated his image, that of a very beautiful and very young man, neither tall nor short, his hair with the bluish tinge of a blackbird's feathers (14/3).

Pink loses its reassuring quality in turning to fire. This regression is marked also at the level of events: his very "turning back"—the action which accompanies the photographic shift—burns like fire. Notice how these disquieting ideas are well wrapped up in metaphor; but the metaphor is strikingly consistent, and identifies from the outset the important motifs.

Shortly after the battle for the necklace, that significant object of value, the following passage creates still more new aspects:

> They looked at each other with a hostile air; she, leaning among her lingerie and lace; he, sitting side-saddle (*en amazone*) on the edge of the bed. He thought, "She has a nerve to talk to me about the wrinkles I may some day have." And she, "Why is he ugly when he laughs, he who is beauty itself?" (14–15/4)

This passage, which again will be fully realized towards the end of the novel, no longer presents hostility purely as metaphor. It is now visible. The two characters are defined by their battle posture, and if Léa is still an integral part of the bed-battleground, Chéri is on the point of departure, of flight. The element of androgyny is more explicit, in the use of the very word "amazon," which might almost be taken in its literal sense here, but which is in fact a catachresis,[10] a dead metaphor. More important is the representation of non-communication. The conflict is verbalized in thoughts of unexpressed antagonism, which focus once again on beauty in its nega-

10. Ducrot and Todorov, *Dictionnaire encyclopédique.*

tive connotations, and, when Chéri reproaches Léa for talking about his future defects, on the conflict between generations. To speak, even to think, of the other in the third person—this is an example of the indirection which characterizes the fundamentally defective relationship between the two rivals. For Chéri, "in revolt and yet submissive, loosely chained, unable to be free" (15/5), the accusation of ugliness is worse than that of malice. If one asks why, most critics answer in terms of the amoral sensuality of Colette's work.[11] But in my opinion this is the result rather than the cause. The drama of ugliness thinly disguises a block to the process of maturation—"unable to be free"—which borrows its form of expression from the aesthetic-sensual domain precisely *because* this domain is already opposed to communication, inaccessible. It is the outside alone which can be interpreted, since the characters are not capable of admitting that the other penetrates into them.

Léa, a pink character beside the colorless Chéri (and Edmée dressed in white!), defends herself with little success against the reproach that she smothers the child with her superiority. This woman, who has just been said to love Chéri *because* he is "unable to be free," and who towards the end will betray her jealousy of the younger woman, resorts to an outright lie in response to the "choir" of *demimondaines* who envy her Chéri: "Let them take him. I don't keep him chained up, and he goes out all by himself" (17/6). On the contrary, she has kept him firmly chained up, in an attempt to escape the impasse created by her finding her true identity precisely in assuming the role of mother. For the character of Léa represents a condensation and a displacement. The numerous old women in the novel, among whom is the "national Harpy" who will be replaced in the second volume by la Copine as Léa's central "other," divide the maternal characteristics among themselves. Léa is set over against the others—the warmth which attaches and yet imprisons versus the coolness, ridicule, and malice which first created in the child this lack, this void, making maturation impossible for him, for want of real existence, of psychic substance. Excess of attachment versus lack of bonding. Léa represents a displacement in that she assumes only a part of the maternal negativity—and the most "positive" part, the bewitchment which is the immediate cause of the fixation—while leaving to others the instances of cold aggressiveness which create the void and prepare the child for the fixation. Léa also represents a condensation, in that she is more than just maternal. She stands not only for safety, and its converse, imprisonment, but also for the daughter. Her own narcissism becomes mixed with that of Chéri, who is her other "myself." Her sensuality is superior to that of her lover-child. She incarnates that paradoxical honesty which is a major issue in the novel, and which she herself defines *a posteriori*:

11. Duquette, *Colette*.

"My poor Chéri. . . . It's funny to think that in losing, you your old worn out mistress, I my scandalous young lover, we have lost the most honorable thing we possessed on earth . . ." (127/109–10).

If Léa's position is ambiguous, it is so not only in the evaluative sense—indispensable warmth versus destructive attachment—but also and above all in the sense that she represents Colette the daughter, rendered impotent by the overpowering mother, and herself incapable of being a mother. Léa has no child, and will lose, through the loss of her relationship with Chéri, her femininity.

Léa's transformation from mother into daughter: in her the struggle between Colette and Sido plays itself out. Attachment to the past, which motivates Chéri (as much as Colette, his double) to cleave to everything about Léa that is maternal, that is dated ("The midday sun came into the pink room, gay, over-decorated, and of a luxury that dated it" 18/8), is equally a problem for Léa herself, and the circular shape of her domain, with its closed pink curtains, as well as of the novel, serves to identify her position as that of the mother—but only for Chéri, not for herself. For her own part, she is just as frustrated as he by the characteristic incapacity of neurotics to grasp the present. She moves back and forth between future and past; hence the flashbacks. After the opening scene, the narrative goes back to the beginning of the affair, when Léa tended the "baby" in his growing pains, and when she was not able to talk with Chéri. But it is in the final scene that the conflict is brought into view in all its clarity. As mother, Léa actively plans her child's future. As child, she despairs that she cannot go back, start again from scratch, recapture the moment before the painful revelation. To replace the adult man, the father, with an adolescent is a way of returning to a past in which love is the chaste but intense love between brothers. As Chéri puts it: "No women . . . so much the better! Say, Léa, are you my brother? Yes?" (36/24)

True, the attempt to occupy the position of mother turns out badly, or rather, too well. After Chéri has left, Léa sees herself reflected, like any mother abandoned by her child, in the mirror which gives concrete form to the split in herself: "A wheezy old woman mimicked, in the oblong mirror, her gesture, and Léa wondered what she could have in common with this old fool" (158/138). The split is inevitable, in that any mother is also a daughter, and those who hold a bit too long onto the role of child will be powerless in later life.

The problem inherent in motherhood is dramatized in the novel with a particular acuteness. The demands are simply too great. The security that everyone needs, of which one sees traces everywhere in the novel, and which is represented in western ideology by the Virgin Mary, the pure mother,[12] has an inevitable reverse side—the destructiveness which is

12. Warner, *Alone of All Her Sex.*

equally invested in the mother, and of which Eve the first woman is the symbol.[13] The chastity of the one, and domination by the other, are equally male projections, but they have entered the consciousness of everyone, men and women, since men have for so long controlled the ideology of the sexes, and since men and women have equally experienced the extreme power-lessness of childhood. Colette suffered this particularly, one may suppose, in that she was a witness to the castrating power of the mother. Did she not see her father, from whom she got her wish to be a writer, triply impotent, with his torn-off leg, his weak character, and his empty notebooks? In the novels, fathers are absent or are mere puppets,[14] though criticism has not perceived clearly enough that fatherly men (Farou, Renaud) alternate with impotent ones (Michel, Alain, Chéri) in this role.

Colette's solution to the problem of the strong mother is multi-layered. Firstly, she sometimes eliminates the mother, a move which has been observed but not explained.[15] The elimination of the mother allows for her substitution by the daughter, but the latter can only fall into the same inherent trap. Léa bears witness to this: after correcting Charlotte, Chéri's mother, she becomes, at the end of the novel, identified with her—an old fool who falls into Charlotte's habit of repeating everything she says ("He's coming back up! He's coming back up!" 157/138). The unity in duality of mother and daughter, celebrated by Colette in her autobiographical texts, is fatally betrayed by the love which comes to set these roles in opposition. They become enemies: Léa and Charlotte detest each other, Léa and Edmée are natural enemies. The contempt for other women criticized by Simone de Beauvoir[16] becomes only too apparent. In this sense, it would be paradoxical to call Colette a feminist. The horror of mothering is at the same time a prime symptom of the converse aspect: contempt for herself in the position of daughter. Denying herself, through a disgust so deep as to amount to a self-destructive taboo, access to the motherhood whose fatal side she has observed only too well, Colette is caught in the impasse personified in Léa. A feminist position becomes impossible for her, since her basic attitude towards femininity is negative. Hence her need to project herself onto male characters (Chéri, Alain), an identification which is arrived at via the position of child.

Secondly, however, Colette assuredly has a side which one may call feminist and which one sees at work in this novel. It shows itself in the way she dares to go beyond binary divisions by projecting herself into all pos-sible positions: parents, children, men, women. Encouraged by her own narcissism, Colette projects parts of herself everywhere, and the novel gains

13. See Bal, *Lethal Love*, Chapter 5, and below, Chapter 9.
14. See Biolley-Godino, *L'homme-objet*.
15. E.g., Duquette, *Colette*, 90–92.
16. Beauvoir, *La force des choses*.

in complexity thereby. Her claiming of the right to express her sexuality, irritating to many male readers who feel themselves called into question by it, points to a sense of powerlessness which she seeks to overcome, projecting it onto the Chéri of the beginning of the novel, and onto Léa as she appears after the affair. At the same time, this claim is one of the leading ideas of the feminist ideology which seeks to conquer the image of Eve. In Colette, this claim plainly arises from unconscious sources, and is only the more convincing for this reason.

Thirdly, Colette does not shrink from representing the fears and frustrations of women. Could one imagine, for example, a more direct evocation of that second, reversed "birth trauma" which is the fear of defloration, than the following, taken from *Claudine en ménage?*

> "Furthermore, I harbored for a long time, and to tell the truth still harbor a little bit, the dread of . . . how shall I put it? One calls it 'marital duty,' I believe. This virile Renaud makes me think, for the sake of comparison, of that big clod Anaïs, who always wanted to put her oversized hands into too small gloves."[17]

In *Chéri*, the image of the ridiculous old women represents the fear of the converse aspect of womanhood, the fear of its ending; Léa's final rejection by Chéri who, once away from her, "filled his chest with air, like an escaped convict" (158/138), depicts the anguish of abandonment; the complaints to the boxer Patron express her sexual frustrations. The self-mastery which gives Léa her maternal superiority serves only to hide her infantile fears.

Finally, the "feminist" side of Colette—which, as I have said, is never other than paradoxical—is visible in the very conflict from which her character suffers: torn between the myths of Mary and of Eve, Léa refuses to choose, and this attempt to transcend a destructive sexual ideology constitutes the feminist heroism of the author, even as it symptomatizes her painful neurotic fixations.

The literary means which Colette uses to exteriorize this unconscious network of ambivalent positions are many. Obviously, the fabula, the story of a love incestuous and chaste, acted out in the milieu of chic prostitutes and half-imbecile bastards, but which at the same time is "the most honorable thing we possessed on earth," constitutes the framework of the complex in question; this only too recognizable story conceals its unconscious sources. The *images*, some of which I have picked out from the first pages of the novel, enrich this framework with troubling nuances. The mirror, which in Lacan's theory constitutes the pivot between the imaginary infancy and the entry into the symbolic order of intersubjective communication, is a key image, figuring this transition in Chéri, as well as the narcissism of both characters which is its precondition. Further, the mirror

17. Colette, *Claudine en ménage*, 14 [trans. by ed.].

thematizes the indirect focalization so characteristic of the work that it is sometimes, and quite rightly, reproached with voyeurism. Since this voyeurism is nothing else than a compensation for the communicative powerlessness of the subject fixated on the image of the primal scene—where the man, for the child who is watching, seems to lose a member, a leg or something else—one begins to glimpse the density of this image of an image. The *language* of the novel is another subtle and effective means of expression: replete on the one hand with negations, on the other with generalizations and repetitions, it represents the non-existence of the subject fixed in the infantile position. If the existence of Chéri is expressed in negative terms, it is because it gets totally drowned in the multitude of particular instances where he loses his individuality, just as Léa's repeating herself at the end makes her get lost in the mass of old women. The *paradoxes* are another way of saying the unsayable, and at the same time they point to a certain level of generality.

Finally, the most striking means is the circular *structure* of the novel. It harks back at the end to its beginning, and both of Chéri's departures, of which the one, supposed to be definitive, proves provisional, while the other is definitive but comes too late (whence his return and his suicide in the sequel) are focalized by Léa. The first departure, "on winged feet," foreshadows the deceptive relief of the second, and in between there takes place a scene in which, with Léa absent, Chéri *and* Edmée see themselves quite appropriately as orphans. And, in the following image, a metonymic metaphor like the ones pointed out by Genette in the work of Proust,[18] a narrative metaphor in that it foreshadows the conclusion, and a *mise en abyme*[19] in that it harks back to the "winged feet" and the whiteness of the beginning, we see that the position of victim is equitably distributed: "She looked, overwhelmed, at this impatient young man, white as a seagull, whose light feet and open arms seemed ready for takeoff . . ." (152/133).

As mother, she destroys; as child, she abandons; Chéri abandons and is abandoned: however differentiated one becomes, one remains "overwhelmed" by the powerful mother. Let us stop idealizing, on the basis of an autobiography which is shot through with this burdensome sense of the superiority of the other, the relationship between Colette and her mother. To assess how much she remained a child, crippled by this relationship, would be a better way of taking Colette and her work seriously.

18. Genette, *Narrative Discourse.*
19. See Dällenbach, *Le récit spéculaire.*

■ 9 ■

Zola and
the Nature of Sin

Brother Archangias, the most misogynist character in Zola,[1] well understood the Apostle "Paul,"[2] to whom the following lines are attributed:

> Let a woman learn in silence with all submissiveness. I permit no woman to teach or to have authority over men; she is to keep silent. For Adam was formed first, then Eve; and Adam was not seduced, but the woman was seduced and became a transgressor. (1 Tim 2:11–14, adapted.)[3]

In the area of seduction Archangias is an expert, and he knows better than anyone how intensely close the relation between woman and the serpent has remained, since their unhappy encounter in paradise: "They have the devil in their bodies, they reek of the devil; they reek of him in their legs, in their arms, in their belly, all over . . ." (71/75).[4]

"Paul" gives only two of the eleven arguments enumerated by Trible[5] in her list of "misogynous" traits drawn, rightly or wrongly, from Genesis 2–3. "Paul's" two arguments are both the most commonly put forward and the most obviously wrong. As a factual report of the story, they do not find support in the text when it is carefully read; even if they did, the conclusion to be drawn from these "facts" would not necessarily be these value judg-

---

1. The following is an intertextual reading of Emile Zola's novel *La faute de l'abbé Mouret* and Genesis 1–3. It parallels Chapter 5 of my *Lethal Love*, bringing the novel into relationship with the text of Genesis at each stage.

2. Current scholarship does not accept the traditional attribution of 1 Timothy to Paul. The quotation marks take account of both the tradition and the scholarship.

3. Biblical quotations are from the Revised Standard Version, adapted where so noted. Biblical quotations not otherwise marked are from Genesis.

4. [Translator's note] Page references are to the French and English respectively. The latter are for reference only—the translations are my own, and deliberately literal.

5. Trible, *God and the Rhetoric of Sexuality*, 73.

ments; and, even if these judgments were justified, there would not be the slightest logical link between them and the prohibition based on them. I argue in each case the opposite: that Adam as male is not the first to be created; that no qualitative priority can in any case be based on mere chronological order; and that, even if the man could pride himself on such a priority, the woman's being a less successful product of divine pottery would by no means imply her incapacity to speak, teach, or exercise authority; and, furthermore, that the two humans transgressed equally.

Though Archangias' summary of "Paul's" argument is a bit simplistic—"It would be good riddance if all girls were strangled at birth" (39/37)—it remains faithful to the structure of the argument, whose most interesting point seems to me to be the *collocation* of the emergence of the female body in narrative signs, and the assumption of moral corruption in the character endowed with that body. I shall show that the proper name is the site of this collocation. The proper name, a textual label which signifies the stability and the continuity of the character, makes the character and the common noun coincide. In other words, if Archangias refuses to refer to Albine by her proper name, it is because the proper name *Eve* makes the proper name Albine superfluous; replacing the proper name *Eve* by, in his opinion, the most pertinent feature of "Eve" as a concept or a common noun, he calls Albine simply *the trollop (la gueuse)*. Paradoxically, his rejection of the proper name—Archangias never pronounces the name *Albine*—shows how the proper name functions in the novel.

Why do modern theoreticians (Barthes) and novelists (Sarraute, Duras, Robbe-Grillet), in their attacks on literary character, militate, after their various fashions, against the proper name, which "can no longer be written," according to Barthes.[6] The central place occupied by the proper name in fictional discourse gives rise to a reading strategy which I propose to call the retrospective fallacy. It consists of retrojecting a complete character, fully defined and unique, *named*, onto the textual elements which have led, gradually, to the construction of that character. The resulting circularity is the fallacy of realism. It is in this way that "Paul" read Genesis, and Archangias shows us the power and the persistence of the retrospective fallacy. But Zola's novel does more; staging, through the character Archangias, the destructive aspect of such a reading of Genesis, it attempts an impossible superseding of this typically Christian reading. From the point of view of the poetics of the novel, this polemical intertextuality should make us pause. For it brings into play the concept of *character*, and, along with it, all such pseudo-stable narratological concepts. The dialogical reading which I shall propose in the following pages is meant to exemplify the self-critical narratology which I advocate, which alone can save a

6. Barthes, *S/Z*, 95.

discipline grown sterile, by placing it in the service of a general critical theory.[7]

There was no Eve in paradise. During the brief period which passed in that place, one can at most discern several phases in the *construction* of this character. First there was an earth creature, after that a woman, then an actant, and it was only after the time in paradise that a being called Eve came into existence. Following the several stages of this construction will enable us to see how Zola reacts to each.

1. THE EMERGENCE OF THE HUMAN BODY

The signs of the female body do not appear right away. First, a sexless creature is formed. The first body, *the* body, unique and undivided, is the body of the earth creature, the work of Yahweh the potter. From 2:7 to 2:20, this creature has neither name nor sex nor capacity to act. It appears as a potential character, pointing, precisely by what it lacks, to the definition of a complete character.

As a description of the concept (humanity, human being) that it signifies, the word *hā'ādām* is very apt. It is derived from the word which indicates the material used in its construction. The earth in its materiality, *hā'ādāmā* or "clod," envelops the creature which partakes of it. In other words, the latter is characterized first of all as *taken from*, differentiated from, a larger milieu. This principle of differentiation is the major feature of the Genesis 1 creation.

The creature has no proper name. The common noun does not become a proper name until much later. The creature is as yet completely passive; it is under the control of its creator, who places it in the garden where the trees are about to appear. In the same way, Serge is carried unconscious to Paradou.

Trible,[8] among others, stresses the sexually undifferentiated nature of this *ha'adam*. Strictly speaking, it cannot even be called androgynous or bisexual, for sexuality does not yet exist. Nonetheless, this is how the later versions understood it. In the more recent account in Genesis 1, for example, God creates humanity as male and female (1:27), and in 5:1–2 this androgyny is explicitly attributed to the being *hā'ādām*. The use of the plural pronoun ("he created *them*") in 1:27 and 5:2 makes a singular, male understanding of the creature in chapter 2 unjustified. What prompts readers like "Paul" to assume that this creature is male, and why do they take this (erroneous) priority as proof of superiority? Unable to read an incomplete character, they complete it, themselves providing the features

---

7. For a full discussion of this issue, especially in relation to the work of Jürgen Habermas, see above, Chapter 1.
8. Trible, *God and the Rhetoric of Sexuality*, 72–143.

that are lacking. It is clear that our Christian friends base their readings on a concept of character of which proper name and sexual identity form an integral part, and which assumes stability in every case. Such a static reading of character is encouraged by a descriptive narratology which aims at *naming*, at pointing out unities, and creates precisely out of this stability the "coherence" which is the criterion of the text's integrity. As a result, it inevitably fails to take account of one of the most interesting aspects of the novel as a genre: its polemic against the literary tradition out of which it was born. Zola provides a striking example of this. Oddly enough, Serge is not the only offspring of undifferentiated *hā'ādām*. Albine when she first appears, as the only inhabitant of Paradou, is presented as a neutral being, a wild, sexless little monkey.

2. THE EMERGENCE OF SEXUAL DIFFERENCE

After this phase of pure existence, differentiation develops. The singular creature becomes plural. However, while readers may be able to complete the character, the character itself cannot. It is Yahweh God, and not *hā'ādām*, who decides that his work is not finished. Once in paradise, "It is not good that the human should be alone; I will make for it a companion corresponding to it" (2:18, adapted). So Serge, as soon as he has glimpsed Paradou, begins to feel ill at ease. Albine will put it precisely: "What you need is to be loved; do you see?" (102/114). The lack of sexual differentiation causes a vaguely resented loneliness, but the being cannot know what it lacks, not having experienced it yet. It takes some time, though, for Yahweh to understand that simply *adding* beings will not suffice. The animals, beings of a different kind, do not *correspond*. Two remarks are in place here. First, Yahweh's error is the first indication of the fact that he is beginning to lose his absolute power and mastery. Second, the problem with the animals shows that the usual translation, "a help(mate) fit for him," is wrong, and not "simply" sexist. This translation renders the animal episode void of meaning. For, according to the myth, it is the tension between the same and the different which creates sexuality. The creature has to be separated from part of itself, in order that the remaining "half," as well as the separated "half," may come into existence.

The earth creature loses consciousness in a deep sleep. This sleep is the death of the undifferentiated creature. It will wake up double, differentiated. This phase of the development is presented by Serge who, after the crisis in which he implores first the Virgin, then God, loses consciousness. Like *hā'ādām*, Serge dies to his untenable innocence, in order to be reborn, painfully and slowly, as a new man: as a man. His aloneness and his childishness have been underlined numerous times by all of the novel's discourses: by the narrator, by Serge himself in his daydreams, and by the judgments of the character charged with the axiological function: his housekeeper La Teuse. She announces that his saintliness is no more than a want of maturity: ". . . he hasn't lived at all, he knows nothing, it's no trouble for him to be as good as a cherub, dear boy!" (31/28). Zola pursues the details of this phase of the creation-construction. After his first glimpse of Paradou, Serge, vaguely ill at ease, is brought by his retarded sister to see her animals. Desirée, with whom he shares an infantile, undifferentiated existence, *shows* him the animals and *names* them. It is during this episode that Serge falls ill and loses contact with reality, leading later to loss of consciousness and memory.

The verb used for the formation of the earth creature was one specific to pottery. The verb in 2:22 refers specifically to architecture and the construction of buildings. The action is more sophisticated and more difficult, and it requires more differentiated materials. The difference would indicate a higher level of creation, and this possibility conforms to the poetics of the Bible. Just as, in the liturgical version of 1:1–2:4a, the creation of humanity is the climax of the creation of the world, so the creation of humanity in the version of 2:4b–3:24 is developed in two progressive phases of perfection. This refutes "Paul's" first argument, based as it is on his first error. The material used no longer consists of dust or clay, but of flesh and bone already enriched with *nephesh*, the life-principle. The result is also "higher"; no longer an undifferentiated creature, but a sexual being, and more precisely a woman: ". . . and the rib which Yahweh God had taken from *hā'ādām* he built into a woman (*'ishā*)" (2:22, adapted). Of the two nouns which in this text designate sexually differentiated beings, *'ishā*, woman, appears first; *'ish*, man, follows later. It is *'ishā* who changes the meaning of *hā'ādām* from earth creature to earth man. In this semiotic sense, the woman was formed first, the man afterwards (*contra* "Paul").

But there is no reason to overstate her case. Just as the man can come into being only by his differentiation from the woman, so she, as a next step in her creation, has to be recognized as different, and in her turn receive from the man the sexual identity assigned to her. Again Yahweh manipulates a character not yet finished, not yet capable of action. He brings her to *hā'ādām*, who, in recognizing the other, assumes his own sexual identity. The recognition of sexuality is worded in his poetry, which constitutes the first human speech to be directly quoted. If the woman is the first to be signified, the man is the first to speak. The attribution of speech to the man, this next step in the creation of humanity, displays the thoroughly equalizing dialectic of the narrative procedure. Alter[9] gives an interesting account of the poetics of quotation in biblical narrative. In this poetics, to which the descriptive mode is totally foreign, quotation is one device of

9. Alter, *Biblical Narrative*, 65–67.

characterization, and is, like naming, closely linked to the biblical concept of humanity. The distribution of speech and names among the different characters is therefore a relevant issue.

The experience of the man who, when he wakes, believes himself reborn, since the presence of the other changes his own being, is put into words by Serge through some sentences which display the intertextual relation to Genesis. "He fancied that he had been born only the day before" (103/116). He asks Albine, "Who are you, where do you come from, what are you doing *at my side*?" (119/134), and, "It was you, wasn't it, who drew me *out of the earth*?" (123/139, my italics). It is through the interrogative form that there develops the recognition of the other as other ("Who are you?"), whose origin poses the problem of existence. The relationship between Serge's three questions is profoundly metonymic: identity ("Who are you?") is a function simultaneously of origin ("where do you come from?") and of the tension between the same and the other: she is there, but she is not himself; she is at his side (*côté*), a condensation of the "rib" (*côte*) from which she originated and of the "companion corresponding" which defines her. And there is condensation again between Albine and the creator: "It was you, wasn't it, who drew me out of the earth?" This question shows that Serge has grasped the essence of creation according to Genesis: differentiation. "Draw out of" is, in this perspective, the very act of creation, while the passive form, "drawn out of," is the essence of humanity's specific existence.

The lyric *hā'ādām* performs is in two parts. First, he recognizes the woman as part of the same *hā'ādām* of which he is the remainder:

This at last is bone of my bones
and flesh of my flesh (2:23a).

After the failures of 2:19–20, this is a joyous celebration of their common nature, their brother- and sisterhood. The man is, then, not the parent from whom the woman is born, as the traditional reading would have it, but rather, if we stick with these family metaphors, her brother. He is the son of *hā'ādām*, she, the daughter. This relationship casts further light on that between Serge and Desirée. Retarded, the latter represents a stage which Serge will now painfully transcend.

After recognizing their similarity, *Hā'ādām* the Second celebrates difference. There are three reasons for referring to him thus. He is the second born, after the woman who has been separated from him; he is the second *hā'ādām*, after the first who was undifferentiated; but he is nonetheless the future King Adam, who will reign, under Yahweh, over the earth, including the woman—but this lies far ahead. The ambiguity of the sentence which now follows is symptomatic:

She shall be called Woman (*'ishā*),
because she was taken out of Man (*'īsh*) (2:23b).

The gender-marked noun *'īsh* seems to pose a problem for my point of view, and indeed Levinas[10] discusses the importance of the two nouns in developing the idea that the very essence of femininity is in woman's secondary origin: femininity, according to him, lies in "this initial afterthought." It would be more convenient for me if the noun *hā'ādām* had been used, so that I could assume the first, undifferentiated sense. The text as it stands leads me to consider an alternative reading. The difficulty may be resolved by supposing that, after the allotropy (the change of physical properties within the same substance), the man assumes that he always had his sexual identity. (This retrospective illusion is understandable in a character just coming into being, but should be eschewed by the modern critic, on pain of falling into paraphrase!) The man focalizes his earlier state out of his present state. Just as adults have no memory of their early childhood, during which they were not yet full subjects, let alone of their prenatal life, the man is not capable of imagining a time when he was not yet a man. This analogy between the man in Genesis and someone just entering adulthood suggests the hermeneutical code of psychoanalysis, which is obviously relevant, but on which I cannot dwell here. At this stage in the narrative development, the noun *hā'ādām* has already been definitively doubled, and the undifferentiated common noun is beginning to take on an appearance of differentiation—still a common noun, but soon to be a proper name.

However plausible and, indeed, acceptable this explanation may be, there is another equally, if not more, plausible possibility. The phrase "taken from," synonymous with Serge's words, does not mean "made out of" but "separated from," "drawn from," "differentiated from." The man is correct. Out of *hā'ādām* (in the first sense) Yahweh made *'ishā* and *'īsh*, by separating the one from the other. Similarly, in the previous phase of the creation, Yahweh made *hā'ādām* by separating it from the rest of the earth, *hā'ădāmā*, which by that separation changed radically: its unity was broken, it became less chaotic, and in losing the part of itself that was potentially human it acquired a potential master and servant. In both cases, a pun stresses difference in similarity, the relation of container to contained being reversed, if you will, by the iconic sign. This is why the same root had to be used.

Both these interpretations are staged in *La faute de l'abbé Mouret*. The amnesia is particularly discernible in that Serge, after his becoming-man, feels that he has to give up the cult of the Virgin. He can no longer conceive of a non-sexual relationship with a woman, for women have become too

10. Levinas, "Leçon talmudique."

radically alien. One might say that Serge and the Virgin have both, in this process, lost their virginity (note the rhyme of Serge and *Vierge*, as obvious as the one between La Teuse and *la gueuse*, "trollop"). From now on, Mary represents the danger which Archangias, who was at once fully aware of the change in Serge, had already seen in her. The second interpretation is manifest in the condensation of creator and creature: "It was you, wasn't it, who drew me out of the earth?" The act performed by Albine coincides with the act undergone by the earth creature. As between the novel and Genesis, the key concept "differentiate" in the one case condenses, in the other separates: the event remains the same, but subject and object, first and second, are different in the two accounts. In Zola's novel, the principle of differentiation brings about a distribution of the functions involved among the characters. Thus the male function is distributed among Serge, Archangias, Fortuné (in binary opposition to Archangias), and Rosalie's father (in opposition on the one hand to the friar and on the other—precisely as father—to Serge). In Genesis, this is how the man is presented by the narrator: "Therefore, a man leaves his father and his mother and cleaves to his wife, and they become one flesh" (2:24). This is the beginning of history. The narrator generalizes, anticipates, and, in anticipating, also looks backward. He invents here the retrospective illusion, and by doing so anticipates the parent-child relationship (for up to this stage there has been no question of parenthood). It must be so: this is how chronology begins.

We can now return to "Paul's" first claim. Although it is possible to assume that, strictly speaking, the woman was the first to exist, since she was the first to be signified, hence the first *character*, I see nothing of interest in such a conclusion. To take this line would be to succumb to a suspect, though very fashionable, ideology, based on attributing an exaggerated importance to the sign, giving it priority over the subject. If the man is the second to be signified, he is the first to signify. If the woman is differentiated first, the man is the first to recognize the difference, and hence to make it significant. This distribution of semiotic roles implies a dialectic equivalence of sign and subject, which mutually constitute each other: man and woman, then, were created at the same time. It was precisely when this semiotic of Genesis was no longer understood that interpretations of the Pauline type could come to the fore, with the well-known consequences.

This provides us with arguments against the commentaries which assume a contradiction between the two creation stories. Alter[11] tries to explain this supposed "contradiction," in a discussion which is highly interesting for biblical poetics generally. This poetics often involves different versions of the same event, sometimes contradictory from our point of view, but hermeneutically complementary. From this perspective, the critic

---

11. Alter, *Biblical Narrative*, 142–43.

distinguishes a realistic (2:4b–25) from a theological (1:1–2:4a) version of the creation. The editors, who, Alter claims, assumed that God must have created man and woman equal, as in Genesis 1, included the "sexist" version of Genesis 2 to neutralize the contradiction between theology and social life. That Alter's view seems plausible is a measure of the extent to which later interpretations have turned Genesis 2 into the sexist Pauline story. As a result, the "equal rights" version has to be explained away, but its return in 5:1–2 renders Alter's explanation/repression problematic. His defense of the paradoxical coherence of Genesis 1–3 seems to me in any case superfluous. Genesis 2 does not contradict Genesis 1. Rather, it provides a specific elaboration of the meaning of "he created them male and female." It is a case of synecdochic composition. What the redactors have done is to bring together complementary texts, one positing the principle of differentiation, the other filling it out by imaginative representation of its concrete consequences.

3. THE EMERGENCE OF ACTIVITY: SIN?

3.1 Awareness of the body

Between ahistorical existence and the beginning of history, the last sentence of Genesis 2 can be considered as a transition: "And the man and his wife were both naked, and were not ashamed" (2:25). This sentence supplies information which prepares for the events to follow. It states the duality of the future characters, and it maps the semantic field of the story: *nakedness* versus *shame*. In fact, it is not a case of simple opposition, and there is nothing "logical" about the way it is developed, as the makers of semiotic squares would have us believe.[12] The sentence portrays, albeit by negation, the evolution of character from unawareness to awareness of the body. This first "inner-view" representation of feelings further promotes the construction of characters. The sentence takes up a few lines in Genesis. Zola attests to the power of the novel as a genre by extending this episode to some fifty pages. He makes of a punctual event a progressive development which implicates the two characters equally, and the slowness of this development, if nothing else, implies a criticism of the Christian view of the seductive woman. Zola's woman, as her very name indicates, is just as naive as the man, and both need a lot of time to grow, mature, come to awareness.

In Genesis, the "logic" of shame requires the presence of the other, of Yahweh, for the characters to come to awareness of their nakedness. Likewise in Zola, it is not the nakedness itself which causes shame, but the appearance of Brother Archangias, which inspires, in Serge first of all, the

---

12. Greimas, *Du sens*.

feeling of *Unheimlichkeit* (the uncanny)[13] which follows so quickly upon his "fault."[14] I cannot help it if this comparison between the two characters, Yahweh and Archangias, is not too flattering to the former; the fact remains that in both stories it is *confrontation* between characters, the appearance of a third party which establishes the "logic," so influential in Judeo-Christian morality, of shame.

3.2 Choice

"What does it mean," asks Albine, "when you dream of a bird talking to you?" (142/161). Why would Zola have replaced the serpent, a crawling and dangerous animal, with a bird, symbol of freedom, in the role of tempter? The bird being also a symbol of sexual desire, the choice makes sense; even so, further explanation is necessary. The difference between the two animals is revealing: for a novelist of the Victorian age, the combination of freedom and sexuality is innovative, while in the mythic context of Genesis, the combination of sexuality and the power to renew life, of which the serpent is the symbol, expresses the most important aspect. Metonymically linked to Albine, the free spirit, the subject of desire and the innocent woman, the bird possesses all the features of the dream-sign: condensation of several meanings, displacement both of the dreaming subject and of the originating symbol, so it can draw together the intertextual threads of novel and myth, while still remaining opaque.

But why was it necessary to change the symbol at all? The reasons are multiple, and they not only shed light on the kinship between the two texts, but also help show what motivates my own approach. Once more it is Brother Archangias who provides the explanation, when he says: "Don't you see the serpent's tail twisting among the locks of her hair?" (180/206). This use of the symbol of the serpent shows that it simply is no longer available for expressing what Zola wants to express. Between the symbolism of Genesis and nineteenth-century France there have intervened not only the entire Judeo-Christian tradition, which began very early to blame the woman, but also other cultural elements of various origin, such as, to give only the most obvious example, the image of Medusa. The result of this inevitable process has been a collapsing of symbolic ambiguity, as unacceptable to the structure of the novel as it is foreign to the symbolism of the myth.

In Genesis, the serpent is an ambivalent creature. Ontologically, it is an animal, but one that speaks (at least at this stage). Narratologically, it is the

13. See Freud, "The Uncanny," and below, Chapter 11, sect. 6.
14. [Translator's note] The word "faute" in Zola's title falls, as Bal points out in the essay, between "sin" and "transgression"—the two English translations I found used these two words for their titles! I have rendered it as "fault" (in quotation marks), so as not to lose the ambiguity.

first being to confront another—the woman, as it seems, but its use of plural verb forms indicates that it is addressing the man too. The bird in Paradou has a more modest function, since, in accordance with the realist tradition, both the prohibition and the temptation are presented as more directly psychological. And Zola illuminates a third, this time moral, aspect of the serpent's ambivalence, disclosing retrospectively a solution to a recognized problem in Genesis. In *La faute de l'abbé Mouret*, the functions of the prohibition and its transgression are distributed between Serge and a number of trees. This plurality of trees is at odds, at first sight, with the single forbidden tree in paradise.

The serpent's cunning is shown in the words "Did God say, 'You shall not eat of any tree in the garden'?" (3:1). By presenting the prohibition as so absolute, so tyrannical, the serpent incites revolt. But it is not so easy to eliminate this "not . . . any tree" as a lie. In 2:16–17 Yahweh apparently said the opposite: *hā'ādām* was allowed to eat of every tree but one. But what trees, in that case, remained at its disposal? In 2:9, the trees are described: Yahweh "made to grow out of the ground every tree pleasant to look at and good to eat and the tree of life in the middle of the garden and the tree of the knowledge of good and evil." The ambiguity of the particle ordinarily translated "and" makes our task no easier. Does the collection of trees consist of only two species, or even of just one? For the verse may be equally well translated by "every tree . . . *that is*, the tree of life . . ." as by "and" repeated several times, or variants like "as well as" or "besides." Westermann[15] holds that there is only one tree described twice. The woman, in her answer, describes the tree in the middle of the garden as the forbidden tree. The question which must be asked is that of the relation between the two complements: "of life" and "of the knowledge of good and evil."

Serge and Albine, in search, as it were, of the forbidden tree in Paradou, find several candidates. One tree would have the following effect: "Only then shall we know everything, shall we be the real masters" (168/192); another will be "a tree of life, a tree under which we shall be stronger, healthier, more perfect" (169/193); yet another gives wisdom of a particular kind: "It was the tree which whispered in Albine's ear what mothers whisper to brides on the wedding night" (174/199). Not only is the single tree here replaced by a plurality of trees, each representing an aspect of the tree of paradise, but another difference is also striking. Whereas in paradise the woman alone answers the serpent, here both characters are in search of the tree—albeit at Albine's insistence, since Serge takes part only reluctantly. This is exactly the aspect of the myth on which the novel casts light. The great final hallucination in the church, where the tree takes on exorbitant dimensions, reveals the reason for this distribution of roles:

15. Westermann, *Genesis 1–11*, 212–14.

There, it grew enormously; its trunk became colossal, until it made the church burst like a belt become too tight. In all directions the branches stretched out huge knots, each of which carried away a section of wall, a strip of the roof.... The great Christ, torn from the cross, hung for a moment from one of the locks of women's hair that streamed down, and then was swept, whirled away, lost in the black darkness, in whose depths it sank with a loud crash. *The tree of life had pierced the heavens*; it overtopped the stars (266–67/276–77, my italics).

The metonymically motivated metaphor[16] "like a belt become too tight" shows clearly, for anyone who is still missing the point, to what a pitch of anguish the symbolism of the tree arouses the man. The locus of his shame, of the taboo, is to be found in his fantasies about his sexual organ.

In the face of the multiplicity of Paradousiac trees, the question the serpent raises about the number of trees in paradise loses its relevance. What displaces it is the question of *why* the number is irrelevant. The reason lies in the relationship between the different aspects of the tree. Whether there were two trees, one bringing immortality and the other knowledge, or whether there was only one, the knowledge in question can be none other than awareness of "the facts of life," as the synonymous use of the verb *yd'* for "know" and "have sex" suggests. Hence the knowledge in question does indeed bring immortality, not to the individual but to the species. So the woman's possible confusion between the two trees is really a sign of wisdom on her part. The three descriptions of the tree represent three phases of the dialectic and progressive description of what is at stake in the prohibition *and* the transgression. In 2:17 the issue is knowledge, including sexual knowledge with its consequence for life; 3:3 introduces the idea of death as the other side of life; and in 3:11 disobedience, or, in another sense, emancipation from blind authority, provides the passage from life to death. By accepting sexuality, humanity can go beyond the infantile fantasy of immortality.

The serpent does not, therefore, contradict Yahweh when it explicates the prohibition. Yahweh said: "In the day that you eat of it you shall die" (2:17). The serpent turns the argument around, without contradicting its latent content, when it says: "You will not die... your eyes will be opened, and you will be like gods, knowing good and evil" (3:4–5, adapted). Indeed sexual knowledge, be it morally colored or not, does "open your eyes," and makes you both die and not die. It makes you live on in the children it allows you to produce. It creates history: the chronological succession of generations in life and death. Since man and woman are always, in this respect, the non-individualized representatives of the species, the difference between species and individuals is not relevant. When "the woman saw that the tree was good ... and ... to be desired to make one wise" (3:6),

16. See above, Chapter 5, sect. 4.

the wisdom alluded to cannot but be the acceptance of the human condition, including death, and the continuity of history that it allows.

So was the serpent right in promising wisdom instead of death, and, even more remarkable, was Yahweh wrong? My interpretation rests on the equal position of these two characters in relation to truth. Both are sly without actually lying. Yahweh stresses one aspect, mortality, the serpent the other, knowledge, of the same idea. Together, they trick the humans into accepting the human condition.

3.3 Action

Serpent, tree, and deity share, therefore, the actantial position of the sender[17] in this first action properly so called. The tree is the source of temptation, the serpent is the active tempter, and God is the prohibitor of the action: the judge. All three provide the signs which the humans have to interpret. This is why Zola can distribute the functions among different trees, and so have no need of Yahweh. The absence of God allows Zola temporarily to disengage the crucial episode from the too-specific context of Judaism (and, by the same token, of Christianity). In place of the different readings offered or suggested, in Genesis, by the combined senders, the trees become here the actual signs, among which Albine and Serge have only to choose. Unluckily for them, there is a breach in the wall of Paradou, which allows the alien character to intervene.

Let us look more closely at Yahweh's position. We have already seen that he long since lost his absolute mastery over his creation. By her act, the woman paradoxically realizes the creation of humanity in God's likeness and, *at the same time*, the creation of God as a literary character in the image of human being. It was likeness to God that the serpent presented to her as the main charm of the tree. This likeness included the free will to act implied in the prohibition itself—which radically alters the meaning of will itself. The motive for the prohibition must be Yahweh's *jealousy* over the possibility of equivalence, and his later reaction proves that the serpent was not wrong. The creator and his creatures, the author and his characters, turn out to be equal antagonists in the fabula in which the author is dramatized. The woman promotes her own status in the narrative. Her disobedience, an independent act, makes her powerful as a character. Not only has she the power to make the man eat in his turn, and hence to make him know (her); she also manages to turn the almighty creator of Genesis 1 into a character with equal status, features, and feelings to the other characters. From now on this creator spirit (1:2) has a body; one that seeks the freshness of the garden, strolls in it and looks for his fellow inhabitants; he has a personality which makes him angry sometimes, and also, later,

---

17. The *destinateur*, in Greimas' schema; see *Sémantique structurale*, 172–91.

afraid (3:22) and jealous. He is no longer in a position to "take" and "put" the human objects wherever he wishes. Speech becomes dialogue, action becomes confrontation. The relation between characters is now basically horizontal, in terms both of space and of actantial power.

Zola, as we have seen, does not bring God into the action. God is not a character; he is only the receiver of Serge's despairing prayers. But jealousy, displaced onto Archangias, remains the villainy in the story. In his pagan myth, Zola condenses God's power, and the malice attributed to the serpent by Christian tradition, with God's jealousy, and the task of guarding the garden (attributed, in 3:22, to the mysterious cherub, and, in *La faute de l'abbé Mouret*, to the monk whose name, Archangias, cannot fail to recall the archangel which the cherub becomes in Christian tradition). Just as acquiring knowledge completes the two primal humans as sexual beings, so with Serge and Albine. The two women in the life of Serge, Desirée and Albine, up to now all too similar, are at a stroke differentiated: Desirée will remain to the end a retarded child—though in an adult body—while Albine progresses, learns, grows.

4. THE EMERGENCE OF CHARACTER: SORROW

It is after this crucial event that the two texts diverge. Paradou was not separated from the world except artificially, temporarily; the pre-Christian myth could be introduced only within limits—the wall of Paradou, with its poorly patched up hole, guaranteed the divergence. Archangias' intervention merely concretized the Christian influence on a myth which had already been irremediably lost to sight.

As we have seen, the woman, in choosing to sin, established a network of actantial positions and initiated the action. Following the logic of the story, the consequences of the human choice are next enacted. The episode consists of a series of interpellations, which, as the converse side of speech, add another feature to the construction of the character. Through these interpellations, Yahweh recognizes, by assigning responsibilities, the actantial position of each character. First he addresses the man, who has betrayed himself by his confession of shame: "Who told you that you were naked?" (3:11). Indeed, the awareness of nakedness was the immediate consequence of the acquisition of knowledge. Speaking and spoken to, focalizing (his shame) and focalized (by judicial authority), acting, the man now participates fully in the narrative process. He tries to blame the woman. Serge, by contrast, leaves this job to Archangias, and refuses the status of a character by remaining silent; but he is also the first to feel shame, when he senses that he is being observed. Next, Yahweh turns to the woman, who shifts the blame to the serpent. When Yahweh subsequently addresses the latter, it is not to acknowledge its status as a character but rather to take away that status. He condemns the serpent without questioning it. It is thrown back into being a speechless animal, and its ambiguity is thereby narratologically removed. This shows that the status of a character can change in mid-story, and that its stability is an illusion.

In contrast to Albine—and here we see Zola's post-Christian reaction in all its ambiguity—the woman in paradise is not cursed. Serge, for his part, accuses Albine just as the man tries to blame the woman: "In you there is only darkness. Your trees distill a poison which changes men into beasts; your thickets are black with the venom of vipers" (226/261). And yet more clearly: "Always the 'fault' was there, Albine's nakedness, dazzling as the sun, lighting up the greenness of Paradou" (231/266). Yahweh is more realistic, and less cruel. Nonetheless, what he says is not without its disturbing side.

> I will greatly multiply your labor and your childbearing;
> in pain you shall bring forth children,
> yet your desire shall be for your husband (*'ish*),
> and he shall rule over you (3:16, adapted).

The use of the word "labor," repeated in the address to the man, suggests that this is a division of labor between the sexes: the man will work for food, for short-term survival, and the woman for children, for long-term survival. These lines specify the consequences of the acquisition of knowledge for the life of the species, but at the same time establish sex-roles. It is the second part of this speech that is especially disturbing. It is tempting to claim, and this would not be contradictory, that the "equal rights" God of chapter 1 is developing here into an ordinary male character, himself affected by the invention of sex-roles. As an ideological agent, he creates "those identities of man and woman, the fictions of oppression,"[18] against which a modern critique claims to struggle.

The relations between the sexes are fixed in terms of the semantic axes of fertility and domination; like all such axes, these are in themselves arbitrary. According to Yahweh's statement, fertility necessitates labor, and domination presupposes desire. But the relation between domination and desire is scarcely "natural." Power and domination establish the organization of social life while, more specifically, the distribution of reproductive roles organizes work. These are exactly the consequences which Serge abhors; the idea of reproducing scares him, and when he works to repair the decaying church it is not in order to "earn his bread by the sweat of his brow" (cf. 3:19); having refused this option when Albine proposed it, it is now precisely in order to go on fleeing from a down-to-earth life that he suffers. Of Yahweh's prediction to the man, Serge retains only the last part,

---

18. Heath, *The Sexual Fix*.

"to dust you shall return" (3:19), which he sees with a perverse desire as the ultimate satisfaction: "Oh, may nothing disturb me in my immobility! I shall remain cold, rigid, with a permanent smile on my granite lips, powerless to descend to the world of men" (254/293). Serge, having passed through Christianity, cannot measure up to the human condition.

It is at this stage that the characters are complete enough to receive the labels which will make them memorable: proper names.[19] It is, again, the woman to whom the proper name is given first, and only to her explicitly. Once more, this priority in the formation of character is balanced by the act of naming, assigned to the man. The name "Eve" which, according to the man, means "the mother of all living" (3:20), is given to the woman in view of her social and sexual role. Like most biblical names, and many literary ones, including Albine, the name Eve is chosen for a reason; it is descriptive, and oscillates between common and proper noun, just as the character oscillates between species and individual. Her character thus emblematizes the very definition of a literary character which, present and re-presenting, subsumes the split, in any case illusory, between the particular and the general.

In giving her this particular name, the man helps determine the character endowed with it: Eve is imprisoned in her maternal function. It is no longer a question of the sexual attraction celebrated in 2:23-24. It is this aspect of the woman that I would like to consider, in order to analyze, as a diachronic narratology must, the evolution of character. It is the very possibility of procreation which repels Serge most—"The hope of being impotent was very sweet to him" (246/284)—because, for him, "After love, there was nothing left but death" (258/297). He speaks truly, accepting metaphorical death for himself ("my granite lips") while at the same time alloting real death to Albine, who must die pregnant with his child—a synecdochic displacement *par excellence*. As for "Paul," his violent reaction is highly suspect. In forbidding women to teach, or exercise the least authority, he denies to them the social side of the maternal function inscribed in the proper name. However, the collocation of an inferior body and moral inferiority, which he condenses in the proper name—accusing Eve and, in her name, all women—stands for him in opposition to motherhood, for he continues: "Yet woman will be saved through bearing children" (1 Tim 2:15). This paradox raises a disturbing question, which receives a double answer in the tradition: Do women deserve contempt in spite of, or because of, motherhood? Christian morality, echoed in the invention of the "pure" motherhood of the Virgin with whom Serge maintains such painfully contradictory relations, seems to opt for the first answer. Psychoanalysis, in stressing the problems the child has to surmount

19. Hamon, *Le personnel du roman*.

because of its too close link with the mother, suggests the second. "Paul" is able to resolve the contradiction by reading Yahweh's verdict not as a realistic description of the female condition, symmetrical with the male, but as a punishment. This is the typical Christian reading which, as we have seen, is by no means compelling. The very invention of virginal motherhood is sadistic and contradictory, but so equally is the invoking of the pain of pregnancy as punishment for a motherhood which is never "pure." Again it is Archangias who has rightly hit upon what Christianity can sanction, if one is so inclined, by way of gratification:

> When she got up, she had blood on her wrist. That made me happy for a week. I can't think of her there on the ground *without getting a tickling in my throat and my belly that makes me burst out laughing* (245/282; I italicize the indications of sexual sadism).

Such interpretations depend on the retrospective illusion. The proper name, the label which makes the completed character memorable, does not necessarily imply all the features previously described and attributed to an entity which was incomplete, and therefore different from the completed character. In lumping together the different experiences through which mythic humanity has gone in the course of becoming, "Paul" cannot avoid contradiction. And retrospective readers even today project all Serge's feelings—his stupefaction before the obviously sexual hallucination of the tree growing uncontrollably in the church; the anguish and desire he experiences at being passively guided into each scary new stage; the dread of offspring which seizes one who knows only the relationship of brother and sister—and the projections they engender, onto the name *Eve* which, in 3:20, describes no more than *the mother of all living.*

5. CONCLUSION

Why, then, is Albine generally identified with Eve, by the novelist himself at the very moment of the "fault," by the critics, by Archangias the cherub, representing violent authority ("His right hand, thrown back behind his head, had not let go of his dogwood staff, which he seemed still to brandish like a fiery sword" 247/286)? If the concept of character is both the cause of the retrospective illusion and the means to its deconstruction, it must provide a key to the dialectic relationship between Eve and Albine. Let us reconsider for a moment the construction of these characters in the two texts.

In Genesis, the existence of a potential character was posited at the outset, but the being portrayed was not yet sexual. Albine, whom Zola at first wanted to call Blanche, is shown as innocent by her name; her "little monkey" behavior identifies her with the animals; she is portrayed, in her integration into the Paradou estate, as a being from *before* history. In Genesis, the character was later sexually differentiated, addressed, endowed with various aspects of subjectivity. It became a subject of focalization, of speech, of potential action, of choice, and of real action. At first, Albine is not differentiated from Desirée, the retarded female; once differentiated, Albine becomes the opposite of Desirée when she takes charge of Serge in order to initiate him into adult life (Desirée remaining in the story as representative of the preceding phase, which Albine has surpassed). The increasing power of the subject is distributed between the two main characters throughout the long process of initiation. Serge's speech represents prohibition, Albine's transgression. This distribution is both similar and different in Genesis. There, the man joined in the action only later in the story, the discourse of prohibition belonged to God, and the causal relation between prohibition and transgression was more direct. The tragedy of Zola's characters lies in their *belatedness*: they are not the first, Paradou is not the whole world, Christianity has succeeded Genesis.

Whereas Albine, despite her education, can live without a past and start again from nothing, as a new character, Serge cannot. This is because he is a double character. He comprises two beings of the past, both Adam and "Paul." He is the innocent child of the paradise story, but also the Christian priest, the successor of "Paul," who "knows" that the story must end in motherhood, and who defines woman in terms of everything leading up to her completed character (retrospective fallacy). Serge's first amnesia, during his convalescence from the "deep sleep," is followed by a second, less spectacular, but equally fraught with consequences. It is the one brought on by his return to the church, which makes him forget the experience of Paradou. After the first amnesia, he speaks like Adam: "What are you doing at my side?"; after the second, he speaks like "Paul." His is a double, alienated discourse. He recasts the Genesis story when he marries Rosalie and Fortuné, the coarse, amoral, almost pagan couple. Not only does Serge pronounce the words of the other, the Christian morality which drove him from Paradou; he also displaces the actantial receiver of his discourse, speaking of eternal love not to Albine, as he did incessantly before, but to people he despises, and who fail to understand. He does speak of love, nonetheless; such will be his discourse from now on. The scene is painfully full of displacements which work together to show the incurability of the priest's alienation.

The woman's part, as we have seen, is distributed between Desirée and Albine. That of the man is divided into powerlessness ("my granite lips") and aggression, sadism ("that makes me burst out laughing")—between Serge and Archangias. The doubled discourse, of pre-Christian myth and of Christian morality, takes on an expressly polemical tone during the final confrontation between the two protagonists and their incommensurable worlds. In this pseudo-dialogue, Albine speaks of paradise and Serge of Calvary, each in monologue, the other being out of reach. In the conflict between two ideologies, Zola gives to the woman the innocent role. The title itself throws the "fault" on the Abbé Mouret. Even if the "fault"—an ambiguous notion oscillating between the moral idea of sin, so little actualized in Genesis, and the anthropological idea of transgression—could not avoid being moralized, and located in the story at the moment of sexual initiation, there was no intrinsic reason to attribute it to Serge alone. So there is a third context in which the "fault" needs to be located, that of the post-Christian polemic whose traces I have tried to bring to the fore. The "fault," in this sense, lies in letting oneself be imprisoned, to the point of being destroyed, in Christian morality, in the Pauline interpretation of Genesis. The Abbé Mouret's "fault" is his not daring to carry through his "fault" to its conclusion. This is a secondary "original sin," an inherent part of the Christian ideology with which Zola is in dialogue. Fighting without illusions, the novelist shows that, in his context, the only possible version of the old story is a post-Christian, post-Pauline one: there is no return to paradise, and the innocent Albine must die rather than, like Eve, taking her role to the next stage by becoming a mother.

In the conflict between the two female characters in the respective myths, and as part of his endless critique of social alienation, Zola stages the destructive character of the backward look, of the retrospective illusion and its Pauline result. He makes use of all the means which cultural history puts at his disposal. The length of the novel as a genre allows him to elaborate a constellation of characters other than that of Genesis, but equally differentiated. The distribution of the features of a character among the different phases of its development is here replaced by a distribution of the features among different characters. The ambiguity is thus preserved, to the extent that the poetics of the nineteenth-century novel permits. The repressive effect of the standardized view of man and woman, as the Christian churches portray them, is criticized in the same gesture. As against "Paul's" *declaration*, Zola presents a *narration*. To "Paul's" *evaluation* Zola opposes a *description*. To a *summary* he opposes a *development*. To a brief and static *generalization*, Zola responds with a long and dynamic *specification*. Aware of the inevitable contingency of the historical moment, Zola reaches back to Genesis across the Christian morality which he seeks to combat while acknowledging its power. Zola's novelistic discourse is itself double. Paradou connotes paradise *and* the South of France in the Nineteenth Century. There is no possibility of an ahistorical setting; this is signified by the poorly-repaired breach in the wall. Serge in his virginity cannot cope with the reality which the myth of Paradou paradoxically represents. Such a double discourse can be expressed only by means of the novel, as the poetics of the age defines it.

Zola's reaction to Genesis, from the other side of Christian morality, shows us, by its awareness of history and poetics, what cultural criticism can achieve. It is to this enterprise that modern narratology needs to contribute in its turn. By using its own concepts in order to subvert them, it can hope to escape from the sterile paraphrase into which a descriptive narratology threatens to fall. It may then be able to transcend the stage where "fictionality" authorizes an avoidance of the question of the relationship between literature and reality, or, to put it more clearly, between culture and ideology. It is not enough to tell oneself, in the words with which Albine tries to reassure the child Serge: "There, there! it's not true, there is no garden. It was only a story I told you. Go to sleep" (112/126).

∎10∎

Perpetual Contest

For Dorrit Cohn

The first autobiographical text written by a woman is the account of the last days of the life of the Carthaginian martyr Perpetua. The text is a favorite of historians and theologians but has not yet been studied with the help of contemporary literary tools. However, inspired by Dorrit Cohn's reflections on the distinction between fiction and (auto)biography on the one hand, and by her analysis of "transparent minds" on the other, I will contend that it is in its literariness—its narrative structure, its fantasy-character, its metaphorical insistence on unavowable themes—that the proto-feminist radicality of the text can be assessed. The most characteristic narrative strategy of literary fiction, not only in the period of realist writing, but also in other periods is the "transparent mind": the account of visions that no one else can see. This article is meant to make the case for such an assessment.

The mode of Perpetua's martyrdom, a contest with beasts, will inform my interpretation of her story. I will start from the premise that in this text the notion of *contest* can be a structural device in more than one way. The idea of contest is applicable to both technical narrative devices and thematic structures, as well as to the interaction between them. The most interesting of all these forms of contest is perhaps the one that affects the status of Perpetua as a narrator: the contest between narration and description. I will speculate that this contest shapes the one that informs Perpetua's choice for this particular martyrdom: the contest between male and female, or rather, the contest for masculinity. The analysis combines narratology, psychoanalysis, and deconstruction in a voluntarily anachronistic appropriation of this unique document which will be defended at the end.

1. DOUBLE INTRODUCTION

The narrative of Perpetua is framed[1] on both ends by contests. In the first paragraph of the text, the contest concerns *time*;[2] in the final episode of the story, it concerns *beasts*. Could there be a common ground between these two contests? And could that common ground in turn draw attention to contests of other kinds in the text? And, finally, could the notion of contest have a much deeper structuring effect on this text than the anecdotal level of the contest with the beasts, and the introductory function of the story itself, suggest? These are the questions I will address in this chapter.

As for the frame of, or preliminaries to, the text itself, the introductory remarks opposing two moments in time, antiquity and "more recent," set up a contest indeed. From "prior claim" and prestige of antiquity on the one hand, to the idea that recent events "contribute equally" to the goals of story-telling, we are confronted with a competition whose outcome is the power of the story which follows. That this contest is not brought to a decision at the end of the narrative is not important; this happens all the time with contests. The contest with the beasts, for example, while not evaluated in terms of victor and loser either, is repeatedly called a contest. In fact, the outcome of the contest between martyrs and beasts is displaced in this case. The martyrs' victory is not over the beasts, but over the devil which the beasts represent;[3] yet victory there is, on the side of those who by definition could not win.

Similarly, the contest between antiquity and recent times does not lead to the victory of recent history but to that of the story that serves as its exemplar. That is, if we take the analogy between the two contests one step further, the story takes the place of one party in this contest, thus undermining the idea of contest itself, just as the martyr replaces the other party in her contest with a force within herself. Hence, although their opponents were declared winners from the outset, neither victor can lose.

Other contests that I will for now only enumerate are, on the level of the textual structure, that between the narration of Perpetua's story by an external narrator and her own account, and, within her own text, the contest between narration of events and description of visions; in Cohn's

1. I distinguish between the beginning and end of the text, in which the author introduces and supplements Perpetua's narrative, and her own testimony proper. I consider the latter the main text, while the former is an ideologically alien (male-religious) appropriation of it.
2. For time as a historical versus a narrative category, see Ricoeur, *Time and Narrative.*
3. The devil is often called "the beast." The actual beasts function as a metaphor of the devil, but that conventional metaphorical relation is modified in Perpetua's divisions. It is remarkable that the explicit metaphorical presence of the devil is related not to the beasts but to a man, the Egyptian, in the last vision, while the actual beast Perpetua is confronted with is a female animal.

terms, between narration of events and psychonarration. On both levels there is an implicit contest between recounting and writing, between narrating and seeing, and between happening and predicting. Within the story there is a contest between old men and young men, between divine and earthly fathers, between the mother-position and the child-position, between pleasure and suffering, and between masculinity and femininity. Among all these contests the crucial one between "Christians" and "pagans" almost gets lost sight of. If a story "about" a contest is set in a structure based on contest, we can happily speak of the contest as an iconic sign, the actual contest with the beast being the *mise en abyme* of the story.[4] But what if the story and what it is "about" compete as well? What if we don't even know what the story is about, since its structure perpetually undermines the dichotomies of form-content, or sign-meaning, in what is maybe the master-contest of this text, its fight against itself?

This sounds like a deconstructionist[5] qualification of the text. Such a qualification is by no means based on some marginal figure. Rather, it is based on a central figure—contest. This figure makes the story a highly problematic self-reflexive text whose initial contradictions generate the others. The subversive quality of this figure is not its particular shape— contest—but its status as central figure. Central, hence constructive, yet figural, hence, supposedly, marginal. The initial contradiction of the text is generated by the problematics of gender played out by Perpetua, whose heroism oscillates between female and male endeavors; this is not surprising since, on the one hand, her heroism is socially framed by a confirmation of her sex, while, on the other hand, her case as exemplar is only possible if she transcends her sex.[6]

2. THE CONTESTED STATUS OF NARRATIVE

2.1 Framing Contests

The very first paragraph of the text sets out to obscure the content of the story to follow. Not only is the result of the contest between antiquity and recent times left undecided, since the story replaces one of the parties; but

4. For the term *iconic sign* or *icon* see Peirce, "Logic as Semiotic." For the term *mise en abyme*, see Dällenbach *Le récit spéculaire*, and Bal, *Narratology*. The passage from Thomas Mann's *Death in Venice* which Cohn quotes (*Transparent Minds*, 50), wherein Aschenbach's hallucinated vision of a tiger is psychonarrated, seems to me a similar case of *mise en abyme*. It asserts the founding importance of vision in the story, both in its insistent use of the verb "to see" and in the destructive power of its actual vision.

5. For a survey of deconstruction as a critical approach, see Culler, *On Deconstruction*. Examples of deconstructionist criticism are legion: see e.g., Johnson, *A World of Difference*; Chase, *Decomposing Figures*.

6. This transcendence is facilitated by the appropriation of the narrative in the frame, but remains problematic nevertheless, thanks to Perpetua's insistence on, and sharp awareness of, her martyrdom as within sexuality.

the function of the story is also left unclear, based as it is on one ambiguity after another. The story is supposed to be a "proof" of God's favor, but "proof" can mean both evidence and test; as an exemplar, the tale must "achieve the spiritual strengthening of man as well" (p. 107),[7] but this can maliciously be read with different accents, depending on whether God, too, needs strengthening—depending on whether the "test" meaning of the word "proof" is joined to its "evidence" meaning. Recounting the exemplars of faith is being opposed to writing them down, the latter activity being geared toward honoring rather than "proving" God, and comforting rather than strengthening men.

The means of comforting is recollection, one of the instances of psychonarration Cohn analyzes: the evocation of the past in a present visionary act, recorded out of time by writing.[8] Writing is then both recording and fixing the exemplar. By the same move, the temporal aspect inherent in narrative, in recounting, disappears; it loses the contest between it and the contingent testimonial narration supposedly prior in time. I will contend that this contest is won by writing, precisely because writing can get rid of time; it is this contest that, by its relation to gender, generates all the others.[9]

The primary contest, not represented but acted out in the story that Perpetua recounts (writes?), is introduced and, again, framed by a remark, not from the narrator, but from God: "The young shall see visions and the old shall dream dreams" (p. 107, adapted). This contest is plural, intricate and self-defeating: it opposes visions to dreams and youth to age. So far, so good; the reader is warned about a thematic contest (age-groups; old men versus young) and a literary one (modes of focalization: to dream versus to see).[10] The remark also opposes the narrated past to the future that initiates it, since it will be in the last days that God will "pour out the spirit," allowing the visions that will be presented as Perpetua's past. This contest between past and future is already complex and contradictory. But the contest between "dreaming dreams" and "seeing visions" is the most interesting one, since it affects the reading of the narrative to follow, which is a narrative of visions.

7. Page references are to *Passio Sanctarum*.

8. A strong example of a text whose recollecting/comforting function predominates over its historical function is the Song of Deborah in Judges 5. See Globe, "The Song of Deborah"; Coogan, "The Song of Deborah"; Bal, *Murder and Difference*.

9. On the "contest" between writing and speech, see Derrida, *Writing and Difference*. On the relation between writing and gender via the "historiographic project," see Bal, *Murder and Difference*.

10. On the term "focalization," which replaces the traditional term point of view, see Bal, *Narratology*. The act of seeing is a favorite case of the "subverbal states" (Cohn, *Transparent Minds*, 46) rendered in psychonarration. It comes close to the ideal of the window, lens, mirror, or camera as metaphor of the transparent mind. As the ideal of platonic deception, as well as of positivist perception, seeing is the ideal mediation between pure subjectivity and pure objectivity.

2.2 Considering Genre

Setting aside the fact that the text is written—by whom?—we can attribute two generic qualifications to Perpetua's text, both limit-genres of literature: autobiography and testimony. Integrating these two, we can approach it primarily as an autobiographical, testimonial narrative, its self-referentiality being its value as exemplar. American slave-narratives belong to this genre, and the difference between a non-autobiographical testimonial novel and an autobiographical one immediately appears when we compare the well-meaning, but in many ways dubious, *Uncle Tom's Cabin*[11] to Frederick Douglass' autobiography. However, the reliability of the testimony is not the only important difference between the two narratives. Somehow, Douglass' narrative is generically different from *Uncle Tom*, and not just because of the voice, the use of "first-person," and the self-referentiality it entails. Making up a story to illustrate a point (*Uncle Tom*) is easier, or so it seems, than illustrating a point with a real life, because the autobiographical narrative lacks the teleology of a conclusion that only the narrator's death could provide. Douglass' narrative is hardly a narrative in the sense that *Uncle Tom* is. It is much more a series of visions, of disconnected events, each of which has a persuasive value. In other words, if we can take Douglass' text as exemplary in this sense, testimony and autobiography work against narrative structure. Cohn, then, is right to challenge the conflation of all discourses as fictional. It is not so much the substance as the structure of a text that makes it fictional.

The generic starting-point of autobiographical testimony, which I assume to be a pretty general reading attitude, entails by itself a number of resistances to narrative. As narrative, it engages the desire for the ending, in conflict with the desire to defer the ending,[12] while as testimony, it freezes narrative stream to still description. Autobiography's self-referentiality and its narrativity are a source of tension in retrospect; that is, when we as readers are in a position to summarize the story—when the story contains its own unnarratable ending—it entails the death of its narrator. Since Perpetua's death *constitutes* her story—that is, her story *as* testimony of her martyrdom—the genre is in contradiction with its own project. That is a first reason why the voice can only be accorded to Perpetua for a brief time, an episode, framed by the voice which will put the testimony to persuasive use, bracketing the autobiographical mode. This is, consequently, why I

---

11. For a feminist critique of this novel, see Tompkins, "Sentimental Power."

12. Peter Brooks' *Reading for the Plot* is an attempt to develop a narrative theory on the basis of the psychoanalytical concept of the desire for ending and the need for deferral. The theory, appealing because it tries to relate form and content in a novel way, fails by its blindness to questions of gender and the exclusive focus on male preoccupations it entails. For my review, see above, Chapter 2.

had to begin, and will have to end, with a discussion of the framing narrative, why I cannot isolate the testimony.

3. A READING OF THE TEXT

3.1 Realism and Paternity

Now what is Perpetua doing when she tells this story? First, there is not really a story. It starts *in medias res*, with "While we were still under arrest," and then it proceeds with a dialogue in which she talks to her father in two terms: the visual—"do you see this vase here?"—and the verbal, the narrative—"Could it be called by any other name than what it is?" (p. 109).[13] Her appeal to realism is well known from rhetorical traditions. We all know that a vase is not a mind; rather, a *body* is often compared to a vase, a vessel. The vase of her body could be filled with either a pagan or a Christian mind. Calling the thing by its name does not have the realistic effect that she seeks. On the contrary, her naming seems to be magic that turns a loving father into a devil ("diabolic arguments," p. 109) who wants to pluck out her eyes.[14]

What this failed appeal to realism also stages is the contest between story and description. Perpetua wants to discuss her martyrdom in terms of the (realistic) description of what she is. Her father's response, however, does not address her in the same mode. Instead, he acts rather than talks, thus prodding the story into movement again. The character of her father functions this way throughout the narrative. The rhythm of the alternation of narration of events and description of visions is related to the father. The presence versus the absence of Perpetua's father inaugurates the staging wherein her visions will take place.

Perpetua's relationship with her father turns out to be very special. He loves her more than he loves his wife and his sons—another contest—and when she does not respond to his love by giving up her faith, he starts to behave quite differently: either hating her or identifying with her, being victimized like herself; maybe, let's face it, he is competing with her. She in turn rejects him, feeling great relief at being separated from him. Later on, she feels sorry for him, a feeling that is invariably phrased as "sorry for his old age." As her own youth is emphasized on many occasions, there seems to be a competition in this domain, a competition introduced already in the Lord's framing prediction: the young shall see visions and the old shall dream dreams. Predictably, the gender-neutral Latin is translated into male language in English, but since in the same statement the distinction between men and women *is* made, this translation is particularly unfortunate.

13. This dichotomy generates tension in this text. For a discussion of the word-image opposition, see Mitchell, *Iconology*; Bal, *Reading "Rembrandt"*.

14. The relationship between blinding and castration-anxiety as established by Freud, "The Uncanny," is evidence for Perpetua's tendency to self-identification as male.

The gender-neutral plural is needed in order for Perpetua to insert herself into the category of the young who see visions.

3.2 Away from Femininity

The position of the relatives in the story gets more complex when we think of the other relatives evoked: her brother and fellow-martyr, her small brother prematurely killed by an illness whose horrifying description foreshadows Perpetua's martyrdom itself, her mother, to whom she speaks in her anxiety, and her baby, who signifies her motherhood as well as her detachment from it. All these characters, except the dead brother, appear at the very beginning of Perpetua's narrative. The movement away from her father toward her motherhood via the evocation of her own mother is however, less a choice *for* motherhood than a choice *away* from daughterhood; it is more negative than positive. Once the baby has been taken good care of, she is not only willing to give him up, but happy to be relieved of this earthly tie. In a traditional, ideological view, this movement away from her father does not lead to her maturity as a "real" woman, a mother that is, but, as we shall see, to her detachment from femininity.[15]

This deviant development is, I contend, what precludes the classic autobiographical narrative from unfolding. Narrative fiction and psychobiography stand at opposite ends of a scale. The series of visions that structure the text, breaking the narrative unfolding in time and each taking away one aspect of Perpetua's femininity, eventually bring out a masculine aspect in Perpetua, as a symptom, a trace, of the difficulty of getting rid of gender. In her first vision, she evokes a ladder, intertextually[16] related to Jacob's ladder. Jacob's dream, I remind you, was a dream of ambition, of promise of election, an election that, in Genesis, could only befall men. This intertextual reference begins Perpetua's contest for masculinity, but that contest does not go very far yet. The dragon, and its obvious association with Eve ("it [her seed] shall bruise thy head, and thou shalt bruise his [!] heel," Gen 3:15, King James Version), reconfirm Perpetua's femininity, as does her brother's leadership. When she arrives in the garden, a substitute father with the same grey hair that her worldly father is pitied for, one who does not reject but praises her choice, is waiting for her.

This father, too, is identified with the nursing mother Perpetua, as he feeds her. The product he gives her—curds, or cheese—mediates between

15. Rather than referring to the many excellent discussions of femininity as either essential nature or social construct, I wish to draw attention here to what I consider a wonderfully sharp piece of feminist thought, Evelyn Fox Keller's book *Reflections on Gender and Science*. Although Keller's study is devoted to the problem of gender as related to science, the way she goes about discussing the issue of gender is exemplary for what I take to be the most fruitful position.

16. The concept of intertextuality was introduced into western critical thought by Kristeva, "Poésie et négativité," and *Revolution in Poetic Language*. For a critical discussion, see Culler, *The Pursuit of Signs*.

pre-Oedipal "natural" milk and culture. When she comes to herself, the taste of something sweet is still in her mouth.[17] Psychoanalytic critics would see a pre-Oedipal, imaginary remembrance evoked by this phrase, and milk-product would become mother-milk. Has the father been eliminated only to reappear as so "good" a father that he becomes a mother? I think that the relevance of this nurturing father lies also elsewhere, in Perpetua's position before him/her. For the development of Perpetua away from femininity, the most important aspect of this taste is its position in the pre-Oedipal realm which brings Perpetua back to the stage *before* sexual difference. But the milk-product is cultured, not entirely "natural"; the regression carries traces of what was left behind.

After this vision, the narrative goes on to describe a second encounter with Perpetua's father. This time his love turns not devilish but marital. He behaves as a suffering spouse rather than as a tyrannical parent. And as a spouse, the role he takes on is less that of a husband than that of a wife. He becomes quite feminine himself, crying, kissing her hands, and shedding tears. The statement that "he alone of all my kin would be unhappy to see me suffer" (p. 113) is highly ambiguous if we look at it within the isotopy of relationships. Does she mean that he alone loves her as a real woman would love, or that he alone blames her for her martyrdom? These two meanings seem contradictory, but are actually compatible, since they function on two different levels of the story—the historical-religious one, with which I am less concerned in this essay,[18] and the gender-oriented one that my deconstructionist-psychoanalytic framework allows me to emphasize.

The third meeting with her father initiates a new phase in the development of their relationship. Carrying her baby now, he seems to be appealing to shared parenthood. The sacrifice he asks of her, on the historical-religious level, is of course the pagan sacrifice of renunciation of her religion; on this level, it is also an allusion to Abraham's sacrifice, since Perpetua, too, is ready to give up her child for her God. This promotes her to the position of the patriarch, the most masculine and the least maternal

---

17. Modern readers cannot help thinking of Proust's famous "involuntary memory" aroused by the taste of a madeleine cake soaked in linden-blossom tea, an episode in *Remembrance of Things Past* that has become the emblematic passage on metaphor and its metonymic motivations. See e.g., Genette, *Narrative Discourse*. The rhetoric of the madeleine-cake episode is discussed by van Alphen, *Bij wijze van lezen*. And to complete this post-modern anachronism: the sweetness left by the cheese can be best imagined if we combine Perpetua's and Proust's experiences in the idea of cheese-cake.

18. My approach to this text may indeed be perceived as aggressively different from the more obviously relevant historical-religious approaches. It goes without saying that my choice does not imply that I find those other interpretations less useful—on the contrary. I have simply chosen to limit myself to the present approach in order to show that, even though the historical-religious approach is more directly obvious, mine can contribute to the realization of the still-vital importance of concerns of gender and its relation to narrative, or more specifically, to psychonarration.

of biblical characters, just as her evocation of Jacob's ambition-dream of the ladder had foreshadowed.[19] The father-become-mother keeps the child, and Perpetua goes to the next phase of her experience, to her next vision, when she is "relieved of any anxiety for my child and of any discomfort in my breasts" (p. 115). She is relieved from all that emphasized her femininity, that is.[20]

3.3 Back Into Infancy

Perpetua's second vision involves another relationship with a relative, her dead little brother. This vision, even more than the first, is descriptive rather than narrative. She sees her brother because she identifies with him: he comes out of a dark hole, as she has herself been locked up in a dark hole—and has come out of it, for that matter. In light of the previous vision which ended with the taste of pre-Oedipal sweetness in her mouth, we can consider both the sex and the smallness of the brother as contributing to Perpetua's development away from gender. If that development is an acceptable suggestion, then we can even see in the wound on his face the symbolic marker of his pre-gendered position, as a possibility of femininity. The water then even suggests a pre-natal memory, stimulated by the long time that has elapsed between this vision and the last time Perpetua saw or thought of the boy. Radical separation, the abyss between them, will be overcome in her next vision.

Perpetua's second vision of Dinocrates, which is the third of the series, emphasizes not only the relief of his suffering by bringing the water within his reach, but also his childishness, expressed by his playing. Between these two visions there is, exceptionally, no narrative interference by the father; only a brief narrative fragment, recounting a single event, is interposed. The event itself, Perpetua's transfer to a military prison, is not without masculine overtones, while the *games* mentioned in this passage will be echoed in the play of the child in the vision, opposing that masculine and guilty play to Dinocrates' genderless, innocent play. It is noticeable that the later description of Perpetua's attitude during her fight with the beasts is more reminiscent of the childish play of her brother than of the masculine game of fighting wild animals. She simply never fights: she wins the game by adopting a dream-like, regressive attitude, the recounting of which requires a most astonishingly "modern" psychonarration. After this third vision, the father intervenes again. He is now overwhelmed with sorrow

19. It is relevant to note that the episode of Jacob's dream, in which the ladder appears, takes place when Jacob is still very far removed from the patriarchal status he will later acquire. The dream—a vision—foreshadows his future, just as Perpetua's visions foreshadow hers.
20. Susan Harvey's forthcoming work on "Transvestite Saints" shows that this withdrawal from gender is a generic feature of medieval saint narratives.

and makes a scene that we would be tempted to call hysterical. The father has lost all of his paternal power, throwing himself on the ground and tearing hairs from his beard. But the most significant change in his attitude regards the contest over words that Perpetua initiated in her first encounter with him. He gives in to her model of representation, ceasing to promote narrative and trying in his turn to use language as magically as Perpetua had. As she recounts it: "He . . . began . . . to say such words as would move all creation" (p. 117).

3.4 Maleness and Pleasure

The fourth vision is the crucial one for Perpetua's development away from femininity, as it is for the contest between youth and age. The vicious-looking Egyptian is not explicitly described as old, but the introduction of the "handsome young men" to be Perpetua's seconds and assistants suggests such an opposition. The Egyptian's mission is to represent the devil, but the devil had been previously identified with her father. He literally mediates between the father, described as diabolic in the first encounter, and the dragon of the first vision, the more traditional representation of the devil.

The key-sentence for my interpretation of the text is: "My clothes were stripped off, and suddenly I was a man" (p. 119). One way of explaining this striking element with reference to the social background would be to invoke chastity. Perpetua being a woman, the following scene would have been impossible. And that scene is one of pleasure. The pleasure of being rubbed with oil, the closest we will come to sexual pleasure, has to be mitigated by the transsexual change. But even then, the desire for this pleasure expressed in the vision is striking enough for a martyr so far only interested in the masochism of martyrdom.[21] I am inclined to make more of it, to see in this transformation the expression of a real desire for masculinity as the definitive discarding of femininity, a desire motivated by the desire for pleasure. This has, of course, a social background: in the pre-text of the ancient Roman world,[22] the pleasure of being naked and rubbed by handsome young men is accessible only to men. In order to accede to that pleasure, Perpetua had to become a man.

This vision, the strongest thematically, is also the strongest discursively, in that it demonstrates most clearly the contest between narrative and

---

21. The term "masochism" is voluntarily anachronistic. Historically speaking, it would be absurd to apply this term to martyrs; yet the combination of suffering and pleasure the term emphasizes is pertinent here. The question, of course, is the nature of the pleasure; in the present case, it is arguably sexual. Hence the appropriateness, if qualified, of the term.

22. Of the various alternative terms to indicate the reality informing texts, van Alphen's proposal *pre-text*, in *Bij wijze van lezen*, seems the most appealing to me, since it implies both a temporal and an anti-mimetic aspect, while also expressing the idea that the text leans on it, exploits it, only to gain its own status in its difference from it.

description. Perpetua says: "Suddenly I *was* a man" (in Latin, "I *am* a man"), not "I became a man." The difference is subtle, but it is the difference between description and narrative. Since description is the visual mode, a specific subcategory of psychonarration, and narrative the historical mode, the mode where events control whose victim she is, Perpetua can only assume power over her life by stepping out of narrative, by promoting description of vision, and by stepping out of the femininity that brings suffering, by *being* a man and enjoying pleasure.

The sexual nature of this scene needs further elaboration. Its sexuality is, again, masculine: the beautifully adorned man of marvellous stature who appears in the amphitheater is inordinately tall not only because he is another incarnation of the father, a function symbolized by his position as arbiter. He is tall also because he represents the sudden growth of the penis in erection. His purple tunic, beltless, with two stripes running down the middle, emphasizes his oblong form without interruptions. Of course, this interpretation, as bold as a voluntarily anachronistic interpretation can possibly be, does not exclude the other, more self-evident interpretations of this figure. One such interpretation would identify him with God. But given the intertwining between Perpetua's search for pleasure and her voyage to God, the motherly father of her first vision, the ambivalence of this figure is not surprising. To push this a little further, if this man figures an erect penis, his head is logically the top, and his feet, to whose attractiveness so much attention is drawn, the testicles. But this positive figure of masculine sexuality is positive precisely in that it carries femininity.

The description of the fight with the evil Egyptian does not represent any form of anxiety or displeasure. On the contrary, the fight is represented as *light*, as an "unbearable lightness of being," beginning with "to let our fists fly" and including actual flying, according to Freud[23] a quite frequent representation of sexual arousal in dreams; there is also a representation of actual intercourse (she "got hold of his head," p. 119). Perpetua comes down to earth in victory, a pleasurable ending of the event. The tall man has now lost his imaginary stature and is simply referred to as "the trainer," while he addresses her as "my daughter." In other words, after this amazing fantasy, Perpetua is back in normal life—as it should be, but isn't "really."

The text we are looking at is so interesting for its passages of psychonarration because it contains the fictionalizing device of representing minds in the *plural*. If one takes a look at the parallel vision of Saturus, a male participant in this voyage toward martyrdom, one can immediately assess the difference. Unlike Perpetua's, his vision is entirely void of any sensuality. The vision is filled with the clichés of paradise: splendid but sexless angels, "rose bushes and all manner of flowers" (p. 121). The angels are

---

23. Freud, *The Interpretation of Dreams.*

wearing white robes like Perpetua's arbiter/trainer/penis, but nothing associates these robes with any gender-related aspect of the angels. Saturus' vision is, like Perpetua's earliest vision, concerned with the contest between old men and young men, a contest that is resolved outside sensuality by the vision of the "aged man with white hair and youthful face" (p. 121) whose feet he did *not* see. The father-figure is multiplied by the elders and aged men who send the martyrs out to play. We recognize this motif from Perpetua's third vision, the one where her *little* brother was cured and as a result began to play. In other words Saturus also regresses back into pre-gendered, pre-historical, pre-Oedipal infancy, but for him this love is simple. If we believe Perpetua's evocations, overcoming gender is a double fight for a woman, who cannot simply go back to infancy but has to move to infancy via masculinity. Why would this be?

3.5 Writing Sexual Difference

In the visions, we see that the regressions always leave a trace, a *writing* of sexual difference. In her first vision, Perpetua identified not only with Jacob but also with Eve, and the milk of pre-gendered identity was already processed, hence, gender-bound. In the second, the dark hole was ambivalent—both frightening prison and secure uterus—and the wound suggesting the female sexual organ was graphically represented on her little brother's face, and deepened by the abyss that separated them. In the third vision, that wound was healed but, emblematically, left a scar. In the final, fourth vision, sexual difference is only overcome after the pleasure of the *other*, male sexual experience, is integrated into the female experience: the erection of the tall man, the transsexual change, and the flying sensation. When she comes down and steps on the devil's head, she has overcome the limitations of her femaleness as well as the wickedness of bad, devilish, fatherly maleness. Compared to Saturus' itinerary, hers is a much more complex and difficult one, as the route toward sexual identity is a more tortuous one for women in a society where maleness is the norm and femaleness the deviation.

Perpetua's last vision is not only the vision of the contest for spiritual victory over bodily mutilation that she will enact in the scene of her actual murder, where she does not even realize that the contest with the beast—the mad heifer—has already taken place. It is not only the contest between the pain of reality and the pleasure of her vision, a pleasure that will replace the pain of her actual martyrdom. It is also the contest for descriptive victory over narrative suffering. However hard they try, the spectators of the contest do not *see* the event of her suffering, and the narrator of the final scene can only explain this by emphasizing Perpetua's absent-mindedness —a regression to both the pre-Oedipal stage and to the vision—that represents her escape from what historical reality tries to do to her.

Historical reality needs the narrative mode to structure its unfolding in time. It is that collaboration between temporality and historical reality that Perpetua chooses to undermine. Her narrative is narrative only to the extent that it shows how poor the narrative mode is, compared to the descriptive mode that takes Perpetua out of time, out of victimhood, into an atemporal realm that is both pre-gendered and pleasurable.

Two moments in the concluding narrative, the final section of the frame, confirm that Perpetua's contest is related to gender not only for herself but also for the others, the lustful sadistic onlookers. At the same time, they emphasize the distinction between narration and psychonarration, between biography and autobiography, between fiction and the realm where fiction-nonfiction is a void distinction: fantasy. First, Perpetua and the other female martyr, Felicitas, are exposed to a female animal, in order for their sex to match that of their antagonist. This contest is set up as a "real" game, with "fair" rules. But when the two women are stripped naked, the mob is shocked to see their female vulnerability. Perpetua is then described as "a delicate young girl," which, as a young mother, she is not "really." By contrasting her to Felicitas, "fresh from childbirth with the milk still dripping from her breasts" (p. 129), the narrator shows that he has understood Perpetua's devolution: her separation from her child—her breasts were dripping there—is seen as a regression to an earlier stage. It is the moment of emerging femininity—adolescence and maternity—that the onlookers are objecting to seeing mutilated, not the suffering of established femininity that they, as amateurs of pornography, would have loved to see.

Perpetua wins this contest, too. The sadism of the crowd, which she had ridiculed right before the spectacle, is frustrated, both by her chaste concern for her appearance, her refusal to let her female body be exposed, and by her dream-like unconsciousness, her refusal to let her suffering be exposed. However hard he tries, the narrator ultimately cannot *write* the martyrdom of this woman. He can only write how she escapes it.

4. CONSIDERATIONS OF METHOD

Although I have cheerfully endorsed the charge of anachronism, my reading of the text is less anarchistic than it may seem, as I hope to argue in this concluding section. I started out by defining a guiding theme—contest—and by specifying a defining genre that challenges established literary categories—autobiographical testimony. The narratological distinction between narration and description encompassed the equally narratological distinctions between telling and seeing and between narration of events and psychonarration. The problematic status of the genre as self-contradictory matched the problematic status of the text as, if I may say so, self-contesting in all senses of the word. Thus, generic and narratological considerations led to a deconstruction of the status of the genre and of narrative from the start.

In a second step, I came to see a relationship between the technical, narrative, and scriptural devices of the text, and the links the narrator and the heroine of the story are involved in. These connections are as self-deconstructive as the previously mentioned ones. The awareness of this problem on the thematic level brought me to a psychoanalytic third step, the examination of Perpetua's move away from her sex. This move was complex for her, because she not only had sex to transcend, but she also had to move beyond it through masculinity. As we have seen, this detour was harder, but also more rewarding because leading to positive pleasure, than the simple, infantile evocation of paradise that represented Saturus' regression.

For an important contingent of feminists—mainly historians—psychoanalysis is an objectionable framework, less for its male biases than for its anachronism. Indeed, the historical contingency of Freudian thought has been amply demonstrated for many of its aspects—although not so much for its major foundations. Interpreting an ancient text within such a framework runs the risk of forcing it into an early twentieth-century bourgeois-patriarchal mold. To this objection, eight answers can be addressed: two defensive, three aggressive, two *ad hoc* and one historical. I will simply enumerate these answers, thus positing, denying, and defending the anachronism of my endeavor.

(a) *The supplementary-relativistic defensive reply.* The historical reality of the text may be partially bracketed but is not violated by my interpretation.

(b) *The universalist defensive reply.* Freud assumed that all people have sexual fantasies, generated by the discrepancy between motoric and mental development of the infant, even if those fantasies are socially and historically embedded and shaped. I have drawn upon one aspect, the "universalist" assumption, while tacitly presupposing the other, its embedding in social reality.

(c) *The relativistic aggressive reply.* Why would we accept all other contemporary models of textual interpretation—no model devised by us can be truly "native"—to confront ancient texts with, and not the psychoanalytic one? What are we denying, when we refuse the latter, about the relevance of sex?

(d) *The post-relativistic aggressive reply.* What position are we taking if we deny peoples in other times and cultures the sexually informed fantasy-life that we then reserve for ourselves? Such a denial involves ethnocentrism.

(e) *The post-modern theoretical aggressive reply.* Why would we be open only to what we know already, to a clone of our own thought, rather than addressing the question of what this "ahistorical" interpretation can bring us?

(f) *The hermeneutical* ad hoc *reply*. The insistence, in *this* text, on family relations interwoven with erotic fantasies suggests that the Freudian framework is relevant.

(g) *The feminist* ad hoc *reply*. Shying away from psychoanalysis is denying the strong concern with gender, and the difficult but particularly fulfilling access to sexual pleasure for women, in the historical context inscribed in this text.

(h) *The historical reply*. "History" involves two sides: the past of the "object" and the present of the "subject." "Seeing" is the most appropriate act to bring these two together. Both need to be acknowledged, in order to let the two interact, rather than pretending to an objectivist position of security outside the object. The historical position of the reader *now*, my own that is, is inscribed in what for a long time was an aporetic problem of reading, but where the lack of feminine subjects has now been overruled by feminism. Hence the need for "wild" readings, as a historical requirement for changing cultural constraints today, readings whose wildness can be compared to Perpetua's wild fantasies: delineated yet stretching the limits imposed upon them.

That Perpetua's move away from femininity would lead her, not so much to give up sex as to enjoy it in the only way she could have access to it, turns this story of victimhood into a story of victory, not only, not even primarily, in the religious sense, but also in two other senses. First, her victory over gender-limitations makes her possibly, in the end, a proto-feminist heroine. Second, her victory over narration makes her in the same sense a proto-post-modern. Thus, the contest set up in the beginning between ancient and recent times, is brilliantly won by her, as she moves way beyond the recent past, into the future of vision and the present of writing.

▪11▪

The Song of the Sirens, or the Narrative of Disjunction

With Ernst van Alphen

... two worlds that have contracted a relationship of sorts. They are close together and even touch one another, ... but they still remain apart, maybe because each world is sufficient unto itself.

Rob Nieuwenhuys

I. GENRE AND FICTIONALITY

Just as the "Once upon a time" at the beginning of a fairy-tale unequivocally indicates that one should not be too particular as to the factual truth of the story, the "From our correspondent," meaning "We have learned from a reliable source," which introduces a newspaper report, denotes that the report ought to be believed. Nevertheless, both formulas, for we may refer to them as such, have another, contradictory meaning, which, though certainly secondary, also contributes to determining the reading attitude. Taken literally, "Once upon a time" supposes the existence—in a distant past—of the elements that are to be presented, and therefore appeals to the "willing suspension of disbelief"—the readiness to defer the question of truth, and still to give a certain credence to what is told within the fictional position. But the introductory formula for newspaper reports also implies that the narrator cannot guarantee the truth of the report. S/he has it at second hand. However reliable the source may be, it remains a source derived from tradition, and thus the report is set in contrast to the eye-witness account.

When, at the beginning of a narrative text, an indication is given of the source or genre—the two often go together—of relative referentiality, or specific fictionality,[1] the reader will adjust his or her attitude with respect to

1. Zoest, *Waar gebeurd.*

242

the story to the promise that such an indication holds. The promise is not binding. On the contrary, it is a strategy frequently employed to frustrate the reader, with respect to the expectations raised at the beginning, by changing genre, or to confuse the reader by running two or more genres into each other. In this way, new genres come into being. Todorov bases his definition of the fantastic on such a hesitation between two modes of reading; Alexandrescu, in his turn, characterizes what he terms the "strange" (*l'étrange*) as a hesitation between a fantastic and a realistic mode of reading.[2] The undecidable accordingly becomes the genre feature. The historical changeability of genres is a given fact of this reader-oriented point of departure, and there is, consequently, no point in approaching questions of genre starting from a universalistic assumption.[3]

In the story "The Sirens," by Maria Dermoût, the issue of indistinct genre is raised. The title alludes to a mythological subject, which is familiar to us from the Western tradition (Homer), yet the story is presented, in the work of this Dutch-Indonesian writer, as a recorded Eastern folktale. The first words are, "The story goes:," which indicates that the reader should be prepared for an authentic Indonesian folktale for which, as we might expect, the framework is the Archipelago, the atmosphere mysterious, and the events on the border between myth and reality. All this we know on the basis of tradition.[4] At the same time it is pointed out that the story is being retold. As a result, a specific communication situation arises, which has implications for the attitude of the reader with respect to, in Jakobson's terms, the code, the context and the sender.[5] On the one hand, they reflect the typical East Asiatic narrative situation[6] in which, during public gatherings, professional story-tellers (sender) pass on the stories still alive in the community on the basis of common knowledge and points of view (context). On the other hand, the Dutch reader is reassured. Apparently there is someone, the narrator, who will be concerned that the reader does not miss the link with a story (code) unfamiliar to him or her. Thus two worlds are brought together, so that we can take our place in the circle of listeners with an easy mind. The words which follow confirm this. With "Not a man, a woman bought the proa," apparent concern is displayed for the understanding of the differences between the two cultures. Evidently, these differences lie in the area of man-woman relationships.

2. Todorov, *The Fantastic*; Alexandrescu, "Le discours étrange."
3. Bal, *Literaires genres.*
4. Nieuwenhuys, *Mirror of the Indies.*
5. Jakobson, "Linguistics and Poetry."
6. Maten, "De schelm als zedenmeester."

In the course of the story, it actually turns out not to be so simple. When the young man makes clear that he too is surprised by the independent behavior of the woman, and when the villagers of an island at which the two protagonists call during their journey also express amazement at the woman's position of power, three cultures prove to be involved: that of the woman, a matriarchy, that of the Indonesian patriarchies, and ours. Neither is the question of genre so simple. It concerns a folktale or traditional story—that which is narrated[7]—but because of the reference to Homer our entire Western tradition is drawn into the story. As a result of this intertextual relationship,[8] the myth is going to constitute part of the traditional story, and the wanderings of the two protagonists become linked with Ulysses' quest. Moreover, the traditional tale itself is an equivocal genre. A story, perhaps true in itself, is fictionalized by tradition. This is familiar to us from the game in which a sentence that is passed on from person to person by word of mouth returns totally distorted. We are also acquainted with popular gossip that often blows up an innocuous fact to mythical (and sinful) proportions. At the same time, the tradition in itself proves, at any rate, that the narrator has not made up the story: a source, albeit anonymous and collective, is quoted. Furthermore, the persistence of the tradition makes the source "reliable": there is no smoke without fire. A traditional tale, therefore, just like gossip, simultaneously contains fiction and truth, or rather, truth in fiction: "somewhere" the invented must be true after all.

Where exactly? The search for the level on which the claim to truth inherent in the genre has a bearing is interpretation. It is, after all, a search for meaning; for a meaning that gives the parties involved in the process the feeling that they have something to do with the story. In Dermoût's story it can be clearly seen that the traditional tale is ambiguous also in this respect. On the one hand, the persistence of the tradition can be founded on the impression that the "original" (true or invented) event has made. The confrontation with the unfamiliar makes belief therein become deep-rooted ("I have seen it with my own two eyes"). On the other hand, it can be recognition that causes the event to have appeal. A deep, unconscious feeling of "So it goes"[9] among the listeners makes the story appeal as "true."

The word "unconscious" has been mentioned. The unfamiliar and the recognizable, apparently incompatible, can exactly reinforce each other at the unconscious level. Verhoeff[10] explains this process as similar to catharsis in tragedy, in which the succession of identification and distantiation

---

7. Gorp, *Lexicon.*
8. Boheemen, "Intertekstualiteit."
9. Alphen, *Van hoe 't is en hoe 't gaat.*
10. Verhoeff, *De Januskop van Oedipus.*

make the purifying effect possible. Both aspects, distance and recognition, are marked in "The Sirens" by stylistic means. Distance is created by stressing the unusualness of occurrences, as, for example, in the opening sentences. An entire scene is devoted to a detailed account of the amazement of the villagers on seeing the strange company: "In the markets on the small islands the villagers held their breath and looked at each other" (p. 264).[11] Recognition is facilitated by interpolations and short sentences that have a "So it goes" tenor: "for cats are fond of drinking blood" (p. 265), "where the sharks are that are fond of drinking blood" (p. 267), "Why should they?" (p. 270). The emphasis on the unusual is, however, clearly stronger. Can one conclude from this that, in this instance, tradition is founded on distance? Another possibility would be to say that the recognition must be hidden deeper, and located more unconsciously. There is, however, a third possibility which we will defend here.

"Usual" and "unusual" denote normative reactions which are connected to the subject. What one person considers usual is exactly what can be strange in the eyes of another. "The Sirens" is based on this subjective instability of norms.

The ambiguity of the genre also takes shape within the story. Both aspects, identification and distance, the usual and the unusual, enter into dialogue with each other, continue functioning next to each other, and even leave the readers free choice to distribute recognition and distance over the characters of the story in their own way. The cultural differences, which will coincide with differences of sex, lead to the development of two lines in the story in which the final impossibility of unity and harmony becomes concrete. The framing formula itself expresses the dialogue between the two lines. This occurs three times. The first time is at the beginning, in the form of a sentence opening: "The story goes." Later, after a first version of the story, with an ending that proves to be false, thereby undermining the true-false dichotomy, it occurs in the form of the end of a sentence: "She did not find the Mainland, the story goes" (p. 264). The two incomplete formulas come together once, in the closing sentence, printed as a separate paragraph, after the outcome of both story-lines has been told: "So the story goes" (p. 272). Between the end of the woman's story and the beginning of the man's there is one blank line (p. 265), which can be taken as an iconic sign of the ultimate division between the two characters. Thus the use of the genre formula itself also signifies the ambiguity of the genre. The incorrect ending of the first version also belongs, after all, to the traditional tale.

11. In the following, page references are to the translation of Dermoût, "The Sirens," appended to this chapter.

2. FOCALIZATION

2.1 External focalization

The ambiguity of the story lies not only in the genre. The narrative technique contributes to it as well. The entire history is embedded within a coordinating view of the external narrator-focalizer, whose task it is to remove cultural differences, or rather to make them explicit so that the Dutch addressee understands the story. This transcultural view is expressed, among others means, in explanatory parts of the text, sometimes in parentheses. A few examples:

1 Not a man, a woman bought the proa (p. 263)
2 That had come about like this (p. 265)
3 Toeangkoe So and So, or whatever he was called (pp. 266, 271)
4 smelt it (hibiscus flowers do not smell) (p. 270)
5 he looked deathly pale, he was dead too (p. 271)
6 took the shipmate up in her arms (he did not weigh that much) (p. 271)
7 in the meadows, as it should be, cows grazed (p. 267)
8 As they are called as far back as the mists of antiquity (p. 267)
9 "have you," but he did not say that in the informal way, he always said "you" in the formal way, "have you never heard it?" (p. 268)

Once again, most of these quotations can also be seen in a different relation. Thus, #1 and #2 refer to the external narrative situation, but #1 also refers to the embedded cultural differences between the woman and the man, whereas #2 indicates a transition between two perspectives (see below). #3, in both occurrences, de-individualizes the young man, and thereby makes his case exemplary. What is said in #4 not only supplies information to the Dutch readers, but also draws attention to the fact that the young man is susceptible to the non-existent, which is of thematic importance in the story. We could go on like this for some time, up to the remarkable #9, in which the narrative situation itself is ironized, but, at the same time, the distance that continues to exist between the man and the woman, in spite of their love relationship, is pointed out. Precisely this double use of formulations goes excellently with the external focalizer's function of bringing together the various embedded views.

2.2 Internal focalization

(a) *The woman.* On a second level of focalization we encounter several views, in the first place that of the woman. In the first section (pp. 263–64), her past history is given, which ushers in and explains her view, accounts for her actions, and necessitates her cultural attitude. Exclamation marks and other idiomatic peculiarities indicate that, generally speaking, the view of the woman is given. She comes from a matriarchal society in which she enjoyed the privileged position of eldest daughter. Of the way things run in that society, the organization of sexuality, apparently exemplary and/or important for the rest of the story, is explained. What the woman turns her back on by leaving is indicated in an elaborate parallelism:

10.   That was why she had left the one large island where she lived.
      Where . . . the "long houses" stood that belonged to the women, high on piles, . . . with beautifully carved ascending ladders.
      Where every night, on the stroke of half past twelve the torches were lit and the men had to leave the women, down the ladders of the "long houses" and further along a dark path . . . a long way into the forests.
      Where she too lived in a "long house" with her mother . . .
      Where she could have had a good life, waiting for her turn to buy a man . . . (pp. 263–64)

We shall have to return later to the meaning of these details, in particular the expression "long houses," constantly occurring in full and in inverted commas. The houses are apparently the domain of the women, where the men are admitted only temporarily. Afterwards they are sent off into the forest.

The woman gives up all this to go on a journey. Her motives are discussed emphatically in a section that precedes #10.

11   The woman had not bought the proa because she loved the sea, she did not love the sea, she was afraid of the sea.
      She loved the vast Mainland that she had never seen, but where she wanted to go, and must and would go (p. 263).

The emphasis on negation and fear, but also on her determination, makes both motives striking. Both her fear of the sea and her obsession with the Mainland recur in the story. The Mainland, written with a capital letter, and thus a kind of proper name, was already referred to earlier like this:

12 It had been called the land of the Tiger, formerly (p. 263).

The "long houses," which the woman leaves behind, are opposed to the Mainland to which she goes (with her cat-tiger). The sea of which she is afraid, the journey over the sea and the flooded land, are located chronologically and locally in between. Whether the preposition "between" introduces a determination of time or place remains otherwise unclear; in the following quotation it deviates from the normal usage for determining position.

13 A proa . . . to sail the straits between the flooded land (p. 263).

There is also a lack of clarity in the use of verb tenses, in the hesitation between iterative and punctual use of past tenses. Thus again, in this uncertainty of "between," we hesitate: events or situations, a slow development or a short, actual history, time or place?

(b) *The man.* A second focalizer on this level is the young man. His view comes into consideration when the woman invites him to become her lover, proposes to buy him. The key word is—how could it be otherwise?—"look."

> 14 The shipmate looked at the woman when she said that. He had looked at her before . . . (p. 265)

Looking, the having of a view, is linked with power in this story. We shall come back to this later. In this instance, his view indicates that earlier he had already, independently, taken up an interest in the woman. Power and initiative go together. Directly after this it is also pointed out that he comes from a different culture:

> 15   Where he lived there were no "long houses," there a woman walked differently, . . . there a woman did not look straight ahead and say this or that; and that a man should just come and lie with her on the couch at night.
>   There a man said that to a woman, . . . looked straight ahead (p. 266).

His view is gone into in the section which follows, expressed in a catalogue of what he likes. He is, it appears, a lover of beauty: the woman, the proa, red flowers. In the description of what he finds beautiful, her looking straight ahead, her power, is also included again. And also:

> 16   and he liked . . . the sea in the white moonlight, and the horizon so silvery and hazily distant—was there land or was there no land? (p. 266)

We find this preference for the diffuse, the ambiguous, again in his adventure with the sea-cows, and his eventual place, in the sea-meadows of the flooded land, stands in sharp contrast to the rocky Mainland where the woman goes in the end.

The final element of his view brings both views, his and the woman's, into a discordant contact with each other:

> 17 The shipmate . . . actually liked anything and everything.
>   Only he did not like the cat.
>   It was as if the woman noticed this (p. 266).

The woman does like the cat—although the verb "like" is not often attributed to her. The reason for their respective antipathy and sympathy is, strangely enough, the same:

18   "Ah! cats are fond of drinking blood!" he said, and he shuddered at
the thought.
"Yes," said the woman next to him, "cats are fond of drinking
blood" (p. 266).

With this, we have also arrived at a central theme of the story.

(c) *The community.* A third embedded focalizer is the village community. Unfamiliar with the characters, their background, and the destination
of the journey, the villagers represent the detached aspect of tradition, the
amazement at the unusual which they, in contrast to the Dutch readers,
"have actually seen with their own eyes":

19 ... the villagers held their breath and looked at each other.
The woman! (p. 264)

The description that follows this introduction contains the grounds to
which their amazement is related:

20 A heavy loose-fitting sarong interwoven with real gold or silver, a
black girdle around her waist, a black silk cloth tied over her breasts,
her black hair combed smoothly, oiled, her face powdered, walking
slowly, erect, looking straight ahead, and: she walked in front! (p.
264)

This resembles the portrait of a priestess. With her ritual posture and walk,
her powdered face and fixed gaze, and all the black, she looks like a
priestess of death. This very solemn, magical, and ominous impression is
summarized in her walking in front, a sign of power. The contrast is
maximal with the gossipy description of the man which follows:

21   Behind her came a man, also so well-dressed, in just such beautiful
clothes—the woman will have given them to him!—a straight
sarong, ... a flower behind his ear (p. 264).

If the woman seemed to be dressed up for a ritual, then the man looks
"adorned." His walking behind is connected with his subordinate position
(he carries the shopping basket). The relationship between the two makes
the villagers curious:

22   He was a young man, younger than the woman, but not so young
as to be her son. Too old to be her son? Too young to be her husband?
Who? What? A member of the family? The shipmate? The lover of
the woman? (p. 264)

The confusion, which is shown here by the numerous questions, is fundamental. Moreover, it is perhaps even stronger for the readers. The latter
know, after all, that at least one of the supposed relationships is correct
(shipmate). The last also soon proves to be right (lover). Why then should

the other possibilities not be appropriate as well (son, man, member of the family)?

The view of these eye-witnesses, including this confusion, bridges the cultural difference between the characters and the readers, and between the characters themselves; they interpret for us, and lay specific stress on the strange and the recognizable. The position of power of the woman is emphasized; she buys, she talks, she looks straight ahead. She buys, amongst other things, hibiscus plants "with red flowers." With these she buys the eroticism of the man—which, just like the man himself, is apparently for sale. Not only the color of the flower, but also the form (a calyx with a sizable pistil), the use (for his adornment), and his penchant for these flowers, make this link, which is likewise made by the villagers:

23 The man wore an hibiscus flower behind his ear.
    He was definitely the lover of the woman! (p. 265)

She talks with the villagers "about the weather and the wind," seafarer's talk then, men's talk. She also asks after the Mainland. The villagers point to all four quarters of the compass, thereby indicating that it is not a single entity, or that they do not know, or that each understands something different by the Mainland. This points to its subjective status. Like "between the flooded land," this is rather strange, at least, as an indication of position. It is added emphatically that the man has no part in this conversation. It becomes him only to listen, and that is what he does.

The amazement of the villagers, who express our questions in their questions, stimulates the advancement of the story. Their view ends in uncertainty, it is then broken off with a blank line, after which an answer is given to their question, as an (apparent) truth:

24   Was the young man really the lover of the woman?

    The young man was the lover of the woman (p. 265).

Here too, however, the genre suggests a different meaning. The truth-claim of the traditional tale was, after all, linked precisely with the gossip-like character of oral tradition. The villagers authenticate[12] the story; they are suited to do this, as a half-related but nevertheless extraneous body, only they too are at a loss. The peremptory tone of what follows seems to refer to a higher, better-informed source. But at the same time a higher degree of fictionality is drawn in, which still only allows alternating focalization through the two protagonists, no longer through outsiders, inside the coordinating view.

The duality, put into perspective by the amazement of the villagers, is

12. Doležel, "Truth and Authenticity."

given shape in the course of the story in the explicit disagreement between the man and the woman about the sea-cows, and in the implicit disagreement about the cat. The position of the animals in relation to both characters gives the key to the interpretation.

3. CAT BECOMES TIGER, SEA-COW BECOMES WOMAN, SHARK BECOMES ?

3.1 The cat

It is said about the cat that it is fond of drinking blood, and that the woman gladly provides it with this. The man finds that creepy. In addition, it is yellow with black stripes. It sleeps with the woman before the man becomes her lover. Subsequently, they lock up the cat. Every night, it drinks some of the blood of the man when the man is asleep and the woman has pricked his finger. In the market it walks beside the woman, brushes against her legs sometimes, is now and then petted by her, then sent away again. At the end, when the man is dead, it has become a tiger through the blood of the man. It now walks in front and leads the woman to the Mainland, to "where she had to go" (p. 271), and where she has now arrived as a matter of course, after having long searched in vain. Thus, the woman's quest comes to an apparently satisfactory end, seemingly at the expense of the man who loses his life.

3.2 The sea-cows

As part of the general duplicity that characterizes the story, it has, moreover, also a double ending. The man falls out with the woman on account of his daily visit to the sea-cows, the sirens of the title. In order to reach them he has to swim quickly across the dangerous deep waters,

25 where the sharks are that are fond of drinking blood, he knew that all right! He could swim faster and also better than the sharks, he said (p. 267).

The sea-cows, in all probability the source of myths of sirens and mermaids,[13] are first described as animals with a fishtail, black heads, bulging eyes, protruding teeth, and only then, through a comparison, to be associated with women:

26 On the front of the body (they were mammals) they had breasts like a woman (p. 267).

After this first onset, more personifications follow: leaning on fins like arms, they raise the upper part of their body "to look out over the water" (in order

---

13. Leach and Fried, *Dictionary of Folklore*, 710, 1013; Graves, *The White Goddess*.

to look for prey? In order to express in their turn a position of power?).
Nevertheless, they are only partially transformed into women. Firstly, still
putting things in perspective, it is said that at night or in the twilight they
"looked somewhat like women," but then, immediately afterwards, it is
stated that they lowed, though drowned out by other sounds,

> 27 of the sea and waves and wind, it was as if they sang, the black women
> under the water, the sirens. As they are called as far back as the mists
> of antiquity (p. 267).

The personification is put into effect by this myth-making. The allusion to
the myth makes the lowing cows not only into singing women, but also into
fatal women, to which only an elect (Ulysses) can listen unpunished. They
seduce the young man with their singing, just as the woman seduced him
with her presents. The relationship is such that the young man can be
compared with Ulysses:

> 28 They did him no harm, . . . looked at him, sang for him (p. 267).

Accordingly, when the woman says to him,

> 29 "The sea-cows will harm you! Sometime one day, they will kill you
> and drink your blood! (p. 268)

There is every reason to have a further look at this *Umwertung* (reversal of
values). The story also has a pleasant ending for the man. True enough, he
dies, but after that he can enjoy everything that he liked at his ease: with a
red hibiscus flower behind his ear, he listens to the singing of the sirens
among which he lies and which sing his own story for him. He is in fact, so
it is said, "a happy man." According to the mythology, sirens are, it is true,
goddesses of death, but they distinguish themselves from their daunting
colleagues, the harpies, through their power of attraction. They represent
the sweet, sought-after, liberating death.[14]

3.3 The sharks

Alongside the cat that becomes a tiger, and the sea-cows that become
women, the sharks play only a minor role. They, like the woman's cat, are
fond of drinking blood, and they live in the sea like the sea-cows/women.
They live in the deep part of the sea that surrounds the proa. In that sense
they are jailers: they guard the captive young man; make it difficult for him
to leave the woman to go to the sirens.

#25 suggests another aspect of the sharks: rivalry. When the young man
can swim faster than they can, he succeeds in reaching his girlfriends.
Later, when he is weakened by loss of blood, he is no longer able to.

---

14. Managhan, *Women in Myth and Legend*, 273.

On the one hand, the sharks are, therefore, thematically linked with both poles of the feminine appeal. On the other hand, they stand for the separation between the two, which is broken at first, and later maintained by a test of strength.

The interpretation of this triangular relationship between the animals, in which the young man looks for his place, can be sought in a psycho-analytical context. The significance of the motives is then made dependent on the partially unconscious relationship between the man and the woman of which they are a symbolic, unconscious, form of expression. But, again, there are two relationships between the two characters. The woman has a relationship with the man, and the man with the woman. *These relationships are not symmetrical.* They stand with respect to each other, as Nieuwenhuys[15] puts it in his characterization of the entire work of Dermoût:

> . . . two worlds that have contracted a relationship of sorts. They are close together and even touch one another, . . . but they still remain apart, maybe because each world is sufficient unto itself.

Only when we see these two relationships in their interconnection with one another, which is to say, on their own, and now and then in contact with each other, can we do justice to the peculiarity of this story. The duality of the genre, the tension between the focalizers, acquires a separate meaning in this way. Therefore, we will discuss the two relationships separately.

4. MAN SEES WOMAN

The shipmate's view of the woman is put into words most directly at the moment that she asks him to sleep with her in future. The man accepts the invitation, not on account of the price that she pays—he comes from a culture in which the man, not the woman, buys a partner—but because he thinks that she is beautiful. His desire for her comes out in a passage in which the looking, the most concrete form of focalization, acquires the dominant meaning of desire.

30 The shipmate looked at the woman when she said that. He had looked at her before, at the way she squatted on a mat, at the way she lay on the couch, the way she rose to her feet and walked, the way she held her head and looking straight ahead said something (pp. 265–66).

In this passage, two forms of looking enter into a dialectic relationship with each other: desire and the exercise of power (looking at someone versus looking straight ahead). By looking at the woman with desire the man

15. Nieuwenhuys, *Mirror of the Indies*, 266.

places himself on her level. Moreover, directly after this passage there follows a train of thought on the cultural background of the man, which explains his self-willed looking/desire, and also raises the matter of the power relationship once more in this context:

> 31   He too came from the one large island. Where he lived there were no "long houses," there a woman walked differently, stood differently, held her head differently, there a woman did not look straight ahead and say this or that; and that a man should just come and lie with her on the couch at night.
>
> There a man said that to a woman, like that, and walked like that, and held his head like that, looked straight ahead (p. 266).

When, with an "All right, if you want it," he subjects himself to the wish of the woman, it is with pleasure and of his own free will.

Besides being desirable, the woman is also strange, which likewise appears from #31. He is surprised at her behavior, which distinguishes itself from what he is accustomed to in initiative and power. In his eyes her behavior is reversed, masculine. As a direct inversion, term for term, it can still be placed: her behavior falls into the same categories as those that are familiar to him. And, apparently, it is to his liking. On a more general level however, the image of the woman, for the reader, is determined in the first place by what happens to the man. For those who identify with him, the occurrences give indirect expression to the general opinion on the man-woman relationship. In this, especially fear plays a large part. It is all terribly creepy after all.

On this level a division comes about between various aspects of the woman. In psychological terms, this division can be imputed to projection. The male imagination projects both fears and desires onto that which arouses those feelings. In this case the woman is desirable and dangerous at the same time. The combination of the two makes her creepy.

She is dangerous in all sorts of ways. She is confining. The man is together with her on the proa. Sharks swim around the proa as jailers. If he leaves her for a moment to go to other women she is jealous. She wants to keep him for herself, and what is more, prevent him from choosing rather than being chosen. On account of her fatal jealousy he does not get the chance to gain the status of subject,[16] to come forward in public, to go into society. She is all-absorbing, as women are often fancied to be in stories.[17] The fear of being sucked dry by the woman is given its most literal form: her small cat drinks his blood. The confinement and the absorption are two ways in which she tries to fix him. The proa symbolizes this fixing in spatial

---

16. Felman, "Rereading Femininity," 32.
17. Berge, "De mannenschrik."

terms. She wants to keep him young, small. When he is too quick for the sharks, so that he can grow towards independence, he is made weak so that he is dependent on her again. Then she will take care of him, wash and feed him, like a child (see also #6). He rejects this regression, but she and the cat are stronger than he is. When he feels weak and complains about his bad dreams—"always the same, I don't know what!"—she presents this as a punishment for his escapades: "Why do you do it anyway! Why do you bathe yourself every day in the sea" (p. 269). In other words (namely those of #29), she wants to make him believe that he has been weakened by "being unfaithful" with the sea-cows, whilst she is the real cause.

These three characteristics, which all indicate a strong mother-fixation (see now #22 again), a paralyzing relationship that makes it impossible for the son to enter the social order, are typical for a pre-Oedipal problem. In this phase the son forms a unity with the mother from which he is not yet able to distinguish himself. The attempt to fly in the face of the danger of the sharks symbolizes the transition to the Oedipal phase. The sharks, which are emphatically presented as rivals in #25, represent the father image against which the growing subject has to react. However, they are exclusively negative, bloodthirsty, and completely in the service of the powerful mother. They drink blood like she does, and by their collective action are deprived of their individuality: her servants, her harem. When the young man proves to be so strong that he is too quick for them, and independently goes to visit his—likewise numerous—girlfriends, his harem, it is no wonder that from their (projected) jealousy the sharks could "drink his blood."

In this case, transition from one phase to the other, from a symbiosis with the mother to independent subjectivity, proceeds with exceptional difficulty. By not only fearing, but also desiring the mother, by voluntarily entering into a love-relationship with her, the young man exposes himself to a confusing situation, which he courts, but in which he also becomes entangled. This is already obvious in #14, whilst in #16 it is indicated precisely how much this confusing, diffuse situation fascinates him. When he starts emancipating too radically he relapses into regression: the power of the mother is as yet too great.

The characteristics that the woman has for the young man also take shape in her demeanor during the day time. As the creepy, night time occurrences represent his unconscious fears (he has bad dreams, but about what?—later it turns out to be about the cat), so these fears are confirmed in the conscious relationship. The woman is subordinating. She exerts power, expressed in the buying, looking, and speaking. These three activities have not been chosen randomly. They represent the three levels of narration: to

18. Cf. above, Chapter 4, sect. 2.1.

act, to focalize and to narrate.[18] Consequently, she has the story in her hands, and thereby keeps the young man unemancipated: she "has all the say."

After this regression (puberty?), however, something drastic happens. The woman gives him a little push, a boost, symbolized by throwing him overboard, and, see, there is no trace of the sharks any more, he can calmly go to the sirens and stay with them.

The attraction of the woman, the source of the desire, is likewise split and divided over various objects. He thinks the woman is beautiful, and the red hibiscus flower that she keeps giving him symbolizes the erotic alliance between them. But the sirens also exert a power of attraction over him with their watery domain, their breasts, and above all their singing. When the mother-lover becomes too powerful for him, the sirens offer a reassuring alternative. In their abundance they can never become individually so strong that they destroy him. Moreover, they represent the mysterious to which he is so susceptible. The woman, who was creepy on account of her inscrutability, contrasts with the sea-cows, strangely enough, on account of her worldly character. She does not hear their singing and denies that they are women. She is seen by the young man when she sits, squats, or lies down. Her power is also expressed in her possessions, her purchasing power. The sirens, on the contrary, live in the diffuse area between the land and the deep sea, among the algae meadows, in the gently washing waves. He is happy in a passive, contemplative attitude. Why is he so happy?

> 32   He not only likes what the sirens sing, he understands what the sirens sing . . . (p. 272).

He does not enjoy himself only as he did previously on the proa, when he really liked "anything and everything." He is now able also to set himself limits and listen within those limits, to understand: to communicate. Now he "has a say." He has joined the symbolic order. And what do the sirens have to tell him?

> 33   They sing about all sorts of things. . . .
> They sing of a proa and a woman and a shipmate and a cat; they sing of a vast Mainland somewhere, and of a Bengal tiger; but he has already heard that once before (p. 272).

Like the story of Ali Baba and the forty thieves, this story bites its own tail. Together with the boy, the reader also knows the story already: the story of an unrealizable desire (the Mainland somewhere) and of the power of the mother (Bengal tiger). But now it has become a story, a story in which he can experience all his fears and desires once again, only in complete tranquility, without having to justify himself, without rivals. The song of the sirens works for the young man as the entire story works for those readers who identify with him: comfortably relishing the horror in your armchair.

5. WOMAN SEES MAN

As the relation of the man to the woman is ambivalent, so too is that of the woman to the man. Likewise for her, he merely represents a phase in her development. However, with that the similarity between the two relationships ends. The woman has a radically different past, other desires, other goals.

For a start, her point of departure in this history is her relationship not with the young man—this only begins to have significance for her much later—but with her mother. The picture that is painted in #10 defines itself now that we interpret the story psychoanalytically. A sentence quoted incompletely in #10 shows this well:

34　　Where she too lived in a "long house" with her mother, who was the head of the family, of all the families in the "long house": the women and children in the house and their men out there in the forest (p. 264).

These "long houses," which, with their quotation marks, are emphatically presented as an image, stand high on piles with beautiful ascending ladders by way of which the men may come in now and then. It is not difficult to see the image of a female body in these details. Where it is said that the "long houses" belong to the women, we can read: the woman has the right to choose. The length of the houses could refer to the length—always too long, gruesomely long—of the natal passage. If the woman does not have the patience to wait until it is her turn to take over the power of the mother, this can point to the fact that she too must free herself from the oppressive bond with her mother, which is an impediment to the development of her own subjectivity.

Her goal, the Mainland, of which no one knows the exact position, is certainly bound up with this initial situation. In any case it lies *elsewhere*. It is linked with a feeling of lost unity:

35　　Once all had been joined to the Mainland: the large island, the small scattered islands, the flooded land in between, one land! It had been called the land of the Tiger, formerly (p. 263).

The innumerable small islands at which the woman calls during her journey continually point out that the unity is still nowhere near being found. They symbolize the disintegration.

It is nostalgia for unity that carries the woman away from her mother. The unity is connected with the tiger. The tiger-cat is her partner in the search for the Mainland, which apparently can only be reached when the young man is dead. What does that mean?

The cat has yellow and black stripes. The woman is dressed in a black and gold sarong. The cat slept with the woman when she still slept alone. On the market, the cat walks beside the woman, even brushing against her now and then. The woman identifies herself strongly with the cat: she feeds it with the blood of her lover. However, when the woman sleeps with the young man the cat is locked up below decks. There it thumps against the hatch. It is possible to see an aspect of the woman in the cat, namely that aspect that must achieve full growth before she can reach her goal. It is an aspect of ferocity, expressed in its thirst for blood, its miaowing, the killing of mice, and of pleasure, as appears from the following description:

36 . . . and licked itself clean with its curled pink little tongue (p. 266).

Both sides come together in the scenes at night:

37 and the cat opened wide its little mouth and caught the drops of blood on its little tongue (p. 269).

The frantic thumping of the cat under decks comes close to the throbbing of the blood in the lower part of the woman's body. Sometimes she permits that, sometimes she does not, but in each case the young man is a *hindrance* with his antipathy to the cat. That seems strange. He is, after all, her lover; surely she should be able to take pleasure in being with him.

That this is not the case is because this story is about two developments and not one situation. The young man represents a phase for the woman, as she did for him. It is the phase of motherhood. She feeds him, takes care of him. When his dependence lasts too long the cat demands its rights. Just as the mother has fed her child, so she now feeds herself on him. She sucks him dry, claims him completely. She does not see at all that, in doing so, she causes him injury:

38   After a while the bleeding stopped, the woman stroked the hand of the man and laid it next to him again . . . (p. 269).

This loving gesture at such a moment, the care she offers him, yes, even the warning, contrary to her own better judgement, that the sea-cows will injure him, all this indicates that motherhood, if carried on for too long, can only be at the expense of the child. At the same time, the woman needs it in order to break away from the influence of her own mother. When she is drifting around at sea, free from all the small intermediate stations (the small islands), and the young man, sucked completely dry, is dead, the woman experiences a moment of existential *Angst*. The cat, still locked up, growls and thumps. It is pitch dark and deathly quiet.

39 It took so long, why did it take so long? The shipmate did not move, sometimes the cat miaowed, the woman held her breath over and over again (p. 270).

A phase is closed, she can start all over again. When it becomes light the proa is lying by the shore of the Mainland:

40   A high, rocky, dark shore and directly behind the rocks a forest— she had never seen such a dark forest before—and further, hills and forest, and even further, mountains and forest, a land, dark, a dark Mainland (pp. 270–71).

Still, she cannot set the cat free. First she has to put the young man overboard, deliver him to his destination with the sirens. Then, the thumping in the hold becomes too powerful:

41 it was as if the proa creaked at every joint (p. 271).

This crisis is experienced by every woman when her children leave her, and her own suppressed desires surface and come to demand their rights. Sometimes this happens so forcibly that the woman is devastated by it, sometimes her life takes a new course and becomes fully her own.

42   It looked everywhere at once with its hot yellow eyes; the woman, the proa, the flooded land on the one side, the sea-cows (there lay the man), the Mainland on the other side, the forests, the hills, the mountains, everywhere forests, again at the woman, growled and with one jump it was off the proa and on the high rocky shore and stood there: it was a full-grown Bengal tiger, golden yellow with black stripes, and terrible to see (p. 271).

Confusion is rampant, the gaze of the tiger, sign of his power, takes in everything that is to be seen within the frame "the woman": her entire life. The tiger is the first to reach the goal. Now that the woman lets herself be led by it, she can cast off the last residue of social constraint, and, still not quite used to it, commence a new life:

43   The woman scrambled clumsily, hampered by her golden sarong, first over the rail of the proa and then up the high rocks to the animal, which was waiting for her. Afterwards, they walked farther afield together, first the tiger, the tiger in front, then the woman, to the forests on the hills, on the mountains of the vast Mainland, where she had to go (p. 271).

Those readers who identify with her can feel relieved. They have recognized the silent dark moment that precedes an important change of course. They have experienced the fear, and although the new is still completely unknown (dark woods), it has already turned out that the tiger, her own desire, however "terrible" it seems, is a good guide.

6. THE TRADITIONAL TALE AND THE "UNCANNY"

When the story is finished, the suspense has passed. The man and the woman each go their own way, and they are both satisfied. Still, it is a creepy story. As Kappers-den Hollander[19] explains in connection with the Gothic novel, a genre much used by women, the creepy impression these stories evoke is caused by a simultaneous feeling of recognition and alienation. In his essay "The 'Uncanny'" ("Das Unheimliche"), Freud explains how the repression of something of which we would rather not be reminded does not entirely hinder its recognition, but transforms it into horror:

> This uncanny is really nothing new or strange, but something that has long been familiar to the psyche, from which it has been alienated only by the process of repression.[20]

What exactly it is that, from the male perspective, is creepy, familiar and alien, is not difficult to guess, as explained once again recently by Ten Berge,[21] and as sometimes occurs with baffling explicitness in stories. An example is the eighteenth-century tale "Le sultan Misatouf et la princesse Grisemine, ou métamorphoses," by Voisenon, in which the terror of the *vagina dentata*,[22] comes in for lengthy treatment, including a dentist who tries in vain to file down the sharp teeth. About this, Freud says:

> It often happens that neurotic men explain that they find the female genitals creepy ("uncanny"). This uncanniness is, however, the entrance to the old home of the human child. . . . Love is homesickness. . . .[23]

To this he adds: "but the prefix 'un' on this word is the mark of repression." He refers thereby to the etymology of the word. The German word *unheimlich*, which, via repression, is synonymous with its opposite, is particularly significant, certainly in connection with the "long houses" in this story. *Heimisch*, "homey," separates into two meanings: on the one hand "safe, snug," with *unheimlich* as its opposite, and on the other hand "hidden,

19. Kappers-Den Hollander, "Nachtmerrie en Ontwaken."
20. Freud, "The 'Uncanny,'" 394 (my translation differs). The German (p. 254) reads: "Dies Unheimliche ist wirklich nichts Neues oder Fremdes, sondern etwas dem Seelenleben von alters her Vertrautes, das ihm nur durch den Prozess der Verdrängung entfremdet ist."
21. Berge, "De mannenschrik."
22. See also my *Lethal Love*, Chapter 2.
23. Freud, "The 'Uncanny,'" 398–99 (my translation differs). The German (p. 259) reads: "Es kommt oft vor, dass neurotische Männer erklären, das weibliche Genitale sei ihnen etwas Unheimliches. Dieses Unheimliche ist aber der Eingang zur alten Heimat des Menschenkindes. . . . Liebe ist Heimweh. . . ."

secret," with "public" as its opposite.[24] The opposite meanings are themselves contrary, so that a peculiar semantic structure comes about:

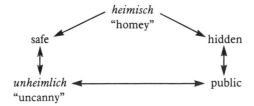

When what was hidden becomes public this can precisely remove what is creepy, as is the case with a successful psychoanalysis. If, however, the familiarity is deformed by repression, the feeling arises that is indicated by this very adequate German word. By, for example, seeing the cat differently than the woman, the young man turns it into a more scary beast than the sharks.

In uncanny stories, states Freud, the borderline between life and death is often overstepped or becomes blurred. This is also the case in "The Sirens." The young man only becomes happy when he is dead, and his new existence seems more like a life beginning than a state of affairs after life's end. He lies in the water among the sirens without moving, and is completely passive. The actual uncanniness of the story, however, does not lie in the double ending, but in the duplicity itself, which, depending on the identification of the reader, makes one storyline recognizable and the other strange. For one reader the sea-cows, among the brownish green algae moving gently up and down, are creepy; for another it is the cat with its small pink tongue, which feasts first on itself, in #36, and then on the man, in #37. With the woman, one is afraid of the sea, with the man, of the cat. Both are uncanny for the same reasons. The sea is often seen as a symbol of amniotic fluid. The young man finds that an attractive idea; the woman, who also fled the "long houses," is afraid of it. The cat/tiger, for the woman the center of her selfhood, her guide, is for the man a gruesome extension, a metonymic image of the entry to the mother's womb, with sharp teeth, and eager to lap up your vital fluids. Actually, the man and the woman are therefore afraid of, and attracted by, the same thing. But the symmetry ends here, for the woman is not only a child, but also a mother and a woman, whereas the man can only be a child.

The uncanny, attractive, and characteristic feature of this retold traditional tale is its lack of unity. Precisely because the two fabulas affect each other, but still have their own development and outcome, this is a remarkable traditional tale, the handing down of which is doubly motivated. Whichever perspective one chooses, both the strange and the familiar will

24. Freud, "The 'Uncanny,'" 376–77 (German, p. 237).

always appeal. Consequently, it is not only an absolutely democratic story, but it also has, through its uncanniness, a cathartic effect which makes it so penetrating, again, for men *and* women. For both it releases a phantasma, as Mendel puts it with reference to popular fiction:

> A dazzling intuition, a short-circuit between the conscious and the unconscious, which is opposed at every point to rational thought. . . . it embraces the external subject, it embraces outside and inside, present and past, desire and reality. . . . a bridge set up for a very brief time between the unconscious and the conscious.[25]

By vicariously experiencing, the uncanny readers of either sex can divest the prefix "un-" of its power, and the "long houses" become familiar again, not ordinary, but acceptable.

This effect can best be achieved with texts from a genre in which the reader presupposes a certain, but limited, degree of fictionality. If the degree of fictionality is high, as is the case in fairy tales, then the story is not really scary, and therefore cannot make the readers experience fear. If the story is realistic, then the same norms count as in real life, and only that will be scary which we would also "normally" find scary. Only in texts from a genre that, like the traditional tale, supposes a double attitude towards fictionality, can the writer extend the uncanny "far beyond what could happen in reality."[26] Then it becomes possible that the man ends in passivity and the woman in activity, and that they are both happy in that condition, because they have overcome the uncanny, their fear. It might well be that for the reader it is this reversal which, on a deeper level than that of the creepy events, makes the story so uncanny. As Felman writes, in a brilliant analysis of Balzac's short story "La fille aux yeux d'or":

> What is perhaps the most uncanny about the uncanny is that it is not the opposite of what is canny, but rather, that which uncannily subverts the opposition between "canny" and "uncanny," between "heimlich" and "unheimlich." In the same way, femininity as real otherness . . . is uncanny in that it is not the opposite of masculinity, but that which subverts the very opposition of masculinity and femininity.[27]

They are not bloodthirsty animals, but, in their dark domain between the sea and the land, they are enticing symbols of this vagueness, which is the most awful: the sirens, so called since ancient times.

25. Mendel, "Psychanalyse et paralittérature," 449. Translated by the editor.
26. Freud, "The 'Uncanny,'" 405 (German, p. 265).
27. Felman, "Rereading Femininity," 41–42.

The Sirens,

by Maria Dermoût

The story goes:

Not a man, a woman bought the proa, a beautiful proa, carved, brightly painted, on the stem the one wide open, the "All-Seeing Eye," tall bamboo masts, which could be lowered when the wind would not come, triangular sails of woven matting, brown and red, which could also be lowered or serve as an awning in storm or rain or too much sunshine or too much moonshine.

A proa with a broad bamboo outrigger on one side and without a deep draught, to sail the straits between the flooded land; with here and there and everywhere small islands, with one large island far away on the one side, and a vast Mainland far away on the other side.

Where?

Once all had been joined to the Mainland: the large island, the small scattered islands, the flooded land in between, one land! It had been called the land of the Tiger, formerly.

The land of the Tiger was not there any more.

The sea was still there, just as it used to be.

The woman had not bought the proa because she loved the sea, she did not love the sea, she was afraid of the sea.

She loved the vast Mainland that she had never seen, but where she wanted to go, and must and would go! That is why she had bought the proa.

That was why she had left the one large island where she lived.

Where, along the river, on the edge of the forest, under the trees, the "long houses" stood that belonged to the women, high on piles with beautifully carved beams, with beautifully carved ascending ladders.

Where every night, on the stroke of half past twelve the torches were lit and the men had to leave the women, down the ladders of the "long houses" and further along a dark path to their own men's quarters somewhere a long way into the forests.

Where she too lived in a "long house" with her mother, who was the head of the family, of all the families in the "long house": the women and children in the house and their men out there in the forests.

And she the eldest daughter!

Where she could have had a good life, waiting for her turn to buy a man that pleased her for so many men's sarongs and headcloths interwoven with gold and silver, which were weighed on the steelyard for their heaviness, to get children, daughters above all! To hear the gurgling river, the rustling of the tall trees, and at half past twelve at night, the crackling of the burning torches and the voices of the men in the dark who climbed down the ladders of the "long houses" and grumbled. Waiting for her turn, after her mother's death, to become the head of the family, of all the families in the "long house."

This woman had not wanted to wait for her turn, she had bought a proa with all that should be on a proa, and a young man as shipmate, and a cat, a striped one, yellow and black, for the mice, she was afraid of mice.

And she had gone sailing on the proa, with the man, with the cat, through the straits between the flooded land and the many small islands, at which she called in turn, in order to search for the vast Mainland, on the other side, days, months, years.

She did not find the Mainland, the story goes.

In the markets on the small islands the villagers held their breath and looked at each other.

The woman! A heavy loose-fitting sarong interwoven with real gold or silver, a black girdle around her waist, a black silk cloth tied over her breasts, her black hair combed smoothly, oiled, her face powdered, walking slowly, erect, looking straight ahead, and: she walked in front!

Behind her came a man, also so well-dressed, in just such beautiful clothes — the woman will have given them to him! — a straight sarong pulled up high, a headcloth, both interwoven with gold — or silver — thread, a flower behind his ear.

He walked some way behind the woman and he had a basket with him in which to carry her shopping.

He was a young man, younger than the woman, but not so young as to be her son. Too old to be her son? Too young to be her husband? Who? What? A member of the family? The shipmate? The lover of the woman? Nobody could tell that by looking at him.

A big yellow and black cat walked beside the woman, it miaowed sometimes and brushed against her sarong and the woman said "Shoo!" to it and it came to walk beside her again.

In the markets of the small islands the woman bought all sorts of sup-plies: fresh drinking water to go in the martavans on the proa, charcoal for cooking on the way, oil for a small lamp at night and provisions for her and the man and the cat: rice and root crops, red peppers, coconuts, cured meat and fish which could be kept for a long time, and sweets and incense and perfumery. She also liked to buy flowers, preferably flowering plants in pots, they lasted long, also on a proa, preferably hibiscus plants with red flowers. The man wore an hibiscus flower behind his ear.

He was definitely the lover of the woman!

And for the cat she bought raw meat on which there was still blood, for cats are fond of drinking blood.

The woman paid with small and large pieces of gold—or silver fabric.

Afterwards she handed out sweets and incense, and stood talking with the villagers in the markets on the small islands: about the weather and the wind and the waterway and about the flooded land (she looked straight ahead) and . . . about the Mainland.

Then the villagers nodded: yes, they had heard of it!

There were some that said that they knew where it was; one said that he had been there once.

But if the woman asked "Where then, where?" they pointed north and south and east and west to all four silent Sheikhs at the corners of the world at the same time.

"Oh well!" said the woman and shrugged her shoulders.

The young man and the cat stood still behind and beside her, they did not join in the talking, they listened.

Was the young man really the lover of the woman?

The young man was the lover of the woman.

That had come about like this.

Not straight away, in the beginning. In the beginning the woman slept on her beautifully painted couch behind the matting of a sail, and the shipmate slept anywhere, here or there on the proa, on a small mat.

If it could the cat went to sleep with the woman on the couch, she did not mind, most of the time.

Once, when they had already been sailing around for many a day past the many small islands, past the flooded land, but still could not find the Mainland, the woman called the shipmate to her and said that he should just come and lie with her on the couch at night, then she would give him the chest with men's clothes, the golden and silver men's sarongs and headcloths, not only for best, for the market, forever; he could weigh the clothes on the steelyard for their heaviness if he wanted to, and she would give him the flower-pots at the back of the proa with the hibiscus plants with the red flowers.

The shipmate looked at the woman when she said that. He had looked at her before, at the way she sat squatted on a mat, at the way she lay on the couch, the way she rose to her feet and walked, the way she held her head and looking straight ahead said something.

He too came from the one large island. Where he lived there were no "long houses," there a woman walked differently, stood differently, held her head differently, there a woman did not look straight ahead and say this or that; and that a man should just come and lie with her on the couch at night.

There a man said that to a woman, like that, and walked like that, and held his head like that, looked straight ahead.

The shipmate thought that the woman looked beautiful in her golden sarong, black girdle, black cloth, the black hair in a knot, against the side rail of the proa, looking straight ahead; and he liked the night sky behind her with moon and stars and the sea in the white moonlight, and the horizon so silvery and hazily distant — was there land or was there no land? — and he liked the proa: the masts, the purple sails and all the beautiful carving and also the golden and silver clothes in the chest, the men's sarongs and headcloths, and the flower-pots with hibiscus plants with red flowers at the back of the proa, he liked red flowers.

He loved all of that.

"All right," he then said to the woman, "if you want it."

He had already lain with a woman on the couch at night, he liked that.

The shipmate, the young man, Toeangkoe So and So, or whatever he was called, actually liked anything and everything.

Only he did not like the cat.

It was as if the woman noticed this.

During the day the cat used to lie here and there on the deck of the proa in the sun and licked itself clean with its curled pink little tongue and blinked its yellow eyes against the light and yawned and slept for a while; but at night when the man and the woman were lying together on the coach the cat was not there.

The young man sometimes wondered: "Where is the cat?" not because he loved the cat, since he did not love the cat. And the woman said that she had locked the cat up below deck where the mice are, to hunt them in the dark.

Sometimes, when the night was silent and there was not much wind and the proa lay still at her anchor-stones and the man and the woman lay still on the couch, they heard the cat.

A bump that sounded like a leap, a creaking, and nothing more except a tiny, tiny crack.

The young man sucked his breath between his lips. "Ah, cats are fond of drinking blood!" he said, and he shuddered at the thought.

"Yes," said the woman next to him, "cats are fond of drinking blood."

Every day, late afternoon, when the work was finished, the proa washed clean and scrubbed for the night, they dropped anchor, somewhere in the shade, close to the flooded land, not too near lest the proa get caught in the sand, near the edge of the deep water.

Then they washed and bathed, to be clean for the night, all three they liked to be clean.

The cat washed and licked itself clean every free moment of the day and the night, the cat was always clean.

The woman raised the sail as a protection and washed herself behind it with sweet water from a martavan; she also always used oil and perfume and lemon, then she was clean and smelled good.

The young man bathed himself every day in the sea, he was a good swimmer.

Every day the woman tried to stop him, but he would not listen to her; he took off his headcloth and his flower and his men's sarong and jumped over the railing of the proa into the sea.

With a few short fast strokes he swam out across the deep waters, where the sharks are that are fond of drinking blood, he knew that all right! He could swim faster and also better than the sharks, he said.

And then he came onto the flooded land, there it was not deep: extensive flat meadows under water, covered with algae as if it were grass, green and brown and very wet; and in the meadows, as it should be, cows grazed.

In the sea-meadows sea-cows grazed.

They grazed in herds, they lay on the bottom in the shallow water and were big and black, with tails like fish, round black heads, small bulging black shining eyes, round mouths with protruding white teeth with which they grazed on the algae. On the front of the body (they were mammals) they had breasts like a woman; left and right of the body, two long fins on which they leaned, as if they were arms, when they raised the upper part of their body; they often did that to breathe above water, to look out over the water.

Not in the bright sunlight during the day; in the twilight or in a haze or at night they looked somewhat like women, these sea-cows.

And they lowed.

Accompanied, muffled, drowned out sometimes by all the sounds of the sea and waves and wind, it was as if they sang, the black women under the water, the sirens. As they are called as far back as the mists of antiquity.

The young man walked towards them, wading through the shallow water and he remained standing near them or he sat down among them, or if it was very shallow, he lay backwards among them.

They did him no harm, they were inquisitive and came closer and in a circle around him, raised the upper part of the body, the heads up, looked at him, sang for him.

After a while he went back again, walking back through the shallow water, quickly swimming across the deep water where the sharks are, and climbed back on board the proa. He was clean after his bath in the sea, took a washed and clean golden or silver men's sarong and headcloth, picked a fresh red flower.

And then the woman said : "Why do you do this, why do you bathe every day in the sea? The sea-cows will harm you! Sometime one day, they will kill you and drink your blood!"

The man laughed. "Since when are sea-cows fond of drinking blood? Cats are fond of drinking blood, and sharks," and turning away from the woman he looked at the flooded meadows, green and brown under the water, and at the black shapes lying under the water, pointed, "and those are not cows, those are women," he said.

The woman stood the way she stood, erect, kept her head straight, looked straight ahead. "Oh well! Beautiful women!" she said slightingly.

"I don't say that they are beautiful," said the man, "no one would say that the black women under the water are beautiful"; and after some time: "They sing, the black women under the water sing; have you," but he did not say that in the informal way, he always said "you" in the formal way, "have you never heard it? If you listen carefully you can hear it as well."

"Oh well," said the woman, "Cows will always be cows, land-cows, sea-cows, cows don't sing, they low!"

The man gave no reply, he stood beside her in his gold or silver clothes and looked past her, smiling.

He loved the green and brown underwater meadows so much, and the black women under the water, and he loved what they sang.

Again, every day, in the twilight, towards dusk, the same thing happened; the woman said this and the man said that and at night they lay beside each other on the couch.

The woman wore (all the women from the "long houses" wore it) a pin, a razor-sharp golden pin, as thin as a golden thread from her sarong; no one could see that she wore such a pin.

Not suddenly, gradually the woman turned herself in the night to get up from beside the man. Carefully!

He lay as he always lay when he slept, his hands right and left next to him, one hand hanging over the edge of the couch; he slept soundly and deeply, and dreamed.

The woman walked as she always walked, but carefully, over the one plank that did not creak, to the hatch, opened it — the hinges were oiled — and whispered "Puss" and the cat, also very carefully, came out from below deck and they walked back together. The woman in her bare feet, the cat on its little velvet paws over the plank that did not creak.

The woman bent over, took the hand of the sleeping man, he did not notice it, and pricked into the top of one of the fingers with the golden pin, so quickly, so carefully, he did not notice it, kept hold of the hand from which slowly drop by drop the blood flowed.

"Puss," she said without moving her lips; and the cat opened wide its little mouth and caught the drops of blood on its little tongue, so carefully, not one drop of blood was lost, and the man did not notice it.

After a while the bleeding stopped, the woman stroked the hand of the man and laid it next to him again on the edge of the couch; he slept, he had not noticed anything.

The cat licked its small mouth clean and the woman took it back to the hatch, closed it behind the cat and went to lie beside the man again on the couch so that he did not notice it.

Again, every day: in the evening twilight, in the night.

One day, when the young man woke up in the morning and sat straight up on the couch, the sun colored everything rose-red: the woman and himself and the proa and the sea and the flooded land and the sea-cows and a small island somewhere and the most distant horizon. With his hand, he rubbed his eyes, his head.

"I dream so strangely sometimes," he said to the woman, "not pleasantly! Always the same, I don't know what!"

He looked pale in the morning.

And the woman said: "Why do you do it anyway! Why do you bathe yourself every day in the sea; that makes you ill, and sometime, one day . . ." and the man said . . . .

And so they said it twice a day now, in the early morning and in the late evening twilight.

The young man was fond of both, of the morning, of the evening, of such a long lovely day! And the night? He did not know whether he liked the night, now; he had also liked the night, and his dreams, before.

The shipmate did not get up from the couch that morning, the woman had got up earlier. When he woke up, he sat straight up again, with his hand he rubbed his eyes and forehead again and said: "I've got it, I have dreamed of the cat, of course, all those nights, I have dreamed about the cat! Why," he swore terribly, "I don't like to dream of that wretched cat!"

He said this to himself, not to the woman, she did not give any reply anyhow; he lay down again on the couch, he looked so pale, time and again he fell asleep.

The woman left the proa riding at anchor that day, she did all the work, she stretched the matted sail, so that the sun did not bother the man, and cooked and brought him food and drink, but he did not want to eat or drink.

She asked whether she should wash him.

"No," he said, he did want a clean men's sarong and headcloth; she gave him these and picked a fresh hibiscus flower.

"Thank you," he said, looked at the flower, smelt it (hibiscus flowers do not smell), stuck the flower in his hair, fell asleep.

When the sun began to go down, in the twilight, he got up, went and leaned against the side-rail of the proa. He could still have walked, he thought, in the meadows under the water near the sea-cows, but he could no longer swim faster and better than the sharks, he knew that all right.

And so the woman did not say this, and the man did not say that. Why should they?

He went to lie down again on the couch, closed his eyes, slept, dreamed, in the evening, in the night, he did not dream of the cat.

The woman did not come to lie beside him on the couch. Why should she? She went to lie somewhere on the proa on a small mat, she did not get up that night, did not prick the man with the pin, she did not open the hatch for the cat. Why should she?

The cat miaowed a few times below the deck of the proa; the man did not hear it, the woman acted as if she did not hear it. It had never been so dark before, no moon, no stars, and there was no more oil for the small lamp; the proa lay still at her stone anchors, the man lay still on the couch, the woman lay still on her mat, the cat was also still now below deck, when late at night a wind rose — not a strong wind, not a storm or a typhoon or such like, the wind — and the proa began to move, just as if a strong current softly carried the proa along through deep water, so deep the stone anchors no longer rested on the bottom.

The woman sat squatted on her mat. If they ran onto the flooded land and turned over and drowned! If they were dashed against a rock or a high shore! But that did not happen.

The proa sailed slowly, her anchors still out, to somewhere, all the hours of the night. A slight jolt! The proa lay still at her anchors.

The woman got up, she walked, groping in the dark, to the couch to wake the shipmate; she could not wake him up, she grabbed hold of his one hand that lay next to him on the edge of the couch, the hand felt cold in hers, she put the hand back again.

Suddenly the cat growled loudly a few times in succession below the deck of the proa.

"Hush cat!" whispered the woman to herself and squatted down against the couch to wait for daylight. It took so long, why did it take so long? The shipmate did not move, sometimes the cat miaowed, the woman held her breath over and over again.

At last, in the very first greyish light, still long before sunrise, the woman saw that the proa lay by the shore, with one side onto it, the broad bamboo outrigger on the other side on the water.

A high, rocky, dark shore and directly behind the rocks a forest — she had never seen such a dark forest before— and further, hills and forest, and even further, mountains and forest, a land, dark, a dark Mainland. The woman looked at the shipmate in the grey light; he looked deathly pale, he was dead too.

The cat below deck miaowed and growled so loudly that it was as if it gave a cry now and then, and jumped up against the hatch.

"Quiet you!" shouted the woman.

She washed herself first, she combed her hair, she brushed her teeth, she powdered herself, she opened a chest and took out her most beautiful sarong woven with gold, her finest silk breastcloth; she pulled the sarong tighter around than usual, the breastcloth as well, and her broad girdle.

Then she walked to the couch, bent down and took the shipmate up in her arms (he did not weigh that much), walked with him to the side-rail of the proa, not on the side of the Mainland, on the other side, close to the flooded land, she braced herself, and threw him in an arc overboard out over the bamboo outrigger and on top of the meadows under the water near the sea-cows that grazed there and turned themselves around.

The cat growled now without stopping, jumped up against the hatch without stopping; it was as if the proa creaked at every joint.

"Yes, yes all right," said the woman, "I'm coming!" and opened the hatch; the cat came out from below the deck of the proa onto the deck, swishing its tail up and down.

It looked everywhere at once with its hot yellow eyes; the woman, the proa, the flooded land on the one side, the sea-cows (there lay the man), the Mainland on the other side, the forests, the hills, the mountains, everywhere forests, again at the woman, growled and with one jump it was off the proa and on the high rocky shore and stood there: it was a full-grown Bengal tiger, golden yellow with black stripes, and terrible to see.

The woman scrambled clumsily, hampered by her golden sarong, first over the rail of the proa and then up the high rocks to the animal, which was waiting for her. Afterwards they walked farther afield together, first the tiger, the tiger in front, then the woman, to the forests on the hills, on the mountains of the vast Mainland, where she had to go.

The beautiful proa remained behind deserted — there were not even any mice left on board — by the shore of the Mainland, until the stormy wind comes that will dash her to pieces.

Every night, in the light of the moon, the light of the stars — maybe even in the dark, but then nobody sees it— a young man, Toeangkoe So and So, or whatever he is called, lies in a flooded meadow somewhere around Malacca way.

In a woven gold or silver men's sarong, pulled up to the armpits like a sheath around him, a small woven silver or gold headcloth tied tightly around the head, a red flower, an hibiscus flower behind an ear.

He lies straight and still in the wet brown and green algae; yet he has not drowned, he is not sleeping either, he is peacefully lying backwards, both his hands are lying next to him. He keeps his eyes open, then he looks through the water.

In a circle around him the black women under the water, the sirens, sing for him.

They sing about all sorts of things . . . .

They sing of a proa and a woman and a shipmate and a cat; they sing of a vast Mainland somewhere, and of a Bengal tiger; but he has already heard that once before.

Sometimes he laughs about what they sing, sometimes he does not.

He lies very peacefully and listens . . . .

He is a happy man that Toeangkoe So and So, or whatever he is called; he will never become old, he will never die any more than he has already died, he not only likes what the sirens sing, he understands what the sirens sing . . . .

So the story goes.

Works Consulted

Alexandrescu, Sorin, "Le discours étrange." Pp. 101-33 in *Sémiotique narrative et textuelle*. Ed. Claude Chabrol. Paris: Larousse, 1973.

Alphen, Ernst van, *Van hoe 't is en hoe 't gaat: Over psycho-analytische en tekst-sociologische ideologiekritiek*. Utrecht: Instituut voor Algemene Literatuurwetenschap, 1982.

———, "Visie of zinsbegoocheling?" Utrecht: Instituut voor Algemene Literatuurwetenschap, 1983.

———, *Bang voor schennis? Inleiding in de ideologiekritiek*. Utrecht: HES Publishers, 1987.

———, "Literal Metaphors: On Reading Post-/Modernism." *Style* 21 (1987): 208-18.

———, *Bij wijze van lezen: Verleiding en verzet van Willem Brakmans lezer*. Muiderberg: Coutinho, 1988.

Alter, Robert, *The Art of Biblical Narrative*. New York: Basic Books, 1981.

———, *Motives for Fiction*. Cambridge: Harvard University Press, 1984.

———, *The Art of Biblical Poetry*. New York: Basic Books, 1985.

Althusser, Louis, *For Marx*. Trans. Ben Brewster. Harmondsworth: Penguin Books, 1969.

Bal, Mieke, *Complexité d'un roman populaire: Ambiguité dans* La chatte. Paris: La Pensée Universelle, 1974.

———, *Narratologie: Essais sur la signification narrative dans quatre romans modernes*. Paris: Klincksieck, 1977.

———, "Mise en abyme et iconicité." *Littérature* 29 (1978): 116-28.

———, "The Laughing Mice or: On Focalization," *Poetics Today* 2 (1981): 202-10.

———, ed., *Literaire genres en hun gebruik*. Muiderberg: Coutinho, 1981.

———, "Notes on Narrative Embedding." *Poetics Today* 22 (1981): 41-60.

———, "Psychopoetics—Theory." *Poetics* 13 (1984): 279-98.

———, *Narratology: Introduction to the Theory of Narrative*. Trans. Christine van Boheemen. Toronto: The University of Toronto Press, 1985.

———, "Sexuality, Sin and Sorrow: The Emergence of the Female Body. A Reading of Genesis 1-3." Pp. 317-38 in *The Female Body in Western Culture*. Ed. Susan Rubin Suleiman. Cambridge: Harvard University Press, 1986.

———, *Femmes imaginaires: L'ancien testament au risque d'une narratologie critique*. Utrecht: HES; Montréal: HMH; Paris: Nizet, 1986.

273

————, *Lethal Love: Feminist Literary Readings of Biblical Love-Stories.* Bloomington: Indiana University Press, 1987.

————, *Death & Dissymmetry: The Politics of Coherence in the Book of Judges.* Chicago: The University of Chicago Press, 1988.

————, *Murder and Difference: Gender, Genre and Scholarship on Sisera's Death.* Bloomington: Indiana University Press, 1988.

————, *Reading "Rembrandt": Beyond the Word-Image Opposition.* Cambridge: Cambridge University Press, 1991.

Barthes, Roland, *Mythologies.* Selected and trans. Annette Lavers. New York: Hill and Wang, 1972.

————, *S/Z.* New York: Hill & Wang, 1974.

————, "Introduction to the Structural Analysis of Narratives." Trans. Stephen Heath. Pp. 74–124 in *Image, Music, Text.* New York, Hill and Wang, 1977.

Beauvoir, Simone de, *La force des choses.* Paris: Editions Gallimard, 1963.

Belsey, Catherine, *Critical Practice.* London: Methuen, 1980.

Benveniste, Emile, *Problèmes de linguistique générale.* Paris: Gallimard, 1966. English trans., *Problems in General Linguistics.* Trans. M. E. Meeks. Coral Gables, FL: University of Miami Press, 1971.

Berge, H. C. ten, "De mannenschrik: Over het motief van de verslindende vrouw in de mythiese verbeelding." *Bulletin* 10 (1982): 91–99.

Bergren, Ann, "Helen's 'Good Drug': Odyssey IV 1–305." Pp. 201–14 in *Contemporary Hermeneutics and the Interpretation of Classical Texts.* Ottawa: University of Ottawa Press, 1981.

————, "Language and the Female in Early Greek Thought." *Arethusa* 16 (1983): 69–95.

Berlin, Adele. *The Poetics of Biblical Parallelism.* Bloomington: Indiana University Press, 1985.

Biolley-Godino, Marcelle, *L'homme-objet chez Colette.* Paris: Klincksieck, 1972.

Blin, Georges, *Stendhal et les problèmes du roman.* Paris: Corti, 1954.

Boheemen, Christel van, "Intertekstualiteit." Pp. 121–30 in Bal, *Literaire genres.*

Boling, Robert, *Judges: A New Translation with Introduction and Commentary.* The Anchor Bible. Garden City, NY: Doubleday, 1975.

Booth, Wayne, *The Rhetoric of Fiction.* Chicago: The University of Chicago Press, 1961.

Bremond, Claude, "La logique des possibles narratifs." *Communications* 8 (1966): 60–76.

————, *Logique du récit.* Paris: Editions du Seuil, 1973.

Brontë, Emily, *Wuthering Heights.* Harmondsworth: Penguin Books, 1965.

Bronzwaer, W., "Mieke Bal's Concept of Focalization: A Critical Note." *Poetics Today* 2 (1981): 193–201.

Brooks, Cleanth, and Robert Penn Warren, *Understanding Fiction.* New York: Appleton, Century, Crofts, 1943.

Brooks, Peter, *Reading for the Plot: Design and Intention in Narrative.* New York: Knopf; Oxford: Oxford University Press, 1984.

Browne, R. M., "Typologie des signes littéraires." *Poétique* 7 (1971): 334–53.

Buuren, Maarten van, "Metaforische beschrijvingen: De presentatie van personages bij Proust." Pp. 47–59 in *Mensen van papier: Over personages in de literatuur (Paper-People: On the Concept of Character in Literature).* Ed. Mieke Bal. Assen: Van Gorcum, 1979.

Carroll, David, *Questioning the Subject: The Languages of Theory and the Strategies of Fiction.* Chicago: The University of Chicago Press, 1982.

Chambers, Ross, *Story and Situation: Narrative Seduction and the Power of Fiction*. Minneapolis: University of Minnesota Press, 1984.

Chase, Cynthia, *Decomposing Figures: Rhetorical Readings in the Romantic Tradition*. Baltimore: Johns Hopkins University Press, 1986.

Cohn, Dorrit, *Transparent Minds: Narrative Modes for Presenting Consciousness in Fiction*. Princeton: Princeton University Press, 1978.

――――, "The Encirclement of Narrative: On Franz Stanzel's *Theorie des Erzählens*." *Poetics Today* 2 (1981): 157–82.

Colette, *La Chatte*. Pp. 141–246 in *Oeuvres Complètes de Colette*, vol. 9. Paris: Flammarion, 1949. English trans., *The Cat*. Trans. Antonia White. Pp. 71–193 in *7 by Colette*. New York: Farrar, Straus and Cudahy, 1955.

――――, *Chéri*. Pp. 13–158 in *Oeuvres Complètes de Colette*, vol. 6. Paris: Flammarion, 1949. English trans., *Chéri and The Last of Chéri*. Trans. unattrib. New York: Ballantine Books, 1982.

――――, *Claudine en Ménage*. Pp. 7–185 in *Oeuvres Complètes de Colette*, Vol. 2. Paris: Flammarion, 1949.

Coogan, M. D., "A Structural Analysis of the Song of Deborah." *The Catholic Bible Quarterly* 40 (1978): 132–66.

Culler, Jonathan, *Structuralist Poetics: Structuralism, Linguistics and the Study of Literature*. London: Routledge and Kegan Paul, 1975.

――――, *The Pursuit of Signs: Semiotics, Literature, Deconstruction*. Ithaca: Cornell University Press; London: Routledge and Kegan Paul, 1981.

――――, *On Deconstruction: Theory and Criticism after Structuralism*. Ithaca and London: Cornell University Press, 1983.

D'Hollander, Paul, *Colette: Ses apprentissages*. Montréal: Les Presses de l'Université de Montréal; Paris: Klincksieck, 1978.

Dällenbach, Lucien, *Le récit spéculaire: Essai sur la mise en abyme*. Paris: Editions du Seuil, 1977.

Damisch, Hubert, *L'origine de la perspective*. Paris: Flammarion, 1987.

Davies, Margaret, *Colette*. London: Oliver and Boyd, 1961.

Dermoût, Maria, *Verzameld werk*. Amsterdam: Querido, 1982.

Derrida, Jacques, *Of Grammatology*. Trans. Gayatry Spivak. Baltimore: Johns Hopkins University Press, 1976.

――――, *Writing and Difference*. Trans. Alan Bass. Chicago: The University of Chicago Press, 1978.

Dickens, Charles, *Dombey and Son*. Harmondsworth: Penguin Books, 1974.

Dilthey, Wilhelm, *Gesammelte Schriften*. Göttingen: Vandenhoeck & Ruprecht, 1919–67.

Doležel, Lubomír, *Narrative Modes in Czech Literature*. Toronto: The University of Toronto Press, 1973.

――――, "Truth and Authenticity in Narrative." *Poetics Today* 1 (1980): 7–25.

Doyle, Arthur Conan, *The Complete Sherlock Holmes*. Two volumes. Garden City, NY: Doubleday and Company, n.d.

Dronke, Peter, *Women Writers of the Middle Ages: A Critical Study of Texts from Perpetua to Marguerite Porete*. Cambridge: Cambridge University Press, 1984.

Ducrot, Oswald, *Dire et ne pas dire: Principes de sémantique linguistique*. Paris: Hermann, 1972.

――――, and Tzvetan Todorov, *Dictionnaire encyclopédique des sciences du langage*. Paris: Editions du Seuil, 1972.

――――, "Structuralisme, énonciation et sémantique." *Poétique* 33 (1978): 107–28.

Duquette, Jean-Pierre, *Colette: L'amour de l'amour*. Montréal: Hurtubise HMH, 1984.
Duras, Marguerite, *Le vice-consul*. Paris, Editions Gallimard, 1966. English trans., *The Vice-Consul*. Trans. Eileen Ellenbogen. New York: Pantheon Books, 1968.
Eco, Umberto, *A Theory of Semiotics*. London: The Macmillan Press, 48–54.
Faulkner, William, "A Rose for Emily." Pp. 167–82 in *These 13: Stories by William Faulkner*. New York: Jonathan Cape and Harrison Smith, 1931.
Felman, Shoshana, *Le scandale du corps parlant*. Paris: Editions du Seuil, 1980.
———, "Rereading Femininity." *Yale French Studies* 62 (1981): 19–44.
———, *Literary Speech-Acts*. Ithaca: Cornell University Press, 1984.
Feyerabend, Paul, *Against Method*. London: New Left Books, 1975.
Flaubert, Gustave, *Madame Bovary*. Ed. Claudine Gothot Mersch. Paris: Garnier, 1947. English trans. Alan Russell. Baltimore: Penguin Books, 1950.
Foucault, Michel, *The Order of Things*. New York: Vintage Books, 1973.
Freud, Sigmund, *The Interpretation of Dreams*. Ed. and trans., James Strachey. New York: Avon Books, 1965 (1900).
———, "Contributions to the Psychology of Love: The Taboo of Virginity." Pp. 217–35 in *Collected Papers*, vol. 4. Trans. Joan Riviere *et al*. New York: Basic Books, 1959.
———, "The Uncanny." Pp. 368–407 in *Collected Papers*, vol. 4. Trans. Joan Riviere *et al*. New York: Basic Books, 1959. (German, "Das Unheimliche." Pp. 229–68 in *Gesammelte Werke*, vol. 12. London: Imago Publishing Company, 1947.)
Friedman, Norman, "Point of View in Fiction: The Development of a Critical Concept." Pp. 108–37 in *The Theory of the Novel*. Ed. Philip Stevick. New York: The Free Press, 1967.
Gadamer, Hans-Georg, *Truth and Method*. Trans. ed. Garrett Barden and John Cumming. New York: Crossroad, 1985.
Gallop, Jane, "Lacan and Literature: A Case for Transference." *Poetics* 13 (1984): 301–8.
Gelley, Alexander, *Narrative Crossings: Theory and Pragmatics of Prose Fiction*. Baltimore: The Johns Hopkins University Press, 1988.
Genette, Gérard, *Figures II*. Paris: Editions du Seuil, 1969.
———, *Figures III*. Paris: Editions du Seuil, 1972.
———, *Narrative Discourse: An Essay in Method*. Trans. Jane E. Lewin. Ithaca, NY: Cornell University Press, 1980. (Trans. of pp. 67–273 of *Figures III*.)
———, "Boundaries of Narrative." Trans. Ann Levonas. *New Literary History* 8 (1976): 1–13. (Trans. of pp. 49–69 of *Figures II*.)
———, "Discussion sur le concept de focalisation (avec M. Bal)." Paris: Ecole des Hautes Etudes en Sciences Sociales, 1982.
———, *Nouveau discours du récit*. Paris: Editions du Seuil, 1983.
Girard, René, *The Scapegoat*. Trans. Yvonne Freccero. London: Athlone Press, 1986.
Globe, A., "The Literary Structure and Unity of the Song of Deborah." *Journal of Biblical Literature* 93 (1974): 493–512.
Gorp, H. van, *et al.*, ed. *Lexicon van literaire termen*. Leuven, Groningen: Wolters-Noordhoff, 1980.
Göttner, Heide, *Logik der Interpretation*. Munich: Wilhelm Fink Verlag, 1973.
Goudeket, Maurice, *La douceur de veillir*. Paris: Flammarion, 1965.
———, "L'oeil du témoin." *Cahiers Colette* 1 (1977): 27–38.
Graves, Robert, *The White Goddess*. New York: Creative Age Press, 1948.
Greimas, Algirdas Julien, *Sémantique structurale*. Paris: Larousse, 1966.
———, *Du sens*. Paris: Editions du Seuil, 1970.
———, *Maupassant. The Semiotics of the Text: Practical Exercises*. Trans. Paul Perron. Amsterdam: Benjamins, 1988.

————, and Joseph Courtés, *Semiotics and Language: An Analytic Dictionary*. Trans. Larry Crist, Daniel Patte, *et al.* Bloomington: Indiana University Press, 1982.

Habermas, Jürgen, *Knowledge and Human Interests*. Trans. Jerome J. Shapiro. Boston: Beacon Press, 1971.

Hamon, Philippe, "Qu'est-ce qu'une description?" *Poétique* 12 (1972): 465–85.

————, *Introduction à l'analyse descriptive*. Paris: Hachette, 1981.

————, *Le personnel du roman: Le système des personnages dans les* Rougon-Macquart *d'Emile Zola*. Geneva: Droz, 1983.

————, *Texte et idéologie*. Paris: P.U.F., 1984.

Hart, Maarten 't, *De aansprekers*. Amsterdam: Editions De Arbeiderspers, 1979.

Heath, Stephen, *The Sexual Fix*. London: Macmillan, 1982.

Hendricks, William O., "Methodology of Narrative Structural Analysis." *Semiotica* 7 (1973): 163–84.

Herrnstein Smith, Barbara, "Narrative Versions, Narrative Theories." *Critical Inquiry* 7 (1980): 213–36.

Hichtum, Nienke van, *Afke's tiental*. Alkmaar, Editions Kluitman.

Houssa, Nicole, *Le souci de l'expression chez Colette*. Brussels: Palais des Académies, 1958.

Jakobson, Roman, "Linguistics and Poetry." Pp. 18–51 in *Selected Writings*, vol. 3. Ed. Stephen Rudy. The Hague, Paris, New York: Mouton, 1981.

James, Henry, *The Golden Bowl*. Harmondsworth: Penguin Books, 1975.

Jameson, Fredric, "Imaginary and Symbolic in Lacan: Marxism, Psychoanalytic Criticism, and the Problem of the Subject." *Yale French Studies* 55/56 (1977): 338–95.

————, *The Political Unconscious: Narrative as a Socially Symbolic Act*. Ithaca, NY: Cornell University Press, 1981.

Johnson, Barbara, *A World of Difference*. Baltimore: Johns Hopkins University Press, 1987.

Kappers-Den Hollander, Martien, "Nachtmerrie en Ontwaken: De Engelstalige Vrouwenroman en de Gothische Traditie." *De Revisor* 8 (1981): 40–51.

Keller, Evelyn Fox, *Reflections on Gender and Science*. New Haven: Yale University Press, 1985.

————, and Christine R. Grontkowski, "The Mind's Eye." Pp. 207–24 in *Discovering Reality*, ed. Sandra Harding and Merrill B. Hintikka. New York: Reidel Publishing Company, 1983.

Ketchum, Anne A., *Colette ou la naissance du jour: Etude d'un malentendu*. Paris: Minard, 1968.

Klaus, Peter, "Description and Event in Narrative." *Orbis Litterarum* 37 (1982): 201–16.

Koehler, Ludwig and Walter Baumgartner, *Lexicon in veteris testamenti libros*. Leiden: Brill, 1953.

Koot and Bie, *Calendar 1977*. Amsterdam: Editions De Harmonie, 1977.

Kress, Gunther and Robert Hodge, *Language as Ideology*. London: Routledge and Kegan Paul, 1979.

Kristeva, Julia, "Poésie et négativité." Pp. 246–77 in *Sémiotiké: Recherches pour une sémanalyse*. Paris: Editions du Seuil, 1969.

————, *Revolution in Poetic Language*. Trans. Margaret Waller. New York: Columbia University Press, 1984.

Kugel, James, *The Idea of Biblical Poetry: Parallelism and Its History*. New Haven: Yale University Press, 1981.

Labov, W., and J. Waletzky. "Narrative Analysis: Oral Versions of Personal Experience." Pp. 12–44 in *Essays on the Verbal and Visual Arts*. Ed. J. Helms. Seattle: University of Washington Press, 1967.

Lacan, Jacques, *Ecrits*. Paris: Editions du Seuil, 1966.

Lanser, Susan S., "(Feminist) Criticism in the Garden: Inferring Genesis 2-3," *Semeia* 41 (1988): 67-84.

Larousse du xxe siècle: Supplément. Paris: Larousse, 1933.

Leach, M. and I. Fried, eds., *Funk and Wagnall Standard Dictionary of Folklore, Mythology and Legend*. New York: Funk and Wagnall, 1949.

Lemaire, Ria, ed., *Ik zing mijn lied voor al wie met mij gaat: Vrouwen in de volks-literatuur*. Utrecht: HES, 1985.

Lévinas, Emmanuel, "Leçon talmudique: Et Dieu créa la femme." Pp. 41-57 in *L'autre dans la conscience juive*. Congrès mondial juif. Paris: Presses universitaires de France, 1973.

Lintvelt, Jaap, *Essai de typologie narrative*. Paris: José Corti, 1982.

Littré, E., *Dictionnaire de la langue française*. 7 volumes. Paris: Gallimard and Hachette, 1963-64.

Lodge, David, *Changing Places*. Harmondsworth: Penguin Books, 1975.

――――, "Types of Description." Pp. 93-103 in *The Modes of Modern Writing*. London: Edward Arnold, 1977.

Longus, *Daphnis and Chloë*. Trans. George Thornley. Cambridge, MA: Harvard University Press, 1955.

Lotman, Jurij, *The Structure of the Artistic Text*. Trans. Ronald Vroon. Ann Arbor: University of Michigan Press, 1977.

Maatje, F. C., *Doppelroman*. Second edition. Utrecht: Wolters-Noordhoff, 1968.

Magny, Claude-Edmonde, *Histoire du roman français depuis 1918*. Paris: Armand Colin, 1950.

Managhan, Patricia, *Women in Myth and Legend*. London: Junction Books, 1981.

Márquez, Gabriel García, *One Hundred Years of Solitude*. Trans. Gregory Rabassa. New York: Avon Books, 1970.

Maten, Erik, "De schelm als zedenmeester." *Forum der Letteren* 21 (1980): 114-25.

Maupassant, Guy de, *Une vie*. Paris: Calmann-Lévy, 1950. English trans. Marjorie Laurie. London: Wyman, 1923.

Mauron, Charles, *Des métaphores obsédantes au mythe personnel*. Paris: Corti, 1963.

McHale, Brian, "Free Indirect Discourse: A Survey of Recent Accounts," *PTL* 3 (1978): 249-87.

Mehlman, Jeffrey, "Entre psychanalyse et psychocritique." *Poétique* 3 (1970): 365-85.

Meijer, Maaike, *De lust tot lezen: Nederlandse dichteressen en het literaire systeem*. Amsterdam: van Gennep, 1988.

Mendel, Gérard, "Psychanalyse et paralittérature." Pp. 206-37 in *Entretiens sur la para-littérature*. Noël Arnaud *et al.*, eds. Paris: 1970.

Mitchell, W. J. T., "Spatial Form in Literature: Toward a General Theory." Pp. 271-300 in *The Language of Images*, ed. W. J. T. Mitchell. Chicago: The University of Chicago Press, 1980.

――――, *Iconology: Image, Text, Ideology*. Chicago, The University of Chicago Press, 1985.

Mooij, A. W., *Taal en Verlangen: Lacans theorie van de psychoanalyse*. Meppel: Boom, 1975.

――――, *Psychoanalyse en regels*. Meppel: Boom, 1981.

Moser, Walter, "Des usages intellectuels de la fête." *Canadian Review of Comparative Literature* 14 (1987): 77-90.

Nieuwenhuys, Rob, *Mirror of the Indies: A History of Dutch Colonial Literature*. Trans. Frans van Rosevelt. Ed. E. M. Beekman. Amherst: The University of Massachusetts Press, 1982.

Nyquist, Mary, "Gynesis, Genesis, Exegesis, and the Formation of Milton's Eve." Pp. 147–208 in *Cannibals, Witches, and Divorce: Estranging the Renaissance*. Ed. Marjorie Garber. Baltimore: The Johns Hopkins University Press, 1987.

Parker, Patricia, *Literary Fat Ladies: Rhetoric, Gender, Property*. New York and London: Methuen, 1987.

Passio Sanctarum Perpetuae et Felicitatis (The Martyrdom of Perpetua and Felicitas). Trans. Herbert Musurillo. Pp. 106–31 in *The Acts of the Christian Martyrs*. Oxford: Oxford University Press, 1972.

Pavel, Thomas, "Origin and Articulation: Comments on the Papers by Peter Brooks and Lucienne Frappier-Mazur." *Style* 18 (1984): 355–68.

———, *The Poetics of Plot*. Minneapolis: The University of Minnesota Press, 1985.

Peirce, Charles Sanders, *Collected Papers*. Ed. Charles Hartshorn and Paul Weiss. Cambridge, MA: Harvard University Press, 1931–35.

———, "Logic as Semiotic: The Theory of Signs." Pp. 1–23 in *Semiotics: An Introductory Anthology*. Ed. Robert E. Innis. Bloomington: Indiana University Press, 1985.

Petersen, Jürgen H., "Kategorien des Erzählens: Zur systematischen Description epischer Texte." *Poetica* 9 (1977): 167–95.

Phelps, Robert, *Colette*. Paris: Fayard, 1973.

Popper, Karl, *The Poverty of Historicism*. Boston: Beacon Press, 1957.

Pouillon, Jean, *Temps et roman*. Paris: Gallimard, 1946.

Prince, Gerald, "Le discours attributif et le récit." *Poétique* 35 (1978): 305–13.

Propp, Vladimir, *Morphology of the Folktale*. Trans. Laurence Scott. Austin and London: University of Texas Press, 1968.

Proust, Marcel, *Remembrance of Things Past*. Trans. C. K. Scott Moncrieff and Terence Kilmartin. 3 volumes. New York: Random House, 1981.

Raaphorst-Rousseau, Madeleine, *Colette, sa vie, son art*. Paris: Nizet, 1964.

Reinhart, T., "Point of View in Language: The Use of Parentheticals." Pp. 169–94 in *Essays on Deixis*. Ed. Gisa Rauh. Tübingen: Narr, 1983.

Rhys, Jean, "Outside the Machine." Pp. 83–106 in *Tigers are Better-Looking*. Harmondsworth: Penguin Books, 1977.

Ricardou, Jean, *Nouveaux problèmes du roman*. Paris: Editions du Seuil, 1978.

Ricoeur, Paul, *Time and Narrative*. Trans. Kathleen McLaughlin (Blamey) and David Pellauer. 3 volumes. Chicago: The University of Chicago Press, 1984–88.

Robbe-Grillet, Alain, *Instantanés*. Paris: Editions de minuit, 1962.

Robert, Paul, *Dictionnaire alphabétique et analogique de la langue française (Petit Robert)*. Ed. A. Rey *et al*. Paris: Le Robert, 1986.

Rose, Jacqueline, *Sexuality in the Field of Vision*. London and New York: Verso, 1986.

Rossum-Guyon, F. van, *Critique du roman*. Paris: Gallimard, 1970.

Sarde, Michèle, *Colette libre et entravée*. Paris: Stock, 1978.

Scarry, Elaine. *The Body in Pain: The Making and Unmaking of the World*. Oxford: Oxford University Press, 1985.

Schehr, Lawrence R., Review of Bal, *Narratology*. *Substance* 55 (1988): 83–84.

Schmid, Wolf, *Der Textaufbau in den Erzählungen Dostoevskijs*. Munich: Wilhelm Fink Verlag, 1973.

Scholes, Robert, "Métarécits." *Poétique* 7 (1971): 402–12.

Schor, Naomi, *Reading in Detail: Aesthetics and the Feminine*. New York and London: Methuen, 1986.

Soggin, Alberto, *Judges*. The Old Testament Library. London: SCM Press, 1981.

Souriau, Etienne, *Les 200.000 situations dramatiques*. Paris: Flammarion, 1956.

Stanzel, Franz K., *Typische Formen des Romans*. Göttingen: Vandenhoeck & Ruprecht, 1969.

———, *A Theory of Narrative*. Cambridge: Cambridge University Press, 1984.

Steiner, Wendy, *Pictures of Romance: Form and Context in Painting and Literature*. Chicago: The University of Chicago Press, 1988.

Sternberg, Meir, *The Poetics of Biblical Narrative: Ideological Literature and the Drama of Reading*. Bloomington: Indiana University Press, 1985.

Suleiman, Susan R., "Introduction: Varieties of Audience-Oriented Criticism." Pp. 3–45 in *The Reader in the Text: Essays on Audience and Interpretation*. Ed. Susan R. Suleiman and Inge Crosman. Princeton: Princeton University Press, 1980.

Todorov, Tzvetan, *The Fantastic: A Structural Approach to a Literary Genre*. Trans. Richard Howard. Ithaca, NY: Cornell University Press, 1973.

———, *The Poetics of Prose*. Trans. Richard Howard. Ithaca, NY: Cornell University Press, 1977.

———, *Bakhtine ou le principe dialogique*. Paris: Editions du Seuil, 1981.

Tompkins, Jane, "Sentimental Power: *Uncle Tom's Cabin* and the Politics of Literary History." *Glyph* 8 (1981): 79–102.

———, ed., *Reader Response Criticism: From Formalism to Post-Structuralism*. Baltimore: The Johns Hopkins University Press, 1980.

Trible, Phyllis, *God and the Rhetoric of Sexuality*. Philadelphia: Fortress Press, 1978.

———, *Texts of Terror: Literary-Feminist Readings of Biblical Narratives*. Philadelphia: Fortress Press, 1984.

Uspensky, Boris, *A Poetics of Composition*. Berkeley: University of California Press, 1973.

Vadée, M., *L'idéologie*. Paris: P.U.F., 1973.

Valesio, Paolo, *Novantiqua: Rhetorics as a Contemporary Theory*. Ithaca, NY: Cornell University Press, 1980.

Van der Ven, Pieter Dirk, *From Narrative Text to Narrative Structure: A Method Examined and Applied*. Utrecht: Instituut voor Algemene Literatuurwetenschap, 1978.

Verhoeff, Han, *Les comédies de Corneille: Une psycholecture*. Paris: Klincksieck, 1978.

———, *De Januskop van Oedipus: Over psychoanalyse en literatuur*. Assen: Van Gorcum, 1981.

———, *Les grandes tragédies de Corneille: Une psycholecture*. Paris: Minard, 1982.

Warner, Marina, *Alone of All Her Sex: The Myth and Cult of Mary*. New York: Vintage Books, 1976.

Westermann, Claus, *Genesis 1–11: A Commentary*. Trans. John J. Scullion, S.J. Minneapolis: Augsburg Press, 1984.

White, Hayden, "The Forms of Wildness: Archeology of an Idea." Pp. 3–38 in *The Wild Man Within*. Ed. Edward Dudley and Maximilian E. Novak. Pittsburgh: University of Pittsburgh Press, 1972.

Willis, Sharon, *Marguerite Duras: Writing on the Body*. Urbana: University of Illinois Press, 1987.

Zoest, A. J. A. van, "L'iconicité métaphorique." Pp. 15–31 in *Comparative Poetics: In Honour of Jan Kamerbeek Jr.*. Amsterdam: Rodopi, 1976.

———, "Le Signe iconique dans les textes." *Zagadnienia Rodzajów Literáckich* 20 (1977): 5–22.

———, *Waar gebeurd en toch gelogen: Over fictie en niet-fictie*. Assen: Van Gorcum, 1980.

Zola, Emile, *La faute de l'abbé Mouret. Oeuvres Complètes*, Vol. 3. Ed. Henri Mitterand. Paris: Cercle du livre précieux, 1967 (1875). English trans., *The Abbé Mouret's Sin*. Trans. Alec Brown. London: Elek Books, 1957.